More Praise for
# THE WORLD'S FASTEST MAN

Named a *Booklist* Top Ten Sports Book of the Year
Named Nonfiction Book of the Year by the Great Lakes
Independent Booksellers Association

"*The World's Fastest Man* offers a fascinating ride. . . . Kranish has done historians and fans a service by reminding us that such immortals as Joe Louis, Jesse Owens, Serena Williams, and Tiger Woods all followed in Major Taylor's wake."

—*The Washington Post*

"Restores the memory of one of the first black athletes to overcome the drag of racism and achieve national renown."

—*The New York Times Book Review*

"A thoroughly researched biography, a compelling social history, a wonderful page-turner."

—U.S. Bicycling Hall of Fame

"A fantastic exploration of the life of an athlete who should be a household name."

—*Pittsburgh Post-Gazette*

"Journalist Kranish weaves the fascinating and interconnected history of the rise and demise of professional cycling with the life story of African American cycling hero [Major Taylor]. . . . Kranish mixes sports and history, along with the realities of racism, in a valuable addition for all libraries with collections touching on those areas."

—*Library Journal*

"[Major Taylor's] legacy was in the quiet athletes, like Jackie Robinson, who endured endless abuse to break baseball's color barrier. And . . . in athletes like Muhammad Ali, who refused to accept limits imposed by white men. It's also in every child, black or white, boy or girl, who jumps on a bike, sprints down a track, or plunges into a pool with one goal: To go faster."

—*New York Daily News*

"A must-read."

—*Peloton* magazine

"A remarkable story."

—NPR's *Fresh Air*

"A welcome contribution to sports history, drawing attention to two extraordinary athletes for whom recognition is long overdue."

—*Kirkus Reviews*

"Both inspiring and heartbreaking, this is an essential contribution to sports history."

—*Booklist* (starred review)

"A sharp-eyed account of a nearly forgotten African American sports legend."

—*Publishers Weekly*

"In this original, surprising, and important new book, Michael Kranish brings a man and an era back to vivid life. The story of Major Taylor—sportsman, bicyclist, pioneer—is in many ways the story of America. Through his speed and his grace, Taylor emerged as a critical figure that showed a world dominated by Jim Crow and abhorrent theories of innate racial disparities that the prevailing climate of opinion was as wrong as it could be."

—Jon Meacham, winner of the Pulitzer Prize and author of *The Soul of America: The Battle for Our Better Angels*

"Michael Kranish has written an extraordinary book about an extraordinary figure whose place in American history could very easily have been lost to us all. But he does much more than illuminate the improbable story of a heroic black athlete. He throws open a window on a nearly forgotten version of America, when a rising tide of hardship engulfed the lives of millions of black citizens, even as hope faintly glimmered. Major Taylor—a superstar at the zenith of his achievements—inspired both black and white Americans and became, too briefly, a last flicker of possibility for a twentieth century in which 'justice for all' might still have become a reality. It is only through works like this that we can see just how much America lost when our society turned so completely down a path of total racial oppression in the twentieth century. We also are reminded of the generations of black Americans whose talents and contributions to our national life were so cruelly suppressed. Major Taylor represents a very different America that could have been—a better one we sadly chose not to be."

—Douglas A. Blackmon, winner of the Pulitzer Prize and
author of *Slavery by Another Name: The Re-Enslavement of Black
Americans from the Civil War to World War II*

"Jack Johnson, Jesse Owens, Jackie Robinson, Althea Gibson—the world recognizes the names of these trailblazers. Now, Michael Kranish shows that a new name should be added to the list. *The World's Fastest Man* is a riveting account of the life of Major Taylor, the cyclist who was our country's 'First Black Sports Hero.' Kranish brings Taylor's story alive with vivid prose and extensive research. This is not just a story about Taylor, it is a story about his times: when racial prejudice blighted the lives of millions of Americans and made their journeys through life far more difficult than they should have been."

—Annette Gordon-Reed, winner of the Pulitzer Prize and
author of *The Hemingses of Monticello: An American Family*

Also by Michael Kranish

*Flight from Monticello: Thomas Jefferson at War*
*John F. Kerry* (with Brian C. Mooney and Nina J. Easton)
*The Real Romney* (with Scott Helman)
*Trump Revealed* (with Marc Fisher)

# THE WORLD'S FASTEST MAN

The Extraordinary Life of Cyclist Major Taylor
America's First Black Sports Hero

## MICHAEL KRANISH

SCRIBNER

New York   London   Toronto   Sydney   New Delhi

Scribner
An Imprint of Simon & Schuster, Inc.
1230 Avenue of the Americas
New York, NY 10020

First Scribner trade paperback edition June 2021

For information about special discounts for bulk purchases,
please contact Simon & Schuster Special Sales at 1-866-506-1949
or business@simonandschuster.com.

The Simon & Schuster Speakers Bureau can bring authors to your live event.
For more information or to book an event, contact the Simon & Schuster Speakers Bureau
at 1-866-248-3049 or visit our website at www.simonspeakers.com.

Interior design by Erich Hobbing

Manufactured in the United States of America

3   5   7   9   10   8   6   4

Library of Congress Control Number: 2019006827

ISBN 978-1-5011-9259-3
ISBN 978-1-5011-9260-9 (pbk)
ISBN 978-1-5011-9261-6 (ebook)

To my family, Sylvia, Jessica, and Laura;
my cycling siblings, Clif, Steven, and Erica;
my mother, Allye;
and in memory of my father, Arthur

# Contents

# CONTENTS

PART THREE

THE FINISH

# THE
# WORLD'S
# FASTEST MAN

PROLOGUE

# Madison Square Garden, 1896

On the clear, brisk Saturday afternoon of December 5, 1896, an unusual pair of men strode to New York City's Madison Square Garden, where thousands would soon assemble for one of the era's greatest sporting events. The first man, Louis de Franklin Munger, was a lissome figure, with a hawkish gaze, a bristle-thick mustache, and close-cropped hair parted at the apex of his forehead. Munger had once been crowned the world's fastest man and now, at the age of thirty-three, his championship days behind him, he was still widely recognized by an admiring public. Everyone called him "Birdie," an appellation that evoked his love of speed and freedom. Now he had new ambitions. The second man, just eighteen years old, was described somewhat mysteriously in press accounts as Munger's "valet." He seemed at first glance a short, slight figure, but a close look revealed a compact body with remarkably muscular legs.

As the pair approached Madison Avenue and 26th Street, the arena—the second of what would be several iterations of Madison Square Garden—came into view. The structure was one of the city's greatest architectural confections, designed by the legendary Stanford White, whose firm was responsible for many of the Gilded Age mansions that lined the most fashionable streets of Manhattan. The Garden's Moorish arches marched down the avenue; a succession of teardrop-shaped cupolas ringed a fifth-story roof garden. High above, an Italianate tower concealed a private apartment and climbed

1

another three hundred feet into the sky. Atop it all, an Augustus Saint-Gaudens sculpture of Diana, a twelve-foot-tall unclothed gilded figure aiming a bow and arrow at the winds, proclaimed to all who could see her from miles around that this was the grandest public palace in America.

Munger and his young friend arrived early, before most of the spectators would stream through the Garden's granite pillars and into the marbled, mosaic entryway. Inside, parquet boards had been laid to create a bicycle-racing oval. More than nine thousand people could be squeezed into the galleries around the track, with standing room for several thousand more. A sliding glass roof opened for ventilation. Within hours, the crowds gathered, and the Garden buzzed with excited murmurs. At eight p.m., a group of racers assembled on the oval and mounted their bicycles. The twenty-five-foot-wide track was sharply curved and steeply banked to a degree that some riders deemed too dangerous. Workmen had applied a coating to the track that failed to cure evenly, leaving it slippery. The crowd noise reached a low roar as the racers readied. One of those at the starting line stood out. It was the teenager who had been called Munger's "valet."

Munger had been a legendary figure at the dawn of cycling, winning world records on a high-wheeler, which typically featured a large, solid wheel in the front and a small one in back. As his career faded in the early 1890s, a new type of bicycle had become wildly popular, with two equal-sized wheels and air-filled tubes. Munger had also raced the early, heavy versions of those models, and he now was in a contest to build the world's lightest, fastest "safety" cycles, as the new bikes were called.

Indeed, Munger had appeared in this arena earlier in the year touting his bicycles as the world's best. Tens of thousands of New Yorkers viewed the wares of hundreds of exhibiters, marveling at the latest racing cycle, or a $5,000 showpiece festooned with diamonds, or an Army-designed model bristling with weaponry. The age of the automobile was more than a decade away. This was the time of the "silent steed," ballyhooed as a replacement for the horse. One of every three patents in the 1890s was related to bicycle manufacture, and more than one million new bikes were expected to be sold in this boom year of 1896. The country had 30,000 bicycle shops and 250 bicycle factories. The main sports of the day were baseball, boxing, and bicycle racing—and cycling was by far the most popular.

Now, as the great annual race began at Madison Square Garden, the crowd focused on Munger's companion standing on the starting line with a lightweight, state-of-the-art bicycle. The protégé was unlike any racer the spectators had seen before at Madison Square Garden. He was a black man. Not just black, the press reported, but "ebony," "a veritable black diamond," "the black meteor." Those were the kind descriptions. He was housed and sponsored by the South Brooklyn Wheelmen, which called him the "dark secret of Gowanus," a reference to the Brooklyn neighborhood of brick industrial buildings where he began his training routes with the club's riders.

The crowd buzzed as they realized they were about to witness a race of white versus black. At stake was much more than a bicycling victory; there was also the prevalent notion among whites that their race was superior. On one side of this contest was a clutch of the world's most experienced racers, all of them white. On the other was the little-known eighteen-year-old who had come to this unlikely moment under Birdie's wing.

His name was Marshall Taylor, known as "Major." The son of a soldier who had fought for the Union in the Civil War, Taylor had raced in amateur competitions but nothing like the vaunted venue of Madison Square Garden. This would be Taylor's professional racing debut. Logic might have dictated such a start should take place out of the spotlight, but Munger had suggested Taylor's professional career would begin at the top on this great stage. There was a band on hand, as usual, and the members looked through their sheaves of music for "Dixie," known as the unofficial anthem of the Confederacy.

How remarkable that Major Taylor was there at all. Six months earlier, in May 1896, the US Supreme Court had decided *Plessy v. Ferguson*, the case of Homer Plessy of Louisiana, who was determined to be seven-eighths Caucasian and one-eighth African, and had sought to ride in the first-class compartment of the East Louisiana Railroad. When he refused a detective's request to move to a blacks-only car, he was arrested for violating the 1890 Separate Car Act, which mandated that blacks and whites ride separately. The Supreme Court upheld the action on grounds that the cars were separate but equal. The ruling effectively accelerated the already heinous racism of the post–Civil War era, institutionalizing Jim Crow laws for decades to come. Only one justice, John Marshall Harlan, dissented, saying "It cannot be justified upon any legal grounds."

One month after *Plessy* and five months before Taylor arrived at Madison Square Garden, William Jennings Bryan stood in the same arena and accepted the Democratic presidential nomination, saying, "We believe, as asserted in the Declaration of Independence, that all men are created equal." Bryan, who nonetheless supported some segregationist policies to woo Southern voters, lost to William McKinley, a former Union officer who would do little to stop the growth of the Jim Crow era.

If the world of sports had its own great dissenter amid this climate of racism, however, it was Munger. He bet his reputation that Taylor could, while riding a Munger-built bicycle, disprove those who believed that blacks were inferior and deserved segregation. Thus the symbolism represented by the starting line was extraordinary. A black man would compete with whites at Madison Square Garden, and may the best racer win.

Taylor wore skintight, woolen racing shorts and a shirt as he pushed his bike to the starting line. He was a son of two worlds: raised first by his poor family of black farmers, then taken in and tutored by a wealthy white family. He was better educated than most of his competitors, despite the insults hurled against him. He aimed to beat them not just with speed, but with knowledge, tactics, and cunning.

The curtain raiser was a series of half-mile races, each five laps around the track. In every heat, the improperly treated surface caused racers to fall or go flying over the handlebars, but they would reappear in the next heat, "legs and arms swathed up in bandages." The crowd cheered wildly as the racers who remained on their wheels dodged their fallen competitors.

Taylor made his debut in the third heat. Riding a bicycle made by Munger, he bolted from the starting line and gained ground with every lap. He won easily to qualify for the final heat, pitting him against several of the world's fastest riders. A starter's pistol fired. Taylor's powerful legs turned the pedals. Quickly, he put ten yards between him and his closest competitor. "Round and round the track whirled the colored rider, pedaling away like a steam engine," wrote the *Brooklyn Eagle*'s correspondent. Taylor swiveled his head to see a racer named Eddie "Cannon" Bald—considered one of the world's fastest sprinters—closing in. Bald was "straining every nerve" to catch Taylor. The crowd surged from their seats to see if Taylor could hold on to his narrowing lead.

In time, the rivalry between Bald and Taylor would be billed by a promoter as the white "Adonis" versus the "great Negro." Bald would swear that he never wanted to "let a nigger beat" him, while Taylor saw Bald as the embodiment of the racism against him. Their rivalry would serve as a microcosm of the greater social history of the time, and come to an extraordinary conclusion for both men.

Taylor's epic journey began twelve years before Jack Johnson, a black man, became heavyweight champion, and fifty years before Jackie Robinson broke the color barrier in Major League Baseball. Yet here he was in 1896, wheel to wheel against white racers. His life would be one of the most singular of his era, a black man who took on Jim Crow, who crested at the height of the Gilded Age that was dominated by elite whites. His name eventually faded, but his story is far larger than one of sports. It is a story of one man's perseverance against relentless waves of prejudice, and of the enduring friendship of two men, one black and the other white, who joined together to push history forward.

Taylor said from the beginning that Munger was pushing not only for the fastest time on the racetrack but also for the larger principle of equality, which victory would help make possible. So, Munger said of Taylor, "I am going to make him the fastest bicycle rider in the world." And that, improbably, is what was about to happen.

# PART ONE

# Acceleration

# CHAPTER 1

# Birdie Takes Flight

Louis de Franklin Munger, a lean, blond seventeen-year-old living in Detroit in 1880, boarded a horse-drawn streetcar, and, as he did most days, joined the masses on their way to work. Nearly half of Detroit's 116,000 residents at the time were immigrants, including many from Germany, Poland, and Ireland, and these strivers and dreamers streamed into the city's belching industrial quarters, a bastion fed by copper smelters and ironworks. Detroit could hardly keep up with its own prosperity, and Munger steadily rose in the midst of an ambitious, confident city. He had been born on an Iowa farm, moved with his family to eastern Canada, and then settled in Michigan, where his father worked in a patent office. All around Munger swirled invention and commerce and movement, the very future that America saw for itself.

Hopping off the streetcar, he headed to a sash and blind factory, filled with the hum of machinery and clouds of sawdust, as the trees of the great northern forests were planed and sanded into window coverings. A typical six-day, sixty-hour workweek paid six dollars. Munger was a laborer at first, then a carpenter, and, by the time he was twenty-one years old, a foreman.

Detroit's population boomed, but not all shared in the prosperity. Even as he rose through the ranks, Munger was little more than a minion in the machinery of an industrial revolution that greatly profited the few at the top. The titans William Henry Vanderbilt and

J. P. Morgan had made Detroit a focal point of their control of the railroads, installing tracks and stations across Michigan; it was said they were determined to serve every town with a thousand people in an area stretching eight thousand square miles. As Munger turned twenty-one, in 1884, he watched the construction of the "pride of Detroit," the Michigan Central Railroad depot, a Romanesque Revival building that seemed as much like a castle as it did a train station, with its three-story tower, turrets, and marble floors. The gentry from New York City and Chicago, as well as the immigrant laborers, were whisked into Detroit, and the city welcomed them into an architectural wonderland of fast-growing neighborhoods.

Munger's life seemed on a straight course of slow, steady progress until one day he saw a local group of men on bicycles racing along a Detroit road. He had always been an athlete, running and rowing. He had ridden an early version of the bike, with iron tires and a frame of wood and steel, known as a "boneshaker" due to its discomfort. (Air-inflated rubber tires were years away.) The Detroiters who caught Munger's eye were atop more sophisticated "high wheel" bicycles, swift but dangerous conveyances that required a rider to hop onto a high seat, balance on a great front wheel and a small rear one, and pedal mostly over roads of dirt and mud. A strong rider could average eighteen miles an hour, surveying the world from the height of a horseman's perspective. Munger bought a high-wheeler and, nine weeks later, after innumerable crashes that would become his hallmark, he was champion of Detroit (although there were not, to be sure, many competitors in these early days). A doctor urged Munger to rest and let his injuries heal, but, as often would be the case, he rejected the advice. He learned that a race to determine the state's fastest rider would soon be held. He bandaged his wounds, entered the race, and won. Then he heard of plans for what was billed as the first one-hundred-mile race on a straightaway course in North America—a "century" in cycling parlance.

On July 10, 1885, Munger and five other men lined up to race along the Canadian shore of Lake Ontario. It was ninety-five miles from Cobourg to Kingston, with a five-mile loop added near the beginning to make it an even century. The usual warning was issued to watch out for sudden obstacles, such as cows and horses, a constant danger for riders going full tilt. A half-mile after the lap's first turn, Munger saw ahead of him a farm wagon drawn by two horses, with a mare and colt hitched to the back. The mare gave "a snort of terror" and shoved the first rider off the road. Munger, who usually was the loser in such encounters, saw it unfold in an instant and managed to jump off his bicycle to avoid the collision. Midway through the race, Munger arrived at a hotel for a short rest, meal, and a massage. He downed steak and potatoes, got his rubdown, exited the hotel after seventeen minutes, and, as a journalist on the scene noted colorfully, "kicked off a man's hat" as he vaulted onto his saddle. Within minutes a horse lunged into the road and struck Munger, who was thrown from his saddle to the back of his wheel and then to the ground, where he lay "knocked out" for ten minutes. The race was lost, but Munger eventually climbed back on his bike and, impressing everyone with his grit, finished in second place. The one-hundred-mile contest had been, according to *Canadian Wheelman* magazine, "in many respects the most remarkable race ever run."

Munger was enthralled with it all—the crowds, the brass bands, the newspaper coverage. The Canadian race was the first leg of a grand tour that he was invited to join, connecting by steamer to the Thousand Islands in Upstate New York, and then to Buffalo, and by bike and train down the eastern United States, through the towns of the Hudson River valley. At each burg, some old soldier would bring out a cannon and light a gunpowder charge to greet the riders. Locals put on their Sunday best, waving flags and cheering, while young ladies pinned boutonnieres to the riders' jackets. Munger soaked it up. A reporter along for the ride recounted that Munger was "an odd genius, brimming over with fun and frolic, and his pranks on the road, on train and on steamer, added greatly to the pleasure of all parties." Munger attached a hose to a water pump and let loose on unsuspecting victims, rang cowbells at all hours, and generally lightened the mood through days of competition, winning him the title of "funnyman of the tour." Yet it was also Munger who, in the middle of a race, would stop to offer help to a rider with a damaged wheel, even if it meant hurting his own chances at victory.

The touring bicyclists ended their journey in New York City, where they checked into the Grand Central Hotel in mid-July. Munger's racing form had improved each day, and he now entered a series of competitions that would raise him to the highest ranks, even as accidents kept coming. A common headline about Munger was "Suffered a violent collision," as one story put it about his encounter with a horse-drawn carriage. He won as often as he flew over the handlebars. In a matter of just a few months, Munger had gone from the factory floor to his first taste of fame. "Birdie," fleet and seeking freedom, was born, and so the nickname would stick. He headed to Boston, where a race was to be held between some of the nation's fastest men.

Munger drew much attention as he arrived in Massachusetts, the hub of the nation's cycle manufacturing. The *Boston Globe* described the twenty-three-year-old racer as a strong, supple, handsome man, weighing one hundred and sixty pounds, and riding a fifty-four-inch-high bicycle called an Apollo. "He is of very merry disposition and everyone he meets is sure to become his friend," the newspaper said. Initially, Munger had planned to compete in shorter races, training for thirty to forty miles per day and "sleeping all he could." But he did so well that he decided to enter one of the most grueling competitions of the era: a twenty-four-hour race.

Munger climbed aboard his Apollo with little sense of what lay ahead. The race began at four p.m. as a steady rain pitted the roads; then a downpour turned everything muddy. The mist rose, and darkness descended. It became "impossible to distinguish objects ten feet distant," the *Globe* reported. After many miles, Munger felt ill and stopped at farmhouses for assistance. Farmers offered him milk and some bread, and he continued on. At 5:40 a.m., having ridden for more than twelve hours, Munger stopped at a Salem homestead, where he was given a rubdown with sweet oil. Limbered and rested, Munger regained his strength. He began to add miles to the course and asked local riders to accompany him to verify his feat. Twenty-four hours after he began, he ended his epic ride in Dorchester. The distance on his cyclometer measured 211 miles, a new national record.

The *Globe* was dismayed. How could local riders fail to win on their own course? "Won by a Westerner," said the headline. "The Twenty-Four-Hour Bicycle Record Broken."

The glory didn't last. A local rider upped the record to 255 miles, and a cycling journal taunted Munger, writing, "Boston wheelmen are wondering why Munger does not come on from Detroit and smash the 24-hour record, as he claimed he would." Munger showed up for another try. All seemed to go well until he collided with some horses, putting him in such pain that he was forced to quit after 17 miles. A few weeks later, "plucky Munger," as the *Globe* now called him, tried again. There was no moonlight, so Munger rigged two lanterns to his handlebars and a third to the hub of his front wheel. The rains were too heavy, and Munger quit after 130 miles. As he left a hotel in Brighton, Munger said he was "not at all disheartened." Two weeks later, he had another chance.

A large crowd gathered outside Faneuil House, a four-story hotel in Brighton. Munger pushed off at 5:00 p.m. on wet roads lit only by the moon. Munger learned a competitor registered a record of 257 miles. All seemed lost as Munger, "by an unlucky accident," fell from his bike and injured one of his knees. He put bandages on his bleeding leg, adjusted his pedals to accommodate his now-altered pace, and climbed back on the cycle. At 4:58 p.m., with two minutes to spare, he registered 259 miles, reclaiming the American record. He dashed up the steps of Faneuil House, stood under the two-story portico, and waved to "the delighted howl of his friends." Newspapers across the country, including the *New York Times*, heralded the news. Munger's name, his pluck, even his disastrous tendency to take "headers" over the handlebars, became the talk of the sporting press.

Munger's victories coincided with the emergence of bicycle racing as a popular sport. Racing ovals, or "velodromes," would soon be constructed across the country, with grandstands for ten thousand people or more. The press devoted several pages of coverage every day to the exploits of top riders. With winter's arrival in Boston, a publicity-seeking bicycle manufacturer, Everett & Co., which made the Apollo at its Boston factory, offered to pay Munger's expenses to New Orleans, where the nation's best riders were training. Munger took the money and headed south.

New Orleans was a booming port city when Munger arrived in 1886, boasting one of the nation's finest networks of asphalt roads. A reporter for the *New Orleans Daily Picayune* told his readers about the "sun-burned, blond young man, weather-beaten and athletic looking," the holder of the twenty-four-hour American cycling record, who had become "a sort of bicycle missionary, travelling around to encourage the sport." Munger predicted that the bicycle would replace the horse as common transportation, telling how riders in places such as St. Louis "use the machine for their regular daily travel, and do not regard it merely as an amusement." The *Picayune* said Munger "has ridden thousands of miles and is one of the finest long-distance riders in the world." He is "the life of every tour" who planned to popularize bicycles in the South, which was well behind the North in adopting the sport. Munger planned to stay in the South for a month or two, during which he hoped to go beyond winning a national title; he wanted to win races that would certify him as a world champion, too.

Munger got his chance two months later. Early on the morning of March 27, 1886, cyclists lined up on St. Charles Avenue, proclaimed by a local promoter to have the nation's smoothest surface, all the better for achieving a world record in a twenty-five-mile contest. Munger mounted his bike and barreled past churches and squares and riverfront. He completed the course in one hour and twenty-four minutes, shattering the world record by nine minutes. For the next two weeks, speculation filled the press about whether Munger could capture the fifty-mile title. Again, he demolished the record. The word spread: Munger was "wonderful," a marvel, one of the greatest sportsmen and competitors. Drawings of Munger atop his Apollo appeared in newspapers across the country.

The only question was what he would do to top it. Then he heard about a trio of local bicyclists preparing to ride from New Orleans to Boston. They planned to grind out nearly two thousand miles in thirty days, an audacious goal considering the challenge of riding high-wheelers and the dearth of good roads, not to mention the difficulties of staying supplied, keeping dry, and finding shelter. They aimed to arrive in time for the opening of the national meeting of the League of American Wheelmen, a powerful group behind the push for paved roads. The three riders—Henry W. Fairfax, C. M. Fairchild, and A. M. Hill—each placed ten-pound bundles over their handlebars that contained clothing, lotions, chain lubricant, needles, thread, and, of course, plenty of bandages. They followed alongside the railbed of the Louisville & Nashville railroad, reached Atlanta, and then took a series of paved, muddy, or sandy roads near the coast, headed through Virginia's Shenandoah River valley, and then toward New England. Often, they pushed their bikes for miles through sand and muck and swamp. They telegraphed ahead and were met along the way by cycling groups, culminating in Boston, where they joined a parade of eight thousand riders of the League of American Wheelmen, one of the biggest gatherings of the nascent sport that had yet been held.

Munger would not be one of those in attendance in Boston. Shortly after winning his races in New Orleans, the League of American Wheelmen conducted an investigation into whether racers who had won records were paid professionals, instead of "amateurs" as the League required. Munger had not received a salary and thus believed he was not a professional. But he had traveled to New Orleans at the expense of Everett & Co., which wanted to capitalize on Munger's fame. To the League, that made Munger a professional. He was suspended, and his latest records were marked with asterisks. When Munger tried to compete in a Detroit race, a group of riders from Cleveland said they would refuse to race against him for fear of being tainted by competing against a professional, and threatened to sue Munger for damages. He had effectively been blackballed from a sport he had done so much to popularize.

As the controversy over his racing status was fanned by the papers in the late summer of 1886, Munger told friends he just wanted to keep on riding and exploring. But how and where? The answer must have gradually dawned on him. On the same page of the cycling journals that had extolled his New Orleans victories, he read about the exploits of an Englishman named Thomas Stevens, who two years earlier had been the first person to cycle across America. Indeed, as Munger was pondering his future, Stevens was in Kolkata, India (called Calcutta by the British), on his way to completing the even more audacious goal of traveling across the world by bicycle. Munger decided that he would be among the first to ride across America, starting in San Francisco, just as Stevens had done two years earlier, taking advantage of wind that generally blew west to east.

While Munger pondered his trip, the literature of cross-country travel spread a romantic vision. A railroad company published a guidebook filled with flowery prose about majestic peaks, towering forests, fast-flowing streams, and endless prairies. Full-page illustrations were published of scenes such as the Great Falls of the Yellowstone River, in the recently created Yellowstone National Park. Munger would have read such volumes with awe and anticipation. Surely the guidebook's prose would make any adventurous soul want to go west, particularly a man whose other option was to return to a sash and blind factory: "Beyond the Great Lakes, far from the hum of New England factories, far from the busy throng of Broadway, from the smoke and grime of iron cities, and the dull prosaic life of many another Eastern town, lies a region which may be justly designated the Wonderland of the World."

This was Munger's kind of world. That year, a new title appeared by Birdie's name in Detroit's city directory: "travel agent." The job description might have been entered humorously, but it fit. Munger would, as the guidebook said, explore the country "with his own eyes upon its manifold and matchless wonders."

Munger would use Stevens's daunting descriptions as a guide. Stevens had taken a steamship from San Francisco to Oakland and worked his way across the Sierra Nevadas by following the tracks and trestles of the railroad. Stevens had hauled his bike up mountainsides and inside snowsheds that covered tracks in particularly treacherous areas. He pressed against the inner walls of the tunnel with his bike to avoid oncoming trains. Stevens had even hoisted his thirty-four-pound bike on his shoulder and traversed railroad bridges high above raging rivers, once dangling the bike over the edge while a train came alongside. He shot at mountain lions and bears, befriended Native Americans, and bunked with Mormon families in which there were multiple wives.

Munger arrived in San Francisco late in that summer of 1886. California had entered the union thirty-six years earlier, and seven states had been added since then, bringing the total to thirty-eight. The first trainload of oranges had just left California on a transcontinental trip. The wars against the land's native dwellers were largely over. Geronimo, the famed Apache warrior, had ended his three decades of battle against the white invaders and surrendered in Skeleton Canyon, Arizona. Tribes were relocated, treaties were abrogated, and many natives who tried to remain on their ancient grounds were killed, captured, or forcibly ousted.

The early roads were built for carts and carriages. Munger rarely found a paved road during the early weeks of his journey. A Scottish engineer, John Loudon McAdam, had invented a mixture of soil and stone that became known as macadam. The first such roads were built in the United States in the 1820s, and tarred surfaces were growing in popularity, mainly in cities. But many of the western roads encountered by Munger were little more than cleared pathways. An improved surface typically was made largely of "gumbo," a clay substance pocked with sinkholes. "The mud and mire was so bad in many places that it was even impossible to walk for any length of time without getting exhausted," Munger recollected. As he told the story, Munger hopscotched from the railbed to Indian trails to rough roads. He struggled on some days to go more than ten miles. He lumbered up mountains and then downhill into the "large unsettled areas of the great West." He likely followed Stevens's example of spending nights in mining camps, Indian encampments, and the open desert.

Munger deviated from the Stevens route by venturing along the railbed of the recently opened Atchison, Topeka and Santa Fe line.

He tried to ride between the rails or along an adjoining path, but for many miles there was little choice but to go directly on the track. Often, he simply pushed his bicycle. It was, Munger said, "more of a cross-country hike than a bicycle ride."

Midway through his journey, in Kansas, he encountered an early fall snowstorm and was snowed in for five days. He then traveled to Chicago, where he got a fresh bike, finally encountered paved roads with some regularity, and made his way along the shores of Lake Erie to Buffalo, which he had visited a year earlier with other cyclists. Here his path became easier. From Buffalo to Albany, he followed the towpath of the Erie Canal, which had been completed sixty-one years earlier and was still considered one of the country's engineering marvels. It ran 363 miles from its western entry on Lake Erie to its eastern terminus at the Hudson River, a route that opened the Upper Midwest to industrial expansion and transformed commerce. Canal barges glided through a series of locks, pulled by mules and horses that trod a clay towpath. As Munger recalled the journey, one of his strongest memories was that his bicycle twice slipped from the clay paths into the canal, sending him plunging into the water toward the stone-lined bottom. Still, he made good time on the towpath and, at the Albany terminus, he headed down the Hudson River valley, past Catskill and Kingston and Poughkeepsie. Finally, after 111 days, he arrived in New York City.

Unlike Stevens, who had ensured wide coverage by sending dispatches to newspapers and magazines, Munger did not write about his epic journey at the time, and it went largely unnoticed. But the transcontinental crossing left a deep impression. Munger had seen firsthand the threads of a disparate and largely disconnected nation, tethered by the transcontinental railroads. He had seen the nation's uneven prosperity, the thriving coasts, the poverty of tribal territory, the vastness of the western desert, and the expanse of the Plains. He had also, no doubt, seen the rising mistreatment of blacks in the growing backlash to Reconstruction. Prejudice manifested itself in other ways as well. Ethnic groups pitted themselves against one another, such as in riots against the influx of Chinese laborers in the West. Munger had both a close-up and wide-angle view of a nation, not from a passing train or a wagon, not related by a newspaper or a romantic guidebook, but from the high seat of a bicycle traveling vast distances over rough ground, with plenty of time to ponder one's own future as well as that of the country.

Around the time Munger completed his journey in New York City, the Statue of Liberty was being dedicated by President Grover Cleveland in New York Harbor. The copper-clad statue depicting a robed woman lofting a torch was modeled on the Roman goddess of freedom from slavery and oppression. Thousands of people piled into trains and nearly every hotel in the city was sold out. Cannons were fired, fireworks lit the sky, and workers in the city spontaneously threw ticker tape out their windows at the procession below, starting a parade tradition.

For Munger, one journey was complete, and another was about to begin. He moved to Chicago, where he made some kind of accommodation with the League of American Wheelmen, becoming a top representative of the organization for Illinois. For the next several years, Munger raced every manner of bicycle and set more records, including one for the fastest hundred miles on a big-wheeled tricycle. He reclaimed his rightful place as one of the nation's greatest cyclists.

Sometimes, however, Munger went too far. One day, he convinced his friend Billy Arthur to take a daring ride with him through a streetcar tunnel under the Chicago River. Suddenly a northbound train entered, and the pair evaded it by moving to the space between the tracks. Then came a southbound train. Munger's friend saw death approaching. "He attempted to ride between the cars, but the track was too narrow, his handlebars touching both trains," the *Chicago Tribune* reported. "He caught the edge of the roof of one car and swung up, abandoning his wheel, which was drawn under the train and badly broken. Were it not for Billy's strong arms and cool head the matter might have terminated fatally." When the *Tribune* reporter caught up with him, Arthur declared, "I will never ride with 'Birdie' Munger again."

Of course, it was Munger's daring, verging on foolhardiness, that made him a bicycle champion. Such instincts worked in his favor one day in April 1889 when he attended a woman's cycling exhibition. A policeman, probably drunk, thrust his constable's stick into the spokes of a rider's wheel, causing the woman to go flying onto the track. Munger rushed to her aid in what a reporter called "the probable saving of the lives" of the fallen rider and another woman, preventing them from being run over by other competitors. The policeman was run out of the arena but soon returned and, incredibly, arrested Munger, who was quickly released when the fracas was sorted out. The following morning, the *Chicago Inter Ocean* called the policeman "an idiot" and saluted "the pluck of L. D. Munger."

As the cycling craze got under way, hundreds of bicycle clubs were created, newspapers and magazines dedicated to the sport were published, and the power of the League of American Wheelmen and its "Good Roads" campaign grew. A petition of 150,000 signatures was prepared for delivery to Congress calling for the construction of paved byways and highways to encourage more widespread use of bicycles. The effort would reach a peak in the middle of 1892. Munger had become a leader of a Chicago cycling club, which was traveling to Washington to join the largest contingent of cyclists ever to assemble in the nation's capital. They planned to parade in front of the White House, meet with President Benjamin Harrison, and demand that millions of dollars be spent to transform the nation and meet the needs of millions of cyclists. Cycling was more popular than ever, and symbolized a nation moving ever more swiftly into the future. But as a sport, it was almost entirely dominated by white men. No blacks competed for the title of world's fastest man, nor was it imagined that any could.

CHAPTER 2

# The Rise of Major Taylor

B y September 1864, the Civil War had lasted three years and five months, much longer than anyone on either side had expected, at the cost of hundreds of thousands of casualties. The war had destroyed innumerable towns and cities across the South, and despite the Union's advance and the surrender of Atlanta, the conflict raged on. The Confederate and Union armies remained desperate for fresh soldiers. On September 30 of that year, Gilbert Taylor of Kentucky enlisted in Company A of the 122nd US Colored Troops, heeding the call of President Abraham Lincoln and the African American leader Frederick Douglass to help Union forces. The twenty-four-year-old joined thousands of other black Kentucky residents, and soon was sent into the heart of the war's decisive battle, on the outskirts of Richmond, Virginia, the capital of the Confederacy.

It is not clear whether Gilbert had been a slave or a freeman, but either way the act of joining the federal army was its own kind of declaration of independence. Gilbert's home state of Kentucky had been at war with itself. The border state, birthplace of Confederate president Jefferson Davis, had the ninth-largest population of slaves. One of every five Kentuckians—226,000 men, women, and children—was a slave at the beginning of the Civil War. One-fourth of Kentucky families owned slaves. Some white Kentuckians wanted the state to remain neutral but keep its slave-based economy, but that was tantamount to joining the Confederacy. Lincoln correctly believed that the state could be decisive, famously declaring, "I hope to have God on my side, but I must have Kentucky." Recruiters from the South and North sought to win over Kentuckians, sometimes dividing families and leading to the archetypal fight of brother against brother. The state's more pragmatic leaders decided that their destiny lay with the Union and, even as they hoped to retain slavery, petitioned to join the Northern forces. Southern sympathizers formed a shadow Confederate government, and Kentucky, as Lincoln predicted, became a bloody center of the conflict. After several years of stalemate, Lincoln finally decided in April 1864 that the Union Army would recruit blacks. Gilbert joined twenty-four thousand of his fellow black Kentuckians enlisting in the Northern forces.

The nature of Gilbert's service is revealed in a passing reference in a letter written years later by his son. Gilbert enlisted under the last name of Wilhite, which matches a listing of a soldier's name in Kentucky archives. Blacks sometimes enlisted under the names of slave owners, or as substitute soldiers, to avoid being recognized under their given name. Gilbert joined a unit that was sent to Virginia, where the war was about to reach its climax.

Gilbert marched with his fellow Kentucky soldiers along the James River, reaching Petersburg as Union forces encircled the city. After the Union broke through Confederate lines, the Northern troops, including the 122nd Colored, headed twenty-four miles north to Richmond, where a siege was under way. The Confederate government evacuated its capital, setting many buildings on fire before they handed the city to Union forces, which took complete control on April 3, 1865. The following day, as Gilbert and his fellow members of the 122nd looked on, President Abraham Lincoln toured the city, walking to the Confederate White House. Lincoln would be assassinated later that month at Ford's Theatre in Washington, shortly before the war was formally declared over. An estimated 620,000 to 750,000 soldiers died from wounds or disease, including at least 36,000 blacks; hundreds of thousands more were injured.

After Richmond fell, Gilbert's unit was assigned to help guard white Confederate prisoners in Virginia. Shortly after the camp was established, two thousand prisoners arrived, followed soon after by another thirteen hundred, overwhelming the supplies and creating a "shameful" and "filthy" condition. Between the tents lay piles of excrement, covered with rags, and dozens died of disease and wounds. One captive wrote that of the several thousand prisoners, there were not one hundred "well men," and that, in the chaotic conditions of the camp, guards shot or bayoneted several prisoners. By June, the 122nd was transferred to Texas, where Gilbert remained until October, when he was discharged at Corpus Christi. For the rest of his life, Gilbert proudly wore his military jacket at reunions and other occasions.

As Gilbert returned home from the war, however, many white Kentuckians opposed letting blacks have their hard-won freedom, and imposed a host of restrictions. Gilbert was still in Kentucky when a federal census taker came to his home in a mostly black neighborhood of Louisville on July 13, 1870. The census worker noted that the head of the household, Gilbert Taylor, twenty-nine years old, was a laborer who could read but not write. His wife, Saphronia, twenty-six, could neither read nor write, and worked as a domestic servant. They had three children, an infant named William, two-year-old Lizzie, and the eldest, Alice, who was seven years old.

Gilbert eventually concluded that the future looked bleak in Kentucky. Shortly after the census taker came to his door, the family moved 115 miles north to Indianapolis, Indiana, where the family settled on a modest plot of farmland. It was there that Saphronia gave birth in 1878 to their second son, naming him Marshall Walter Taylor.

Gilbert Taylor could not support the family solely by working their farmland, so he found a job as a coachman for one of the most prominent men in Indianapolis, a railroad superintendent named Albert Southard. Gilbert often brought along Marshall, and the youngster quickly found a friend in Southard's son Dan. The two boys were about the same age and shared a love of games and sports.

The Southards, who were white, recognized how happy Dan was to have a playmate and soon arranged for Marshall to stay with them for long periods. The two boys were given the same type of clothes, dressing like twins, and received the same education. To an eight-year-old boy, this was equality. Marshall was practically adopted by the Southards, living a life that could not have been more different from his parents' painful years in Kentucky. By this "freak of fate," as he later put it, Marshall had privileges available to few other children, white or black.

"We soon became the best of friends, so much so in fact, that I was eventually employed as his playmate and companion," he wrote years later. "Dan had a wonderful play room stacked with every kind of toy imaginable, but his work shop was to me the one best room in the whole house, and when there I was the happiest boy in the world."

*The happiest boy in the world.* When Marshall returned to his family and their house and farmland, he encountered resistance, as his father seemed to disapprove of his close relationship to the Southards. His mother, deeply religious, allowed it so long as Marshall adhered to Baptist teachings. Marshall did not yet comprehend the underlying divisions between black and white; when he played with Dan and the other boys, all seemed fair and equal.

One of Marshall's greatest joys was borrowing Dan's bicycle. It was beyond the means of the Taylor family to buy a bike, but Dan soon arranged for Marshall to be given one of his own. Marshall spent hours riding and practicing stunts on the bicycle, standing on the seat while riding, dismounting over the handlebars. One day, Taylor took the bike in for repairs at the Hay & Willits bicycle store in Indianapolis, where he performed one of his stunts. The owner, a kindly man named Tom Hay, was so impressed by Marshall's cycling wizardry that he cleared space outside for Taylor to perform more stunts. Soon a crowd gathered, and as Taylor recalled it, the police eventually had to be called to clear the street for traffic.

Hay hired Taylor, who began wearing a military-style uniform in which to perform his tricks. Perhaps it was one of his father's old Civil War jackets, which Taylor would grow into, or an olive-green set of livery clothing. In any case, the boy had a military look and soon everyone was calling him by a new nickname, "Major" Taylor.

• • •

Major had found yet another home, and another white benefactor, in Tom Hay. Major swept the shop floors and earned six dollars a week performing tricks and selling bicycles. He rode for miles every day— becoming faster and stronger with every passing month. Dreaming of racing, he eyed a gold medal in the window, which was awarded for a ten-mile bicycle race. He held the medal in his hands, pinned it on his jacket, and imagined what it would be like to earn such a prize. When race day came in the summer of 1890, eleven-year-old Taylor was among the crowd who came to witness the great event. Hay was there as well. "Thinking to inject a laugh into the race for the benefit of the thousands that lined the course, Mr. Hay insisted that I take my place on the starting line," Taylor wrote later. "I rebelled, but he fairly dragged me and my bicycle across the road."

"Come on here, young man, you have got to start in this race," Hay told Taylor, who began to cry at the thought. Whispering to Taylor, Hay said, "I know you can't go the full distance, but just ride up the road a little way, it will please the crowd, and you can come back as soon as you get tired."

Hay's encouragement served to be a springboard. After being given a fifteen-minute head start based on his youth, Taylor battled against hundreds of cyclists, inspired to prove Hay wrong. Feeling "very tired" and sure that his knees would be "torn out of their sockets," Taylor was surprised when he noticed some riders coming alongside him. "As they drew closer, I recognized Mr. Hay among them. He had the gold medal that was hung up for first prize and dangled it in front of my eyes as we rode along." Hay told Taylor that he had a mile until the finish. As Taylor later recalled it, the sight of the medal prompted him to ride "like mad" across the finish line, feeling "more dead than alive," after which he wobbled with such fatigue that he lost consciousness.

"The first thing I saw" upon regaining his senses, he recalled, "was that big gold medal pinned on my chest." He raced home to show the reward to his mother, who laughed and cried at her son's accomplishment. The local newspaper aimed at black readers, the *Indianapolis Freeman,* proudly reported in August 1890 that "Master Major Taylor is without doubt the expert wheelman of his age, in the state, both for fancy and speed."

Major was enthralled with this new life centered around the bicycle. One month later, Taylor traveled by train to Peoria, Illinois, 209 miles northwest of Indianapolis. Cyclists from around the country arrived for an annual race at Lake View Park, where three thousand spectators gathered. Taylor had probably come along in his capacity as an employee of Hay & Willits. The star attraction was one of the world's most famous racers, Arthur Zimmerman of New Jersey, who often competed against Birdie Munger. Taylor had read about Zimmerman and was thrilled at the chance to witness one of his heroes close-up. Zimmerman, six feet tall and svelte, won two races, including a ten-mile event.

Following Zimmerman's victory, riders under sixteen years old lined up. Now it was Zimmerman's turn to watch a remarkable race. A reporter for a Chicago newspaper, the *Herald*, wrote that "quite a sensation was created when Major Taylor, a little colored boy of eleven years, appeared as a contestant." Taylor lost by a yard, taking third place against older, stronger contestants.

It had been an extraordinary week in Peoria, and there was one more dramatic moment that would affect Taylor's life. An English rider, Herbert E. Laurie, had recently traveled to the United States with a new kind of tire called a pneumatic—the air-filled tube that revolutionized transportation. At the time of Laurie's arrival in the summer of 1890, most American cyclists still used solid tires.

A Scottish-born veterinarian based in Ireland, John Dunlop had pondered the problem of solid tires two years earlier. Dunlop's son had complained that he always lost tricycle races to the other neighborhood boys. Could his father, a tinkerer, make a better tire? His son wanted "more speed, and it was solely to give it to him that I finally perfected the pneumatic tire," Dunlop said years later. In between his doctoring of cows and horses, the white-bearded veterinarian experimented. Finally, he struck upon a solution: the elasticity of confined air. By putting air in a sealed rubber tube, he could create a lighter tire that would also ride more smoothly and speedily. He ordered rubber sheeting from a supplier in Scotland, at a thickness of one thirty-second of an inch. He rolled it into a tube, shaved the edges with a pocketknife, and sealed it with rubber cement. Then he made a hole and inserted a smaller piece of tubing from a baby bottle to create a valve. He stretched the rubber around a circular frame of wood fifteen inches in diameter and covered the tire with a piece of taut linen taken from a lady's dress, which he tacked into the wood. Then he inflated the newfangled tire with his son's ball pump and conducted a test. He went to a building where horse carriages were stored and rolled his pneumatic invention across the floor. It bounded toward the wall and bounced back. Then he did the same thing with a solid tire, which barely made it to the wall before wobbling on its side. The pneumatic era had begun. Dunlop ordered more rubber, made more models, and finally put the new tire on his son's bike. On midnight of February 28, 1888, with the moon in partial eclipse, his son rolled onto some of Ireland's roughest roads. His son was delighted and "found he could quite easily beat all the other boys in the neighborhood," Dunlop recalled. "The terrible vibration transmitted by the solid tire had been eliminated."

Dunlop made a refined model, replacing the wheel's wooden rim with high-tension, bendable steel, and swapping the linen with cotton. He asked a local bicycle racer to test it against the fastest riders. The racer with Dunlop's pneumatics easily won every match. The Dunlop Company was soon created to make tires, and wheels would never be the same. Thus did Herbert Laurie, the English rider, cross the Atlantic with Dunlop's invention on his bike. In races at Niagara Falls and Hartford, Laurie bested Americans who rode solid tires. It so happened that one of Laurie's next stops was Peoria.

As Taylor recalled it years later, the announcement that Laurie would ride on pneumatic tires was greeted by "hoots and jeers." Race officials decided that Laurie could not ride on his pneumatics at the main event, lest he have an unfair advantage. Sure enough, even though he was paced by the speedy Zimmerman, Laurie lost the race because he was forced to ride with solid tires. Three days later, however, Laurie was allowed to ride in a special race in which all the bicycles with pneumatics were allowed. He won easily, setting an American record for the fastest mile. The pneumatic was a revelation, and the jeers turned to jubilation. It was a moment, Taylor wrote, that "revolutionized bicycle racing, and the manufacture of bicycles simultaneously." Munger, too, was thrilled by the possibilities of the pneumatic tire.

Only later would historians recount how the invention of the pneumatic tire had a devastating impact on those who lived in the regions where rubber was harvested, particularly in Africa. This was most evident in the Congo, controlled by Belgium's King Leopold II, who oversaw a swath of African landscape larger than England, France, Italy, Spain, and Germany combined. The king made the Congo his personal empire. Leopold originally wanted the land for its ivory, but after Dunlop's invention spread, the king's vision turned to the Congo's potential as the world's great rubber producer. Rubber became one of the world's most valuable commodities, popular in everything from gaskets to electric wire insulation. By the late 1890s, rubber industry profits of seven hundred percent were common, made on the backs of slave laborers. In the days before cultivated rubber grew on plantations, the king's workers traveled across the Congo, from village to village, holding women as hostages and rounding up the men, who were ordered to search for vines that produced the wild rubber. The harvesters often used crude methods, draining sap and spreading it across their bodies to enable it to coagulate. When the work was done, the slave drivers sold the women hostages back to village men "for a couple of goats apiece." It is a cruel twist of history indeed that the bicycle, a symbol of freedom for so many, helped unleash a reign of terror. What began with the bicycle boom, followed by an even greater demand for automobile tires and other products, would play a role in the deaths of millions of Africans who died during the often-brutal efforts to harvest rubber.

There would be another cautionary tale from Dunlop's experience—hardly on a par with genocide, but still one that years later would affect Taylor and Munger. It was the lesson of patents and the protection of inventions. Dunlop sold his patents and made about 50,000 pounds (worth about $8.2 million in 2018 US currency). But the buyers made far more, and fights over valuable tire patents would continue for decades.

Taylor, meanwhile, discovered that, for all his acceptance in the Southard family, he was not truly welcome in the white man's world. The lesson came one day when he went to the local branch of the Young Men's Christian Association, intending to strengthen himself for cycling. The YMCA was founded on what it called Christian principles and the desire to build character, but the Indianapolis branch refused to admit blacks. The local YMCA, like many other institutions, instead suggested to blacks that they build their own facilities. The racism stunned Taylor. While he had proven to be the best athlete among his peers, "there was only one thing . . . I could not beat them at, and that was when we went down to the Young Men's Christian Association gymnasium," Taylor wrote late in his life. "It was there that I was first introduced to that dreadful monster prejudice, which became my bitterest foe from that very same day, and one which I have never as yet been able to defeat. Owing to my color, I was not allowed to join the Y.M.C.A., and in consequence was not permitted to go on the gymnasium floor with my companions."

The parents of his white friends "even with their powerful influence were unable to do anything about it," Taylor wrote. "I could only watch the other boys from the gallery go through their calisthenics, and how my poor little heart would ache to think that I was denied an opportunity to exercise in the same manner as they, and for really no reason that I was responsible for." It was the first significant impact on Taylor of the ascendancy of what would become known as the Jim Crow era, the infamous legal codification of racism, named after the minstrel song "Jump Jim Crow," sung by a white man in blackface makeup.

One day the Southards announced they were moving to Chicago. Taylor wanted to go with them, but his parents insisted he move back home. Taylor was devastated. "I dropped from the happy life of a 'millionaire kid' to that of a common errand boy, all within a few weeks," Taylor wrote.

So it seemed that, at around thirteen years old, this was the life that lay ahead, a return to a poor farming family with few prospects. Soon, however, a new mentor would appear in Taylor's life, a cyclist once crowned the world's fastest man, who went by the name of Birdie Munger.

CHAPTER 3

# The President
# and the Cyclists

A light rain fell on the sultry morning of July 19, 1892, as Birdie Munger joined thousands of cyclists swarming across Washington, parading their newfound power as one of the nation's most important interest groups. President Benjamin Harrison, who had invited the group's leaders to the White House, watched as cycling regiments from across the country rode down Pennsylvania Avenue.

Many Americans rarely strayed more than a few miles from home, especially in rural areas. The transportation options were horse, carriage, streetcar, and train. Automobiles were still years away. Bicycles, at this moment, represented a revolutionary step forward, but Munger had seen the poor condition of the nation's roads during his cross-country trek, and he joined others in Washington in calling for change.

As a Chicago leader of the League of American Wheelmen, which had more than one million members nationwide, Munger wanted nothing less than to remake the country with the bicycle at the center. The group called for the nation's rutted dirt roads to be graded, straightened, and paved. Editorials in *Good Roads* magazine, published by the League, urged the federal government to spend millions of dollars to build the arteries of a fast-growing nation. The cyclists were backed by a petition signed by 150,000 people—one of the largest of its kind in the nation's history to that point—urging Congress to create such a network of roads. The petition was wound around two wheels made of oak that reached a combined height of seven feet and weighed six hundred pounds. The League hoped Harrison would become an enthusiastic supporter, but he hardly seemed the kind to embrace revolution.

Before becoming president, Harrison had been a one-term senator from Indiana. As it happened, his Indianapolis home on Delaware Street, a two-story, sixteen-room Italianate mansion, was located about six blocks east of the modest dwelling occupied by the Taylor family. The Republican Party didn't nominate their candidate for the presidency until the eighth ballot, and he lost the popular vote in the general election by 100,000 ballots. But the quirks of the Electoral College system made him victorious. He stood five feet and six inches, a portly, bearded figure with penetrating blue eyes and a manner so cold, so stone-faced, that he was known as the "human iceberg."

His starting days in office were markedly inept. "I do not mistrust the future," Harrison had said in his inaugural address. Yet he refused to turn on the new electric light switch at the White House for fear that the newfangled invention would electrocute him. He picked not a single Southerner for his Cabinet. Instead, he alienated party bosses by rejecting most of their choices and insisted on picking a Cabinet that looked like him, all fellow Presbyterians, mainly Civil War officers.

Still, to families such as the Taylors, he would have sounded visionary about race relations when he said, "Shall the prejudices and paralysis of slavery continue to hang upon the skirts of progress?" Some believed it meant that Harrison, a former Civil War general who had worked to help elect Abraham Lincoln, intended to fulfill Lincoln's promises to the twelve percent of US citizens who mainly were descended from Africans forcibly brought to the Americas as slaves.

Harrison wanted the black vote for his party, and so he relished the idea of ensuring that the Fifteenth Amendment guaranteeing equal voting rights for all men would be enforced. But Harrison's belief was deeper than crass political opportunism. True to his roots as a "radical Republican," Harrison dreamed of providing millions of dollars to poor Southern schools, hoping that the money would be used to improve literacy among blacks. Without such federal support, Harrison knew, it was unlikely that many local Southern school districts would educate black citizens.

Harrison's family legacy demonstrated the difficulty of confronting the issue. He was the great-grandson of his namesake, Benjamin Harrison V, a slave owner and signer of the Declaration of Independence, which declared that "all men are created equal" even while it (and the subsequent Constitution) effectively enshrined the rights of whites to own slaves and denied equality to blacks. He was the grandson of former president William Henry Harrison, also a slave owner, who had served only one month in office before dying of pneumonia. Harrison grew up on his grandfather's farm, where a sixteen-room mansion was set on the bluff of the Ohio River. As a young boy, Harrison learned that the farm was on the dividing line between slavery and freedom. On the Kentucky side of the river, many blacks were enslaved. If they could cross the river to Ohio, where Harrison lived, blacks could be free, and he frequently saw slaves running through the thickets on the family farm as they sought freedom. Harrison fought for the North in the Civil War, joined Sherman's march to Atlanta, and went into politics with a vision to build upon Lincoln's legacy. In speeches, Harrison recalled how blacks "were brought here in chains," lived under "a cruel slave code," and had been "subjected to indignities, cruelties, outrages, and a repression of rights such as find no parallel in the history of civilization." As president, he pushed time and again for voting rights and education for blacks, and he promised never to be silent on the issue. Still, blacks and their white supporters were right to be skeptical, having seen similar efforts fail repeatedly since the end of the Civil War.

Attacks on Harrison for being too radical underscored the odds against him, even with a Republican-controlled Congress. Many Southern politicians were trying to undo the post–Civil War policy of Reconstruction, enacting a series of Jim Crow laws. Harrison's effort to secure voting rights and educational aid for blacks repeatedly failed amid opposition from Southern Democrats, and his enthusiasm cooled. The harsh reality was that Reconstruction had been dismantled, promises had been broken time and again, and blacks could count on little from either party.

All these political crosscurrents were in the background as Harrison walked onto the White House portico on that rainy July morning to greet the cyclists. They were a powerful political constituency, and Harrison needed their support. In the lead was the Washington Military Cyclists Corps, riding in regalia, muskets slung over their shoulders. Dozens of cyclists had already passed the White House by the time Harrison arrived. An impeccable dresser, the president wore a frock coat, dark trousers, and a silk hat.

Given all his other troubles, Harrison was pleased to focus on the jobs that had been created by the bicycle industry. "The parade broke all records, being the largest turnout of cyclers ever seen in this country," the *New York Times* reported. The cyclists rode four abreast as they passed by the president, who waved in return. Dressed in suits, with medals hanging from their necks, many cyclists twirled Japanese parasols, having been given this unlikely gift from a wheel manufacturer.

The clattering of hundreds of cyclists and their machines, working in unison like some fantastic mixing bowl, became louder and louder as the wheelmen churned their way past the White House, riding up the boulevards designed by Pierre L'Enfant and toward the Capitol, where Washingtonians lined the streets. A group of a hundred women led the parade "and attracted considerable attention by their graceful riding," as the correspondent for Washington's *Evening Star* put it.

Some religious leaders, apparently alarmed at the independence provided by the bicycle, preached against the device as the work of the devil. The League of American Wheelmen tried to mollify the churches and discussed a ban on Sunday races. But for every opponent, there were advocates who promised that a ride in the country could cure any ill. The day before Harrison met with the cyclists, hundreds of wheelmen in England attended a sermon on the importance of "Sunday recreation," in which a church leader advocated riding as the ideal complement to devotion. To sit on Sundays could lead more to rust than rest, the church leader said. "There was true recreation in cycling and enjoying the beauties of nature as seen in verdant fields, luxuriant woods and smiling orchards," reported the London *Telegraph*, in describing the sermon.

The bicycle was at this point mostly used by wealthier urban residents. A new model cost $65 to $150, although prices would eventually drop with mass production. Still, for lower-income Americans, including many blacks, cheaper used bicycles became available. By comparison, a horse could cost up to $200 and require $150 a year for food and stabling. For those blacks who could afford it, the bicycle helped free them from Jim Crow laws that restricted their access on some public transportation systems.

The bicycle parade had been the brainchild of the Wheelmen and its president, Colonel Charles E. Burdett, who organized the campaign for a national road network. Burdett took his lobbying straight to Harrison, joining him on the White House balcony as the cyclists paraded before them. At one point Harrison turned to Burdett and said, "If wheelmen secure us the good roads for which they are so zealously working, your body deserves a medal in recognition of its philanthropy."

After a day spent lobbying the president and members of Congress, the riders gathered in the Georgetown section of Washington, where a race was held alongside the Potomac River to Cabin John Bridge, a distance of eight miles. From the Georgetown docks, many of the cyclists took the steamers *River Queen* and *Macalaster* and other vessels across the Potomac to watch races held on what was then called Analostan Island (later renamed Theodore Roosevelt Island in honor of the twenty-sixth president). Analostan, which previously had been a training ground for black soldiers during the Civil War, now was used regularly for cycling meets. Eventually some four thousand spectators ringed the track as the rain abated.

As racers approached the starting line for a series of preliminary heats, one man in particular drew notice from the crowd: the lean, mustachioed figure of Munger. Having set the standard by which all riders were judged in the early days of cycle racing, Munger was still adjusting to the much faster "safety" bike, with its equal-sized wheels. Ten days before arriving in Washington, Munger had finished second in a New York contest that determined the American champion in the ten-mile race. Everyone expected Munger to "capture at least one prize," the *Evening Star* reported.

Despite its name, a "safety" bicycle hardly ensured safety; racing on narrow, crowded tracks was one of the most dangerous sporting activities of the day. A group of opposing riders could gang up on the strongest rider, forming a pocket around him and preventing him from gaining a victory. Worse, an unscrupulous opponent—and there were many with so much money on the line—could lightly touch the wheel of another rider, causing the victim to fly over his handlebars. The track was a dangerous place, with riders killed or maimed every year. Tempers flared and nerves frayed as riders jockeyed for the slightest advantage. The rain-slickened track was "absurdly narrow with sharp, dangerous turns," as one newspaper put it.

Munger started strongly, winning the first heat. But in the second heat he either hit a slick spot or someone pushed him, and he went flying off his cycle. Munger hurt his thigh, had a cut under his eye, and his bicycle was wrecked. As newspaper writers wondered whether Munger would return for a second and final day of racing, Munger and other members of the Chicago bicycle contingent donned white suits and joined several thousand cyclists for an evening of celebration of their cause. Tables were set up on the lawn of the Columbia Athletic Club, which operated the athletic fields on Analostan Island and owned a clubhouse on 14th Street. As hundreds of Chinese lanterns illuminated the evening, and the cyclists were entertained by the Overman Wheel Band and the Mandolin, Banjo and Guitar Club, Colonel Burdett declared the bicycle would change the world. It would be central to every branch of trade and all manner of warfare. One man rose to say that at first he thought it "ridiculous" that a woman would ride a bicycle, "but times had changed."

On the following morning, Munger awoke stiff and sore from the fall he had taken the previous day. By the time the cyclists arrived at the Analostan Island track, the *Times* reported, "most of the events had very slim fields of starters, the calamities and accidents of yesterday having apparently frightened most of the riders off."

But Munger was back—and would fare even worse this time.

During a two-mile race, another rider fell "and Munger went over him, landing with great force." He was "painfully injured," while his three bicycles needed, as the *Washington Post* put it, "the attendance of the cycling veterinarian."

His illustrious career was almost over, but Munger did not want to quit. Three months later, on September 13, 1892, he showed up at a race in Springfield, Massachusetts, where 750 top cyclists were trying to create new world records. Munger again took a hard fall, and he blamed it on a fellow rider, Carl Hess. The two met in the dressing room, exchanged violent threats, "resulting finally in Munger striking Hess a blow in the face," the *New York Times* reported.

The fight ended Munger's chances at a top finish. He entered a few more competitions, but his days as the king of the sport were over. Seven years had passed since he had broken the twenty-four-hour cycling record in Boston, and many prizes had come since then. Now Munger began to think about two things: building a bicycle factory, and finding someone to manage who could become the new champion.

In pursuit of both of these endeavors, Munger, now twenty-nine years old, would find his way to Indianapolis, a growing center of the bicycle industry. He would, per chance, meet a cyclist who was gaining fame at an astonishingly young age: Major Taylor.

## CHAPTER 4

# Birdie and Major
# in Indianapolis

A week after Munger slugged his competitor at the Massachusetts race, he showed up for the annual contest in Peoria, Illinois, where Taylor had won third place two years earlier. Munger's career was essentially over, and a reporter covering the meet wrote that Munger was not expected to do well "because of his poor racing in the East of late." But Munger had recovered from his recent injuries and stunned the field by winning the one-mile race on September 27, 1892, for which he was awarded a $300 piano. Munger's transition from his championship days had been difficult, and reporters wrote about him in valedictory terms. One journalist said, "it would take columns to describe L. D. 'Birdie' Munger, the fast Chicago rider, the most wonderful rider in some respects. He is the hardest rider on the path, the best natured, the shrewdest, the best loser we ever saw; always ready to do the hard work or the clowning, as may strike his fancy." But the story made clear the twenty-nine-year-old was no longer the best; that title had now been seized by the twenty-three-year-old Arthur Zimmerman, whose riding was "more brilliant than that of any other man," winning American championships in 1890, 1891, and 1892, and who would go on to win more than a thousand races.

Munger set a new goal: he would become a leader of the industry by making the new bicycles on which future champions would ride. Munger, in fact, had always loved to invent and build. His father, Theodore, had been issued patents and spent many hours tinkering with inventions in Detroit, and Munger was known as a master mechanic. For the rest of his life, he would be obsessed with patents of tires and wheels, no doubt inspired by the story of John Dunlop's invention of the pneumatic tire. So, shortly after the race in Peoria, Munger moved from Chicago to Indianapolis and opened the Munger Cycle Manufacturing Company. Indianapolis was already one of the nation's centers of bicycle production, including a company that specialized in manufacturing rubber tires, using imports of a South American rubber tree called the Pará, as well as the Indiana Bicycle Company, which was sprawled across eight brick buildings.

Indianapolis boomed with factories and mills, many strung along canals and the banks of the White River. A network of railroads connected at a downtown station, carrying goods and passengers from coast to coast. The National Road, commissioned by Thomas Jefferson to expand the nation westward, bisected the city as well, carrying all manner of horse-drawn traffic and bicyclists.

Around the nation, some of the leading inventors put their energy into building a better bicycle. In Detroit, Henry Ford, an avid cyclist, used bicycle parts to create what he called a "quadricycle," the forerunner of his mass-produced automobile. In Dayton, Ohio, Orville and Wilbur Wright opened the Wright Cycle Co., launching a line of bicycles that would later give them insights into building airplanes. The Wrights' top bicycle sold for $65.

Munger, needing funds in his bid to join such illustrious entrepreneurs, got in touch with three cousins who lived in Indianapolis, brothers Augustus, Anderson, and Orlando Bruner, whose background was in sewer contracting and the laundry business. Augustus became the company president, Anderson vice president, and Orlando treasurer. Munger became the company's manager and, due to his fame and knowledge of cycles, it was his name that was attached to the company.

• • •

Munger's firm took over a three-story brick building at the intersection of Fort Wayne Avenue and North Delaware Street, employing ninety people, and using a sixty-horsepower steam engine to produce about four thousand bicycles per year. The factory stood seven blocks northwest of one of the city's best-known landmarks, Monument Circle, which featured a nearly completed twenty-eight-story-tall memorial to Indiana veterans, the hub around which Indianapolis spread. Nearby stood the elegant Renaissance Revival–style domed state capitol, its Beaux Arts embellishments echoing the US Capitol. Between the monument and the state house, a circular building called a Cyclorama had been built in honor of Civil War veterans. In this time before movies, people flocked to such buildings to take in a 360-degree view, and this one featured a painstakingly produced depiction of the Battle of Atlanta, an event still vivid to many. Eventually, as interest in viewing the war scene faded, bicycle racers were allowed to train inside the structure, giving the original name a double meaning.

Across the nation, bicycle factories ran twenty-four hours a day, and still the demand outstripped supply, giving Munger his opportunity. Soon, according to a boosterish history of Indianapolis published at the time, Munger created "one of the largest and finest cycle factories in the world," with its name becoming "as familiar as Shakespeare or Robinson Crusoe." The company promised to spare no expense to make what it called "the lightest wheel on earth."

"The Munger!" proclaimed one of the ads. "Wait for it! It is a stunner!"

Taylor worked in a bicycle store a few blocks away from Munger's factory and surely knew of his arrival. Taylor's world lay mostly within a few square miles: his family home on the outskirts where an African American community of small houses and scattered farms had been established; the Southard mansion nearer downtown; the shops on Pennsylvania Street, dubbed Bicycle Row, where Taylor had worked; and now the Munger factory. Taylor could easily walk or bike to it all. After leaving his job at the Hay & Willits bicycle store, Taylor worked for an industry pioneer from England named Harry Hearsey, who ran his business from a two-story building on Bicycle Row. Many custom-ers were nervous about learning to ride on busy streets, so the store offered a second-floor room with "padded walls" where lessons were conducted, and the inevitable falls softened. (It was Mark Twain who, after describing his many crashes as he learned to ride a high-wheeler, wrote: "Get a bicycle. You will not regret it, if you live.")

One day, Munger visited Hearsey's store. Munger had heard of Taylor's early racing victories and seen his cycling tricks. Now he met Taylor, and suggested that the "Major" try one of his bicycles. Taylor came to Munger's factory and, soon enough, accepted a job. The young cyclist considered Munger "one of the greatest riders that ever sat in a saddle." Taylor's job included helping out in what was known as Munger's "bachelor quarters," which a journalist at the time described as "famous throughout the cycling world," a favorite haunt of visiting racers. As Munger later told it, he was the first to notice Taylor's true potential, and offered him a job as "cook, chambermaid and general man of all work."

Munger wanted to produce the lightest, strongest bicycle ever made, marketing to an elite clientele. Hundreds of patents were filed on ways to make bicycles lighter, speedier, safer—many of which would later be applied to auto production. The frames were assembled using the highest quality steel tubing, reinforced at the joints. The hubs, around which the wheels spun, were made from another high-quality grade of steel. The tires were wound around wooden rims. The cranks and pedals were developed with newly patented fastenings. All of this, as Munger advertised, created a sleek, strong, fast-running bicycle that he called—with only modest hyperbole—the world's finest. Munger's top model would soon sell for $100 or more.

Taylor at first was given the task of caring for Munger's own bicy-cle, cleaning and lubing and polishing. As Munger watched Taylor's riding skills, he presented him with one of the company's finest mod-els, which weighed fourteen pounds, remarkably light even by mod-ern standards. Taylor was so enthralled with the gift that he could not stop riding it. After that, Munger said, Taylor spent his time at the racetrack instead of cleaning the chambers. Munger "stormed and stormed, but it did no good," he later recounted. One day, Munger went to the track to "see for himself what the 'Major' was doing." To Munger's astonishment, his stopwatch showed that Taylor finished a mile in two minutes and nine seconds.

The world record at the time was two minutes and seven seconds.

Munger could barely believe what he was witnessing. It confirmed everything he had dreamed as he planned the production of his elite product. Now his little-known assistant was riding a Munger-produced bike at a nearly world record pace. Munger, realizing that Taylor could provide invaluable promotion for the company, put him in a series of races, and always found him at the front. Munger and his racing friends soon invited Taylor on their training rides. Taylor joined them on journeys that stretched as long as a hundred miles. The other cyclists, unaware that Taylor had informally come close to a world record, soon realized Taylor's skill as he often sped ahead of them. Years later, Taylor recalled how Munger "became closer and closer attached to me as time went on. Had I been his own son he could not have acted more kindly toward me." He had gone from being a "millionaire's son" with the Southard family to being all but adopted by the man who had been the world's fastest cyclist. Throughout his life, this would be a pattern, as he simultaneously faced the most brutal racism but also was embraced by a series of benefactors who were impressed by his talent and treated him without regard to race.

Soon, another hero arrived. The great Arthur Zimmerman was coming to Indianapolis to compete in a race that had attracted riders from across the nation. Munger invited Zimmerman to stay at his bachelor quarters and asked Taylor to fetch the champion at the train station.

The arrival of "Zimmie," as he was known, was the talk of the city. Two weeks earlier, Zimmerman had set two world records in races in Chicago, including the fastest mile, and now hundreds turned out to greet him. The local newspaper, the *Sentinel*, gushed that racers had come from across the country to try to wrest the championship title from Zimmerman, creating a contest "far superior to anything of the kind ever seen in the world," with "every race for blood." As Zimmerman stepped off the train, a brass band played, and a welcoming committee stood nearby. Taylor, who recognized "my hero" from pictures printed in the local newspapers, worked his way through the crowd. Perhaps Zimmerman remembered seeing Taylor race at Peoria several years earlier, but Taylor was now fourteen years old and had grown considerably since then. Taylor explained he had come at Munger's behest. Zimmerman smiled, shook Taylor's hand, asked his name, and invited the young admirer to join him on the carriage ride to Munger's home. Taylor wore the gold medal that he had won in a ten-mile race, prompting Zimmerman to ask about the feat. The two talked nonstop all the way to Munger's. Arriving at the bachelor quarters, Zimmerman warmly greeted Munger, and the conversation turned to Taylor.

"I am going to make a champion out of that boy some day," Munger said, admonishing Taylor to refrain from cigarettes and liquor. If Taylor lived a "clean life," Munger continued, he would "make him the fastest bicycle rider in the world." Zimmerman told Taylor that if Munger predicted such greatness, "I feel sure you will scale the heights."

Soon, another champion rider, Willie Windle, arrived at Munger's home. The diminutive rider, nicknamed "Wee Willie," had battled against Zimmerman and Munger during the heyday of high-wheel races. Here, at one dining table with the teenage Taylor, were three of the world's fastest riders.

If one evening could be said to affect the course of Taylor's life, this would be the one. Munger was the mentor, advising Taylor, providing him with a bike and a path forward. Zimmerman was the future role model, telling Taylor how he raced in Europe (something Munger never did) and became world champion by following a strenuous training schedule that Taylor would adopt. Indeed, Zimmerman was in the midst of writing a short book called *Points for Cyclists with Training*, one of the earliest and most sophisticated manuals that laid out how to prepare for strenuous athletic competitions. Taylor listened as Zimmerman talked about how to breathe and rest; how to tuck the head in an aerodynamic position and pedal with the proper cadence; when to save energy and when to leap into a last-minute sprint. It was, Zimmerman wrote, a "gradual fitting of the human frame to undergo the severest physical exertion." Taylor would later write how proud he would be if, one day, people thought of him as a "black Zimmerman."

The third racer at the table, Windle, had an extraordinary story to share with Taylor. Windle had grown up in a small town called Millbury, about six miles south of Worcester, Massachusetts. His father, Thomas Windle, like Taylor's, had fought for the North in the Civil War, and barely survived battles and malaria. When the elder Windle returned to Massachusetts, he became a Republican Party stalwart and a large property owner, running a woolen mill. That gave "Wee Willie" the opportunity to focus on his passion of bicycle racing and, like Taylor, he emerged as a star at a young age. Eight years earlier, in 1885, when Windle was fourteen years old, he had learned about Munger's exploits in Boston, setting the twenty-four-hour racing record. Windle acquired a unicycle and, to strengthen his agility and put more power in his legs, he rode it eight miles from his home in Millbury to his school in Worcester and back, just as Taylor had strengthened himself by riding to and from his job at the bicycle store. At fifteen, Windle entered a three-mile race around a half-mile track at Worcester's Agricultural Park. As a newspaper later related, Windle "was then supposed to be simply a young fellow who thought he could ride. People thought differently when the race was over." Windle beat the county champion and went on to win race after race. At one point, he won fifty consecutive races, was declared world champion in a Canada meet, and, a year before this dinner gathering, had beaten Zimmerman in a one-mile race in Springfield, Massachusetts, winning a $1,000 piano. Zimmerman had also beaten Windle in a memorable race in which Windle's saddle broke at the halfway point. All of these tales were likely discussed as Taylor served the men their dinner and then joined them at the table. Taylor was just shy of his fifteenth birthday, the same age at which Windle had started his career. There likely was discussion at the dinner about the opportunities available in Worcester—less prejudice against blacks, and a thriving industrial base for manufacturing. Windle, only twenty-two years old at the time of this dinner, already lived in an opulent home and had earned enough money to construct a racing track on his property. Inside his home he stored $10,000 in prizes, including "diamonds in abundance, pianos, bicycles and enough silver to furnish a good-sized banquet hall," according to an account in the *Worcester Spy*. He was already thinking of switching to a business career, as Munger was in the process of doing, and in fact would stun the racing world by riding his last professional race just three months after the dinner at Munger's home.

Years later, Taylor said there was one thing he remembered above all else about the evening. He had seen none of the prejudice in this troika that he found in so many "would-be champions" in Indianapolis. "The thought flashed through my mind that men can be champions and still broad-minded . . . towards me, a colored boy." These men were "too big" for prejudice, and that thought remained "fresh in my mind" for years to come. As he talked over dinner with these three idols, Taylor felt himself "the proudest boy in the world."

The next morning, August 24, Taylor accompanied the three racers to a track at the state fairgrounds, where several thousand people crowded into the grandstands around a racing oval. After many heats were run, the anticipation built for the main event, a one-mile championship. Zimmerman and Windle were the top contenders, but Munger, now near full retirement, decided to test himself and joined the field. Even if Taylor had wanted to ride, he could not; the meet was sponsored by the Zig-Zag Cycling Club, which allowed only white riders. It was a symbol of the times. Days earlier, a few hundred blacks and whites had gathered in a nearby city to celebrate Emancipation Day. Lincoln's proclamation was read, and the editor of the Indianapolis black-oriented newspaper, *The Freeman*, delivered a speech titled "The Condition of Progress of the Colored Race Since the War," urging that the "peculiar brand of prejudice, known as 'American,'" be eliminated. The editor, W. Allison Sweeney, said that white industrial captains were refusing to employ blacks. The whites in the audience "cringed with shame at his just and withering reflections," Sweeney's newspaper recounted. Yet as the race at the fairgrounds got under way, no protest was made that blacks were excluded from competing. Taylor watched intently as his heroes moved to the starting line.

At stake was a diamond-encrusted gold cup and the potential to break the world record. A strong wind blew from the west. Taylor served as valet, helping Munger and the others get ready for the start. Zimmerman took off at a torrid pace, capturing first place in world record time of 2 minutes and 12¾ seconds, 3 seconds faster than the mark set a year earlier. (This one-mile race record was calculated differently than the one Taylor had nearly matched in his performance under Munger's watch days earlier.) Windle came in fourth and Munger placed out of the standings. As Zimmerman held aloft his gold cup, the crowd serenaded him with chants of "Zimmie!"

Munger rarely competed again. Instead, he would focus on making the world's fastest bike and fulfilling his vow to make Taylor the world's fastest man. But first Taylor would have to battle the racism that had been growing in the wake of the failures of Reconstruction.

President Benjamin Harrison's reelection campaign had ended in defeat. Blacks had been unenthusiastic and did not vote in the numbers that he needed. He had failed to use federal powers to stop lynching, which was growing more widespread, or to pass legislation designed to support black voting rights, or to finance schools mostly attended by blacks. Now he returned to his Indianapolis home.

Years earlier, Harrison had seen Munger and thousands of other cyclists mass by the White House in their call for better roads. Now Munger's factory was ten blocks south of Harrison's home, and the ex-president got caught up in the cycling craze. Harrison "will dignify the sport of wheeling," reported the *Washington Post*. Harrison intended to learn to ride, and he purchased "a Bicycle suit," a fashionable outfit of gray Scotch checks, "with stockings to harmonize," enabling him to participate in a "healthful and invigorating" endeavor that "will undoubtedly prove of great benefit to the former President of the United States."

Meanwhile, the Democratic administration of Grover Cleveland soon proved even worse for blacks than Harrison. Cleveland viewed the Reconstruction era as a failed experiment, and he did not use his power to enforce a constitutional amendment that guaranteed voting rights for blacks. Instead, he expressed confidence—against decades of evidence—that Southerners would do what was best for blacks. "I have faith in the honor and sincerity of the respectable white people of the South in their relations with the Negro and his improvement and well being," Cleveland said. Southerners "do not believe in the social equality of the race, and they make no false pretense in regard to it. That this does not grow out of hatred for the Negro is very plain." He went so far as to say that he was impressed that Southerners had "forgiven the blacks" for what happened during Reconstruction, which Cleveland called the "spoliation of the white men of the South." Only in due time, Cleveland believed, would the races live in harmony. Not surprisingly, Cleveland's patronizing message was taken by many whites as a license to impose new restrictions on blacks and effectively reverse the policies of Reconstruction. The federal government would not as readily come to the aid and defense of blacks, as was done during Reconstruction. Across the country, state and local governments, as well as private institutions, now took their cues from the political direction in Washington and denied basic rights to black citizens. In many places, racism was escalating with what seemed to be the government's tacit approval.

Taylor felt this resurgent racism directly. In early 1894, he learned that the League of American Wheelmen (LAW) was preparing to vote on a proposal to ban blacks from membership. The meeting would be held in Louisville, where his parents had lived until they moved to Indianapolis. The LAW sanctioned many professional bike races, and Taylor was concerned the proposed ban on black members would mean he could not race in the League's contests. Until now, efforts to ban black membership had been put to votes and failed. This time, the sentiment in the club indicated that the ban might pass. Munger headed to the meeting in Louisville and was likely in the audience when a Kentucky leader of the League, Colonel William Watts, argued for banning blacks.

"We understand no good in an organization of this kind can be done by mixing the races," Watts said to the assembled membership. His proposal was simple: the word "white" would be inserted as a qualification for membership. Many delegates interrupted his speech with applause, and the measure was approved by a vote of 127 to 54. While the vote was secret, the Massachusetts delegation announced later that it had unanimously opposed the ban.

The outright racism stoked Taylor's ambition and outrage. Just fifteen years old at the time, he wrote one of the most revealing letters of his life. Sarcastically describing himself as "illiterate"—he was, in fact, more literate than many Americans, black or white—he urged other blacks to speak out. (At the time, the illiteracy rate was fifty-seven percent for blacks and other minorities, and thirteen percent for whites.) He wrote to the cycling magazine *Bearings* that he didn't want to be part of an organization that excluded his race, and he boldly warned that blacks would form their own organization.

> *I am a cyclist; further, I am a negro. I have hesitated a long time, but now I think it high time for some one of my color to say a few words. . . .*
>
> *Negroes who wish to mix with white men are not so plentiful as you think. This great United States government has elevated us, given us education and strength to act for ourselves—for which we are very grateful—but we are still a race as different from others as God first made us.*
>
> *As cyclists we are still young, but as pleasure seekers we are old. Sociability is at least one half of a negro's life and we know that we cannot derive a portion of our existence in the social circles of the white race. We want nothing from south, north, east, or west but that which we are entitled to, and that is certainly not membership to any white man's league of wheelmen.*
>
> *I trust that you will find space in your valuable paper for this letter, that it may be an opening shot in the way of "putting up," instead of "down," the "son of Ham," as he grows interested in cycling. Hoping to hear from the colored cyclists as a body in the*

*near future, I still remain a true lover of what is right for both, yes
for all, classes.*

*Yours truly, Major Taylor (colored cyclist)*

The letter made Taylor an even greater target of racist attacks. Dozens of cartoons were published depicting Taylor in the worst stereotypes. Two months after Taylor's letter was published, the magazine *Cycling Life* published a cartoon showing an ape riding a bicycle, titled "Fast Black." A writer in Chicago's *Referee* magazine, who used the anonymous name of Phoebus to deliver a racist tirade, told readers of the sports journal that Watts and his League of American Wheelmen should be applauded for standing up against the "enthusiastic lovers of the blacks."

"The negro has little interest in anything beyond his daily needs, his personal vanity and a cake walk or barbers' ball now and then," Phoebus wrote. "The darkey is essentially a creature of today . . . he is a lazy, happy-go-lucky animal wherever he is . . . his lack-brain carelessness . . . the negro, outside of a few lemon-hued and saddle-colored specimens with enough white blood to make them cheeky, have no wish to belong to the L.A.W. and mighty few of them have the necessary $2 to spare." Phoebus then addressed a writer who had pointed out that even the antislavery leader Frederick Douglass wouldn't have been allowed to join the League. Phoebus responded dismissively that Douglass was not actually black because he had "the blood of exceeding brainy families." Phoebus said he was weary of whites "whose only acquaintance with the black man is in the matter of 'a shine, boss?'" The League "does not need" blacks, Phoebus concluded.

Such was the racism that Taylor endured; indeed, Taylor's rising prominence likely played a role in the ban. Munger responded to the ban by escalating his support of Taylor, finding places that would accept him as a contestant. It would long be a subject of speculation why Munger fought so hard for Taylor. Munger was "true as a die," said a writer for the *Chicago Tribune*, "always ready to make a sacrifice of himself for the benefit of another man." Munger's family had grown up in parts of Michigan and Canada where many blacks fled from slavery to freedom, giving Munger familiarity with them. Munger himself simply said he believed that Taylor had the right spirit, temperament, and talent for racing, regardless of race. What was clear was that Munger was the ultimate iconoclast, more determined and free-thinking than many others.

For his part, Taylor "will do anything in the wide world for Munger," a journalist wrote, and Munger "has complete power over him." The ban only increased Taylor's desire to show that a black man could compete and win against whites. Up to this point, Taylor had viewed his efforts mostly as a sporting contest. Now, he cast them in greater, societal terms. His white friends, he wrote, weren't just trying to help him win. They were, Taylor wrote, "fighting for a principle as well as for my personal success." Those words would define Munger's role in Taylor's life.

Munger now began training Taylor in earnest, sending him to local high schools and colleges to run in preliminary heats with local racers. Taylor rode the bicycle made for him by Munger and won easily. His slender legs grew thicker and sinewy. An opportunity for a bigger test arose in the summer of 1895, when a local promoter announced a seventy-five-mile race, longer than any Taylor had run. It was a race likely to draw national attention and had a prize worth $300. But white riders would never knowingly let Taylor participate. As a result, Taylor wrote later, "due wholly to the fact that I was colored, the greatest secrecy surrounded the arrangements for this event." A plan was hatched that required Taylor to hide in the bushes and join the field at the crack of the starter's pistol.

Thirty-six of the area's fastest riders, all of them white, gathered at the starting line, unaware of Taylor's presence. Taylor stayed just behind the field for a few miles but was soon spotted by racers who called him "vile" names. As he caught up with the leaders, several tried to push him to the ground, but Taylor stayed steady, profiting from years of experience as a trick rider who could teeter without falling. Then some racers threatened to kill him if he didn't turn back. Taylor again stayed steady. "I decided that if my time had come I might just as well die trying to keep ahead of the bunch," Taylor wrote later. Speed could beat any threat, at least for the moment. With thirty miles to go, he jumped through an opening amid the leaders and made a "feverish dash" that he hoped would give him a wide lead. Every mile put him farther from a gang that he was convinced wanted to kill him. Passing through a thinly inhabited road, weeping willows on one side and a cemetery on the other, he momentarily envisioned this would be the spot for his tormenters "to carry out their dire threats." He pedaled furiously. A hard rain began to fall, muddying the road and slowing him just as he saw a group of riders clumped in the distance. He feared he might be attacked. Instead, it was a friendly group waiting to pace him toward the next town, helping Taylor finish far ahead of the field. The race promoter, a real estate developer named George Catterson, handed him the prize of a deed to a house lot, which the soaked Taylor tucked into his pocket. Later that day Taylor proudly presented the deed to his mother, who hadn't known beforehand that her son would compete in the seventy-five-mile race. She made Taylor promise "that I would never ride such a long race again." It would be a promise that he could not keep.

As the white riders vowed to keep him out of their contests, Taylor won a race against a hundred local black riders for the right to compete in a blacks-only championship in Chicago. Arriving in Illinois, Taylor read in the *Chicago Inter Ocean* that "great interest is centered on 'Major' Taylor" because he recently had won a seventy-five-mile race through mud and rain.

Taylor learned he would be competing against a man who was widely thought to be the nation's top black rider, Henry Stewart, the "St. Louis Flyer." A larger, much more muscular man than Taylor, Stewart ridiculed the sixteen-year-old from Indianapolis. Taylor overheard the taunts and began to feel nervous and weak, writing later that "it was the first time in my life that I had experienced such a reaction." The challenge made him "determined to beat Stewart at any cost." Taylor won the race by ten lengths of a bicycle and then won a rematch. Taylor now felt "very certain that no rider, regardless of his size or physique," could shake him. He yearned for the right to compete against the best racers, white or black. As he worked at Munger's factory and cleaned the bachelor quarters, Taylor revealed his desire to Munger, who backed him wholeheartedly.

One day, someone at Munger's firm asked why he gave so much attention to "that little darkey." Taylor, Munger replied, "was an unusual boy . . . he has fine habits, is quick to learn, is as game a youngster as I have ever seen, and can be relied upon to do whatever he is told. He has excellent judgment and has a remarkably cool head. Although he is sixteen years old he can beat any boy in the city right now. He is improving every time I go out with him."

Munger's explanation did not satisfy other members of the firm, perhaps his cousins who held top management positions. Taylor wrote later that some unnamed directors of the company "strenuously objected to Mr. Munger's befriending me simply because of my color, and I was inadvertently the cause of Mr. Munger's severing relations with the firm." As Taylor told the story, Munger's attachment to him was so strong, and the objections by the partners were so severe, that Munger decided he had no choice but to leave Indianapolis. There may have been business or family reasons for Munger's abrupt departure from the city. But Taylor believed Munger had left after being angered by racism. In the fall of 1895, Munger told Taylor that he was going to build a new life in Worcester, Massachusetts, near where his friend and former racer "Wee Willie" Windle lived. He asked Taylor to join him.

Taylor saw no future in Indianapolis, and now he faced the loss of yet another mentor. He went home, won the reluctant approval of his parents, collected his belongings and his custom-made bicycle, and headed for the station. A crowd of friends awaited Munger and Taylor as they prepared to board the train to Massachusetts. As they departed, Munger made a defiant vow. One day, the pair would return to Indianapolis, with Taylor crowned "champion rider of America."

CHAPTER 5

# No Such Prejudice

The passenger train carrying Munger and Taylor from Indianapolis pulled into Worcester's Union Station in September 1895. The city of nearly 100,000 people fifty miles west of Boston was the proverbial melting pot, filled with immigrants from nearly every corner of Europe, as well as black migrants from the South. They labored in the heart of the country's industrial revolution, in sprawling smoke-belching factories that produced shoes, clothing, textiles, and machinery. The workers mostly lived in tightly packed "triple deckers" in dense working-class neighborhoods. Nearby but a world apart, the moguls who owned the factories lived in spacious mansions, situated on lush lanes and boulevards.

The Blackstone River wound through the city, railroads crisscrossed in every direction, and horses and buggies clattered on the streets. Church spires rose above the landscape, from Catholic to Congregationalist, and the recently opened Lothrop's Opera House attracted acts from across the country. Theater and orchestral performances were held at the elegant Mechanics Hall. A city set upon seven hills, Worcester was dotted with parks, ponds, and lakes, providing a respite from its industrial core.

Within weeks of his arrival, Munger took over the massive plant of the New England Steel Company, a seven-acre site on Bloomingdale Street that sat in the shadow of Union Station's two-hundred-foot-tall Norman-style clock tower and directly next to the freight tracks and a coal elevator. He called it the Worcester Cycle Manufacturing Company. He converted the former steel factory's network of open hearths and casting equipment into machinery that could produce thousands of bicycles. Workers soon filled the complex, producing the lightweight bicycles for which Munger would be known.

Immigrants had long been attracted to Worcester, fleeing violence or economic hardships in their homelands. Jews escaped Russian pogroms and built a new world on Water Street, living in tenements above small shops. The Irish fled famine and built the Blackstone Canal. Armenians escaped a series of massacres in the 1890s (which foreshadowed the genocide of 1915), and reestablished their community, their churches, and culture. French-Canadians came south to work in factories, accompanied by a sizable number of Scandinavians and Germans. They were attracted by busy operations such as the Washburn & Moen's North Works, a wire manufacturer that at one point employed more than two thousand people. Working side by side in hot, smoky, loud factories, speaking an array of languages and following diverse religions, the men and women of Worcester gained a reputation for their willingness to labor under the most difficult conditions as long as the pay and benefits were good. One family member told another back home, more and more relatives crammed into the triple-deckers, and the city and its businesses grew in the classic American fashion. The city had a liberal reputation, welcoming people of every ethnic group and race, befitting its history as a stop on the Underground Railroad. Still, just beneath the surface, tensions simmered between groups such as Swedish Protestants and Irish Catholics, and old Yankees and new immigrants. Those clashes, however, seemed a long way from the deeper racism and insularity that had prompted Munger and Taylor to leave Indianapolis. They were delighted at their newfound opportunities. Munger promptly set about spending his investors' money, and Taylor worked for him as a machinist's assistant. All the while, Munger made time to keep his promise that he would train Taylor into the world's preeminent cyclist.

Shortly after their arrival, Munger took Taylor to 10 Elm Street, one of the most elaborate buildings in Worcester, a four-story structure in the center of downtown that looked like an amalgam of a castle and a French chateau, richly ornamented, with a brick façade, triangular rooflines, and topped by a rounded two-story turret. This was the YMCA, one of the finest in New England. Inside was a two-story gymnasium, ringed by an indoor running track. It was just four years earlier that James Naismith had invented the sport of basketball at a YMCA in nearby Springfield, and the Worcester building was one of the earliest to have a full-scale court. A natatorium—a swimming pool—filled an underground level. As Taylor walked into the gym, basketballs were arrayed near the hoop, and gym equipment was scattered throughout.

Taylor's entry was more than a visit to an extraordinary training facility; it was nothing less than a symbol of being truly free after being banned from the YMCA in Indianapolis. Here in Worcester he was welcomed, and he trained for many months. Taylor recalled it vividly.

"I was in Worcester only a very short time before I realized there was no such race prejudice existing among the bicycle riders there as I experienced in Indiana," Taylor wrote. "When I learned that I could join the Y.M.C.A. in Worcester, I was pleased beyond expression. . . . I shall always be grateful to Worcester as I am firmly convinced that I would shortly have dropped riding, owing to the disagreeable incidents that befell my lot while riding in and around Indianapolis, were it not for the cordial manner in which people received me."

Munger left Taylor in the hands of Edward W. Wilder, the physical director of the YMCA and a basketball enthusiast, who created a rigorous training program. The idea of exercise for the masses was still something of a novelty, and magazines of the time published stories about the wonders that could be achieved in the gym. The higher classes, who performed little physical labor, had been encouraged to exercise, but it was the creation of the YMCA and similar organizations that promoted such recreation for the masses, many of whom were adjusting from the transition from farms to factories or offices. Around the time that Taylor entered the Worcester YMCA, *Munsey's Magazine* published an article about a similar facility, assuring women that they, too, could benefit from exercise. "You see that girl?"

an instructor was quoted as saying. "She came here two years ago, pale faced, with no chest at all; her shoulders were bent, her throat was thin, and showed ugly cords; her carriage was exceedingly bad." Now after rigorous exercise that included swinging from ropes, climbing ladders, and pedaling on a bicycle-type machine, the woman had undergone a "remarkable" change; her chest was strong, her bearing erect, and she had turned into a "very pretty girl." Within a few years, a magazine called *Physical Culture* was launched, and the first "physique contest" in America would be staged.

Taylor studied books and consulted other cyclists about the best training methods. None was more important than the 1895 volume coauthored by Arthur Zimmerman, the hero he had met in Indiana. In *Zimmerman Abroad and Points on Training*, the champion detailed what he called a "training science," which included instructions on what to eat, how to exercise, and what not to do. Go to sleep early. Do not drink or smoke. Ramp up training gradually. Get constant rubdowns to prevent stiffness. Keep "everlastingly at it. Going around the track, mile after mile, does become monotonous, but the coming flyer, if he would succeed, must cultivate patience." Taylor followed it all, particularly Zimmerman's closing, inspirational thought: "Nothing can be more admirable to look upon than the form of a thoroughly well trained athlete. The cultivation of the physical powers that God has placed latent in man is as honorable and commendable as the cultivation of the mind."

Around the same time, chemist Wilbur Atwater released his study of the impact of food on athletic performance. He found bicycle racers to be the ideal subjects, and he studied some of Taylor's eventual competitors to learn about their nutrition. He constructed a contraption on which a cyclist—whose diet was carefully cataloged—would pedal on a machine and breathe into what he called a respiration calorimeter. The cyclist pedaled for hours as his metabolism was studied. From this work, Atwater provided the US government with nutrition guidelines, and cyclists gained scientific information about the number of calories they should consume for peak performance. The highest-performing athletes, he found, consumed twice as much protein as the average farmer. At a time when the eugenics movement suggested that blacks were inherently inferior, Atwater said that a person's intellectual and moral condition is "largely regulated by their plane of living . . . how they are housed and clothed and fed." Atwater urged a reduction in consumption of fatty foods and an increase in exercise. The focus on types of caloric input was, for its time, a revolutionary idea, and later adopted by the US Department of Agriculture and the US Olympic committee. Taylor would incorporate many of the ideas into his rigorously planned diet.

A photograph of Taylor at this time showed him with little visible musculature, a shirt falling loosely over his body. Nobody would have picked him out of a crowd as a top athlete. Taylor's legs were sturdy, but his upper body was relatively weak. Strength on a bicycle came not just from legs, as seemed obvious, but from a strong core. This was a common problem for cyclists: while the chest got little workout during riding, a top rider needed superior strength in that part of the body to excel. Taylor spent hours using the Whitley Exerciser, a pulley system of cords that was advertised at the time as the best way to expand the chest, shoulders, and back. Taylor lifted weights and clubs that resembled bowling pins. He rode his bicycle on Worcester's hills, up and back, until he bested his prior record. He spent hours with sparring partners in a boxing ring, finding it a powerful way to strengthen his arms and reaction time. His aim, he wrote, was to become "physically perfect."

Taylor also worked on his breathing, enlarging his lung capacity and improving his timing for the greatest exertion, crucial for sprints. This would be the key to Taylor's success: he was more disciplined, and better physically developed, than any of his competitors. He became obsessive about his diet. As he later wrote, he became convinced that it was "a matter of ounces over or under my normal weight" that would be the difference between victory and defeat. He consumed protein-rich meals of raw eggs at an astonishing rate. He never touched alcohol or smoked. After months of training, photographs showed Taylor looking strikingly muscular in his upper body, now in harmony with his already-thickened legs.

It was during this period that he created a test. Amid the hills of Worcester, one of the greatest challenges for cyclists was the steep climb of George Street, a narrow thoroughfare paved with cobblestones that threaded uphill amid commercial buildings with a top grade of twenty-four percent. Word spread that Taylor would attempt the climb, "and a big crowd was on hand to see me make my initial attempt," Taylor wrote. He made it on his first try, and fifteen minutes later, he did it again.

Taylor soon felt ready for his first significant race, described in the *Worcester Spy* as a ten-mile contest "open to colored riders living within a radius of 25 miles of Worcester." The prizes included a twenty-one-inch-high silver cup, provided by Willie Windle, the famous racer Taylor had met in Indianapolis. "Everybody was anxious to get a glimpse of the chap from whom his friends expected great things," the *Spy* reported. "Young Taylor has not been in the city very long, and, as he is an unassuming, modest sort of chap, it is not very generally known that he is the champion colored rider of the United States." While there was no such official title, the *Spy* reporter recounted Taylor's victories in places such as Indianapolis and Chicago and calculated that he had earned twenty first-place finishes in significant contests. The story was one of the longest and most prominent yet written about Taylor. The role of Taylor's mentor was highlighted as well. "Were it not for Munger," the writer concluded, Taylor "would never have come to this city." After a month in Worcester, Taylor told *Spy*, he was convinced he wanted to stay.

Munger served as race referee, sending the riders into a stiff wind with a shot from his starter's pistol. Some three hundred spectators, most of them local cyclists, lined the streets. Taylor won easily, accepting the trophy from "my old hero, Willie Windle," he later wrote. But he wanted a chance to race against the best cyclists, regardless of skin color. Taylor trained all winter, and on New Year's Eve he was the star attraction of a celebration by Munger's company, which had recently opened a second factory, this one in Middletown, Connecticut. He showed off his trick riding, which would later give him a strategic advantage in track racing against the world's best competition. After riding up an angled, eighteen-inch-wide plank to a height of six feet, Taylor rode across a narrow platform to a staircase, then rode down the fourteen steps, leading one observer to say that he was "without a doubt, unequalled in this part of the country, as a trick rider."

At seventeen years old, Taylor had accomplished much in his racing career, but he was still largely untested against the world's greatest racers. He wasn't yet ready, but Munger had a daring plan that would take them both to the center of the nation's cycling craze, New York City.

# CHAPTER 6

# The Bicycle Craze

By the beginning of 1896, Munger's booming business had led him to establish factories in Massachusetts and Connecticut, and now he opened Manhattan sales offices on Wall Street and in Midtown. He also planned to operate a large booth at a massive bicycle exhibition in Madison Square Garden, with Taylor playing a major role. Munger advertised in the *New York Times*, promoting the "Birdie Special" and promising immediate delivery of "the best bicycles on the market." Taylor and Munger entered the increasingly crowded metropolis at a moment of historic transformation. New Yorkers had embraced the bicycle, viewing it as the essence of technology and liberation, like nowhere else in America. Indeed, nowhere else needed it as much.

Every morning, hundreds of thousands of clerks, telephone operators, accountants, traders, and all the other facilitators of industry streamed to Manhattan, many of them crossing the East River by ferry or the Brooklyn Bridge. New construction methods using iron beams enabled taller buildings, jamming more people into the city; several hundred structures, many of them served by new types of elevators and pipes, reached at least nine stories, topped with water tanks. Joseph Pulitzer, the owner of the *New York World*, built what was briefly the world's tallest building in 1890, a 309-foot structure near City Hall topped by a gilded globe. In 1894, that was exceeded by the Manhattan Life Insurance Building at 348 feet. By comparison, the Statue of Liberty and its pedestal were a combined height of 304 feet. By the time Munger and Taylor arrived, New Yorkers thronged to board street-level trains and elevated railways that could barely contain them. The first subway in New York City would not open for another eight years.

Most people were used to the relatively slow-moving world dominated by horses, which could proceed at a walking gait of around four miles an hour, a trot of eight miles per hour, a canter of perhaps seventeen miles per hour, and a brief gallop of thirty miles per hour. But for city transportation, towing a buggy or a streetcar, the slowest of these speeds was typical. More than 150,000 horses plodded through New York City, each dumping twenty-two pounds of manure daily. Tons of excrement piled up on the streets, drawing flies and exuding an overpowering filth and stench, which pedestrians inevitably referred to as an ungodly, noxious carpet of crap. The bicycle was, by comparison, sleek, speedy, and clean, a symbol of the future. An average bicyclist could go ten to fifteen miles an hour, and some much faster. For $65 or more, a new bicycle could be purchased, providing not just a conveyance, but freedom to go as one pleased, under one's own power, liberated from horses and stench and the frustrations of an overwhelmed transportation system.

From 1890 to 1900, the bicycle boom years, New York City's population more than doubled from 1.5 million to 3.4 million. Immigrants crowded into dangerously packed tenements, which were subject to disease and crime, and many worked fourteen hours a day, six days a week at one of thousands of sweatshops. Block after block of storefronts advertised in languages from the Old Country.

Civic leaders tried to keep up through waves of innovation. New York City had transformed itself from a gas-lit, steam-powered, metropolis into an electrified world, created by the likes of Thomas Edison, who favored close-to-the-source direct current, and George Westinghouse, who developed a system of alternating current, which brought power from distant places. The streets were planted with tens of thousands of wooden poles, strung with power lines and telephone wires, strands of a changing world. The system of poles had barely been completed when the city decided to replace them with underground cables, dug by thousands of mostly immigrant laborers, enabling the city to be brightly lit at night, which led Broadway to be known as the Great White Way. A network of steam power hissed underground as well, puffing upward little geysers of emission, vented here and there, coughed into the streets. A dozen telephone exchanges operated throughout the city, each handling 150,000 calls daily, most of them for businesses.

Manhattan, leading the nation in electrification and communication, grew even greater as a center of commerce, and as it created enormous wealth, the social classes became more stratified; the leaders of industry—the old establishment and the new robber barons—lived uptown in an array of Fifth Avenue mansions, handsome brownstones, or ten-room apartments in lavish buildings lining Central Park, all of them electrically illuminated and secure from the masses. The commoners, meanwhile, toiled for long hours at low pay to make the city hum. Hundreds of thousands of immigrants poured through Ellis Island, which opened as a transit point in 1892, providing a vital source of labor in sweatshops and back offices. Many mixed uneasily, living and working in separate worlds, initially belying the image of a melting pot. Desperately poor Eastern European Jewish refugees, mainly from the Pale of Settlement in western Russia, formed a new world on the Lower East Side, sometimes clashing with the Italians and the Irish and even the wealthier stock of German Jews. All told, shortly after Brooklyn joined Manhattan, in 1898, as a borough of New York City, the metropolis's German-born population was 320,000. There were some 290,000 Jews, 275,000 Irish, and 250,000 Italians. Blacks had increasingly emigrated from the South, but they were one of the city's smallest minorities; about 60,000 out of 3.4 million people, and with relatively few representatives in the power structures of business and government.

The influx of immigrants and Southern blacks stoked a backlash of nativism and racism, further segmenting a deeply divided society. An English scientist, Francis Galton, publicized the idea of "eugenics," meaning "good in birth," suggesting that society should seek to "unite . . . those who possessed the finest and most suitable natures, mental, moral and physical." A blatant racist, he said blacks did not have "patience, reticence, nor dignity." His views were embraced by many Americans who cited the eugenics movement as justification for the imposition of laws that denied blacks equal rights, and led some states to outlaw racial intermarriage. Rather than band together against the attacks upon them, some immigrant groups looked down upon another.

The upper classes were largely secreted in their world of mansions, clubs, and churches, the latter typically Protestant. The Irish and Italians, typically Catholic, as well as blacks and many Jews, were generally excluded from this world.

For this brief moment in time, the bicycle craze crossed every class and ethnic group. There were 4 million bicycles in the United States in 1896. Automobiles, by comparison, were the rarest of vehicles; a mere three hundred existed in the United States at the time, including a handful in New York City, and most of them were singular oddities in various forms of testing. A bicycle-making pair of brothers, Charles and Frank Duryea, had offered the first rudimentary automobile for commercial sale, an undertaking publicized in Manhattan a year earlier in a six-car race sponsored by *The Cosmopolitan* magazine. The Duryea brothers drove two of the cars as thousands of spectators lined Broadway to view the novelty of a motorized vehicle. Another rider promptly crashed into a man riding a bicycle near 74th Street, and he was arrested for dangerous driving. A magazine, *The Horseless Age,* was launched to chronicle what it saw as the inevitable future of transit. Still, widespread auto ownership was years away. Henry Ford's first attempt at building an automobile, the Quadricycle built with bicycle wheels, would not be tested until mid-1896, and it had no brakes and could not go into reverse.

If an individual wanted to get around independently, the bicycle was touted as the best option. By the early 1890s, tens of thousands of cyclists wound their way through the city. A contemporary writer described a world in which the streets "swarmed with riders. Business men rode down to the offices on bicycles, and many of them took spins in the Park before breakfast. The great avenues of our larger cities were made extremely picturesque in the dusk of evening by the endless line of bicyclists whose lanterns in the darkness produced the vivid effect of a river of colored fire."

Increasingly, many of these riders were women, horrifying some and delighting others. Charlotte M. Smith, the president of the Women's Rescue League, arrived in New York City during 1896, taking up residence in the Astor House, and warned that cycling would lead women to lose their scruples. "I don't say every woman who rides a bicycle is immoral," she said. "I don't say bicycling is immoral. What I do say is it has a tendency to lure young girls into paths that lead directly to sin."

But as women's groups pushed for the right to vote (which would not be ratified as the Nineteenth Amendment for another twenty-four years), the bicycle was seen as a means of liberation. A Latvian immigrant to the United States, Annie Cohen Kopchovsky, who called herself Annie Londonderry, had recently claimed to be the first woman to ride a bicycle around the world, although questions would be raised about how far she actually pedaled. Recounting her trip for the *New York World*, she wrote that it was possible only because she had forgone skirts and worn bloomers, a billowy version of knee-length pants, which gave her "a certain degree of independence which I had never before experienced." Organizations called "rational dress societies" sprang up to advocate that women be allowed to wear bloomers. It was one of many factors that led to calls for equality, and it was said that women were "riding to suffrage on a bicycle."

Frances Willard, the president of the Woman's Christian Temperance Union and one of the most famous women in America in the early 1890s, saw the bicycle as a symbol of independence for her sex, a view reflected in the title of her autobiography: *How I Learned to Ride the Bicycle*. A woman on a bicycle was no longer in the shadow of a man; she traveled without assistance, permission, or even awareness of the opposite sex. It was seen as revolutionary.

"Let me tell you what I think of bicycling," suffragist leader Susan B. Anthony said in 1896. "I think it has done more to emancipate women than anything else in the world. I stand and rejoice every time I see a woman ride by on a wheel. It gives a woman a feeling of freedom and self-reliance. It makes her feel as if she were independent. The moment she takes her seat she knows she can't get into harm unless she gets off her bicycle, and away she goes, the picture of free, untrammeled womanhood." The *New York Herald*, in a story winking with sexual overtones, exulted that men could enjoy seeing "pretty girls on wheels" and expressed thanks that "leading society have at last taken up the cycle as a fashionable fad" because women were gradually unbundling their layers of clothing. "Just for a moment you are startled by an apparent chance resemblance. You recognize a neck, for instance, that you have seen swathed in tulle or lace."

Gradually, as thousands of cyclists became millions, the upper strata realized that something had changed, that the bicycle could replace the horse, that it represented the future. They made it their own. Many of the day's sports had first developed among the upper crust; so it had been for tennis and golf. Initially, the bicycle was "severely frowned upon" by the elite. Then, at a landmark gathering of the gilded in Newport, Rhode Island, bicycles were provided for a ride and "received the august stamp of metropolitan society's approval," as a writer for *Munsey's Magazine* put it in 1896. The writer marveled that "the bicycle was adopted by the masses before it was taken up by society—a marked reversal of the usual order of things."

Two hundred and fifty of New York City's wealthiest people launched the exclusive Michaux Club, which counted Rockefellers, Roosevelts, and Vanderbilts among its members. The club, named after a French bicycle maker, served as a social spot and an "up town cycling academy," as one magazine put it. Entering the Michaux, initially housed in a former armory at Broadway and 52nd Street, a member wandered through club rooms and entered a ballroom encircled by two balcony-style verandas. On one balcony, finely dressed men and women chatted; on the other, an orchestra played. On the rink below—the "riding floor," it was called—the members danced astride their bicycles. Bowling pins were arranged as an obstacle course. Like equestrians on a field, the men and women of the Michaux Club mounted their bikes and pranced about, riding as if in slow-motion to the tempo, elegance supplanting speed. Ladies put one foot on a pedal, another on the floor, and pushed off. Others arranged their dresses astride the seat, taking care to avoid the chain. More members joined the act, creating a colorful circle of synchronicity, to which the spectators on the balcony politely applauded. The highlight was a replication of the Virginia reel, in which the best riders performed intricate moves previously practiced upon a horse. William Rockefeller, a leader of the Michaux Club, declared that "the bicycle craze is still extending, and no telling where it will end." He was pleased that his son, Percy, had also joined the club and guessed the reason: "a number of his young girl friends ride there."

It was the age of extravaganzas designed to attract the masses, of carnivals and circuses and vast exhibitions, and the bicycle seemed the perfect vehicle for one of the greatest yet. Promoters dreamed up a plan to hold the exhibition in Madison Square Garden in what they hoped would be the greatest bicycle shows ever.

Munger purchased a prime spot to show off his bicycles, and he brought Taylor along as his assistant.

A snowstorm swept across Manhattan as Munger and Taylor and thousands of others headed for Madison Square Garden for the show in January 1896. The Beaux Arts building was financed by a consortium of Gilded Age titans, among them J. P. Morgan, Andrew Carnegie, and P. T. Barnum. In the six years since its opening, the great hall had housed odiferous horse shows, vacuous boxing matches, and political gatherings. This bicycle exhibition, however, was the largest ever held in the hall. More than three hundred bicycle makers displayed their wares at the weeklong show, attracting an average daily attendance of seventeen thousand people, ranging from the lowest-paid workers to the upper classes. Even Morgan, who lived in a three-story Italianate-style brownstone at the intersection of Madison Avenue and 36th Street, made his way ten blocks to the south, arriving at the Garden that he had helped finance. Morgan, who owned all or part of dozens of railroads, purchased a bicycle, confirming the craze now reached every class. It was, the *New York Herald* reported, "gloomy news for the horse and livery business."

As Munger and Taylor walked through Madison Square Park, beacons of the changing era surrounded them. The nation's largest billboard, illuminated by fifteen thousand lights—at a time when many lower-income people in New York City did not even have one bulb burning at home—loomed over the park, advertising resorts on Coney Island. The blocks around Madison Square Garden had gradually been transformed from a row of elegant residences to an array of stores, theaters, and hotels. One of the city's most elegant hostelries, the Hoffman House, stood a block from the Garden, on Broadway between 24th and 25th Streets. The hotel was famous for its high-ceilinged Grand Saloon, with seventeen bartenders always on duty, serving drinks from a bar that dominated a long hallway, flanked by intricate columns and illuminated by a row of chandeliers. Turkish rugs covered the floor, and one wall had an eight-foot-high painting of four naked women teasing a half-human animal from Greek mythology. The painting, *Nymphs and Satyr*, caused a scandal, which meant, of course, that it was one of the first things that many visitors went to see. On this day, many of the Hoffman's guests were in town to attend the bicycle show.

Now, even with the snowstorm, so many people were drawn to the Garden that it was proclaimed that a space twice as large could have been filled. Munger and other industry leaders were confident the craze was only beginning. The number of bicycle companies had grown from thirty to three hundred in the prior six years, and the number of bicycle-related patents had soared. But there were warning signs that the business—and all of industry—was changing. Corporate cartels now ganged up on smaller companies. A circle of Gilded Age titans swooped in wherever they saw new opportunities. Basic market economics dictated that the rapid expansion of the industry would set off competition that forced prices downward even as bigger companies employed technological advances that made manufacturing cheaper. Smaller firms such as those run by Munger could be at risk if demand didn't keep increasing. And that was without accounting for the possibility that motorized transport, from motorcycles to automobiles, might siphon customers in the future—something not nearly as far off as many imagined.

But at this moment, it seemed that the boom was boundless, and Munger and Taylor were at the center of it.

The pair entered the hall, greeted by a dazzling spectacle. Banners hung from the ceiling, potted palms were placed throughout the hall to add an air of elegance, and the aisles were so jammed with customers that authorities had to open the doors early to accommodate the masses. The spectators flooded the aisles, and attended carnival-like exhibitions of "fat men, Indian chiefs, bloomer girls and the like." Munger stood under a swath of his company's banners and could see his dream of being an industry leader becoming reality.

Taylor looked on, wide-eyed, as many of the great racers made paid appearances on behalf of their sponsors. Taylor didn't know it at the time, but Munger had been thinking of entering him in the nation's most prominent race, to be held months later in Madison Square Garden. The best riders in the world would compete, and none was more famous and beloved in the United States than a rider who was at that very moment the star of the bicycle show at the Garden. Few could imagine that this man, Eddie Bald, would soon face his stiffest challenge from little-known Major Taylor.

PART TWO

# The Jump

# CHAPTER 7

# The Rivalry Begins

E dward C. Bald was known to all as "Cannon" Bald for his ability to propel himself at an astonishing speed when approaching the finish line. Growing up in Buffalo, New York, he had
been a low-paid worker with few prospects for fame or wealth, having "wielded a cleaver in his father's butcher shop." He learned to
ride by delivering the produce on his bicycle when he was in his early
teens. Cycling with the extra weight of the packages had taught him to
pedal hard; a better training regimen could hardly have been devised.
He began racing when he was sixteen years old and soon became
the fastest sprinter in America, with a star quality that attracted out-
sized attention. Inevitably, he was described as tall and dashing, with
a square jaw and deep-set eyes. His hair typically was parted in the
middle, slicked back or carefully combed to an upside-down V across
his forehead, but sometimes it was mop-like, nearly falling to his eyebrows. Now, at twenty-two, he was on track to earn a remarkable
$10,000 in race winnings in 1896, more than almost any other athlete
in America. Of all the athletes at the bicycle exhibition that year, Bald
was the most popular.

The *New York Journal* published an illustration of Bald at the exhibition in a long-jacketed suit and cravat, looking like a Broadway star,
which he aspired to be. Bald was shown in the *Journal* illustration
leaning on a lectern, surrounded by a crowd of fashionably dressed
patrons, men in suits and hats, woman in dresses that flowed to the

floor. Bald "proves one of the most attractive exhibits," the newspaper said, alluding to the interest he induced among the ladies. Bald's race-track earnings were supplemented by an array of savvy commercial deals. He represented the nation's largest bicycle company, Pope Man-ufacturing Co., headed by the famous Colonel Albert A. Pope, and his visage appeared on a variety of products. A full-page ad declared, "A Sturdy Champion is Eddie 'Cannon' Bald," boosting a bicycle brand called the Barnes White Flyer. A song sheet tribute, "The White Flyer Two-Step," featured his photo on the cover.

Taylor, by comparison, received only the barest mention in the press, his name printed in tiny typeface in a list of attendees at the bicy-cle exhibition. The seventeen-year-old was almost entirely unknown compared to the illustrious Bald. Yet as the summer of 1896 unfolded, it became increasingly clear that Taylor was on a course to face the sport's greatest and most marketable star. In July, Bald returned to his hometown of Buffalo to inaugurate a new cement track, "banked scientifically and perfect in every detail," racing before five thousand fans who roared so loud they would have drowned out "the din of a boiler foundry," as a cycling magazine put it. Shouting "Eddie!," the throng cheered as he raced against New England's Tom Butler, stand-ing when the two neared the finish line. Then, when Bald made his signature move, propelling himself like a cannon ball to win by less than a foot, the crowd chanted, "Cannon Bald! Cannon Bald!" Bald smiled and waved in return. By the time the summer racing season was over, Bald would be declared the national sprint champion. He was deemed unstoppable.

As Bald won race after race in officially sanctioned meets, some of which barred blacks, Taylor entered whatever contest would accept him. He began in his adopted city of Worcester on May 9, 1896, one of three black riders who joined twenty-seven white men in the ten-mile race.

As Taylor wheeled his bike to the starting line at Park Avenue and Grove Street, he was met by the largest crush of people ever to assem-ble in Worcester. Streetcars were overwhelmed and the expected crowd of ten thousand had swelled to an astonishing fifty thousand. The *Telegram*, which sponsored the race, reported that everyone for miles around had shown up "except men in the accident ward of the city hospital and a woman who broke her leg in her hurry to get started for the race." Thousands of people walked to the course, and more than four thousand rode their bicycles, which were parked by every available tree and post. Along with the ordinary citizens, according to the *Telegram*, was "a great outpouring of society people, who came in their splendid carriages, and took just as much interest in the race as did the poor and humble who had to walk several miles to get there, and who stood in the dust of the rich folks' carriages, and took it all good naturedly, so long as they could see what was going on."

The riders lined up nine abreast, as operators from the local telephone company provided updates to the offices of the *Telegram*. Taylor was heralded by the *Worcester Spy* in overwrought prose as the "colored champion road rider of the world" whom teammates called "a sure winner." Taylor's performance, however, was underwhelming, perhaps because he got tangled up with other riders at the start. He finished in sixth place, a respectable showing, but one that earned only a sentence or two in the coverage. For all the hoopla, it was just a local race against middling competition, and Taylor was training for a stiffer challenge.

As the Worcester race took place, the US Supreme Court considered a case that would have a direct impact on Taylor and every other black in America.

Four years earlier, Homer Plessy, a biracial man whose ancestry was seven-eighths European and one-eighth African, bought a first-class ticket for the "whites only" train car in New Orleans. Plessy was asked by railroad officials to move to the car set aside for blacks. He refused. Authorities arrested him for violation of the Separate Car Act. Plessy's lawyers argued that the law violated the Thirteenth and Fourteenth Amendments, which respectively prohibited slavery and granted equal protection of the law to all citizens.

The case was heard by the Court on April 13, 1896. Now, five weeks later, the decision was announced. The vote was 7–1, upholding the Separate Car Act—and by extension the Jim Crow laws that were based on the rationale that separate facilities could be equal. In writing for the majority, Justice Henry Billings Brown said that the court rejected the idea that "enforced separation of the two races stamps the colored race with a base of inferiority." He blamed blacks for seeing things that way.

The lone dissenter, Justice John Marshall Harlan, punctured the majority case. "The white race deems itself to be the dominant race in this country," Harlan wrote, continuing:

> In view of the Constitution, in the eye of the law, there is in this country no superior, dominant, ruling class of citizens. There is no caste here. Our Constitution is color-blind, and neither knows nor tolerates classes among citizens. In respect of civil rights, all citizens are equal before the law. The humblest is the peer of the most powerful. The law regards man as man, and takes no account of his surroundings or of his color when his civil rights as guaranteed by the supreme law of the land are involved. It is therefore to be regretted that this high tribunal, the final expositor of the fundamental law of the land, has reached the conclusion that it is competent for a state to regulate the enjoyment by citizens of their civil rights solely upon the basis of race.

The ruling would be one of the most consequential in American history, all but normalizing racism and undoing much of what had been achieved since slavery ended with the Civil War. Jim Crow laws flourished, and states, particularly in the South, were emboldened to create two societies, dominated by whites. It would not be until 1954, in the case of *Brown v. Board of Education*, that the principle of "separate but equal" would be overturned.

At the time, however, the ruling received little notice. The day after the decision, the *New York Times'* front page featured stories about a steamer that had sunk in Baltimore's harbor and the retirement of an

Indiana senator. To find news of the *Plessy* case, a reader had to turn to page 3, to a column headlined "News of the Railroads." The lead item was about a Department of Agriculture regulation on the handling of livestock. The second item told how the Illinois Central Railroad won the right to limit the number of stops for its passenger trains. Finally, the third item, with the subheadline of "Louisiana's Separate Car Law," told in a spare two paragraphs that the US Supreme Court upheld the right of a railroad company "to provide separate cars for white and colored passengers." The item noted that Harlan had delivered "a very vigorous dissent," saying that he had argued there was no right to "regulate the enjoyment of civil rights upon the basis of race." It would be just as reasonable and proper, he said, for States to pass laws requiring separate cars for Catholics and Protestants.

Two weeks later, the *New York Times* provided the first significant national report about Taylor. He had been working at Munger's factory in Middletown, Connecticut, about eighty miles southwest of Worcester, and trained in the nearby hills. Munger told the *Times* that he was "elated" with Taylor's progress. "The natives who saw the 'Major' skimming over the sandpapered road marveled at his speed," the *Times* reported. Munger then entered Taylor in a test against some of the best racers in the East. Taylor began the competition in a one-mile race, lining up with eleven other sprinters. "Naturally I was nervous in this, my first tryout, but was all primed to go," Taylor wrote. Instead of trying to take the lead at the start, Taylor deployed a common but risky tactic. He rode in last place to conserve energy for the first half of the race. Then, with three-eighths of a mile to go, he sprinted past the pack, "gaining six lengths on them before they realized what had happened," Taylor wrote. He won the race, received a "wonderful ovation," and was awarded a gold watch, "which I promptly presented to my friend Mr. Munger in appreciation for some of the kindnesses he had extended to me."

He came in second in his next race, winning a dinner set that he sent to his mother. Then came what Taylor called "one of the greatest tests," a twenty-five-mile race in Irvington, New Jersey, which featured a hundred and forty of the nation's top riders. Taylor rode just behind the race favorite when someone threw "a pail full of ice water in my face" one-half mile before the finish line. Taylor could not recover in time, and he came in second. He wondered later whether the incident was by "accident or design." Taylor soon had another chance, competing in a twenty-five-mile contest on Long Island against sixty top riders. This time, the tactic used against him involved two riders colluding during the race. The pair alternately sprinted as they tried to tire Taylor, but after "they used every trick," Taylor tried one of his own. He pretended to be exhausted, and let the others go. A half-mile before the finish line, Taylor went into a full sprint and won by six lengths. He had learned hard lessons and further developed his arsenal of tactics.

Munger had once vowed that he would not return to Indianapolis with Taylor until his protégé was a champion. But Munger had business in the city, and he took Taylor with him. As they arrived, they learned that a star rider named Walter Sanger intended to try to set a one-mile record before an "immense throng" at the newly opened Capital City Track, an oval across from the state fairgrounds. Munger snuck Taylor into the arena's dressing room. Sanger set his mark and, with the crowd still buzzing from the feat, Taylor suddenly emerged on the track with some white supporters. Taylor keenly felt the pressure on his white friends, who would be ridiculed if he failed to break Sanger's record. Munger was in on the plan, watching from the sideline. Taylor was paced by white friends who rode tandem bikes. Latching onto the slipstream created by the tandems, Taylor tore around the track, five laps to the mile, and finished at two minutes and eleven seconds. He beat Sanger's record by a remarkable seven seconds. Then, after a rest to regain his strength, he decided to show he was capable of another extraordinary feat. He rode without a pacemaker for a single lap and beat a mark set on a similar Paris track by two-fifths of a second. The crowd gave Taylor one of his "most flattering ovations," and the young rider was mobbed by his friends as he made his way back to the dressing room.

Munger was delighted, but most of the racers who had entered the competition that day were outraged. Several taunted and threatened Taylor, saying he should never have been allowed on the track, and the friends who smuggled him into the facility were castigated. A group of local white racers responded to his extraordinary feat by saying they would try to ban him from competing again in Indianapolis. Munger was now thoroughly convinced that his prodigy was ready for a far bigger stage, and the pair returned to New York City, where cyclists were preparing for one of the world's greatest cycling spectacles. They decided Taylor would compete in a six-day race at Madison Square Garden in December. Taylor had just a few months to prepare for his most grueling test yet.

Throughout New York, bicycle clubs hired young men to tend to the members and keep their quarters clean. Taylor got a job with one of the area's most competitive groups, the South Brooklyn Wheelmen, whose members made him an attendant at the club's headquarters at 278 Ninth Street, in the Park Slope neighborhood. The group was composed of several hundred men, all of them white, most of them well-to-do businessmen, with an average age of thirty. In addition to its brownstone headquarters, the club maintained a property in the Thousand Islands in Upstate New York and sponsored far-flung trips. The club leaders had recognized Taylor's extraordinary talent, and he had quickly gone from being considered a "mascot" to its fastest rider.

Brooklyn was a particularly welcoming place for bicyclists. The nation's first bicycle-only pathway, Ocean Parkway, ran five and a half miles from Prospect Park to Coney Island, which Taylor regularly traveled. When a major section of the path opened in June 1896, coinciding with Taylor's training, a parade was held with 10,000 bicyclists and 100,000 spectators, packed five people deep. Flags and bunting hung from buildings along the route. Led by Park Commissioner Timothy L. Woodruff as grand marshal, riders dressed in all manner of costume, including the "bloomer girls" who startled onlookers with brightly colored pants, and the more traditional ladies in flowing dresses and parasols.

Taylor's training with club members helped him increase his speed and endurance, and his confidence grew about competing in the six-day race. Some riders believed that the contest would take ten years off their life, and warned against it. Taylor could have started his professional career more modestly, but the race would be chronicled by journalists from around the world, and even a modest showing would draw extraordinary attention to him—and the Munger brand of bicycle that he would ride.

Taylor, however, needed a license from the race promoters to participate, and it seemed unlikely they would accept a little-known applicant, especially one who was black. Taylor nonetheless called on the pair of promoters of the six-day contest: Patrick T. Powers, a former baseball manager who was president of the Eastern League; and James C. "Big Jim" Kennedy, who was the former manager of the minor league Brooklyn Gladiators, and had covered baseball for the *New York Times*. Given that bicycling was more popular than baseball at the time, the pair made much of their money promoting bicycle contests and other sporting events at Madison Square Garden, where they maintained an office. As Taylor walked in, he faced two grizzled, rotund men whose primary objective was to make as much money and draw as many fans as possible. There was no precedent for allowing a black racer—not to mention such a young and relatively untested one—to compete in the most difficult bicycle contest ever conceived.

They listened to Taylor's plea and brushed him off. The promoters "contended that the presence of this little negro would not be right at a race; it would stir the whole of New York," according to a contemporaneous account. They suggested he go "to shine the Fifth Avenue gentlemen's shoes."

Taylor insisted he had the right to race. It was a turning point. Taylor's participation in this race would in hindsight be the most crucial factor in jump-starting his career. As the discussion continued, the promoters had an epiphany. The publicity value of a rare white versus black race, with all its controversy, might dramatically increase interest. The promoters relented, and Taylor walked out of their office with his racing license.

• • •

As Taylor continued training with the South Brooklyn Wheelmen in preparation for the big race, the nation was roiled by economic and political woes. A Depression that had begun in 1893 continued to disrupt the economy, and the presidential campaign between Democrat Williams Jennings Bryan and Republican William McKinley was tearing the nation apart. Bryan ran a poorly financed campaign as an outsider, savaging the Gilded Age titans who occupied the Fifth Avenue mansions and dominated Wall Street with their cartels. McKinley, who was funded by some of those very titans, including J. P. Morgan, had $3.5 million in campaign money, five times as much as Bryan, and he used it to push for a gold standard and a pro-business policy. It was, as Edwin G. Burrows and Mike Wallace wrote in *Gotham,* "a grand climatic showdown between 'the People and Wall Street.'"

On August 12, a sweltering day, Bryan appeared at Madison Square Garden, four months before Taylor would race in the venue. The Democratic candidate delivered a two-hour speech, reading laboriously from a text, thundering about his belief that a reliance on the silver standard would increase the value of currency and thus make people richer. A silver dollar, he effectively said, could be worth two dollars when cashed in. Bryan should have had a natural constituency among the working class of New York, but he was so focused on silver that he spoke of little else. McKinley's backers took advantage of the widespread support of business leaders, who in turn got their employees to join them. On the Saturday before Election Day, 750,000 residents turned out in New York City to witness 100,000 McKinley supporters march in step with the Sound Money Association, a group promoted by Morgan and his fellow multimillionaires.

As Taylor watched the campaign unfold, he would have paid special attention to the subject of race relations. Bryan, in his Madison Square Garden speech, said he believed in the Declaration of Independence's clause that "all men are created equal," and vowed that "government officials shall not, in making, construing or enforcing the law, discriminate between citizens." McKinley, an Ohioan who fought for the north in the Civil War, was the preferred candidate of most blacks, including many in the South who were not allowed to vote due to Jim Crow restrictions. He had condemned lynching and was briefly seen as the "best friend" of black Americans, as one historian put it. McKinley won the presidency, but he made only token appointments of African Americans to modest government jobs, and race relations worsened.

A month after the election, as New York City prepared for the six-day race, a muscular, mustachioed occupant of a townhouse at 689 Madison Avenue, near Central Park at 62nd Street, rode his bicycle to work. He pedaled about four miles downtown to 300 Mulberry Street, a modest five-story building that housed the Central Department of the Metropolitan Police. The thirty-eight-year-old man dismounted, climbed the steps to the arched doorway, and headed to his desk, situated near a fireplace that, in turn, held on its mantel a large, rectangular clock. Swiveling from his desk, Theodore Roosevelt, the New York City police commissioner, could open the shutters on an oversized set of windows, and gaze at the traffic of horses, carriages, and bicycles. Five years before he became president of the United States, Roosevelt was in charge of fighting crime and the bicycle became a key to his strategy. Shortly after taking office in 1895, he established a "scorcher squad" of twenty-nine cyclists whose members, he later wrote, showed "not only extraordinary proficiency on the wheel, but extraordinary daring." The bicycle officers frequently chased after criminals or runaways, overtaking their horses and carriages. "They managed not only to overtake but to jump into the vehicle" and capture their prey, Roosevelt wrote in his autobiography. One of Roosevelt's most powerful riders could hold on to his handlebars with one hand while grabbing a horse's bit in the other, preventing a criminal's getaway. One desperate man lashed his horsewhip at the pursuing officer, to no avail; the bicycle officer stayed steady and jumped into the man's carriage, capturing him. Even professional cyclists "who deliberately violated the law to see if they could not get away from him" were caught by Roosevelt's rider.

Thirty-six blocks, a little over two miles, separated Roosevelt's home from Madison Square Garden, and he kept a close watch on plans for the six-day race. To Roosevelt, the contest's duration was inhumane, and several years later as governor he would sign legislation to limit riders from spending more than twelve hours a day in competition. For now he just wanted to keep order as the city prepared for the race, which inevitably would attract an array of thieves and charlatans. The race itself also was of great sporting interest to him. Like so many New Yorkers, Roosevelt soon heard about the young man named Major Taylor and would come to be one of his great admirers.

The year that had begun with the bicycle exhibition at the Garden was now set to end in the same venue with the sport's greatest event. The political bunting was gone, replaced with banners advertising the six-day race. It was at this point that Munger had arrived at the arena with Taylor, with many spectators seeing the former champion accompanied by the little-known "valet" at his side who would soon become so famous. Thousands of spectators arrived from throughout the city, combining the disparate classes and ethnic groups into the arena. With contestants from around the world, many in the crowd could cheer for their native son. The city's black population had the rarest chance of all, to root for a member of their race against white opponents.

First came the preliminary races, including the half-mile contest in which Taylor made his debut. He pushed his bike to the starting line of the twenty-five-foot-wide oval track, with its steeply banked curves still slick from a treatment designed to smooth the wooden course. Taylor won his qualifying heat, and now he lined up against some of the world's fastest racers for the final round. It was here that Taylor first faced the man who would become one of his greatest rivals, Eddie "Cannon" Bald.

The starter's gun cracked. Taylor took off, leading for the first of five laps, and then another and another. Taylor was ten yards ahead when he looked back at Bald and realized his lead was shrinking. Taylor pedaled furiously, crossing the finish line alone, savoring his first professional victory—or so he thought. Somehow, he didn't realize he had gone only four laps, not the required five. As Taylor slowed down, halfway through what he thought was a victory lap, the crowd yelled madly that he had not finished. Bald had been given a second chance and, at full speed, he sped from behind, about to overtake Taylor. The crowd shrieked and Taylor suddenly realized his mistake. Tucking his head in an aerodynamic position, Taylor bolted forward, and this time it was he who seemed shot from a cannon. Bald had expended his energy too soon and couldn't catch up. The South Brooklyn riders who had trained with Taylor cheered, and the crowd roared. The band struck up "Dixie." Taylor, the *Eagle* told its readers, "was easily the hero of the evening."

Bald was mortified at being defeated by "the black boy whom Birdie Munger used to carry around as his mascot." Speaking to a cycling journalist after the race, Bald said, "Now, wouldn't that kill you! They'll all be saying that I'm the only crackerjack in the game what'd let a nigger beat him. Hully gee! But that's tough." The journalist understood the historical significance, writing that Bald realized that "for years to come [Taylor] will be pointed out as the colored gentleman who licked Eddie Bald."

Taylor collected his prize, equivalent to about five months of an average salary at the time. "I immediately wired the $200 to my mother," Taylor recalled later. "This was my first money prize." This grand triumph, however, was merely the prologue to the main event: six straight days of cycling around the track, racing that would test any man beyond reason. One could not compare a half-mile sprint of five laps to a race of six days. Several dozen of the world's best riders, having watched the young racer win his first professional competition, now knew that Taylor was no fluke, and they took aim at him.

The race was due to begin one minute past midnight. The crowd had grown from the five thousand who witnessed the early sprints to a capacity crowd of more than twelve thousand. Widespread newspaper coverage of Taylor's victory and the historic participation of a black racer in the full event had helped swell the number of spectators. The city was in the midst of one of the great newspaper wars in American history, and the six-day race received immense coverage. Joseph Pulitzer's *New York World* reported that it had the highest circulation that year, selling 568,000 copies on an average Sunday, compared to 100,000 for the *New York Tribune* and 80,000 for the *New York Times*. The *World*, whose headquarters had briefly been in the world's tallest building, featured detailed coverage, including separate stories with headlines such as "The Major Doing Well." The era of widespread sports photography was a few years away, but many newspapers published extensive drawings of the racers, including Taylor, who was depicted in the *World* wearing "a gaudy new costume" that included a beanie-type hat. The newspaper also published an illustration of a man carrying a bucket and a brush with the description "Major Taylor's Trainer, Ready for Business." William Randolph Hearst's *New York Journal*, a chief competitor to Pulitzer's two-cent *World*, charged a penny and gained many readers just in time to provide extensive coverage of the six-day race. The *New York Times* produced regular if more staid coverage, as did the *Telegram* and numerous cycling publications. The *Brooklyn Eagle* covered Taylor extensively as the hometown favorite, calling him "the most graceful rider of all [who] sits on his wheel as if he were a part of it."

Anticipation swept the Garden. Hundreds of lightbulbs hung from the arena's superstructure of girders and pillars and twinkled along rooflines. Smoke from cigars and cigarettes drifted upward as the arena pulsated with the crowd's thunderous noise. The band played in quick tempo. An assistant came to Taylor's side, holding his bike by the handle, ready to push the teenager to the starting line. The wooden racing oval creaked. The racers breathed deeply.

Taylor looked up and saw Eddie Bald. The man he had vanquished was not willing to participate in the six-day contest; he was built for short distances. Instead, Bald was dressed in his street clothes and holding the starter's pistol. Taylor, too, should have refused to race; he was too young and inexperienced for such an inhumane test of endurance. But in receiving his license, he had agreed to the six-day contest, so he had no choice.

The absence of Bald hardly diminished the competition. Taylor had a new field of top racers to contend with. The thirty other racers included the long-distance champions of France, Germany, Ireland, England, Scotland, Wales, and the United States. Taylor, at eighteen years old, was in fine form, but was hardly expected to perform well among such competition. As Taylor later recalled it, "the older riders, who were fully matured and thoroughly developed, could stand the loss of sleep better than I." His greatest difficulty, he said, would be staying awake.

Taylor had collected stray horseshoes that he had found during a recent training ride, and he nailed these talismans of good luck to a pole of his tent, which had been set up to accommodate brief rests. To this collection, he added a rabbit's foot and a "voodoo charm," one newspaper reported.

Each rider's distance would be tracked carefully by counting their laps. Trainers provided water regularly, and riders stopped for meals several times a day. Other than that, strategies varied widely. Some riders believed it was best to go as long and steady as possible before stopping, while others took regular breaks and rode hard. Taylor's initial strategy was to ride for seven hours and rest for one, going as much as three hundred miles in a day, about the distance from Washington to New Haven, Connecticut.

One by one, the contestants entered, serenaded by a regimental band with a song of their country as they took a ceremonial lap. A Welsh rider strode to the starting line, wearing dark trunks and a pink shirt, representing the colors of the Prince of Wales. A Scotch rider entered to the tune of "The Blue Bells of Scotland." An Englishman arrived as "Rule Britannia" played, and an American was greeted with "Yankee Doodle." Finally, it was Taylor's turn. The crowd anticipated his arrival, bursting into applause "greater than any that had before," the *Brooklyn Eagle* reported. The band struck up "Suwanee River," with its lyrics about "longin' for the old plantation" and "Oh, darkeys, how my heart grows weary," but Taylor paid no attention as he took his warm-ups around the track.

Bald held the pistol in the air. "Are the timers ready?" he asked, and received confirmation. "Are the starters ready?" The racers signaled affirmatively. Bald fired the pistol, and the racers began slowly, jockeying for position.

Taylor rode eighteen hours on the first day, becoming so exhausted that Munger agreed to find a doctor. It was a ruse to keep Taylor riding; there was no doctor coming. Taylor hoped to sleep for at least an hour, but Munger woke him after fifteen minutes. Even that was too much; Taylor's trainers told him he had slept fifteen minutes over his schedule.

Taylor began the second day in eleventh place. Nearly half of the riders had dropped out, too exhausted to maintain a reasonable pace. Taylor, despite his protestations, was described by the *Eagle* as the "freshest looking man on the track." He was twenty-five miles behind the leader. The consensus, according to the *Eagle,* was that Taylor "hardly has the endurance to stick it out for six days," given that he was the youngest rider. But by the end of the second day, Taylor rose to fourth place among the eighteen remaining riders.

On the third day of the race, Taylor could barely continue. His body "was like ice," one trainer said. He beseeched his trainers for sustenance. "How do you expect a man to ride who hasn't had a bite to eat in fourteen hours?" Taylor said, although he had just eaten a "big meal" an hour earlier, a reporter recounted. "You fellows want me to stay here until my leg drops off so you can take it to the doctor," he said. One of his trainers gave him a glass of water, mixing it with powder that supposedly cost $65 an ounce, saying the concoction would allow Taylor to stay awake for the rest of the contest. "Later I found out also that this powder was nothing more than bicarbonate of soda, but it kept me going for the next 18 hours without a wink of sleep," Taylor wrote. The crowd loved him. After Taylor returned from a brief rest, he was given a bouquet. Taylor played to the crowd, smelling the flowers, holding them above his head and smiling broadly. The band struck up "Dixie" to wild cheers. However, as Taylor settled onto his bike, he was so tired that he lost his usual perfect form. His back, normally flattened to ease wind resistance, bowed enough to be noticed by a reporter. A pillow was fastened to the handlebars so that Taylor could rest his chest against it, allowing him to pedal without raising his head. Taylor dropped to ninth place by the end of the day.

Taylor looked around for Munger but couldn't find him. The newspapers described Taylor as doubled over in pain, wincing in agony, mindlessly wandering across the track due to lack of sleep, and being carried off in a trainer's arms. At one point, delirious and hallucinating, he told his trainers, "I cannot go on with safety, for there is a man chasing me around the ring with a knife in his hand." Then, after eating a steak and sipping water from a funnel-shaped can, Taylor acknowledged the crowd's cheers. The tobacco smoke grew so thick, the dust and grime so great, that the racers were coated in dirt, leading Taylor to say one of the white riders could "pass as his brother." They could not tell if it was day or night, and sometimes could not even see all the way around the track. The riders could barely breathe until the skylights were finally opened. The promoters had been so confident about the popularity of the contest that on these last couple of days the price of admission was doubled to a dollar, and the stands nonetheless swelled to their capacity of twelve thousand, with another five thousand forming a line that "mobbed" the doors and stretched far down Madison Avenue, the commoners and high society patrons equally anxious to get inside. Interest in the race was "developing into a fever," reported the *New York World*. The Garden shook amid the stomping and cheering. The crowd was "remarkable," the *World* reported, and Taylor's popularity "grows every minute."

Some of the most experienced riders faltered. Albert Schock of Chicago, who had pioneered the use of a stationary bicycle trainer and had won the six-day contest three years earlier, "had been slumbering along" when he suddenly fell on his head. Fred Forster, a German, foolishly tried to sprint just when he needed to conserve energy, swerved across the track, hit the railing, and flew off his bike, landing in front of a gaggle of reporters, who watched a trainer awaken the rider with ammonia. Forster pressed forward a few yards before collapsing. Only Teddy Hale, who was described in the *New York Journal* as an Irishman who spun his bicycle's chain "like a thing possessed," seemed at full strength.

By the fourth day, Taylor rested more than the others, but he made up for it by sprinting past his competitors. Then, on the fifth day, Munger returned from dealing with business matters. Taylor revived at the sight of his friend, which filled him with such "ginger" that he taunted other riders. A reporter for the *New York World* overheard it all.

"Hit it up there," Taylor called to one rider, urging a faster pace.

"Go 'way yet, ride in a wagon," the rider responded.

"Come, don't drop dead in your tracks," Taylor yelled to another rider.

"You're not so warm," the competitor replied. The riders "were all laughing and yelling" and doubled their speed as Taylor continued to challenge them.

Taylor could barely compete. Leaning against his pillow, he fell "fast asleep while on his wheel," the *Brooklyn Eagle* reported. He awakened abruptly, pulled his bike to a railing, and dozed, seeming "oblivious to everything about him." Taylor soon returned to the track, but as he rounded a corner, he fell over and went flying twenty feet across the boards. He did not sprint again that day. Someone gave him a flower arrangement of the kind laid at cemeteries, with the label "Gone but not forgotten." That, however, was anything but the case.

Taylor mounted his bike on the sixth and final day, determined to finish. With thirty minutes to go, he collided with another rider, "and he collapsed utterly," the *Brooklyn Eagle* reported. "Try as they would, his trainers could not get him on his wheel again." The crowd roared its encouragement as Taylor, his knee bruised and swollen, remained slumped against a railing. His race was over. He had traveled 1,787 miles, joining the other riders in shattering a previous record for a six-day contest. It was a remarkable feat for the young man who once promised his mother he would never again ride a race as long as seventy-five miles. He finished in eighth place, but no one had expected him to finish the contest, much less win. The crowd's noise was so great as the racers crossed the finish line that they drowned out the band, which serenaded the winner, Teddy Hale. The "greatest bicycle race in history," as one newspaper put it, was over.

One of Taylor's assistants came onto the track, cradled him, and carried him away. For his effort, Taylor was given a $125 prize, a large sum for the day, but $75 less than he had received for winning the preliminary half-mile heat. He returned to Brooklyn, where he slept and ate prodigiously, and then, when he was strong enough, took the train to Munger's Connecticut home to fully recover and plan his future.

Taylor had become a star, his victory in the preliminary half-mile sprint and his survival in the six-day race showing that he could compete against any racer, in any type of contest. He was a sprinter, not a long-distance man, and for the rest of his career he would focus mostly on shorter contests. Taylor had used the race to send a message: a month after having turned eighteen years old, he was one of the world's best riders. White competitors had begun the six-day affair treating him as an amusement. Now they saw him as their most serious threat.

# CHAPTER 8

# "Major Taylor's Life in Danger"

There comes a time in the life of the greatest athletes when the jump is made, the leap from being an ordinary competitor to the kind of star who is expected to win no matter what; indeed, to thrive when the odds against victory are highest. For Taylor, "the jump" had a double meaning, as his greatest skill was just that—shocking opponents with his sudden burst of energy and power just when they thought they had defeated him. He had become famous for the jump when he vaulted ahead of Eddie Bald in the half-mile sprint at Madison Square Garden, and ever since that moment, Bald plotted how to stop him.

The two met repeatedly, each winning their share of races, and much attention was focused on a contest in Worcester. The *Boston Globe* taunted Bald, saying he had been beaten "time and again" by Taylor. Bald was determined not to let that happen now. In the first match, a twelve-man, one-mile sprint, he narrowly beat Taylor. Next came a two-mile race. As Taylor sprinted around a bend in the track, he was crowded by other riders. Forced into this "pocket" at high speed, Taylor hit a post and rocketed off his bike. His arms and legs were severely cut, and his front wheel was broken. Somehow, Taylor got up and walked his bike across the finish line. He filed a protest against another rider, who was disqualified.

It marked the beginning of a new, dangerous pattern that would haunt Taylor for much of his career. Taylor's competitors made him a marked man, cutting him off, trying to knock over his bike, hoping to make him crash at full speed. Taylor soon realized that every time he went on the track, his life was endangered.

As Taylor won matches throughout the East, from Maine to Pennsylvania, the threats and illegal tactics against him continued. A local newspaper described how Taylor had been pushed off a track, with the writer admonishing the culprits: "Major Taylor is a quiet, honest gentleman. He is better educated than the majority of men who he meets in the professional ranks. He is deserving of at least fair treatment."

Taylor often stressed that there were many whites, like Munger, who went to extraordinary lengths to support him. In Philadelphia, when Taylor could not stay at the same lodging as his white competitors, a Virginia racer named Fred Schade came to his rescue. Schade, a rosy-cheeked racer with a "luxuriant growth of blond hair," was such a star that he had arrived at a race in a private railroad car attended by servants. At the Philadelphia meet, Schade had rented a cottage near the racing track. Learning that Taylor had no place to stay, Schade invited him to stay at the cottage, along with black attendants "who could not get quarters at any of the hotels." Taylor performed well, qualifying in all his heats. At first, the crowd hissed at his victories over white riders, "but his repeated successes turned the tide in his favor, and before the big meet was over he was the star of the tournament." Still, Taylor held something back for the final races, "as if he were afraid of receiving bodily harm," according to a reporter at the scene.

A writer for the *New York Sun* admonished Taylor's competitors and called for an investigation into attacks against him. "Taylor rides in all his big races in deadly fear of his racing companions," the *Sun* said, citing what it called a "conspiracy." At a Massachusetts race on September 10, 1897, after Taylor easily won a preliminary bout, he failed to show up for the final heat. A referee determined that Taylor "was afraid to ride" but refused to excuse his absence. Taylor entered the final heat "reluctantly" and "made no effort to win." The *Sun* concluded that "Taylor now ranks with the fastest men in this country, but the racing men, envious of his success and prejudiced against his color, aim to injure his chances whenever he competes. This conduct robs Taylor of many chances to secure large purses and endangers his life." Taylor had no doubt that white racers were colluding against him on account of his race.

Asked if it were true that his life had been threatened, Taylor confirmed it to a reporter for the *Worcester Telegram*, saying he had a "dread of injury every time I start in a race . . . they have threatened to injure me and I expect before the season is finished they will do so."

As Taylor pasted stories about his accomplishments in his scrapbooks, which eventually would collect articles from more than fifty newspapers around the world, one headline stood out: "Major Taylor's Life in Danger."

Munger watched all of this with growing fear. He had never doubted Taylor's talent, and he had provided protection on many occasions, standing by the rider's side, offering him shelter and support, and lecturing competitors. But it seemed to be of no avail. The attacks increased amid a growing national climate in which more Jim Crow laws were enacted. Munger became convinced that Taylor's skin color would prevent him from competing. It was at this fragile moment that Munger came up with a desperate idea that he hoped would rescue his prodigy.

Munger held in his hand a bottle of ointment that was supposed to transform a black man into one who looked white. The lotion would be rubbed everywhere on Taylor's skin. Advertisements in African American newspapers showed before and after pictures of how a black person looked white after the treatment, which was claimed to be "harmless." A black would look "four or five shades whiter" over the entire body.

At the time, the promoters of color-changing products promised to discreetly deliver the lotions. "Black Skin Remover: A Wonderful Bleach Face," said a typical ad in the *Colored American*. Other ads suggested that combining the lotion with hair straightener would make blacks more likely to gain employment and acceptance by whites. "White People spend millions to beautify themselves," said an ad by the Chemical Wonders Company. "Colored people should make themselves as attractive as possible." The products were marketed as if they were for beauty, but the underlying message revealed much about society and prejudice at the time. The ads proved nothing about the products' effectiveness, but rather perpetuated a pernicious marketing of racism, playing on the fears of those blacks who felt pressured to take desperate measures they believed were needed in order to survive a Jim Crow society.

Taylor, fearing he would be unable to enter races, was not immune to these pressures. He agreed to let Munger make an experiment of him.

Munger and an associate, Fred Dickson, poured the skin-changing lotion over Taylor. Day after day, the chemical experiment continued, and Taylor's skin seared in pain. As he later recalled it, "Birdie Munger . . . tried in various ways to make me white, innumerable times by scaring me nearly to death, and on one occasion by the bleaching process. On that occasion, my hair turned red almost by the action of the cream and the skin was nearly burned off me. Then I thought I was going to die." Munger and Dickson were so horrified by the result that they "looked like ghosts before they got through with me."

Munger recalled it similarly, saying Taylor "was one day refused entry to a race owing to his color. We told him that we would bleach him and make him white. He took us at our word and submitted to an operation. The mixture was poisonous in the extreme. It was a sort of cream, and for days and days we poured it on the lad. His hair turned a sort of red, and his skin did seem to be turning whiter and whiter. But the solution was working to the detriment to the lad's health, and we had to stop it. He has never been as dark, though, as he was before the operation."

Three days after Munger's chilling account of bleaching Taylor was published in the *Detroit Free Press*, Taylor entered a race at what seemed to be a safe venue, a county fair in Taunton, Massachusetts, fifty-three miles south of Boston. Few states had been more hospitable to Taylor than Massachusetts, where officials had gone to great lengths to make sure he could participate regardless of his skin color. Robert Teamoh, an African American cyclist who was simultaneously a member of the Massachusetts House of Representatives and a reporter for the *Boston Globe*, had won passage of one of the nation's strongest antidiscrimination laws. The bill included a provision that said discrimination was prohibited in places such as skating rinks "or other public amusement," which covered the velodromes used for cycling competitions. Anyone who discriminated in such places based on race was subject to a fine of up to $300. The bill seemed designed to support racers such as Taylor, but some of his competitors still objected to his presence. The conflict came to a head as Munger escorted Taylor to the race in Taunton, where a victory could help launch Taylor into the race for the national championship.

An extraordinary crowd of twenty-five thousand people gathered to watch the one-mile contest on September 23, 1897. Taylor raced hard but ended in second place. It seemed uneventful, but as Taylor prepared to dismount, the third-place finisher, William E. Becker, thrust his hands around Taylor's throat, and choked him "into a state of insensibility," as Taylor recalled it. Police pulled Becker away. The stunned crowd watched as Taylor lay motionless on the track. Munger rushed forward, trying to revive his friend, but for fifteen minutes Taylor was unconscious. Word spread that Taylor had died. Finally, Munger revived him, and the pair walked off the track. The attack made headlines across the country. "Choked Taylor," said the *Boston Globe*. "Major Taylor Choked into Insensibility," said the *Cleveland Gazette*.

Becker later claimed that Taylor cut him off. His excuse was accepted by the League of American Wheelmen, which then fined him $50 for his physical attack of Taylor. Becker, with contributions from some fellow white racers, paid his fine and quickly rejoined the racing circuit. It was a small price to pay, a journalist wrote at the time, noting that Taylor's competitors "would gladly sacrifice $50" to get Taylor off the course.

As the racing season moved south and west, the top riders took a train from city to city, and Taylor boldly joined them. But Taylor was barred from entering most of the races. In New Albany, Indiana, across the river from Kentucky, "the white southern riders refused to get up against him and openly threatened him with violence," prompting the referee to cancel the contest, which Taylor was "a moral certainty" to win, the *Boston Globe* reported. Seeking to practice on a Louisville track, Taylor was told that blacks were barred under a Jim Crow law. Taylor entered contests in more hospitable cities such as Detroit, but his season was over. As he returned to Worcester, he lamented that despite being "at the top of my form," he was not able to fight for the championship.

The title of national champion—hollow as it was—went to Eddie Bald.

Munger, meanwhile, faced his own crisis. The bicycle boom had led him to expand rapidly, running overtime shifts in Worcester and ramping up the Connecticut facility. He had opened his two showrooms in New York City. In February 1897, Munger brought seventy bicycles to New York's National Cycle Show, including the "Royal Worcester," which was bathed in electric light under purple banners. Advertisements for Munger's bicycles appeared in newspapers and magazines, and the business boomed. But by mid-1897, more companies competed for the business, forcing prices to drop. Munger announced a ten percent pay cut to workers at his Connecticut factory. Workers went on strike and vowed to return only if they received their regular wages. "When this was refused most of them took their coats and left the factory," a local newspaper reported. Munger resigned, and the plant was idled with five thousand unfinished bicycles. It was a scene that Taylor, who often worked at the Connecticut factory when he wasn't in training, either witnessed or soon heard about. The company factories in Massachusetts and Connecticut had piled up nearly $700,000 in liabilities. The debts could not be paid, a sheriff took possession of the assets, and a judge put the company into receivership. Munger, however, was not personally liable for the debts, which were held by bondholders and other interests, and he shifted his focus to making tires for the just-emerging automobile business.

• • •

Just as Munger's Connecticut factory was on the verge of its shutdown in mid-1897, Taylor recorded in his notebook that his mother, Saphronia, had died. He returned to Indianapolis to attend the funeral, briefly reuniting with his family. From his earliest races, Taylor had sent his mother many of his prizes, and promised her that he would hew to his Baptist upbringing. Six months after his mother's death, on January 14, 1898, the nineteen-year-old pledged to do more than give his financial support, writing that he had "embraced religion."

But just as he was rejected by so many because of his skin color, he found that his co-religionists did not embrace him. He sought membership in a black congregation in Worcester, John Street Baptist Church, founded fifteen years earlier by a group of Southern migrants. To his dismay, they refused to admit him as a member "on account of his business as a bicycle rider," which the leaders found unholy. Taylor fought the rejection, stressing that he would refuse to race on Sundays, but church leaders dismissed his appeal, telling him to come back in a year. It was a dark time: burying his mother, being rejected by the black Baptists of his adopted home, being unfairly denied entry into contests, which hurt his place in the overall standings, and watching Munger lose control of the bicycle factories.

Taylor considered a life beyond racing, and amid the stories he put in his scrapbook about triumphs and travails, he pasted a clipping about a speech by a minister headlined "A Colored Orator." It told the view of the Reverend C. S. Smith of Tennessee, who believed that "the greatest need was development of mental and not physical powers; that one theological college was of greater value than a hundred industrial schools." At the same time, Smith said, a black person should find the strength to use racism to his advantage, and "fully appreciate the feeling against him, which will urge in his mightiest efforts."

No one could have given a mightier effort than Taylor, but he feared his dream of a national championship was over because he would never be allowed to compete on fair terms.

Taylor's story might have ended at this moment if it were not for a brash Broadway and boxing promoter named William Aloysius Brady.

# CHAPTER 9

# The Fighting Man

On the night that President Abraham Lincoln was assassinated, April 14, 1865, Terence Brady, the founder of the *San Francisco Monitor* and one of the nation's most ardent racists, a supporter of Southern secession and the continuation of slavery, publicly declared that "it served Lincoln right." That, at least, was the recollection of his son, William Brady, who called his father one of the "principal inciters" of lawless mobs that roamed San Francisco on that night.

As the elder Brady spewed his contempt for Lincoln, "a mob sprang at my father, dragged him down from the stand, and would have hanged him," but he was rescued by federal troops in the area, the younger Brady wrote later. Undeterred, the mob broke into the *Monitor* and wrecked the machinery, before heading to another pro-South newspaper headquarters and "demolished" it. Brady's father was imprisoned at Alcatraz, successfully sued the city for failing to protect the *Monitor*, and was awarded $30,000. Freed from prison, he snatched his three-year-old son from his wife and took William to New York. The elder Brady eventually lost his fortune, and died when William was fifteen years old.

Destitute and alone, Brady made pennies by shining shoes, hawking newspapers, and running errands. He was drawn to sports, and he focused his attention on boxing and baseball. He went to see the odd spectacle of six-day "walking matches" at Madison Square Garden, a precursor to the manic bicycle races of the same duration and venue that would later become so popular. He got a job as a newspaper sports reporter and became expert on every fix and ploy and crooked angle. Returning to San Francisco, he was drawn to the theater and became an actor, stage manager, and producer, whereupon he made his way back to New York, and became one of the city's leading promoters of sporting events and theatrical productions. Before his career was over, he would make and lose several fortunes, produce 260 shows, represent two boxing champions, and promote bicycle racing. The titles of his two autobiographies summed up his life well: *Showman* and *The Fighting Man*. He wagered huge sums of money on people he believed in. He said he had "the rare quality of discerning quality in others." He preferred to fail spectacularly than attempt small, low-risk ventures. "Never tackle anything but champions," he wrote. "Nothing else is worthwhile." He admired the underdog, having risen from newsboy to a denizen of Park Avenue. He played the role of showman with panache, dressed in the finest suits, his thinning hair parted in the middle and combed back, revealing a high forehead above arched eyebrows. He rejected his father's racist views, seeing the struggle of blacks as akin to his own desperate attempt to survive in the city as a boy without means or a father.

Fortuitously, Brady was at the bicycle races in Madison Square Garden in 1896, sending the results to a newspaper, when he saw the young Major Taylor beat Eddie Bald in the preliminary match, and then run strong in the six-day contest. Brady, as it happened, had formed a partnership with the two promoters who had granted Taylor his license for that race. Now, in 1898, Brady consistently made headlines. He promoted a wrestling match in the unlikely venue of New York City's Metropolitan Opera House at Broadway and 39th Street because Madison Square Garden was booked. When one of the wrestlers broke the rules by punching his opponent in the face, Brady hopped into the ring, got mixed up in the fight, and was "hurled through the ropes" as the crowd screamed. "Pandemonium reigned, and for ten minutes there was danger of a stampede," reported the *New York Times*.

Six blocks away, near the intersection of Broadway and 33rd Street, Brady promoted a play at the Manhattan Theatre called *Way Down East*, which became a hit. If nothing else, Brady knew how to draw an audience. He remembered Taylor, and he learned that the cyclist was being denied the chance to enter races and lost a shot at the championship. Brady wasn't necessarily motivated by altruism. He knew, from his father's experience, the passions stirred by race. The public, Brady wrote years later, feasted on "having an orgy of freak shows . . . I was one of the people who gave them whatever lunacy they happened to be craving at the moment." He envisioned Taylor drawing thousands of spectators who would, as they did at Madison Square Garden, be tantalized at the prospect of a black matched against a white. Ideally, Brady would turn the Bald versus Taylor storyline into the main attraction. The fact that Taylor's competitors tried to avoid him would become a selling point. At this height of the bicycle craze, as Brady later recalled it, "small boys knew by heart the records of Cannon Ball Eddie Bald, the Adonis of the wheelman, [and] Major Taylor, the great negro rider . . . a champion streaking round the track hunkered over on his wheel in one of the old-time thirty-mile races was the epitome of human speed. And dangerous."

Brady brushed off those who sought to exclude Taylor based on his skin color. If the League of American Wheelmen wouldn't let Taylor race, he would create a new organization that would. And that is what he did. Taylor became a charter member of Brady's American Cycle Racing Association. But Taylor would race only when Brady thought he was ready. Munger had done an extraordinary job bringing Taylor to this point but was busy with his financial problems. Brady, a student of rehearsal from his efforts in boxing and the theater, decided that Taylor would focus on training during the winter so he would be ready to compete during the next racing season.

Brady assigned an experienced trainer, Willis Troy, a white man who had once worked with Arthur Zimmerman, to work with Taylor. Troy had hoped Taylor could train in Belleair, Florida, just south of Clearwater on the state's west coast, where other elite riders had assembled and were setting speed records. The town had become the opulent center of winter cycling, featuring the just-opened Belleview Biltmore Hotel, which included a 13,000-square-foot ballroom and 244 rooms. Six-day bicycle races, like the one Taylor had participated in, were held on the grounds, and cyclists from around the world competed there. Taylor had proven he belonged in such an elite setting.

Here, however, Brady's well-conceived plans went awry, and he was no better at fighting racism than many before him. Objections were raised about having a black rider in Belleair, and Troy eventually settled on an alternate location, Savannah, Georgia. None of the nationally recognized riders trained there, but it did have a popular cycle racing track, good roads, and warm weather, and that would have to be enough for Taylor. Troy wrote the officials in charge of Savannah's Wheelmen's Park and received permission for Taylor to train there. The city's population of sixty-four thousand was slightly more than half black, giving Troy confidence that Taylor could blend in. In fact, the city was riven by racial tension. Months earlier, President William McKinley had appointed John Deveaux, one of the city's most prominent blacks, to be the chief customs inspector. It was one of a handful of such appointments designed to appease blacks who were disappointed the Republican president had not stopped the spread of Jim Crow laws or put an end to lynching. Deveaux was a publisher whose black-oriented newspaper had said that "no decent Negro could afford to support the Democratic Party since it was the party of Jim Crow, disenfranchisement, and proscription in general of the Negro." The city's white establishment was overwhelmingly Democratic and feared Deveaux and his egalitarian beliefs. The Savannah Cotton Exchange and Board of Trade passed a resolution that characterized blacks as "inferior beings" and expressed concern that having Deveaux in the job would "hurt business."

Savannah's blacks were outraged, and on December 22, 1897, in a brave public show of unity in the South, more than a thousand attended a meeting in support of Deveaux. The blacks passed their own resolution, reminding whites that Deveaux had served at the Customs House for nineteen years and had been a port collector for another four. Moreover, the resolution said, Deveaux had helped people of all races in Savannah when the city was struck by yellow fever, "remaining at his post and distributing thousands of dollars for the relief of citizens without a single penny being unaccounted for." Whites were asked to "set aside their prejudices." As for the idea that having a black man in the job would drive away business, blacks responded that there should be no concern "about the color of a man's skin as long as business was conducted properly." Deveaux's appointment was assured when the city council supported him, but the matter left bitter feelings among many whites, a tension that Taylor and his backers apparently knew nothing about.

Troy, for his part, had hoped to avoid surprises by going to Savannah early and making sure Taylor would train without incident. Still, as a precaution, he booked lodging under his own name for himself and Taylor.

Trouble began as soon as Taylor arrived.

Whites in the boardinghouse where Taylor was supposed to stay objected to a black occupant, and Taylor was forced to find alternative accommodations. Then, when Taylor went to the Wheelmen's Park, a group of white riders barred him. Some of these white riders trained on a "triplet"—a three-seat cycle that could set a blazing pace. Taylor, now nineteen years old, was determined to train, so on the following day he rode into the country along with Troy. They headed from downtown Savannah on Louisville Road, which sliced through farms and forests to the west. Soon, Taylor pulled alongside the triplet and asked the riders if he could follow.

One of the white riders told him there was no way they would be "pacing niggers," and the trio unleashed a storm of epithets against him, threatened his life, and demanded he leave the road. It was a dangerous setting: Taylor, outnumbered, in a remote area of Savannah, where he was unknown. Stoic by nature, Taylor had a tough, righteous side that made him a fierce competitor, and the taunts only emboldened him.

"Alright then," Taylor responded, and he pulled in front of the triplet. The riders tried to pass him, but they could not, and Taylor "led the triplet a merry chase back to town and through the principal streets, much to the cyclists' disgust."

The next day, Taylor received a death threat, accompanied by a crude drawing of a skull and crossbones:

*Dear Mr. Taylor,*
    *If you don't leave here before 48 hours, you will be sorry. We mean business—clear out if you value your life.*
(signed) White Riders

The *Savannah Tribune*, an African American newspaper that had been run by Deveaux before he became chief customs inspector, learned about the incident and defended Taylor. The newspaper wrote that the "cowardly writer" of the death threat against Taylor was "like a midnight assassin" and should be prosecuted. No record of such prosecution was subsequently noted in the newspaper. Taylor had no choice. Lynchings were a real threat; at least 127 would occur nationwide that year, including 12 in Georgia, and most of the victims were black. A trumped-up allegation was often given, such as "paying attention to a white girl," and a man could be hung from a tree. The number of race-based beatings was far greater, and many crimes were never recorded.

Taylor's life was in more danger than ever. Troy received a similar letter, warning him against being associated with a black man. The pair headed back to New York, publicly insisting that it was because of an upcoming race, not the threats against them. But weeks later, Taylor told a reporter that the threats did cause him to leave. "I knew I had no right south of the Mason and Dixon line, but I did not think the feeling was as strong as was shown," Taylor said. "It is useless for a colored person to attempt to get along in the South, for the feeling is so strong that only a race war will settle it."

Now, as he struggled to figure out where he could train, white riders in the North ganged up on him. One of the nation's most prestigious facilities, Woodside Park in Philadelphia, where national championship races were to be held, banned him. The track's manager, Tom Eck, had announced in April 1898 that "We shall bar colored riders and, unfortunately, Taylor is included." He blamed it on the fact that the League of American Wheelmen had banned black members, even though it had allowed Taylor to race. Now, however, Eck—who had helped instigate the League's ban on blacks—announced that its members "will not make matches with Taylor, not that they are afraid of defeat, for he proved last season that he could win only occasionally from the best men, but they object on general principles to competing against him." The racing forms included a stark notation: "for white riders only." Taylor wrote later that he learned that "the color prejudice was not confined to the South."

This was the point at which another man might have quit, with so many forces arrayed against him. Taylor, instead, had an epiphany. Never again would he consider that he would be better off if Munger could bleach his skin white. Prejudice against him turned into motivation. "My color is my fortune," Taylor said in April 1898, shortly after returning from Savannah. "Were I white I might not amount to a row of shucks in this business."

Once again, Taylor vowed to make Munger's declaration come true, that he would become the world's fastest man. If only he could find a venue that would let him ride a fair race. "I was especially determined," he wrote, "to go after the Championship of America in the season of 1898."

# CHAPTER 10

# A Rematch
# with Eddie Bald

The New York and Manhattan Beach Railway traversed Brooklyn's Sheepshead Bay, circled a racing track, and stopped at a station at the Atlantic Ocean's edge. The latter part of the journey was a spectacular voyage on what was known as the Marine Railway, built upon pilings that seemed destined to fall victim to the swirling waters below. That, in fact, would eventually happen, but for now it was the most convenient way for the elite of New York City to disembark at the resort called Manhattan Beach and its two miles of sandy beachfront. Nearby, tens of thousands of working-class people gathered amid the carnival atmosphere of Coney Island, with its amusement rides and food stands. But here was a world apart, an enclave known as the grand Manhattan Beach Hotel. The Queen Anne–style building sprawled just beyond the dunes; only a promenade and a greensward separated it from the spray of the Atlantic Ocean.

The hotel was a Gilded Age extravagance of turrets and balconies and verandas, rising four stories, and providing an astonishing 2,350 single bathhouses and 350 units suited for groups of six bathers. The manicured grounds, with flowering gardens and emerald lawns, included an Excursion and Picnic Pavilion and a concert shell. Guests strolled in their elegant ensembles on an oceanfront esplanade. Near the hotel, Brady opened a cycling velodrome, surrounded by grandstands that could seat thousands. Brady sent Taylor and his other clients to train there and, eventually, to hold a series of spectacular contests. Brady stocked his new American Cycle Racing Association with a handful of the world's best riders, trainers, and equipment. Sometimes it seemed like a crew of misfits. Aside from Taylor, the most notable racer was Jimmy Michael, a Welshman whom Brady described as a "pink-cheeked midget hardly out of short pants" who nonetheless was a "streaking wonder." Each racer had the kind of raw talent that Brady valued.

Brady knew that racers often had poor eating and sleeping habits, so he established an innovative program to ensure that the members of his association were in the best condition. He leased a Sheepshead Bay estate called The Homestead, which had a spacious cottage where Taylor and other riders could lodge, as well as a barn and hennery. "Neither effort nor expense will be spared" at the facility, the *Brooklyn Eagle* reported. A "first class chef" prepared meals designed for top athletic performance, and a manager kept watch to ensure the riders got the proper exercise and rest. It was a short walk from the estate to the Manhattan Beach Hotel and the racing track.

The setting was spectacular, but the track was frightful, whipped by ocean winds, even more dangerous than the slick wooden track that had been erected in Madison Square Garden. To Brady, the threat of catastrophe was a lure for spectators, and he played it up. Taking a punch in the face from a boxing champion might be easier than falling from a bike "on the big concrete oval that our outfit built on Manhattan Beach," he wrote.

Brady's favorite training tool was the use of pacesetters, who rode elongated "multicycles" with extra seats and riders. Taylor and other racers would follow in the pacesetter's slipstream, like birds that follow the leader in a flock flying in a "V" formation. The riders knew the slightest error could send them hurtling into the pacesetter or onto the pavement. Even a slight deviation from the slipstream was disastrous. The air suddenly would become heavy, as if a turbine had been turned on, working against the rider who had broken from the flock. It was an art, riding in the slipstream, staying precisely in rhythm, inches behind the rider in front; the closer you hugged the wheel in front of you, the more the slipstream worked to your advantage, unless, of course, you lost a moment's concentration, or your heart raced slightly too fast, or a competitor brushed his tire against yours or threw his elbow against you, or trapped you in a pocket, and then all was lost. The trick was to stay strong while letting your opponent seize the lead until you took it yourself as the finish line came closer.

Preparing for the race required endless training, giving you the speed and strength needed to bring you home. Shortly after returning from the South, Taylor wrote about his training regimen and lifestyle in a story for the *New York American*. It was a great mistake to ride constantly, he wrote. It was far better to ride in a methodical way, which could be a series of sprints and easy laps, complemented by weight training. Sometimes he added rides at moderate speed from Brooklyn beyond the city limits to outer areas of Long Island to boost his endurance. Equally important was good nutrition and abstention from smoking and alcohol. Stay in condition "all the time."

Taylor would need all of his training as he prepared to race at the Manhattan Beach track. His main opponent would be Eddie Bald.

The morning of May 21 dawned ominously, with leaden skies, slanting rain, and winds whipping across the track at Manhattan Beach. Then the clouds blew over, specks of blue appeared, and some thirty-five hundred spectators piled into the grandstand. Bald and Taylor—the white Adonis and the great Negro, as Brady had called them—lined up for the one-mile race along with a pack of others. It was, the *New York Times* reported, "one of the finest fields of professional cycle racers that has ever pedaled in competition in the East." Bald had "come out of his winter seclusion" and was cheered by most of the crowd. They set off at a brutal pace. Taylor kept strategically behind until close to the end, when he bolted ahead, bursting through at a "red-hot" pace to win the contest.

Bald countered by easily winning the second heat. But when it came time to race the third, decisive heat, Bald looked depleted. He sat up halfway through the race, indicating he was giving up, drawing boos from the crowd, and finished last. The rest of the field dashed to the finish, and Taylor seemed to win, but the referee declared he had lost "by a finger's width."

Still, Taylor gained enough points to remain in the hunt for a championship.

Shortly afterward, Taylor again beat Bald, this time in a two-mile race in Utica, New York. Bald won many races that didn't include Taylor, and the two spent much of the year in a seesaw battle for the most victories. Taylor attracted wide notice as he pushed for a national title. An Indianapolis writer, recalling that Taylor's boasts of his talent had been met locally with "allowance," said that he had "clearly demonstrated that he is the equal of nearly any man," notwithstanding the "remarkable odds" against him.

Two months after his Manhattan Beach triumph, Taylor headed to a much-anticipated race in Cambridge, Massachusetts, at the recently constructed Charles River Park track, a state-of-the-art twenty-acre facility with covered grandstands on Massachusetts Avenue that accommodated ten thousand people. Yet even in Cambridge, as favorable a venue as Taylor could find in the United States, the undertone was ugly. A band struck up a popular tune—"The Warmest Baby in the Bunch"—which included lyrics such as, "You'll all be dazzled when see dis member; you'll think that you've been drinking nigger punch." Then the band serenaded Taylor's competitors with the song "All Coons Look Alike to Me," a ragtime ditty by a black minstrel composer, Ernest Hogan, who profited from the million-selling score but came to regret it. The cover image of the sheet music showed seven stereotyped blacks and the subtitle "A Darkey Misunderstanding." Taylor had no choice but to stand with his bike during the performance. The competitor for whom the song had been played, Eddie McDuffee, rode around the track to great applause, clasping a bouquet in his hands. Taylor and McDuffee shook hands at the starting line, put their heads down, and waited for the thirty-mile race to begin, longer than Taylor's preferred one-mile sprint matches.

## A REMATCH WITH EDDIE BALD

Two teams of pacers emerged on the track, composed of five men each on newfangled five-saddle bikes called "quintiles," providing power for a faster-than-ever dangerous pace. McDuffee easily won the thirty-mile contest, and Taylor decided once again that he should stick to his speciality of sprints, in which his toughest opponents often were those who sought to bar him.

One day, as Taylor prepared to race in Wilkes-Barre, Pennsylvania, he learned that promoters had caved in to white racers and banned him. For months, Taylor had told reporters that he feared for his life. Now, with encouragement from onetime newspaperman Brady, he increasingly used the press as his ally, forcefully speaking out against the tactics. Reporters, especially in the North, eagerly quoted him at length. In a typical interview, Taylor attacked the Pennsylvania promoters, saying they lacked "the backbone to allow me to ride in the race in which they had once invited me." Brady, meanwhile, used the press to put pressure on Philadelphia promoter Tom Eck, who had previously prevented Taylor from competing and threatened to do so again. Brady convinced Eck to change his mind, arguing that Taylor would be a major draw, and a race with Bald was arranged. More than seven thousand people packed the grandstands at Tioga Park on July 17 to see two dozen of the world's fastest racers compete. The winner would be known as the fastest one-mile racer and collect points toward becoming the year's overall champion.

"Cannon Bald!" the crowd chanted, as Eddie Bald headed to the starting line. Then came the "hated rival," Taylor, as the *Philadelphia Press* put it. Some of the other riders crowded with Bald, and Taylor could only wonder if a plan against him was being hatched. After a series of preliminary heats, Bald and Taylor and a number of other riders lined up for the final. They set off at a fast pace, circling at increasingly high speeds. Suddenly, several wheels touched, and one rider went flying in front of the grandstands. Taylor found himself bunched in a middle pack, pinned in by his competitors. He was stuck in the dreaded "pocket," surrounded by opponents who sought to keep him from jumping into the lead.

113

Taylor had spent much of his career battling to get out of pockets. He perfected a technique in which he lay across his handlebars and suddenly accelerated, which became known as his famous "jump." Years later, he revealed that one strategy he had used was in "strict violation of the rules," but was his most effective answer when opponents tried to seal him in a pocket. His opponents' tactics were "nothing less than an attempt to kill," and he felt he had to respond. "My answer was this: I was always on the defensive, they were the first to violate the rules by forcing me in a pocket." To extricate himself, Taylor wrote, he sometimes touched the wheel of one of the riders who sought to trap him, giving a "side slap with my front wheel by a quick jerk of my handle bar." That would momentarily "frighten" his opponent "and invariably cause him to swerve out a trifle," enabling Taylor to "instantaneously" escape. He never caused another rider to crash, he wrote, even though he used the tactic "hundreds of times." The trick didn't always work, and sometimes it was Taylor who crashed. Other times he avoided being in the pocket by trying to lead a race from start to finish. But that was exhausting and often failed because it denied him the benefit of riding in a slipstream, and he rarely tried it when facing top competitors, as on this day.

Taylor seemed trapped, struggling to get out of a pocket set by several riders. He looked ahead and saw Bald escape from the middle pack and, in the homestretch, race toward the lead. Bald "was coming in as a champion never come before," the *Philadelphia Times* reported.

The chants went up even louder. "Cannon Bald! Cannon Bald!"

Then Taylor made his own jump. To the crowd's amazement, the *Press* said, here came "the little form of the colored wonder." Taylor had surged out of the pocket. Thousands in the crowd stood. Taylor suddenly passed Bald "like a flash" and crossed the finish line, victorious by several bicycle lengths. The crowd was stunned.

A new chant went up: "Taylor! Taylor!"

Taylor collected the local newspapers and clipped the stories about his conquest, pasting them into his scrapbook. "Taylor Beats Champion Bald," said the *Press* headline." Newspapers across the country, which received reports by telegraph and an increasing network of long-distance telephone cables, simultaneously reported the results. "Major Taylor Carries Off the Honors at Philadelphia," said the headline in the *Los Angeles Times*. Taylor was now the National Mile champion and was on his way, he hoped, to being named the year's fastest rider.

As Taylor departed Philadelphia and headed for a meet in Asbury Park, New Jersey, he had time to reflect on how far he had come. Five years earlier, he had been Birdie Munger's valet in Indianapolis, and he had been thrilled to be sent to the train station to pick up his hero, the cycling champion Arthur Zimmerman. Now, as Taylor arrived in Asbury Park, there was none other than Zimmerman himself, turning the tables and waiting for him at the train station. Zimmerman, who lived in the area, was recovering from a serious illness. He had followed Taylor's exploits and arranged for this reunion. Zimmerman invited Taylor to stay at his home, and the former and future champions talked for hours about cycling. Zimmerman was slated to be the starter for an afternoon race in which Taylor would again compete against Bald and others. Zimmerman went with Taylor to the track, looked at him gravely, and delivered a message: Taylor must repeat his feat.

"I am very anxious to see you win the championship event this afternoon," Zimmerman said, "and I feel sure you will, even without a suggestion from me. However, I have one to offer, which aided me greatly in my heyday, and I trust you will give it consideration."

Zimmerman walked to a spot on the track where he advised that Taylor make his "jump" into the lead, halfway to the last turn. "If you can lead the field into this turn, nobody can pass you before you cross the tape," Zimmerman said. "I made all of my successful sprints from this identical spot."

Taylor lined up with Bald and the other top riders. A victory here would help Taylor gain ground on Bald in the race for the year's championship. The standings were based on the results of each race, so any victory by Taylor against Bald was doubly important, gaining extra points for himself while denying them to his chief rival. The first three laps were "as hotly contested as any I ever rode in," Taylor wrote later. At the last lap, the pacemaker left the course, and the riders were on their own. Taylor kept a steady eye on the track ahead, remembering Zimmerman's admonition about where to take the lead. He approached the spot. The other riders pedaled furiously. Taylor thought of his childhood hero and suddenly made his jump, winning by inches.

Of all his victories, Taylor said, this one was among the most meaningful, having come in front of his hero. "I have never seen a more happy man in my life than Arthur A. Zimmerman as he shook my hand warmly at the conclusion of the race," Taylor wrote. The two men went to a telegraph office and sent the results to Munger. As Zimmerman walked by Taylor's side, he repeated again and again: "Our friend Birdie Munger was right."

Taylor then returned by train to his boyhood home of Indianapolis, competed in several races, winning second and third places, and was feted by old friends. He climbed in the national standings. Now he stood on the cusp of overtaking Bald.

Brady did all he could to stoke the Taylor-Bald rivalry. He offered $1,000 for a rematch and hoped to get his chance when both men raced in Buffalo. But Bald had had enough. He refused Brady's challenge, fearing a loss to Taylor would hurt his shot at the 1898 championship. Taylor responded angrily, and began to publicly berate Bald. "I want to race these men," Taylor said. "Were they not afraid of me they would come forward." Speaking to a reporter from the *Worcester Telegram*, Taylor said that Bald had drawn "the color line . . . and refused to ride" against him. The real reason for Bald's refusal, Taylor said mockingly, was that "he was afraid of getting licked."

Brady decided it was time to create a new rivalry. He chose Jimmy Michael, the Welshman known as the "midget." In order to lure Michael to race in the United States, Brady agreed to guarantee the extraordinary sum of at least $22,500 for the 1898 season, which would make him one of the world's highest-paid athletes. Michael hardly looked worth it, weighing slightly less than a hundred pounds. But he was one of the world's fastest racers, the "champion of all champions," and had the potential to be an even bigger drawing card than

Taylor or Bald. To make up for his diminutive size, Michael trained ceaselessly, prompting one journalist to write that "the daily work of this little rider would kill many men twice his size."

Michael woke at seven, ate breakfast, and went on a ten-mile walk. Then he rode fifteen miles behind a pacesetter. After lunch, he walked another five or ten miles, then rode another ten behind a pacesetter "at a record-breaking clip," as the writer for the *Boston Globe* recounted it. Then, after supper, Michael walked another five miles, and then "he skips rope from 2000 to 3000 times. Fifteen minutes with dumbbells ends the day's work." This, of course, was at odds with Taylor's admonition that too much riding weakens the rider for the race. Now the two racers' methods would be tested.

The contest between Taylor and Michael was set for the sweltering, windless afternoon of August 27. Bald saw it as a slap, insisting that Michael had promised to race him, not Taylor, in his first match. "Well," Brady said in return, taunting Bald, "when Michael races Taylor, he will be up against the best man" in the cycling world.

The winner would be determined by whoever won two of three one-mile contests. Michael preferred longer races, wearing out his opponents over long distances, while Taylor excelled in sprints such as this one. Thousands of spectators thronged along the guardrails and in the grandstands, and the race was readied. Two teams of five men each mounted their five-saddle quintiles, struggling to steady the ungainly bicycles, while Michael and Taylor prepared to follow the pacemakers. The quintiles set an astonishing pace, five men feverishly turning the pedals and picking up speed, as the racers tried to keep up behind them. Taylor was just about to pull ahead when his team's quintile broke down, leaving Taylor on his own. Michael, paced by his blazing quintile, raced ahead for the victory. Now Taylor had to win both remaining races to be declared the victor. The quintile was fixed, and the second heat was under way.

Twice, a chain snapped on one of the pacing machines, forcing a false start and prompting much anxiety. Finally, the quintiles worked to perfection. In his trademark style, Taylor kept his chest flat over his bike, arms extended to the handlebars, upper body nearly motionless, head down, eyes straight ahead. Taylor lovingly described the science of the sport, and the poetry of the motion. "With a light, quick motion of the ankle," Taylor wrote, he could "not only produce a maximum of efficiency, but by constant practice it would produce an easy, graceful celerity of motion that is pleasing to the eye. It would also conserve the rider's energy for the final lap where it is most needed."

A mile took three laps around the oval. Taylor and Michael were even after the first lap, when the pacesetters handed off to another team. Taylor and Michael had to stay apace with the new teams or risk losing ground. "The slightest miscue means certain defeat," Taylor wrote later about the handoff. He and Michael "were both struggling for dear life to hold on to our big machines as the pace was waxing hotter and hotter with every turn of the pedals." Taylor felt his strength ebb in the last lap, and he could see the rear wheel of the quintile "getting away from me, inch by inch." Michael was slightly ahead. Taylor's elbow was almost touching Michael's.

"C'mon, c'mon!" Taylor's coaches pleaded.

Taylor was a yard behind his quintile, much too far, and threatened to fall out of the slipstream entirely. Then, shockingly, Michael began to scream to his pacemakers: "Steady, steady!" He couldn't keep the pace. Taylor could not believe what he saw; it was, he later wrote, "the psychological turning point of the race." He had convinced himself that Michael would beat him. Now, he believed he could win.

"Go, go!" Taylor called to his pacemakers, who picked up their speed in response. It was, Taylor recalled, "a glorious sensation to see victory now within my grasp, when only a few seconds before inevitable defeat stared me in the face." Taylor sprinted past his pacemakers and finished in victory, and the grandstand crowd erupted. Next came the third and decisive heat. Michael looked drained. He sat up in his saddle and, midway through the race, conceded the contest.

Taylor not only won the $1,000 prize, but his fastest heat, in the third contest, set a world mark, racing at 34.81 miles per hour, finishing the mile in one minute and forty-three seconds, beating the record by two seconds. Mindful of the role played by his pacesetters, all of whom were white, he split his earnings with them. They initially refused payment, saying his thanks were enough, but he insisted it was a team victory. Taylor wrote that if a single rider on the pacesetter wanted to prevent a black man from winning, he could have easily done so by slowing just momentarily. Skin color was "neither a burden, handicap or drawback in this instance," Taylor wrote of his teammates, thanking them for having "respected me as a man."

Taylor was applauded with "tumultuous shouts" from the crowd, while poor Jimmy Michael, his reputation shattered, "was hissed by the spectators as he passed the stand, dispirited and dejected by Taylor's overwhelming victory," according to the *Richmond Times*.

Taylor could now, briefly, claim to be the world's fastest man, but only in this narrow category of a one-mile race with quintile pacesetters. Brady seized the moment, declaring to the crowd that he would pay up to $10,000 for Michael and Taylor to race any distance up to a hundred miles. A rematch was, indeed, held a few weeks later, but at Michael's preferred contest of twenty miles, and he easily won. Still, Taylor's initial victory over Michael firmly established him as one of the nation's greatest athletes.

Once again, the race to be national champion focused increasingly on Taylor and Bald. Taylor gained ground as he won in New Haven, Connecticut, while Bald was injured and unable to compete. Taylor picked up six points, putting him just behind Bald, who remained in first place. Then Bald and Taylor faced off in Philadelphia, racing before a crowd of ten thousand.

Taylor easily won the first heat, a one-third-mile sprint. As he headed to the dressing room, he ran into an angry gaggle of competitors who wanted to prevent him from participating in the next race, a two-mile contest. One of them "threatened me with bodily harm if I dared start in that event," Taylor wrote later. He hadn't planned on competing in the next contest, but he "decided on the spot" that he would do so. He ignored a warning that his competitors planned to gang up on him and knock him to the ground.

The worst nearly happened as the race unfolded and Bald sought to "pocket" his rival, providing an opportunity for his coconspirators to elbow Taylor and send him flying. But Taylor worked his jump to perfection, escaping the pocket to victory. A racer who saw Taylor repeatedly perform the move marveled at his technique. Taylor rode "very low, his nose almost touching the handlebars" as he made his escape. "He manages to jump through . . . so quickly that it is impossible to close in on him," the racer, Howard Freeman, wrote. "The fact that most of the racing men hate him is anything but encouraging. Eddie Bald threatened to thrash him several times this season, but owing to interference he did not get a chance to disfigure the Major's black countenance." Freeman included an illustration that he drew of a white racer jerking his elbow against Taylor's head.

Taylor savored the victory, especially because "I had thwarted the 'frame-up' planned by my fellow riders." This time, as he reached the dressing room, his competitors seemed in awe, replacing their threats with accolades for his remarkable speed. It was, Taylor wrote later, the first time his main competitors had congratulated him. He wrote hopefully—too hopefully, it turned out—that a match of "true sportsmanship" could overcome racism.

Taylor had nearly reached his goal. He had sent a message to the country that undermined racist theories, and his exploits were increasingly followed as an example in African American newspapers. The national championship would likely be determined by just a couple of remaining races. Taylor coveted the prize, the *Philadelphia Press* wrote, "for it means to him fortune and favor the country over and the world over in fact." Bald, however, wanted this championship, which would have been his fourth straight, "more than he wants anything else on earth." To do that, he would have to come up with a new plan to eliminate Taylor from competition.

# CHAPTER 11

# In Pursuit
## of the Championship

One week after their race in Philadelphia, Taylor and Bald joined other riders for contests in Trenton, New Jersey. If the League of American Wheelmen wouldn't ban Taylor, Bald announced, then he would create a group that would. The other white riders agreed and, as Taylor watched in dismay, promptly elected Bald as chairman of the newly established American Racing Cyclists Union.

Taylor lashed out, as he often did, in an interview with his home-town newspaper. "They have hung together so well that they have shut me out of tracks," Taylor told the *Worcester Telegram*. "They went to the promoters and said, 'We will ride if you don't let the nigger ride,' and now they ask me to join them against the league." Taylor, how-ever, soon regretted his refusal to join Bald's union. He realized that if the other riders created the group without him, he would be shut out of even more races. He didn't want to win the championship if it wasn't by defeating Bald and other top racers. Some of the members of the new union, meanwhile, realized that Taylor was needed to help draw big crowds. Taylor was assured—falsely—that the union would not allow Sunday racing. With deeply conflicted feelings, Taylor left the League of American Wheelmen and joined the union headed by his nemesis, Bald.

Still unresolved was how the national championship would be

determined. Bald led Taylor by a narrow margin at this point, and it was decided that contests sponsored by the union would be added to the existing standings. The winner would be determined by a few remaining races in an area of the country that had long been unfriendly to Taylor.

Bald's union scheduled its first important races in St. Louis and Cape Girardeau, Missouri. A year earlier, Taylor had been barred from competing in the state, where a pre–Civil War law had prevented blacks from being taught reading or writing, and it remained one of the nation's most segregated places. Now as Taylor stepped off the train in St. Louis, he was told he could not sleep and dine in the same hotel as the other riders. He was sent to stay with a local black family. Being on a strict diet, and reluctant to ask his hosts to accommodate him, Taylor went into St. Louis each day to eat at the restaurant at Union Station. But after several meals, the manager "rudely informed me that I would not be welcomed henceforth." The manager ordered the headwaiter, who was black, not to serve Taylor. The waiter, who knew of Taylor's fame, refused. The manager immediately fired the man, and a distraught Taylor was forced to leave. The abuse was an ominous beginning to Taylor's new life in the union, which had failed, just like the League, to provide him with equal housing or other accommodations.

Taylor saw the competition in St. Louis as another chance to show that blacks deserved equality. He and Bald won separate heats in a five-mile race, setting up a showdown between them. But the final was postponed by darkness, and the union scheduled a makeup match the next day, a Sunday. Taylor was aghast, believing that the union had violated its agreement with him, but he stood by his religious convictions and gave up his chance to gain points in the championship tally. Bald lost his race, setting up one last contest in which Taylor conceivably could overtake him and become champion. The race was to be held in Cape Girardeau, 118 miles south of St. Louis. The *Boston Globe* reported that Bald led in one category—total points, calculated by adding up his first, second, and third place finishes. Bald had accumulated 185 points, giving him just a two-point lead. Taylor led in percentage of wins, having taken eight first places, compared to five for Bald. It all came down to this one last contest.

But Taylor, angry about his treatment, decided he wouldn't participate. He prepared to leave when the promoter of the Cape Girardeau race, Henry Dunlop, approached him. Dunlop told Taylor that he owned the hotel near the racecourse and promised that there would be no color line drawn against him. Dunlop said "he sympathized with me in the rough treatment at the hands of the hotel and restaurant men . . . and he promised me faithfully I would receive the same treatment and attentions in his hotel as the rest of my fellow racers." Moreover, Dunlop said, the black residents of Cape Girardeau had put up $400 to help sponsor the race, and they—and the promoter— were most anxious that Taylor participate. With these assurances— and the possibility that he still had a shot at winning the national championship—Taylor headed by train south for the decisive race of the season.

Taylor arrived at the Riverview Hotel, which Dunlop was expanding into a "sanitarium," as such facilities were called then, where guests could receive a variety of health treatments. The hotel had a dodgy reputation, with reports of prostitution on the premises. Dunlop, who was described in a local newspaper as having "made a trip around the world on a bicycle," a questionable claim, had just built a quarter-mile bicycle track near his hotel. In time, this would become one of the state's most popular courses, and the coming race was crucial to Dunlop's promotional plans. Bald and the other racers checked into the Riverview and began their training. But Taylor was given a familiar story: Dunlop was "sorry," but Taylor could not stay there on account of his skin color. Dunlop offered to put Taylor up with a local black family, something Taylor had reluctantly accepted many times before. But this was too much. Taylor was a national figure, just a few points away from being national champion, and he had watched a black St. Louis waiter stand up for him, getting fired rather than follow orders not to serve Taylor.

Taylor had no choice but to stay overnight with the local black family. But in the morning, instead of preparing for the race, he headed to the train station and purchased a ticket for Worcester. He would no longer accept the color line or the false promises. As Taylor prepared to board his train, Dunlop and some of the riders ran after him, beseeching him to race. Dunlop knew that Taylor was a major draw, and he didn't want to give up the $400 provided by black residents for the match. Taylor was told that if he refused to race, not only would he lose his shot at the title, but would also be "barred forever from the racing tracks of the country." His career would be over.

Taylor was unmoved. He boarded the train and headed home.

Bald also did not race at Cape Girardeau—for a most peculiar and deeply egotistical reason. He had convinced himself that he was not only a champion cyclist, but also a future star of Broadway. He had gone from being a butcher's son to earning tens of thousands of dollars, a superstar before the phrase was coined. He believed his own publicity that he was the handsomest and most beloved man on the racing circuit, and convinced himself that he could use his fame to catapult himself into a career as an actor and producer. He had agreed to finance a play called *A Twig of Laurel,* named for a champion's crown, which mixed a story of romance and bicycling, and he found the perfect lead actor: himself. So, instead of competing in this last important race, he headed to New York City to attend rehearsals. Bald was billed as the "leading attraction of the play," and a premiere was slated for October 31, in Wilkes Barre, Pennsylvania.

The decisions by Bald and Taylor not to race in Cape Girardeau added to confusion about who was deemed champion. Taylor believed that he deserved the title based on having won the greatest percentage of races, but Eddie Bald and others also claimed it based on cumulative points. Either way, Taylor felt he had been cheated out of a clear shot at the title, and many agreed with him.

As Taylor made his way to Worcester, the national press, much of which had been friendly to him, heard about his treatment. The *Philadelphia Press* said that Taylor "is entitled to every human right." The *Cycling Gazette* said it was too late to ban Taylor, even as it regretted his rise. "It is, of course, a degradation for a white man to contest any point with a Negro," one editorialist wrote. "It is even worse than that and becomes absolute grief and social disaster when the Negro persistently wins out the competitions."

The union refused to back down, banning Taylor and fining him for failing to race in Cape Girardeau. Taylor also faced a fine from the League of American Wheelmen, which he now hoped to rejoin. Taylor refused to pay either fine, meaning he could not race in the United States. This seemed the end.

While many racers wanted nothing to do with Taylor, bicycle manufacturers saw him as a valuable spokesman. A company based in Waltham, Massachusetts, hired Taylor to ride and promote its new "chainless" bicycle. The owner, Walter Sager, paid a $150 fine that enabled Taylor to rejoin the League of American Wheelmen. Sager's new type of bicycle had the benefit of an enclosed mechanism that turned the wheels, eliminating the chance that dirt could build up and cause friction. Sager offered Taylor $10,000 if he could ride a mile in one minute and thirty seconds, which would spark a publicity bonanza for the new type of bicycle. That would require Taylor to beat the world record by slightly more than two seconds. On November 16, in near-freezing conditions on a Philadelphia track, Taylor tucked into position behind pacesetters, pedaled at a searing rate, and broke the world record by one-fifth of a second. He could not go fast enough to earn the $10,000, but his performance was nonetheless a triumphal moment that earned him wide acclaim. Taylor had "astonished the wheeling world," said the *Boston Globe*. Sager's invention was soon discarded because it was too difficult for a rider to change gears, but Taylor had ridden it triumphantly.

Taylor's prize, however, still eluded him. It was one thing to ride alone on a track in a newfangled bicycle and set records. He wanted a fair fight against the best riders. He vowed that in 1899, he would beat Bald and every other racer and be declared the national champion.

On New Year's Day of 1899, Taylor walked into John Street Baptist Church in Worcester, which months earlier had rejected him as a member. It had dealt this blow to Taylor even though the congregation had an entirely black membership and he was a devoutly religious man and one of the leading African Americans in the city and, indeed, the nation. The church deacons had summarily rejected him because he was a bicycle racer, which they presumed superseded Sunday worship and was, in their view, ungodly. For months, Taylor had tried to convince the deacons that his cycling and his religion were compatible. He was deeply pained that even as he regularly battled white racists like few other blacks of his day, he also had to battle the black church that he wished to join. He had promised the deacons that he would never race on Sundays, a promise that had cost him a shot at the national championship he so greatly desired.

The deacons had learned about all of this, and on this new day of a new year, they relented. "They recalled with Christian pride that he refused to participate in Sunday riding," reported the *Boston Globe*. Now Taylor was warmly welcomed. His self-ban on Sunday riding would cost him tens of thousands of dollars in potential prize money and would later be questioned because many of Taylor's supporters worked six days a week and could attend cycling contests only on Sundays. Taylor never regretted his stand. "The one thing I shall never do is race on the Sabbath," Taylor said. "I am not a religious crank nor anything else excepting a man who has his own ideas as to right and wrong, and who, believing as I do, that cycle racing on Sunday is not right will refrain from taking part in any contests on that day."

Eddie Bald had a different dream. The *Brooklyn Eagle* gushed that his play, *A Twig of Laurel*, was "being rapidly booked for a tour of thirty weeks." Crowds would flock to see a production in which Bald "wins a girl and a fortune," featuring an on-stage bicycle race for the third and final act. The play would show how a boy, from a family that suddenly lost its great wealth, was discovered racing through the mountains. Then he starts winning races, finds the girl of his dreams, and makes a new fortune from his cycling skills. Bald, the *Eagle* wrote, "is confident of success in his experiment, although he has had no experience as an actor."

Bald began in smaller cities, arriving in town with an entourage and looking "more like the son of a bank president attending university" than a bicycle racer. He wore a finely tailored brown suit, patent leather shoes, and what was invariably described as "a large diamond ring."

The show opened to great anticipation in the fall of 1899. A critic from the *Binghamton Herald* put it as nicely as possible: Bald's "elocution was not quite what it should be, but this will improve with experience." The critic from the *Binghamton Leader* was less kind, and his review was published in Bald's hometown Buffalo, New York, newspaper. "Bald possesses no intrinsic talent as an actor," the *Leader's* critic wrote, calling him "nervous and uneasy . . . always diffident and shy . . . he has yet to master the first rudiments of acting." Bald was "slovenly in action and stiff in repose." He "did not look at the audience, as it made him dizzy." Acting, the critic continued, "isn't child's play." Even if Bald overcame his deficiencies, there was another problem. The play was "bad, bad to the core . . . the fellow who wrote it up ought to be ashamed of himself." The main redeeming quality was that the bicycle race in the third act was "very realistic"— racing being the thing that Bald knew something about. As for the audience, it was "meanly small."

For three weeks, Bald played lesser cities as he tried to find his voice. He never did. After a performance in Utica, New York, a critic wrote, "Eddie can ride. He cannot act." Weeks of rehearsal were needed, but hardly worth the effort because "it would be almost impossible to conceive a poorer constructed play." Still, Bald went ahead with a week's engagement at Boston's Grand Opera House, where most of those in attendance were from cycling clubs.

Bald vowed that he would keep his commitment to appear for six months, through the end of May, which meant he would be unable to train or compete in races. He publicly insisted that he had financial backers, but it turned out he had funded the production with $8,000 of his bicycling winnings, and he was losing money on many nights. He couldn't afford to lose more. In December, he announced he had quit the stage and would returning to cycling.

Instead of training, however, Bald gallivanted. He joined forces with one of the few athletes who may have been more famous than himself, Tod Sloan, the most celebrated jockey of the day, as well known for his speed on the track as the zest with which he cavorted with women. Raised by foster parents in a poor home in Kokomo, Indiana, the diminutive Sloan had made a fortune during the early years of his racing career, including a series of wins riding for the royal stables of Great Britain. He would be portrayed as the "Yankee Doodle" character in a George M. Cohan musical on Broadway, serve as a model for an Ernest Hemingway story, and be accused of gambling on his own races. He was said to have a "hypnotic influence" on horses, and his free-flowing lifestyle appeared to have the same impact on humans. He owned a yacht and a magnificent home on Brooklyn's Sheepshead Bay, and traveled the world in style, smoking his favored large black cigars, often with a fetching actress at his elbow. He had invested so wisely—and, some suspected, perhaps benefited from throwing races that he bet on—that during his time with Bald he collected a $400,000 check from a Wall Street firm, making him wealthier than some of his sponsors. He was, in other words, the perfectly wrong companion for a bicycle racer trying to recover from a disastrous theatrical debut.

Sloan and Bald rented their own train car for a journey to California, packed it with trunks of clothing, bicycles, dogs, and hunting traps, and stopped in towns along the way, in what amounted to a rolling party caravan, attended by valets. After a few days of duck hunting in southern California, they reached San Francisco, where each rented "the swellest apartments in the biggest hotel." Bald threw all-night, alcohol-infused parties, egged on by Sloan, who felt himself "bigger than the president of the United States."

The hotel where Bald stayed, the 750-room Palace, epitomized the emergence of San Francisco at the turn of the century. The city was at the center of the state's booming economy, with bustling markets by the seaport, a burgeoning metropolis of tall buildings (many of which would be leveled in the 1906 earthquake), and a transportation network that carried crops from the San Joaquin Valley across the country. Huge fortunes were made and lost in the city's stock market, which traded the shares of gold and silver mining companies. The boisterous mix of seafarers, fortune seekers, and prosperous merchants proved all too alluring to Bald. Temptations abounded, and Bald did not resist. He was, the *Brooklyn Eagle* wrote, "a very lavish dresser and liked the flesh pots." He had won championships for three years in a row, abandoned his training for the stage, and was now out of shape, acting in a "wild and reckless" manner, and "spending money lavishly." The *Buffalo Commercial* tracked down a trainer who visited Bald in California. "I tried to reason with him," said the trainer, Arthur Willatts. "I told him he was foolish to blow all of his money so recklessly, just to have a good time." Bald would not listen.

Yet Bald continued to serve as president of the American Racing Cyclists Union. It was in that capacity that he dealt yet another severe blow to Taylor. The union dropped any pretense that it would allow Taylor to compete. Taylor was devastated, having set a goal that he would defeat Bald for the national championship. He called Bald's group an "outlaw" organization. But for all of Bald's personal failings, his group's power was ascendant, and Taylor would have to find other ways to compete. Taylor had been thinking about a revolutionary new way to race, and now he pursued it.

Taylor's idea had its roots in a unique event a few months earlier, at Charles River Park, in Cambridge, Massachusetts, where Taylor had frequently raced: an automobile exhibition. Only a handful of car models had been produced by this time, and very few Americans owned an auto. The noisy contraptions were prone to disasters such as exploding steam tanks, dangerous hand cranks used to start the engine, and gasoline-fueled conflagrations. A rider had died of a heart attack on the same track, while trying to steer an out-of-control car. On this day, November 9, 1898, five of the finest new vehicles were set to compete in a race, one car at a time around the track. No one was sure if automobiles would become widespread or, if they did, how they would be powered.

The contestants rode an array of auto designs. First was a De Dion-Bouton from France, a racing car powered by an engine under the front hood. Then there were four American buggy-type vehicles: a Haynes-Apperson powered by gas, a Riker electric, a Whitney steam car, and a Stanley Brothers prototype, which would become known as a "Steamer."

After the De Dion-Bouton and the first three American cars made their rounds, it was time for the final contestant, F. E. Stanley, a bewhiskered man in a black outfit, and his Steamer. His twin brother, F. O. Stanley, worked the mechanism that provided the steam to power the contraption. Suddenly, F.O. let the car go, and F.E. raced around the track. No one thought this late entry from the Stanley brothers had a chance, certainly not against the French racing car. The Steamer circled the track, faster and faster. The Stanleys not only won the race, but also set a world record for the mile of two minutes and eleven seconds. Until this day, the Stanleys had been hobbyists. After winning, they decided to go into the fledgling automobile business. Just eight months later, the Stanleys produced a Steamer that became the first motor vehicle to drive to the top of New Hampshire's 6,288-foot Mount Washington, the Northeast's highest mountain. Publicity about the feat helped propel the idea that automobiles could go almost anywhere. The race to build a car for the masses accelerated, led by a number of companies that until then had focused on building bicycles. The arc of the transportation age was about to shift dramatically, from bicycles to autos. But for this moment, the two modes of transportation intersected, and Taylor seized the opportunity.

Cyclists who had been relying on teams of quintile bikes to pace them around the track contacted the Stanleys, asking if their company could retrofit a bike with a steam engine. The Stanleys were intrigued. Building a steam-powered bicycle would force them to develop the smallest possible engine, and that knowledge could then be transferred to the production of a car. They were contacted by Eddie McDuffee, who had often competed against Taylor, and they agreed to build the first such machine for him.

McDuffee intended to shock the racing world. One of the Stanley brothers agreed to bring the machine to Philadelphia and stay for a week to make sure it worked properly. McDuffee initially was supposed to race against Taylor in a fifteen-mile race, riding behind his Stanley steam machine, while Taylor was loaned a French-made De Dion-Bouton gasoline-powered pacing bicycle. But both machines failed, and the contest was rescheduled for a Massachusetts track. The McDuffee-Taylor rivalry soon became big news. Round pins were distributed with pictures of the two men that said: "Black Vs. White. Taylor Vs. McDuffee. Charles River Park. June 17th '98. Purse $1500." More than seventeen thousand fans gathered in Cambridge for a duel that would feature motorized pacers. McDuffee's Stanley machine went a mile and a half before it spewed water and sputtered to a stop. Next Taylor's borrowed gasoline-powered machine also failed. The crowd "left the ground with a bad taste in their mouth." But each failure led to tinkering improvements, and McDuffee soon set a world record with his Stanley. Taylor had seen the future.

It was at that moment that Birdie Munger reentered his life.

Munger, who had established an automobile tire company, had been following the efforts to exclude Taylor. He realized that riding behind a motorized pacing vehicle—against only the clock—was a way for Taylor to continue competing. Cycling fans were newly energized by the addition of motorized pacers, especially after a daring racer, Charles Murphy, rode on boards laid down between the tracks and over the crossties of the Long Island Railroad. He took advantage of the slipstream behind a steam locomotive, which enabled him to ride a mile in just under a minute, giving him the nickname "mile-a-minute Murphy."

The prospect of motorized pacing also fit Munger's plan to plunge into the automobile business. He could, he believed, learn much about automobiles by studying the motor that drove the newfangled pacers. He tinkered with the new vehicle, which would be known as a "motocycle," a power-assisted bicycle, without the r of motorcycle, which was yet to become widespread. He felt certain that Taylor could ride behind a steam-powered motocycle and become the world's fastest man. The two agreed to join forces once again. Taylor bought a duplicate of McDuffee's machine, and Munger returned to help manage his career while also serving as chief mechanic for Taylor's new steam-powered bicycle. Plans were made for the two to meet in Chicago, where an attempt at the world record would be held.

On a July day in 1899, the old friends reunited in Chicago and tested the new machine. The motocycle was a scary, unwieldy, complicated contraption, bristling with rods and valves, puffing with steam, forever breaking down. Constructed from a bicycle built for three riders, its middle seat had been removed to allow for gas tanks and an engine. Pressurized air pumped the gas into a boiler, where it was "ignited in about a hundred jets of flame that pass in and around the three hundred or more small copper tubes in which the steam is made." An engineer sat in the rear seat, controlling the speed with a handle. The driver sat in the front seat, struggling to control the 456-pound machine as it made its way around the track, all while trying to keep Taylor directly behind. The machinery turned the wheels at least 2,700 revolutions per minute. "The machine will travel faster than any human beings have ever been carried on the earth's surface," marveled a writer for the *Brooklyn Eagle*. Yet it failed to work properly so often that "Munger is sick of the thing," a journalist on the scene reported. Without it, Taylor stood no chance of setting a world record.

Finally, after many tests, all seemed ready at Chicago's Ravenswood track. The driver and engineer mounted the motocycle, and Taylor took his place behind it. Munger looked on from the sidelines. Then all went haywire. The exhaust pipe blew out repeatedly, the boiler leaked, and the pipes clogged. Taylor dismounted, wrapped himself in his bathrobe to stay warm, and "gazed with contempt on the 'infernal machine,'" wrote a journalist. Munger blamed the motocycle riders for mistreating the contraption, saying they handled the machine like "cows."

Finally, again, all seemed ready, but Munger would not let Taylor ride unless the motocycle was "perfect." Another cyclist made a test run behind the motocycle, which promptly blew out a tube. After yet another trial run, Munger finally allowed Taylor to take his position. This time, the motocycle performed well, and Taylor tucked behind it, pedaling as close as he could to gain the advantage of riding in the slipstream. It wasn't enough. Taylor just barely missed making a world's record. Taylor's next attempt would have to wait. The following day was Sunday, and Taylor would refuse to race. Munger became convinced that if he could overhaul the motor, the machine would run faster, and Taylor could gain the world record.

Munger could do the repairs on the next day, but Taylor insisted that Munger abide by his ban on not working on the Sabbath, even if that meant losing a chance at the record. It was one thing for Taylor to refuse to race on Sunday, but this was a new wrinkle, prohibiting Munger from doing work on a Sunday on grounds that it would benefit him. Munger knew that Taylor's contract with Sager's company required him to set a record or he would get "no money," but Taylor "would not give in, and even threatened to go home if I persisted."

Munger found a friend to take Taylor to church. During the several hours that Taylor was away, Munger secretly repaired the motor. Then, on Monday morning, he pretended to fix the motor, working on it for a few minutes and pronouncing that he had easily fixed it. The race was on.

As Taylor pulled his bicycle to the starting line, he looked up to find Munger in the driver's seat of the motocycle. Munger had been so angry at how the machine had been driven that he decided he would do it himself. It may have been the first time Munger and Taylor raced jointly, and here they were with the world record at stake. After a warm-up lap around the track, Taylor took his place behind Munger's motocycle. Munger ran some test laps on the rough track. He finally signaled Taylor that he was ready. The timekeepers snapped their watches in unison, and, with a great jolt, Munger's vehicle bolted from the starting line. The motocyle burst forward faster than anticipated. Taylor was a yard behind, too far to get the full benefit of the slipstream, but he eventually advanced so much that "only a faint strip of day could be seen between his front wheel and the hind wheel of the motocycle."

Munger and Taylor circled the track once, then again. As they approached the third and final lap, the motocycle's speed increased, and Munger yelled to Taylor, "Now spurt!" Taylor pulled abreast of the motocycle, and the pair passed the finish line almost simultaneously.

Five men held stopwatches to ensure there was no doubt about whether a record had been broken. The announcement came: Taylor and Munger had done it. The crowd screamed. A new world record had been set. Taylor had cycled the mile in one minute and twenty-two and one-fifth seconds, beating the mark by one second.

"I could hardly believe it when they told me the time," an ebullient Taylor said afterward.

Munger exulted, saying, "I knew Major could do it if the machine would pace." He predicted Taylor would go even faster in his next attempt. "The boy has got it in him."

Only later did Taylor somehow learn that Munger had secretly repaired the motor on Sunday. He "was quite put out when told of the fraud," Munger said.

The motocycle would soon be transformed into what later generations would call a motorcycle, no longer built atop a jury-rigged bicycle, but a new vehicle from the ground up. Lessons learned from the operation of the motocycle would also be applied to automobiles. The race was on to determine whether automobiles would be generated by steam, electric, gasoline, or other means. Only in retrospect would it be clear that from the day that bicycles were paced by motors, a major step had been taken to move the nation into the auto age.

Taylor's performance positioned him for the ultimate goal: world champion. While he was boxed out of competing against many of the best riders in the United States, he qualified to compete in the annual world championship, which was to be held shortly—and conveniently—in Montreal. Taylor hoped that rivals who refused to race him on American soil, including Eddie Bald, would not be able to resist the chance to compete in Canada for the world title.

In the United States that summer, thirty-eight blacks were lynched in the South. James K. Vardaman, a newspaper publisher and a candidate for governor of Mississippi, campaigned on a white-nationalist platform that included a ban on education for blacks. In a typical comment, he said the nation was cursed by blacks, contending they were "a lazy, lying, lustful animal which no conceivable amount of training can transform into a tolerable citizen." (Vardaman lost that election but won the governorship five years later and then became a US senator.) His racist rhetoric was widely echoed. It was in this atmosphere that Taylor's competitors tried to keep him off the racetrack, and he headed north of the border.

Canada at the time was still deeply intertwined with the British government; a change in the Constitution had to be approved in London, and fifty-eight percent of the population had roots in Britain, with another thirty-one percent of French descent. The country was largely rural, with the majority of residents lacking running water or indoor plumbing. French-dominated Montreal was the largest city with a population of 268,000. A pressing issue of the day was the influx of non-British immigrants, who were seen as taking precious jobs from the locals. In a country of 5.1 million people, there were only 17,000 of African descent. A black Canadian-born boxer who moved to the United States, George Dixon, had won a world bantamweight title nearly a decade earlier, but no American-born black had won a world sporting title, and a cycling world championship would be considered a heroic accomplishment for any athlete. That was the challenge that now lay before Taylor.

While Canada was far less diverse than the United States, the nation welcomed Taylor as it had few sports figures before him. Little mention was made of his race, and rarely in a detrimental fashion. No one tried to ban him from competition; there was only criticism of white riders who refused to race against him. Bald and some other top white riders from the United States refused to come to Montreal. Still, the majority of racers were from the United States, and some of the best from England, France, and Australia also arrived. While Taylor was disappointed that he would not be racing against some of his greatest rivals, he treasured the chance to compete on what he considered the greatest stage. It was the moment he had been waiting for his entire career. "My one outstanding motive was to win the World's Championship," he recalled.

On August 10, in what one newspaper called "the largest crowd ever seen in Montreal," more than eighteen thousand people packed the stands at Queen's Park racetrack, and another five thousand could not get in. Taylor, fresh off his record-setting performance in Chicago, was widely portrayed as the best racer in the field. One Montreal newspaper said Taylor, who was "very pleasing looking" and "probably the best developed man on the track," quickly became a crowd favorite. In his first race, a half-mile sprint, Taylor stayed behind during most of the race, then used a burst of speed to leap ahead of his competitors— or so nearly everyone seemed to think. "It was the opinion of 18,000 people in the grandstand that Taylor was the winner by at least a foot," wrote one Montreal journalist.

The judges awarded him second place, leading the crowd to scream in "vigorous protest."

Taylor asked the judges if it was their "honest decision" that he had come in second place. They assured him it was.

"Well, all right, if that is your verdict, gentlemen, I shall have to abide by it," Taylor said. "But I know I won."

As Taylor walked away from the judges, the crowd grew angrier. People began to shout Taylor's name, and the chant went through the crowd in waves, "Taylor! Taylor!" For a half-hour, the Canadian spectators yelled "scathing remarks to the judges." Then word went through the crowd that everyone who believed Taylor had won should stand. Before long, "every man woman and child had arisen," a Montreal newspaper reported. The judges held firm.

Taylor considered his next chance in his one-mile specialty, "the greatest race I had ever been called upon to contest." He was "a trifle nervous" because he faced "the most formidable racing combination known in the cycle racing world"—a pair of American brothers, Nat and Tom Butler. The Canadian champion, Angus McLeod, and a French racer, Gaston Courbe d'Outrelon, rounded out the field, but it was the Butlers whom Taylor feared most. He had lost the half-mile race because he had been caught too long in a pocket formed by his rivals, and this time he vowed not to be ensnared.

Taylor and his competitors stood at the starting line, and a "most dramatic solemnity" hushed the crowd. The pistol cracked, and the Butler brothers set a torrid pace. Suddenly, on the second lap, Taylor found himself nearly in a pocket, escaping "only by the narrowest margin." Nat Butler led the pack, with Taylor just behind, and Tom Butler hugged his rear wheel. McLeod and d'Outrelon were just behind. As the five racers rounded the bend, McLeod made his move, dashing toward the front. Taylor joined the sprint, and pulled ahead of McLeod. Taylor now had the lead, but he saw the Butler brothers gaining on him. Working together, one of the brothers would be in position to win unless Taylor could stop them both.

The homestretch loomed. Taylor made a racer's move of quickly peeking under his arm to see who was following, rather than swiveling his head back and potentially losing a second while craning backward. The Butlers burst forward, and "our three wheels were almost abreast," Taylor wrote. He had to make "that last supreme effort" if he was going to win. He relished the moment. It was a fair fight. No elbows would be thrown—the Butlers had always treated him right. The fastest man would win. "I bolted for the tape," Taylor recalled, and suddenly he burst through it. The crowd roared. Taylor was "elated," feeling he had beaten "the cream of the cycling world."

In the United States, when he had taken a victory lap, the band often struck up a condescending song, belittling him by playing "Dixie" or some other tune with racist overtones. But here in Canada, he heard something upon his victory that had never been played for him: "The Star-Spangled Banner."

"My national anthem took on a new meaning for me from that moment," Taylor recalled. "I never felt so proud to be an American before, and indeed, I even felt more American at that moment than I ever felt in America."

Taylor had "but one regret," he wrote, "that my manager, Mr. Munger, could not be present to actually witness his remarkable prophecy," that Taylor would become "the fastest bicycle rider in the world." The championship was "a big victory for him as well, not only for his confidence in me as a rider, but also on account of his ideals and true sportsmanship for which he stood." Taylor also won a two-mile championship. He turned down a request to run a race in which no prize money was offered, which Taylor viewed as an insult, although it did not stop some racist American writers from claiming he was afraid to race. That mattered little. He was celebrated in headlines around the globe: Major Taylor was the world's fastest man. He was three months shy of his twenty-first birthday.

Every possibility lay in front of Taylor, if only he would continue to race outside the United States and its systematic racism. Taylor, however, had one more goal. He returned to the United States, and, despite many efforts by racers who employed their usual tactics against him, he won enough races to be declared national champion later that year. It would be much noted that Bald and the members of his union, drawing the color line, competed for their separate national championship, which was won by a racer named Tom Cooper. Still, Taylor's national and world titles made him one of the most famous athletes in the world, confounding racists who had belittled him, and those who tried to deny him the opportunity to race. "The colored boy . . . has astonished the world," wrote the *Chicago Times-Herald.*

Munger, meanwhile, received the news he had been awaiting: he was given $600,000 to start a new company in the automobile business.

As a new century loomed, Taylor and Munger seemed on top of the world.

The triumphal moment would not last.

# CHAPTER 12

# "A Race Run for Blood"

Shortly before Christmas of 1899, a French journalist and sports promoter named Victor Breyer arrived in Boston and sent word that he wanted to meet Taylor. Breyer was a classically handsome man, educated in England and cultured in France. He sported a thick mustache and a straw hat, with piercing eyes and an athletic build, and he elegantly filled his tailored suit, cuffs perfectly extended. A journalist, cycling promoter, and bon vivant, he had come to the United States with some of his country's top cyclists to compete against Americans. But his real mission, it seemed, was to convince Taylor that the time had come to race in Paris.

In France, the center of the racing world, promoters salivated at the chance to sign him, and no one was more aggressive than Breyer. He had seen or heard about every top racer in the United States. He was only interested in signing one man. "Taylor is the rider of all riders we want to see in Paris," he told the *Boston Globe*. He would not "give a cent" for any other.

Taylor, for his part, was "burning with such a strong desire to come to France," and he agreed to meet Breyer for dinner at a Boston hotel. The pair, joined by some French racers, talked for hours, and it seemed a deal would be struck. Breyer suggested he would offer Taylor $10,000 if he would agree to participate in a number of races, and more could be earned if he won the contests. It was one of the most generous sporting contracts of the time. There was a catch, of course. Breyer insisted that Taylor race on Sundays. Taylor reminded the Frenchman that he could not race on that day, and the prospect for a deal faded—but did not yet die. After dinner, Breyer watched Taylor win an exhibition at a nearby velodrome, and was even more impressed. In a report for the journal *Le Vélo*, Breyer praised Taylor and suggested a deal would be forthcoming.

"We met the negro at last," Breyer wrote of Taylor, extolling him as "very well behaved" and with "very correct manners." Breyer had "high hopes of persuading him to overcome his religious scruples of racing on Sundays."

News that Taylor might agree to spend the season in Paris created a sensation. "The flying Negro!" wrote Robert Coquelle, another French journalist and promoter working to sign Taylor, in the sporting publication *La Vie au Grand Air*. The "beautiful black" was "the perfect cyclist." Not only was he "the best sprinter in the New World," but also a man of extraordinary strength and character given "the antipathy that exists on the other side of the water for people of color."

As Taylor weighed his decision, he faced new pressures from an old foe.

The same week that Breyer met Taylor, Eddie Bald returned from Europe, having spent all of the $10,000 he had carried with him on "a good time." He had "lost my appetite" for racing, he said upon returning to New York. Yet he needed money and he announced that he planned to race again. He promptly set about finding a way to exclude Taylor as a competitor.

Bald's union had become increasingly powerful, and it forced the League of American Wheelmen out of the business of sanctioning races. That meant that Taylor could not race in 1900 unless he paid a fine of $500, which he had deemed unfair. As a result, Taylor faced the loss of his income and his chance at competing.

"Major Taylor, the fastest of them all, has been the victim of a game of freeze out," wrote his sympathetic hometown newspaper, the *Worcester Spy*. Just months after the newspapers had been filled with stories of his national and world championships, they published a series of dire headlines: "Lost in shuffle! Major Taylor is at the mercy of his enemies," said one. "Little Hope for Major Taylor. Appears to Be Permanently Barred From All Racing," said another. The *Spy* expressed outrage, writing, "The riders have drawn the color line; it is unconstitutional, un-American, unsportsmanlike. It is wrong in the abstract, unrighteous in the concrete."

Taylor carefully clipped the article and pasted it in his scrapbook. Beneath it, these words appeared:

Yield not to discouragement.
Zealously labor for the right,
And success is certain.

While Taylor pondered the offer to race in France, Breyer stepped up the pressure, saying the cyclist must "come at once" or the proposal would be withdrawn. American newspapers began to report that Taylor had given up his "religious scruples" due to "love of fame and thirst for coin." This was more than Taylor could stand, and he rejected the offer. "Taylor Refuses $10,000; He Won't Race On Sunday: Negro Cyclist Is Offered a Large Guarantee for French Season, but Does Not Accept," reported the *New York World*. A drawing accompanying the story showed a perfectly sculpted, bare-chested Taylor, hands extended to his head, showing off his shape.

Other promoters similarly tried to persuade Taylor. Mark Braun, who represented Paris track owners, went to Worcester to visit with Taylor and spent several days seeking to convince him to come to France. Taylor told Braun, as he had told Breyer and so many others, that he would accept as long as he didn't have to race on Sundays. So strong was Taylor's objection that Braun said he was "now certain that Major Taylor will not cross the ocean."

Taylor defended his decision in a letter to a New Hampshire newspaper, while acknowledging that the temptation was strong: "It isn't as though I had lots of money and could afford to say I don't need to race on Sunday, and I am sure if the general public knew my heart as God knows it, they would appreciate what I am doing even better than they do."

• • •

Notwithstanding his complaint that he needed money, Taylor was, in fact, one of the wealthiest blacks in Massachusetts. He had long wanted to buy a home in Worcester, a city that had embraced him—or so he thought. He felt an urgency to find a spacious accommodation because he had learned that his eighteen-year-old sister, Gertrude, was suffering from tuberculosis, and he had agreed to let her live with him in Worcester.

A new development of solid, two-story homes was being constructed in a neighborhood called Columbus Park, served by a streetcar line, a much more elegant locale than the tightly packed working-class triple-deckers that had proliferated in the city. But no blacks lived in the neighborhood, and the builder wanted to keep it that way. Taylor was indignant. He had as much right to live there as anyone else, and he had the ability to pay in cash.

He contacted a real estate agent, John Maher, to buy the house from the builder, Charles King. Taylor's identity would be kept secret. Maher, sympathetic to Taylor's plight, arrived at King's home in the winter of 1900 and said he had a client who wanted to buy a house on Hobson Avenue. King said the price was $3,000. Maher counteroffered $2,800, and the two agreed on $2,850. A meeting was set for the next day, with Maher agreeing that his client would show up to sign the paperwork.

The next morning, Maher brought a check for the full amount, and kept reassuring King that the buyer would arrive any minute. King said he "wanted to wait and have a talk with the purchaser." Soon, Taylor did arrive, but Maher did not explain that he was the buyer. King assumed Taylor was a workman, and he signed the deed, "thinking that everything was all right, since the certified check paid me everything that was coming to me."

The following Sunday, King learned he had sold a house to a black man. "I was so surprised I could not contain myself," King said later. There were false stories that Taylor had secretly married and thus needed the house. In fact, Taylor's sister moved into a bedroom on the second floor of the home. Her tuberculosis worsened, and Taylor comforted her day and night. Members of his church and other friends also visited regularly, seeking to boost Gertrude's spirits. Taylor's neighbors watched the procession of people to the home with disdain. A number of neighbors marched to King's office and protested.

"There are colored persons, sir, a whole house full of them, sir, right in the midst of our neighborhood," said one of the residents. "You have sold your house to a colored man, and, worse than that, sir, to a sporting colored person! We are going to sue you for damages."

The controversy became state, and then national, news. "Major Taylor Shocks Society," said a sarcastic headline in the *Boston Post*. "His White Neighbors Object," said the *New York World*. "Major Taylor's Rich Neighbors" said a headline in the *Chicago Tribune*. "Worcester Suburb Stirred Up Over the Colored Cyclist." Taylor was asked if he would sell the house back to the builder for a $2,000 profit. Taylor suggested $11,000, nearly four times what he paid for it. In fact, he did not intend to sell for any price. "I don't know why I haven't as much right to buy a little place and get some furniture as any man in town," he said. Unlike countless other blacks of lesser means and fame, who were blocked from white neighborhoods across the nation—often to the proverbial "other side of the tracks"—Taylor won his right to remain in Columbus Park, thanks in part to the scorn heaped on Worcester by the press.

The two-story house, built in the Queen Anne style with Colonial Revival influences, was spacious and finely detailed, with a circular window on the second floor above the entryway. A triangular roof stood above the front porch. Opening a heavy wooden door, a visitor entered the vestibule. To the right was a parlor, at the rear of which were two French doors, each with fifteen panes of glass, that led to the living room. Walking to the back of the house, the visitor entered a large kitchen, and then turned the corner into a formal dining area with built-in cabinetry. Intricate wooden floors had been laid throughout the house in a variety of patterns. Heading out of the dining room, a visitor came to an elaborate oak staircase, with a large ball atop the newel post, leading to the three bedrooms of the second floor. It was a prominent home in one of the city's newest and finest settings. Taylor could walk to a nearby pond, gaze at the foothills, and ride his bike on a rapidly growing road network.

But for Taylor, the housewarming days were filled with sorrow. He spent much of that winter comforting Gertrude. Her illness caused her to leave school in January, and she spent the next four months confined to her bedroom in Taylor's house. She died in April at nineteen years old, and a grief-stricken Taylor pasted a poem into his scrapbook beneath clippings about her death.

> Sleep, oh, sleep!
> The Shepherd loves His sheep!
> Fast speedeth the night away
> Soon cometh the glorious day
> Sleep weary ones, while you may—
> Sleep, oh, Sleep.

Taylor took Gertrude's body on the train back to Indianapolis for burial, and briefly reunited with the rest of his family. Then he returned to Worcester, where the second-floor bedroom that had been occupied by his sister was draped in black. He needed to restart his racing career, but his sister's death had "driven thoughts of everything away." Emotionally drained, he spent weeks rearranging his household, sorting his sister's belongings. He was in no mood to pay the $500 fine that would enable him to race again because he thought it had been unfairly levied. Nor was he willing to back down on his refusal to race on Sundays in order to race in Europe.

In the end, the fine was paid in a face-saving measure by the Iver Johnson bicycle company, which agreed to sponsor Taylor for the season, and he resumed training. It would take Taylor weeks to get back in shape, and even local backers believed he had no chance of competing for his second straight national title. "Out for Championship This Year," said the headline in the *Worcester Telegram*.

Taylor's restart was dismal. During a New Jersey exhibition, Taylor committed his most common mistake, thinking the race was over one lap before it was finished. Reporters were so used to Taylor making this mystifying flub that they began referring to it jocularly as a "Major Mistake," and it dogged him throughout his career.

By mid-July, Taylor was ready for one of the most emotional moments of his career. He returned to Indianapolis, where his father planned to watch him race. Thirty-five years earlier, Gilbert Taylor had fought for the North in the Civil War, and had witnessed the liberation of Richmond, the destroyed capital of the Confederacy. The war was still a vivid memory for most families. The North had been served by 2.2 million members of the military, 364,511 of whom had been killed, and the South had mobilized as many as 1.5 million soldiers, 133,821 of whom were killed. The country had not yet healed from the war's divisions. A clue to the impact of Gilbert Taylor's military service on his son's outlook can be found in a scrapbook that Major Taylor kept of his racing exploits. Pasted among these stories of his victories and defeats is a letter to the editor of the *Worcester Spy*, titled "Colored Troops." For nearly a page, the writer told how US military leaders had relied on black fighters, but that such soldiers had received little in return. The black soldiers were asked "to stop a bullet" but had "no hope of promotion but simply a right to die for your country . . . you tell him to his face he is incompetent to command. You would employ him as you would a bulldog."

The black veteran should live in a country where "color does not count." Many veterans, the writer continued, had without help from whites acquired wealth, and they had excelled in the fields of law, science, and medicine, "but the bar remains, the insurmountable barrier of color."

Now Gilbert Taylor, white-haired and proudly wearing his old military jacket, arrived with several veterans with whom he had served in the Union Army, settling into the stands to watch the cycling contest. His son, who had battled so bravely on the racing track, seemed daunted, even a bit petrified, by his father's arrival. The surprising truth was that Gilbert Taylor had never seen his son race professionally. Gilbert had never seemed impressed by what he had heard about his son's accomplishments, and Taylor, like many sons, yearned for his father's approval.

The races were held at the Newby Oval, built two years earlier to be one of the world's finest velodromes. The facility was constructed by Arthur C. Newby and his partners, who included Carl Fisher, who would become famous for his development of Miami Beach. The quarter-mile curved track was covered with white pine boards nailed into the ground. Grandstands held more than eight thousand people, and sometimes as many as twenty thousand spectators spilled onto the grounds.

The evening of July 18 began poorly, as Taylor lost a half-mile race. His only other entry was a two-mile contest divided into two heats. Taylor easily won his preliminary bout. In the final, his main competition was Owen Kimble, a Louisville native whom Taylor considered one of his most racist opponents. "Kimble felt that in order to uphold those inherited ideals of his forefathers, he was obliged to hate me with a genuine bitterness and do his utmost to defeat me every time we met," Taylor wrote. Unlike some racers, Kimble never used unfair means, like a thrown elbow, to win, Taylor said. He channeled his racism into a mad energy that made him one of Taylor's stiffest competitors. For seven laps, Taylor's mission was to avoid being caught in a pocket. As Taylor approached the eighth lap, hearing the bell that signaled the final quarter-mile, he "shot up the banking," streaking out of the pocket and above his competitors. Then he swooped down at the northeast turn, took the lead, and "pedaled like a fiend." Kimble took after him, but Taylor had opened a lead of three lengths and won the race. It was, Taylor wrote, "one of the most sensational rides I ever made," and the crowd gave him a standing ovation.

His father was not so enthralled.

"Well, son, there is one thing I don't understand," Gilbert Taylor said as he congratulated the victor in the dressing room. "That is, if you are the fastest bicycle rider in the world, as the newspapers say you are, why in time don't you beat those white boys further at the finish line?"

146

"Well," Taylor replied, taken aback, "I won by a couple of lengths, didn't I?"

"Yes," Gilbert Taylor said, "but I expected to see you leave them so far behind that you could get dressed and come out and see the rest of them fight it out for second and third money."

Taylor tried to explain that he wasn't as fast as the newspapers said, and his father "readily agreed." Then Gilbert Taylor asked why his son had to start "way back in last place," unaware that Taylor was put there because of his perceived advantage in what was known as a handicap race, giving competitors a better chance to compete. Why, Gilbert Taylor asked, were "all the white boys" placed ahead of him at the starting line? Taylor's father was convinced his son "was being picked on again" because he was black.

Taylor seemed newly energized by the victory in front of his father, and he excelled in the weeks that followed, winning a half-mile sprint in Worcester and a quarter-mile in Newark, New Jersey. A much-hyped contest was held in Hartford, Connecticut, against W. S. Fenn, a rider nicknamed the "boy wonder." Fenn briefly sprinted ahead of Taylor, drawing gasps from the crowd, until Taylor easily took back the lead and won by three lengths.

Just seven months had passed since newspaper headlines described only gloom for Taylor, and his odds for rejoining the racing circuit deemed nearly nil. Now he was back and in complete control, just as his competitors had feared. At the end of the season, the points were tab-ulated, and Taylor had won the national championship by a stunning margin of 40–20 over his nearest competitor. Bald had failed to regain his form and hadn't come close to breaking into the top standings.

With the race for the annual championship over, Taylor still felt the need to compete directly against Bald, but that was impossible because his rival "drew the color line." The "next best choice" was Tom Cooper, who was one of Bald's closest allies. A handsome, ruddy-faced onetime pharmacist from Detroit, Cooper was widely considered one of the world's best racers. He agreed to face Taylor in what was seen as a contest to determine who would be the best American rider to face the top racer in France, the legendary Edmond Jacquelin.

Cooper had previously lost to Jacquelin, and he hoped that by beating Taylor, he would once again attract the interest of French promoters. Taylor, meanwhile, saw the race as his own chance to be chosen to compete against Jacquelin.

Cooper's trainer, Tom Eck—who once banned Taylor from racing in Philadelphia—did everything he could to unnerve him. After making sure both racers were within hearing distance, Eck spoke insultingly to Taylor's trainer, Bob Ellingham. Taylor never forgot the snub.

"Well, Bawb," Eck drawled, "Tawm will now proceed to hand your little darkey the most artistic trimming of his young life. In this first heat Tawm is going to give the Major his first real lesson on the fine point of the French style of match racing. . . . I have cautioned Tawm that in the best interest of the sport and for the good of all concerned, not to beat the little darkey badly."

Taylor smiled as Ellingham responded: "It is true, Mr. Eck, that Major Taylor has never raced in Paris. . . . What he may lack in track strategy he will have to make up in gameness and speed."

In fact, Taylor was a strategic genius. During the warm-ups, he had studied Cooper's bike and determined that his rival was using a 108-inch gear. (The sizing is measured by dividing the number of front ring teeth by the number of rear cog teeth, multiplied by the diameter of the drive wheel. An experienced racer such as Taylor could determine this at a glance.) Taylor knew that the large size meant Cooper intended to power his way to victory while using fewer revolutions of the wheels. Taylor countered with a 92-inch gear, which meant he had to turn more revolutions to surpass Cooper. It was Cooper's brute strength on a large gear versus Taylor's aerobic ability to ride at a higher cadence on a smaller gear. Taylor had to keep close behind Cooper as the finish line neared, then use his highest cadence and strength to reach top speed just before the end, enabling him to burst ahead and win. Wait too long, and there was no way to catch the leader. Push at full speed too early, and Cooper could retake the lead. Gears, cranks, timing, and the nanoseconds that determine the difference between victory and defeat—all of this was in Taylor's mind as he listened to Cooper's trainer deliver the sneering lecture about strategy.

The winner of two out of three heats would claim the $500 prize. The two sped away and, after three laps, Cooper tried to take an outside position and head for the top of the banking, in preparation for making his move. Taylor knew it was coming. He timed his counterattack, beat Cooper to the high position, and spun at the highest cadence he could maintain, suddenly streaking ahead just as Cooper was ever-so-slightly stalled as he climbed the banking. Taylor's tactic was so perfect that he soon gained ten lengths on Cooper with a lap and a half to go. As he headed for certain victory, he recalled Eck's taunt that Cooper would try not to beat him too badly. Taylor, who had never before tried to humiliate a competitor by padding an obvious lead, was so angry that he violated his usual principle. "Riled by that taunt I kept right on tearing to the tape," he wrote. "This was the first time I ever really tried to distance an opponent."

The second race had a twist: it was led by pacemakers. Taylor closely followed the pacemaker's wheel through the first seven laps, took the lead and won the race—or so he thought. Repeating his most common error, Taylor miscounted and thought the race was over a lap early. Slowing, he heard the bell signaling the final lap, and he found Cooper by his side. The pacemaker pulled away, and as the two racers sprinted toward the finish line, Taylor suddenly pulled ahead at the last moment, winning by a half-length. Taylor had done it, winning two races and thus the match. As Taylor claimed his victory, his mind flashed to the evening four years earlier, when he had miscounted laps but still won his first major race by outsprinting Eddie Bald. He could not get his longtime rival out of his head. Now he took great satisfaction in beating Cooper, whose prejudice against him was just as strong as Bald's. "Had the purse been $5,000 instead of $500 it would have been a mere bagatelle compared with the supreme satisfaction that I felt over my defeat of Tom Cooper," Taylor wrote. "If ever a race was run for blood, this one was."

A few days later, Taylor returned home, where he attended a social sponsored by the AME Zion Church. Years back, he had been a poor boy in Indianapolis, wearing hand-me-downs on his small body frame.

Now time and money and athleticism had made him into a marvel of a man: muscular, handsome, well groomed, clean shaven. He took great care in his clothing, being able to afford the most fashionable suits, usually of three pieces, a watch on his wrist, a hat to be doffed upon entrance. He delighted in sitting at the piano, playing popular tunes and composing his own music. He wrote poetry and became an amateur photographer, using both skills to record the world around him—a world that he had already seen more of than most people. He was also a man of deep faith, entrusting that God would watch over him as he regularly risked his life in such a dangerous sport. Walking into the church social on this night, he surely drew the eyes of many, and one of those who took notice was a striking young woman named Daisy Victoria Morris.

Daisy was born in 1876 in the small river town of Hudson, New York, about 130 miles north of New York City. There, she saw the same entrancing views as the famed artist Frederic Church, who lived in his hilltop estate Olana, five miles south of town, drawing the romanticized, panoramic landscapes that made him a central figure of the Hudson River School. Daisy's mother, Mary, was black and had been in a relationship with a white man whom she described as English. Daisy's middle name of Victoria was also that of the Queen of England at the time. The father disappeared from the scene, his name lost to history, and Daisy apparently never knew him. Her skin was light-colored, her hair was long, and she on occasion was described as white. An 1880 census shows her at four years old, living with her brother, Paul, fourteen; her thirty-five-year-old mother; and her fifty-five-year-old grandmother, Charlotte, a washerwoman. The family lived during Daisy's childhood at various addresses on Diamond Street, parts of which were known for having several houses of prostitution (there is no indication that the family had anything to do with the practice), and also an area where many African Americans lived. She said years later that she attended Hudson Academy and then another school, where she was an athletic standout, according to a flattering magazine account she later provided. When Daisy was nineteen, her mother died, and she became a ward of a man who was described in a contemporaneous account as her uncle, the Reverend Louis H. Taylor. He lived in Hartford, Connecticut, and she stayed with him for three years, serving on the social committee of his Pearl Street AME Zion Church. (The reverend was no relation to Major Taylor.) She was "very prominent" in society, and was "an important factor" in plays and concerts, according to the account she provided to a magazine. When the reverend moved to Worcester to become the minister of that city's African Methodist Episcopal Church, he took Daisy with him, and for several years, Daisy lived in a boardinghouse by the church and worked as a housemaid. She was many of the things that Taylor seemed to seek in a potential wife: tall, beautiful, musical, theatrical, athletic, educated, cultured, and committed to her religious faith.

At the time, Worcester was home to 1,100 blacks out of its population of 117,000 people. Many were former slaves who had fled from the South and discovered that Worcester was an abolitionist haven, one of the most "radical" cities in New England. Taylor had gotten to know a number of them, and he put clippings about their lives in his scrapbook. The community centered around two main black churches: the AME Zion Church led by Reverend Taylor, and the John Street Baptist Church that Major Taylor attended. The reverend was one of the most vocal civil rights leaders in Worcester, delivering speeches in which he urged blacks to participate in politics. Similarly, the Reverend Hiram Conway, the minister at Major Taylor's church, urged blacks to become more outspoken in the political world. Together, the two reverends deeply influenced their respective congregants, Daisy Morris and Major Taylor.

Daisy could hardly have failed to have heard about the most famous black man in Worcester, and Taylor likely had heard about her. On October 11, just a few days after he beat Cooper, Taylor attended the church social and made a tantalizingly brief notation in his notebook: "Daisy Morris." The courtship, however, did not start smoothly. Daisy's family initially was not pleased, as "she was raised in a family that didn't approve of cycling," her daughter recalled years later.

Until this moment, there had been no confirmed word of a woman in Taylor's life, although a number of newspaper stories had speculated whether he had been secretly married. Taylor had been astonished at the interest in his personal life, but from the day he made the notation in his notebook, Daisy Morris would be at the center of his thoughts.

Meanwhile, after the initial travails, the year had almost been too easy. The press was again filled with speculation: if Taylor wanted real competition, not to mention a big payday, there was only one man in the world—the Frenchman Edmond Jacquelin—who seemed his equal. Breyer, who had tried a year earlier to convince Taylor to race in Paris, had sent his business partner, Robert Coquelle, to America, and now it was Coquelle's turn to try to persuade the racer. Coquelle visited Taylor at his Worcester home and found that the racer's father was in residence.

Gilbert Taylor was fascinated by the French visitor, and he pointed out two photographs on the wall of his son's home. The first was of Theodore Roosevelt, then the governor of New York, in his Rough Rider outfit. The second was of Booker T. Washington, the black leader. Washington, who had been born into slavery, was known for his "gradualism" approach to racial equality, viewing whites and blacks as being "as separate as the fingers," yet he said they could work together for "mutual progress." Appealing to Southern whites, he said in his famous 1895 "Atlanta Compromise" speech that blacks would "make blossom the waste places in your fields, and run your factories. While doing this, you can be sure in the future, as in the past, that you and your families will be surrounded by the most patient, faithful, law abiding, and unresentful people that the world has seen." Washington effectively endorsed the idea of separate but equal, and his emphasis was on providing blacks with educational opportunities equivalent to those offered to whites, which he said would gradually result in acceptance and integration. He put his theories to work by founding Tuskegee Institute in Alabama, where blacks could receive what he considered to be a practical education. Many of the Gilded Age leaders of the day, such as Andrew Carnegie, contributed tens of thousands of dollars.

In admonishing blacks to work for their own improvement and not revolt fruitlessly against a white establishment that could so forcefully suppress them, Washington faced divisions within his race. The philosophy was rejected as too subservient by black leaders such as W. E. B. Du Bois, who had grown up 109 miles to the west of Worcester, in Great Barrington, Massachusetts. Du Bois said it left the wrong impression that "the South is justified in its present attitude toward the Negro because of the Negro's degradation." Over the years, the conflict between the two would escalate, and Du Bois wrote in his book *The Souls of Black Folk* that "Mr. Washington represents in Negro thought the old attitude of adjustment and submission."

Taylor found much to follow in the philosophies of both men. He entirely agreed with Washington's focus on improving one's abilities, as well as the call for equal education, which he had been denied. But he did not endorse Washington's emphasis on working within the existing societal structure based on separation. Taylor followed Du Bois's belief in fighting for absolute equality, whether it was within cycling competitions or hotel accommodations, and speaking out in the press on countless occasions when he felt he was mistreated for racial reasons. There is no doubt that Taylor endorsed Du Bois's declaration that "The problem of the twentieth century is the problem of the color-line," a summation of segregation that Taylor frequently echoed. Time and again, Taylor rejected any notion that separate facilities could be equal, and it was yearning for fair treatment, as well as a desire to face the world's toughest competition, that led him to seriously consider the offer to race in France.

After pointing out the portraits of Roosevelt and Washington, Gilbert Taylor asked Coquelle whether Paris was as beautiful as American cities.

"Oh much better! Major will be able to tell you all about it later on because I hope very much to be able to take him over to France," Coquelle responded.

Coquelle then repeated the offer that Breyer had made months earlier: $10,000 in exchange for Taylor's agreement to race on Sundays. It was, Taylor later said, "the greatest temptation of my life." He said that since purchasing the house, he had gone $1,500 in debt and he feared never being able to race again in America. Still, Taylor, with his father by his side, could not violate his promise. He refused Coquelle's offer, insisting he would never race on a Sunday. Coquelle was stunned but finally understood that Taylor would not go back on his principle. The two negotiated until they came to a compromise: Taylor would receive $8,000, and he would not have to race on Sundays. Taylor agreed, but then he demanded more money, which so incensed Coquelle that he announced he had "cut off all negotiations." Taylor changed his mind and accepted, and the deal was struck.

Taylor knew that if he wanted to prove once and for all that he really was the world's fastest man, he would have to travel across the Atlantic Ocean to confront the one racer left who he needed to beat. That man, Edmond Jacquelin, awaited him in Paris.

# CHAPTER 13

# A Black Man in Paris

A cold rain swept New York Harbor in the early hours of March 5, 1901, as Taylor headed to a pier where one of the world's grandest ocean liners, the SS *Kaiser Wilhelm der Grosse*, was being readied for passengers. It was a striking vessel, its hull painted in bright red, in the middle a band of black, and the white deck topped by four sand-colored smokestacks. That the ship existed was a matter of good fortune. Nine months earlier, fire had erupted in a cotton warehouse along the wooden piers at Hoboken, New Jersey, setting off explosions of vats of oil and turpentine, spreading flames to the massive steamships along the docks, trapping hundreds of sailors and passengers, and engulfing the ships. Dozens leaped through portholes or from the decks to escape the flames, only to die as they plunged into the harbor. As the fire reached the *Kaiser*, setting it aflame in several places, Captain Heinrich Engelbart managed to unleash her from the moorings; tugboats pulled her away from the docks, and fireboats doused the flames as she sailed up the Hudson. Three other vessels suffered massive damage, and more than two hundred people were killed. Engelbart was a hero, awarded a gold medal by the Volunteer Life Saving Association for protecting his ship and hundreds of souls on board. Now he was at the helm during Taylor's voyage.

The rain turned to a steady snow, borne by northeasterly winds, as Taylor prepared to leave North America for the first time in his life. The newspapers that morning were full of news about the inauguration of the second term of President William McKinley, who had been sworn in the day before. Theodore Roosevelt, the former police commissioner and New York governor who had followed Taylor's career closely, had become vice president.

McKinley's reelection was hailed as a sign of continuity at the turn of the century, and that might have been comforting for many, but McKinley's inaugural address occurred as Jim Crow laws continued to undo many of the gains blacks thought they had made. This harm seemed to have escaped the president's grasp, or at least his willingness to confront the issue. Instead, he told the masses that the divisions of the Civil War had been healed, and said in a comment that history would prove utterly wrong, that "these old differences less and less disturb the judgment." Days afterward, a white mob in Texas burned a black man at a stake, following a similar horror a month before in Kansas. Alabama was on the verge of rewriting its constitution to reestablish white supremacy, as would other former Confederate states. Thus Taylor's leaving was at a historical pivot point. The grandiosity of the Gilded Age, the march of modernity, was all around him, underscoring the contrast with regressive racial politics. Few blacks of his era could have seen the disparity more dramatically than Taylor on this morning as he joined an elite rank of passengers on the docks.

Taylor arrived with an assortment of bikes, wheels for different racing conditions, spare handlebars, pedals, and other custom and hard-to-get parts. A porter hauled his enormous trunk, emblazoned: *Major Taylor, American Champion*. He was without those most familiar to him. Munger and Brady stayed behind. Taylor had initially planned on bringing Daisy, but the couple decided that it was best if he focused on his riding and he went without her. Instead, Taylor was accompanied by a trainer, William Buckner, a black man in whom Taylor said he had the "most confidence." (Buckner was so respected that he would subsequently be hired by the Chicago White Sox, working in the weight room with white baseball players who so greatly valued his regimen that they insisted on his employment even as the team banned African Americans from the field.)

Somewhat mysteriously, Taylor traveled incognito, which initially led to fears he had failed to sail. In fact, he was there, under the name "Worcester," either to avoid publicity or out of concern that he might be refused entry, as had happened at so many hotels and restaurants. Yet he was sent off by an ensemble of well-wishers, who had arranged for a massive floral arrangement in the shape of a bicycle wheel to be placed in his cabin. The twenty-three-year-old champion was ensconced in one of the 206 first-class cabins, a rare enough setting for an African American at the time, let alone one who had recently had to deploy subterfuge to buy a home in a neighborhood of whites. (Another first-class passenger was Kid McCoy, the colorful champion boxer who, when he pretended to be ill, prompted an opponent to ask, "Is this the real McCoy?")

The promise of the new century, in which speed and technology were poised to bring the world closer together, lay before Taylor as he wandered through the great ocean liner. Here was the world's first four-funnel ship, built four years earlier, and it continued to compete with vessels operated by the Cunard and White Star line for the title of fastest to cross the Atlantic. The 660-foot-long *Kaiser* carried fifteen hundred passengers and nearly five hundred crew members. It seemed a seaborne palace. Taylor walked through grand rooms designed in the Baroque Revival style, past statues in their gilded settings. He strolled along hallways and promenades where portraits of the German imperial family were interspersed with intricate tapestries. He saw a smoking salon that resembled a Black Forest inn and ate in a massive dining room that reached through several decks, capped by an airy dome.

The last cargo was loaded at 6:30 a.m., and the final passengers boarded shortly afterward. At 10:00 a.m., the vessel set sail, bounding east through the seemingly infinite expanse of the North Atlantic. Taylor planned to train with Buckner throughout the six-day journey. But his first transatlantic crossing, through extraordinarily choppy seas, left him "terribly shaken" and unable to eat for the first four days. "If the steamer had turned around, I would not have thought of protesting," Taylor said. Only in the last couple of days could he eat and train properly. Finally, in the early morning of March 11, the

*Kaiser* landed at the foggy French port of Cherbourg, where he met journalists and took a train to Paris.

As Taylor neared the capital, he quite naturally wondered how he would be received, a question made more urgent by the fact that many Parisians had just seen an "Exhibit of American Negros" at the city's world's fair, which lasted six months and attracted 50 million visitors, at a time when France's population was about 39 million, few of whom had met a black person. Created by W. E. B. Du Bois, the exhibit was designed to give visitors a positive impression of African Americans. Du Bois had first encountered prejudice as a Massachusetts schoolboy, when a white girl refused to accept a greeting card from him. "Then it dawned upon me with a certain suddenness that I was different from the others . . . shut out from their world by a vast veil." Thereafter, he wrote, he had "no desire to tear down that veil, to creep through; I held all beyond it in common contempt, and lived above it in a region of blue sky and great wandering shadows." He moved to Georgia. He devoted his life to studying and promoting his race, which had brought him to the Paris exhibition.

The world's fair sprawled along the banks of the Seine in the shadow of the Eiffel Tower, which itself had been constructed for a similar event a decade earlier. The exhibit on black Americans had been prompted by Du Bois's friend Thomas Junius Calloway, who had written of the need for Europeans to see blacks as productive members of society. "Everyone who knows about public opinion will tell you that the Europeans think of us a mass of rapists, ready to attack every white woman exposed, and a drug in civilized society," Calloway wrote in seeking support for the Paris exhibit. "How shall we answer such slanders?"

The answer was the Du Bois exhibition, paid for with a $15,000 appropriation from the US Congress, which fit seamlessly into this Paris Exposition's effort to create a humanistic sensitivity about unfamiliar parts of the world. The display relied first upon logic, with charts and maps demonstrating the growing economic status and literacy of blacks in Du Bois's home state of Georgia. Visitors learned about the number of patents granted to blacks, and the hundreds of newspapers and magazines produced by African Americans. The display backed up its argument with an emotional series of photographs, showing homes, businesses, and churches "that defied the image of blacks as impoverished, lazy, and ignorant—stereotypes held by many white Americans," according to a history of the display. The photos showed blacks as people of "dignity, accomplishment, and progress." The exhibit would be, Du Bois said, "an honest, straightforward exhibit of a small nation of people, picturing their life and development without apology or gloss, and above all made by themselves." Du Bois, wearing a top hat and morning coat, oversaw the exhibit in Paris. Taylor, arriving four months after the exhibit closed, exemplified the qualities that Du Bois wanted to display, and was a world champion athlete as well. There was, it appeared, no better emissary.

Victor Breyer, the French racing promoter and journalist who had previously sought to convince Taylor to come to Paris, awaited his arrival at the Gare Saint-Lazare. It was shortly after one a.m., but as Taylor bounded off the train, he was full of energy. He jumped to the platform and reached out his hand. "Hello, Mr. Breyer, how are you?" Taylor was "all smiling, with a mouth wide open and two big eyes that shine like carbuncles," Breyer wrote. Taylor had recovered from the gale-tossed voyage and his health was "excellent." He was delighted to be in France at last, declaring he had wished to come for years. "He wants to see everything, to visit everything," Breyer wrote in *Le Vélo*.

Breyer escorted Taylor on the half-mile journey from Saint-Lazare to the Hotel Scribe, one of the city's most famous and luxurious hostelries, across from the Palais Garnier opera house, and a stroll from the Grand Palais and Jardin des Tuileries. Taylor passed by cafes where clutches of Parisians still sat on chairs around circular tables, smoking and drinking and talking late into the night. The city was an architectural feast of palaces and churches and cafes, with apartment buildings lining the avenues, windows flung open, lightbulbs twinkling. The elegance of the boulevards, the edifices adorned with friezes and caryatids and pediments and domes, signified the Parisian desire to be nothing less than the center of civilization. How far, indeed, it all was from Taylor's life in Worcester, with its flat-roofed triple-deckers and brick factories and simple churches and modest, workmanlike ambitions. Here, as Taylor approached the Hotel Scribe, he could see the magnificent opera house, a masterpiece of the Second Empire and Beaux Arts style, completed twenty-six years earlier. Stepping into the lobby of the Hotel Scribe, which slightly curved around a city block, Taylor had entered the inner sanctum of Paris society. The Scribe housed the exclusive Jockey Club, where a white stone staircase ascended to a hall lined with portraits of the gentlemen who came there to gamble and to lounge in leather chairs in Le Salon des Sports. In the hotel's Grand Café, the world's first motion pictures, exhibited six years earlier, using a celluloid process called Cinématographe invented by the Lumière brothers, had shown workers leaving their factory in Lyon.

Taylor entered his suite around three a.m., and he slept for a few hours until he heard the shouts of a mob below. Pulling back the curtains, Taylor looked down on more than ten thousand people in the streets. "He did not dare go out, thinking that the crowd came for him," wrote promoter Robert Coquelle. He snuck out of the hotel via a back door. Only later did he learn that the crowd had come to support the former president of the South Africa Republic, Paul Kruger, who was staying at the same hotel during his exile from his homeland, which was in the midst of the Boer Wars.

Indeed, Taylor arrived as Europe seemed wracked by constant crises. On the second day of his voyage, Kaiser Wilhelm II, namesake of the ocean liner on which he had traveled, had been hit in the head by a fishplate in Bremen by a would-be assassin. The emperor suffered a bloody wound below his left eye. In Russia, a senior member of Tsar Nicholas II's administration survived an assassination attempt. In England, Queen Victoria had died in January after a sixty-three-year reign, giving way to her son, King Edward VII. France, where revolution thirty-one years earlier had led to the establishment of the Third Republic, was in the midst of a period of relative stability and power, with its colonial empire expanding into Asia and Africa and domestic prosperity escalating.

As its motto of *Liberté, Égalité, Fraternité* underscored, France strived to present itself as a land of freedom and expression and individuality. The nation celebrated art and sport and culture and sex and music with a joie de vivre at the height of the Belle Époque, the "beautiful era." The Paris of 1901 that greeted Taylor was a world drawn in bright brushstrokes of Impressionism and Postimpressionism. The saturation of colors seemed to put everything in movement, dazzling the public, which had tired of the sober, staid classical world of yesterday. Two weeks after Taylor's arrival, Parisians were enthralled by an exhibition of the works of Vincent van Gogh, the Dutch Postimpressionist painter who had moved to France and become a leading member of the avant garde, but who suffered from depression and had killed himself eleven years earlier. Now his landscapes and portraits and still lifes, recognized as works of genius, drew throngs to a retrospective at the Bernheim-Jeune Gallery.

The Impressionists often depicted an exuberant life behind the scenes, amid the picnics and boating parties and canal rides and cancan girls and music halls and gastronomic excess and everything else that made France unlike any other place in the world. The palette was reborn in Paris, or so it seemed.

Taylor soaked in the city. On his first full day in Paris, he lunched at his hotel with his trainer, Buckner, and they headed to the offices of *Le Vélo*, where he signed the guest book and spent hours with his promoters, Coquelle and Breyer, and the journal's staff. Then, day after day, Taylor visited restaurants and cafes and museums. He strolled down the Avenue des Champs-Élysées, taking in the architectural grandeur, the crowded cafes, the boulevards teeming with finely dressed Parisians. He knew not a word of French, but with guides at his side he roamed for hours. One day, he climbed the Eiffel Tower, and on another, he spent all afternoon on the hill of Montmartre, where a journalist said he stood "in ecstasy evoking the magnificent panorama of Paris." Taylor returned to his hotel, brimming with delight, like countless Americans in Paris before and since. "I found Paris as I imagined it," Taylor wrote in a column for a French journal, *La Vie au Grand Air*. "A great and beautiful city where art reigns supreme."

Taylor wrote with keen interest about the horse-drawn, double-decker omnibuses that traversed the streets, bursting with passengers. Stepping belowground, he was awed by the Metropolitan, the subway that opened a year earlier in conjunction with the Paris Exhibition. He took a ride on the line at Cours de Vincennes, where executioners once used their guillotines during the Revolution. "It is remarkable in every respect," Taylor wrote of the underground railway, with its art nouveau entrances that spread upward like a peacock's plumage. While Boston's subway had opened three years earlier, New York's system would not serve riders for another three years. Neither would match the Parisian system for its elegance and efficiency.

France had also become the center of the emerging automobile industry, and Taylor was invited to one of the city's most exclusive venues, L'Automobile Club de France, housed in a palatial five-story building at the Place de la Concorde. The men's club had been created six years earlier, when France had three million horses and two hundred motor vehicles, and was run by a handful of aristocrats who saw a future dominated by the auto. The twenty-three-hundred-man club featured several of the city's most luxurious restaurants, a library, billiard room, eight-hundred-seat theater, and a massive hall. After being honored in one of the club's most elegant rooms, Taylor marveled at his seat at the center of Paris society. "Never would I have thought of finding a club so richly installed," Taylor wrote. "The dining rooms, the garage, the auditorium are truly splendid." He pondered purchasing a French automobile, wondering what his fellow Worcester residents would think if he returned home with a sixteen-horsepower machine.

For now, however, bicycles were supreme. They were everywhere, and—unlike the exclusive worlds of the Jockey Club and Automobile Club—available to anyone. The craze was subsiding in the United States, but in Paris it reached greater heights than anywhere. Some of the most famous artists of the day were among the most avid lovers of the sport. Pierre-Auguste Renoir, the Impressionist painter, rode a bicycle until he fell and broke his arm, leading him to swear off the two-wheeler. Auguste Rodin, the sculptor, bought two top-of-the-line bicycles for a total cost of 1000 francs at a time when one of his artworks sold for 1200 francs. He was said to have had trouble staying upright but nonetheless rode for years.

Many French painters were drawn to the imagery of the bicycle. Léon Comerre produced a particularly evocative portrait, depicting a young woman standing proudly by her bicycle, wearing tan pantaloons and a silky white blouse, her left hand gripping the handlebar and her right clasping her white hat, on a wooded trail in a Paris suburb. The painting, *Cycling at Vesinet*, would later be on prominent display at the gallery of the Petit Palais, where it would be described as an example of how the bicycle facilitated the emancipation of women.

The most famous chronicler of the bicycle in France may have been Henri de Toulouse-Lautrec. A genius who stood only four feet eight, with stunted legs that forced him to walk with a cane or use a wheelchair, he captured the beauty and decadence of Paris. He famously painted the Moulin Rouge, the cabaret of cancan girls that came to symbolize the most outrageous elements of the city, with its famous windmill out front. Another favorite subject was cyclists. He often attended races at the Velodrome Buffalo and Velodrome de la Seine, and was employed by a company that built bicycle chains. He painted the Welsh rider Jimmy Michael, whom Taylor had famously defeated at Manhattan Beach. In a painting for the Simpson cycling company, he drew dozens of cyclists in the background at the track, using a blurring effect to suggest their speed. In the foreground, a cyclist sped in the slipstream of a pacing bicycle. Lautrec even sketched Taylor's hero, Arthur Zimmerman, who had won the sprint championships in Paris a few years earlier, showing him holding his bike in one hand in an olive-colored drawing Lautrec titled *Zimmerman et sa machine*—Zimmerman and his machine. Taylor, who seemed as impressed by the city's art as anything, could not have failed to see the cycling posters produced by some of the city's most talented young painters.

As Taylor wandered through the city, he was astounded that "one never sees blacks in Paris." Indeed, despite its proximity to Africa, there were relatively few blacks in France by the time Taylor arrived, and some were treated as oddities, "paraded in cabarets and human zoos to satisfy the curiosity and prejudices" of Parisians, according to one account of the period. Taylor was told that there was one black who had become famous in Paris. He was called Chocolat, and Taylor decided to pay him a visit.

Chocolat was the stage name of a former slave from Cuba who had been known only as Rafael. Chocolat had developed an act with a British clown named George Foottit, starting in the provinces, and the duo became so successful that they were invited to perform in Paris at the Nouveau Cirque, the New Circus, a theater-in-the-round with an array of box seats owned by the cofounder of the Moulin Rouge. Chocolat was the first black performer to take such a leading role in a French circus, and he, too, was painted by Toulouse-Lautrec. In one typical act, Chocolat appeared on stage in a red jacket with coattails, white breeches and socks and gloves, a foil for his white partner, Foottit. In another routine, Foottit repeatedly prepared to shoot an apple off Chocolat's head, but the apple continually fell off, and Chocolat stole bites before he replaced it, to the howls of spectators. The mock anger, the prancing around, the feigned horror of facing a gun that ends up spraying water—it all delighted the Parisians who applauded from their comfortable seats. Still, for spectators who had little or no exposure to blacks, the performance could reinforce a negative impression. Chocolat was repeatedly slapped for supposed mistakes, and fit the stereotype that many whites had about blacks. He coined the phrase "Je suit Chocolat" whenever something unexpected occurred. It became a Parisian catchphrase that was sarcastically understood to mean "I am deceived." As the years went by, Chocolat would try to change the perception others had of him, seeking Shakespearean roles. On the day that Taylor saw him, the cyclist sat with journalists from the publication *L'Auto Vélo*, and Chocolat celebrated the American's arrival. Taylor laughed "heartily," a journalist wrote, as Chocolat performed his "hilarious mimicry" and sent "friendly glances" to the racer, to "whom all the spectators' eyes turned."

The French were used to seeing a black man as a circus spectacle and subservient to whites. Taylor, by contrast, was promoted as a black man who could prove himself superior to some of France's greatest heroes, its cycling champions. His arrival, an American journalist wrote, was a test of France's "national character." Taylor's promoter, Coquelle, took the hype to new heights, writing that Taylor was "expected as the Messiah."

Yet even when Taylor's hosts spoke of him glowingly, some inevitably sought to liken him to having the qualities of a white man, instead of celebrating his heritage. This was an insidious slant that Taylor heard often. The speaker may have thought it was a compliment but the subject of the comment was justified in viewing it among the worst racist slurs. Breyer, for all the good that he did for Taylor, was among those guilty of this practice, describing Taylor's face as "much more pliant and pleasing than that of vulgar negroes whom we generally see." Taylor was well spoken, clothed, and educated, Breyer wrote, and his "immaculate whiteness, contrasting with his shiny black skin, will cause a sensation on the boulevard."

Taylor was recognized everywhere in Paris. A common refrain was "That must be Taylor, for it isn't Chocolat." Taylor's picture and details of his life story were published throughout France. He adorned magazine covers, newspaper front pages, and posters. "Everyone knows what he eats and drinks and where he goes to have his shoes blacked," an American correspondent marveled. Daisy sent a postcard that mentioned no street, needing only to say: "Major Taylor, World's Greatest Cyclist." A French newspaper published her picture, with the caption saying she was a "charming" woman of mixed-race heritage. It suggested playfully that she was not without apprehension about Taylor's arrival in "the modern Babylon" of Paris.

To some, Taylor's refusal to race on Sundays or to drink alcohol made him appear a sober, staid figure. This was hardly the case. Taylor had a reserved countenance, mindful, composed, and dignified. He had spent years holding back his anger at the attacks against him, usually taking his vengeance on the racing course. His love of speed and competition provided a channel for his outrage. His belief that he was leading a fight against injustice for millions left him protective of his reputation; a fault in him would be deemed one against his race.

One day, after Taylor moved from the Hotel Scribe to the Hotel Malesherbes, a French reporter found him in the lobby at the piano, attired in his usual evening dress of suit and tie, playing a popular Tin Pan Alley tune called "Hello! Ma Baby," which had been composed by an American duo two years earlier and had been a sensation at the Paris Exhibition. The song told the story of a man who could only reach the love of his life on the telephone, a device relatively few people possessed. (It would be another twenty-six years before the first transatlantic telephone call.) Taylor was no doubt thinking of Daisy as he sang:

> "Hello! ma Baby,
> Hello! ma honey,
> Hello! ma ragtime gal.
> Send me a kiss by wire,
> Baby, my heart's on fire!
> If you refuse me
> Honey, you'll lose me
> Then you'll be left alone
> Oh baby, telephone
> And tell me I'm your own."

The French reporter found that Taylor had a "remarkable voice" and was a "perfect" musician, endearing him further to the public. The story was accompanied by extraordinary photographs of Taylor. In the United States, Taylor had been photographed and sketched before, of course, but most of the images were often lower-quality posed pictures or drawings. Now, in France, Taylor's arrival coincided with the introduction of what would be called photojournalism. He attracted the attention of one of the nation's preeminent photographers, Jules Beau, who would be considered the first widely published sports photographer. Beau, thirty-seven years old and the owner of a Paris studio, is credited with more published photographs of Taylor—including many during competition—than any other photographer.

He had perfected the use of halftone photography, which, when combined with flash powder for optimum lighting, captured details and helped create vivid action shots. Such photos could be printed faster to meet newspaper deadlines. Taylor became one of most photographed people in France. The images remain the most indelible portraits of Taylor, as he stares boldly into Beau's camera in a studio shot or races against French champions. That Taylor's arrival coincided with technological advances in photography would play a crucial role in publicizing Taylor throughout Europe.

The impact of photography, in fact, was one of the most unexpected and important turning points for Taylor's career. At a time when African Americans were widely caricatured—and Taylor was simultaneously the subject of some racist drawings in France—the photographs provided an irrefutable counterpoint, showing him as a model of musicianship, sportsmanship, and athleticism. In *La Vie au Grand Air,* a series of photographs showed a finely dressed Taylor playing the piano and mandolin, as well as pictures that displayed him in only his shorts and another that highlighted his sculpted legs, the finest the reporter had ever seen. His musculature was so well formed that he was described in various accounts as resembling a "bronze statue," whose physique was "better than all description." The French, indeed, seemed obsessed with studying Taylor's body. A reporter for *Le Vélo* arranged for Taylor to be examined by a team of doctors, who employed the latest scientific tools in their quest, including an X-ray machine, which had been invented six years earlier by a German physicist. "They declared that Major Taylor was a true masterpiece of human academy," said the report. Amid all the words about Taylor's vitality and ideal form was a focus on sexuality. "Naked, as some photographs have shown," *Le Vélo* said, apparently referring to the picture of Taylor in his shorts, "the Negro is . . . almost perfect, and it is difficult to conceive in a man a happier alliance of strength, suppleness, and elegance." American readers saw some of these remarkable images, and they could read of Taylor's exploits in stories carried across the sea. It was thirty-six years after the Civil War, and many Americans still had vivid memories of the era of enslavement and of the bloody battlefields photographed by Mathew Brady. Taylor's emergence was shocking or heartening, depending on one's perspective. After being all but evicted from many American racetracks, his reemergence in France was a revelation—and, to some, a new threat.

A few days after he arrived in Paris, Taylor was escorted by his promoters to a most unique institution, the Café L'Esperance, on the Avenue de la Grande Armée, the boulevard that links the Place de la Porte Maillot with the Arc de Triomphe. The Café was the center of the Paris cycling scene, patronized by the star athletes and their fans. Taylor had clipped pictures of France's best riders, studying them so that he would know who they were if he happened upon them at the Café or the velodrome. He knew all about the Café from a book coauthored by his idol, Arthur Zimmerman, who was the last great American racer to enthrall Paris. In the book, *Zimmerman Abroad and Points on Training*, the great racer had lovingly described his experience in Paris, "the city of all cities." Zimmerman recalled "her people, her customs, her streets and salons, cafes and gardens . . . the cycling part of Paris [was] unique and extreme and totally unlike that of any other city." Zimmerman wrote how, one day, he took a seat in one of the city's twenty-five thousand cabs, and his companion said to the driver, "Café L'Esperance, Avenue de la Grande Armée," and they sped along the boulevards and monuments, passing multitudes of well-dressed bicyclists. Zimmerman recounted his recognition of counts and barons and ministers, all riding their bicycles. "I believe that they wear better clothes on the wheel in Paris than they do in . . ." Before he could complete the thought, they reached the Café, which Zimmerman referred to as the "Mecca." He marveled at a parade of elegant young ladies, dressed in bell skirts "showing a most startling expanse of fancy-colored hosiery," and another wearing "the trouser variety." The Café was one of several institutions in this prominent part of Paris known as Cycle Row, which had "more depots, salesrooms and shops devoted to the bicycle trade than any other street in the world," extending from the Arc de Triomphe, down the Avenue de la Grande Armée, to the gates of Neuilly, an area just west of central Paris. Zimmerman had walked through the Café entrance, past the sidewalk tables where "near all France seems to live" in seasonable weather, and into what he called the world's most popular place for cyclists, into the "midst of its Bohemian smoke and noise." All of the great names of cycling were assembled on any random day, sipping red wine amid the sound of clacking billiard balls, clinking glasses, and conversation and laughter. Maps of Parisian cycling routes adorned the walls, and talk of wheel size and gearing mechanisms and racing champions filled the air.

Now, six years after Zimmerman's book was published, Taylor walked into the same scene, the most anticipated American racer since his hero raced in France, instantly recognized and rousingly greeted. The owner sent around champagne and was astonished that Taylor wanted only water. It was five p.m. precisely, and amid the commotion Taylor went out onto the terrace. At that moment, none other than Edmond Jacquelin—the Frenchman whom Taylor had come to race against—steered a car along the Avenue de la Grand Armée. Stopping at the Café, Jacquelin recognized Taylor and bounded to the terrace. Jacquelin was introduced, and within five minutes they were "the two best friends in the world," or so it seemed to Taylor's promoter, Coquelle, who observed it all.

"I was led to understand that you were a very large man for a sprinter, but did not expect to find a giant as you are," Taylor said. To the bemusement of those around him, Taylor produced a tape measure and examined him.

Jacquelin, in turn, was surprised Taylor was only five foot seven and weighed 154 pounds.

"I did not expect to find a very large man, but you are really smaller than I was led to believe," Jacquelin said. "Nevertheless I can see that you are remarkably well formed and will probably give me a hard race."

Taylor measured Jacquelin's legs, prompting the Frenchman to say that Taylor's were actually bigger.

"Ah, but yours are stronger," Taylor said.

"That's not the point," Jacquelin said. "I am afraid that yours may be the quicker."

• • •

Shortly after his arrival in Paris, Taylor had headed to the velodrome where, in two months, he would face Jacquelin. He planned to store his bicycle and learn the contours of the track, the kind of reconnaissance mission that was vital to his success. As he arrived at the Parc des Princes, he found a soccer match under way. Slowly, the crowd recognized Taylor and began a chant: *"Vive Major!"* The teams on the pitch stopped their play, ran to Taylor, and began a chorus: "Hip, hip, hurray!" The spectators raced toward Taylor, throwing their hats and strands of confetti in the air, joining in the celebration. Taylor had not intended to ride, but he finally borrowed a bicycle and, for five minutes, led "a long procession" as the crowd continued to shout his name, leaving him "more and more bewildered," Coquelle wrote. Finally, Taylor made his way to a series of cabins reserved for cyclists, and chose the one next to Jacquelin's. Then he returned to his hotel, dots of confetti still clinging to his head. Not since the days of Zimmerman, Coquelle marveled, had there been such a welcome for a foreign racer.

For days, Taylor was anxious to return to the track for training, but the weather turned against him. A cold rain drenched Paris, followed by days of wind and snow and ice. Taylor's bicycle lay dormant. He trained as best he could indoors. He attacked a punching ball, lifted a set of pin-like weights, and stretched. Every night, back at the hotel, he collected articles from the French press, cutting and pasting them into a scrapbook, along with postcards, pictures, and other mementos of his visit. He carried a camera and took pictures whenever he could.

One day, restless from being off the bike, he awoke at six a.m., "questioned the sky with uneasiness," and headed to the velodrome. The cold, icy ride to the suburb of Auteuil left him anxious about the conditions. A small crowd had gathered at Parc des Princes, and Taylor walked with his bicycle to the track. He shivered so badly that he headed back to his cabin. "I am an African, not a European," Taylor said time and again, protesting the conditions. Finally, he emerged, wearing the number 13 on his jersey, a number rejected by most other riders as unlucky, but which had proved providential for Taylor time and again. He mounted his bike, stretching flat-backed to the handlebars, and began to pedal. The crowd applauded, but the performance was brief, and Taylor quickly donned his racing bathrobe to stop the shivering.

For days, Taylor woke to check the weather, anxious to return to the track, but the cold and rain and snow continued. The temperature eventually warmed and Taylor resumed his training on the track, but he was hardly prepared for his first real challenge. He had agreed to race first in Berlin, where his arrival was promoted nearly as heavily as it had been in Paris, and race against some of the best European riders. He had initially viewed it as a warm-up for his race against Jacquelin, but his lack of time on the track had left him vulnerable. The German champion was anxious to knock Taylor from his pedestal before he even got his chance in Paris.

A day after arriving on the overnight train from Paris, Taylor walked onto the Friedenau Sportpark Velodrome, about five miles southwest of Berlin, and again confronted unfavorable weather. He shivered in the freezing temperatures as he surveyed the cement track, which was infamous for buckling as water expanded and froze in the crevices. He didn't take a practice sprint on the course until race day. More than twelve thousand spectators, men in suits and hats, and women in long dresses, filled the grandstands on this Easter Monday. Thousands more crowded the oval interior. Much of German high society was in the audience, as well as Chancellor Bernhard von Bülow. The stadium had opened four years earlier with a Grand Prix of Berlin won by Willie Arend, who was now the German champion and had been training for weeks to race against Taylor.

The other racers began talking to one another in their native languages, leading Taylor to suspect they were plotting against him "because they knew I could not understand them." The race began as Taylor expected, with strategic slowness. Then, unexpectedly, Arend bolted around the pack and streaked toward the finish. Taylor almost caught him but wound up in third place. The crowd exploded in what Taylor called "the greatest demonstration I had ever seen on a bicycle track." Thousands stormed the track, tossing their hats in the air, chanting Arend's name. The champion was hoisted on shoulders and presented with a "monster horseshoe of roses." Then, to Taylor's continuing astonishment, the spectators filed into a line "in perfect order" as they sang "Watch on the Rhine." Stunned at his loss and the crowd's response, Taylor was caught amid the masses as the verses were sung:

> The cry resounds like thunder's peal,
> Like crashing waves and clang of steel:
> The Rhine, the Rhine, our German Rhine,
> Who will defend our stream, divine?

Taylor was his usual sportsman self, seeking out Arend and congratulating him. But he could not conceal his rising ambition and confidence, even on this gloomy day. "Down in my heart, however, I felt it would not be long before the tables were reversed," Taylor wrote.

Arend's defense came three days later. With the publicity from the first match, the promoters drew an even bigger crowd. This time, the weather was warmer, and Taylor felt prepared for another surprise attack by Arend. A second German and a Dane rounded out the field. Taylor told his trainer, Buckner, to mark a spot from which he would be expected to launch a final sprint. He made sure his opponents knew that the mark had been set, expecting them to eye the mark as the place he would make his jump. It was a strategic trick. Taylor let his opponents pass the mark at an all-out pace, and he remained in position behind them. Then, at a mark that he set only in his mind, he burst past them and won.

What happened next stunned Taylor as much as the outpouring for Arend three days earlier. The crowd applauded Taylor just as loudly, and the band played "The Star-Spangled Banner" as he took a victory lap around the track, an extraordinary moment, even if little remembered by history. Another thirty-five years would pass before Jesse Owens, the African American runner, famously won four gold medals in the Olympics at another Berlin stadium as Adolf Hitler looked on, amid the Nazi eugenics movement and its promotion of a genetically pure Nordic race, which set the stage for the Holocaust.

• • •

A week later, after training in Paris, Taylor arrived in Belgium for a race against that country's national champion, Louis Grogna. As usual, Taylor had checked into his hotel and asked for room number thirteen. Many Belgians wanted to see Taylor because they had never, or rarely, seen a black person. But when Taylor's race was postponed, many in the crowd said they had come to see the color of Taylor's skin. Until now, the only place many people who lived "in the provinces" had seen a black person was at the circus, Taylor's promoter Coquelle recalled years later. "They all went to the hotel where [Taylor] was staying," and only after Taylor appeared on the balcony was the crowd satisfied. "They had seen a negro!"

The idea that most provincial Belgians had never seen a black person underscored the great psychic distance that the country had maintained from its huge colony, Congo. King Leopold II had made Congo his personal domain, and the source of much of his fortune, through his barbarous efforts to collect natural rubber, which was essential for bicycle tires, among other things. The king's forces had committed countless atrocities. Disease was rampant, uncooperative villagers were slaughtered, and many populated areas were destroyed by Belgian troops. In the year that Taylor raced in Belgium, more than 500,000 Congolese died from diseases related to Belgian rule. In all, as many as 10 million Congolese may have perished from a combination of atrocities and disease during Leopold's reign. Yet at home, many Belgians were so removed from their king's complicity in the deaths of millions of Africans that Taylor's appearance presented them with their first chance to see a person with black skin.

For Taylor, his time in Belgium was nearly a disaster. When the race was rescheduled, he found Grogna to be a formidable opponent. He was to race three heats against Grogna, and the first to win two would be declared the winner. Taylor won the first heat. But in the second match, Grogna gave Taylor "the surprise of my life." The two racers played cat and mouse, as each slowly pedaled around the banking, daring the other to launch a sprint. Taylor let Grogna sprint first, believing he could catch him, but Grogna was so powerful that he beat

Taylor by two lengths. No one, Taylor wrote, had done that to him in all his years of racing. His objective in these races had been to face spirited competition to prepare him to face Jacquelin in Paris. "The thought kept running through my mind that if Grogna defeated me in the third and final heat of this race in the same manner my invasion of Europe might just as well end then and there," Taylor wrote.

Taylor decided to employ one of his "cleverest tricks." He would race as if he would once again let Grogna slip down the banking into a sprint, but at the last minute would jump first. The strategy worked, and Taylor won by a length, breathing a sigh as he won one of his most difficult races. Grogna "was the last stumbling block." Taylor would go on to win more races in the following weeks, but the only rival who now mattered awaited him in Paris.

## CHAPTER 14

# "The Terribly Dangerous and Beautiful Races"

A s France awaited the great match, Edmond Jacquelin's cocky attitude had gone too far. He wasn't training hard, it was said. He was in Nice, practicing his new hobby of automobile racing. He was in Turin, Italy, losing bicycle races to unknown riders. He chafed at questions about his preparedness, or lack thereof. He was appalled that after so many victories, he was expected to lose to *"le Negré."* But as he learned of Taylor's victories across Europe, he began to train in earnest. "What will I have to do to overcome the half-dozen" journalists who "every year make it a pleasure to doubt me?" Jacquelin wrote. "I wanted to convince them forever."

No one doubted Jacquelin's natural sprinting power. A prodigy, the twenty-six-year-old had earned the Triple Crown of racing the year before, declared world champion, French champion, and Grand Prix winner. Attention focused on Jacquelin as he prepared to race in Nantes, France, in early May. Taylor competed at the event—but not against Jacquelin—and settled into the stands to study his rival. Jacquelin easily won his race against the Danish champion, Thorvald Ellegaard. Jacquelin, too, watched Taylor, impressed by "his astonishing feline suppleness, the ease of his start," but did not find him "extraordinarily fast." Taylor was no Zimmerman, Jacquelin concluded. Playing his psychological game, Jacquelin spent weeks deni-

175

grating his opponent, saying Taylor now faced a much stiffer challenge than beating other Americans. "Here, it will change," he said.

The Frenchman's insults intensified the anticipation of a race promoted in *L'Auto Vélo* as one of the greatest in the country's sporting history.

> It is nothing less, in fact, than the decisive struggle between the two men who were able, one on the New Continent, the other on the Old, to secure . . . supremacy undisputed and undeniable. In truth, today the title of world champion is at stake. Today will be the fight of two types of athletes absolutely different. One, Jacquelin, is the powerful man, extraordinarily muscular. A bull's neck, a broad torso, solidly built into a colossus. Thighs like two steel columns, legs like two formidable pillars. The other, Major Taylor, is the thoroughbred, or rather the greyhound. . . . The body is wonderful, a broad chest, a woman's waist, two thighs on which the long and supple muscles stand out, then thin and unobstructed knees, and finally, under wonderfully made legs, surprisingly thin ankles, as fine as the wrists of a Parisienne. Jacquelin starts in force, packs in force. Major Taylor starts in flexibility, packs in flexibility.

Racial implications were drawn in story after story. The French publication *Le Vélo* published an essay titled "*Noir et blanc*"—Black and White—in which it tried to dissect the meaning of the looming contest. The author, Paul Hamelle, said that while Taylor "is surrounded by mystery because of the color of his skin," it was clear he was an even better rider than his record indicated, given how his white rivals often ganged up on him.

Hamelle wrote that he had a "crazy idea": Taylor could win because he was black. The Major's color, which was a disadvantage for him in America, "will be an advantage on this side of the water." Hamelle said he saw how "the white man, struggling against the black man," would become "disoriented." How would Jacquelin "read" what he called Taylor's "silent mask," the emotion and expression so hard to deduce,

THE BOSTON TEAM.

Major Taylor faced many barriers to being
one of the world's greatest athletes. As a
teenager, he was a scrawny five feet seven
inches and faced competitors who were taller,
stronger, and more muscular. He was a black
man in a sport dominated by whites, and was
often banned from racing under Jim Crow
restrictions or physically attacked in races.
His enemies portrayed him in the press with
stereotypes in an effort to denigrate him and
other blacks. In 1897, a thin Taylor joined
four white veterans on a Boston team.

1

2

3

Louis de Franklin "Birdie" Munger, a former world champion racer, was astonished when he saw Major Taylor ride a mile just two seconds slower than the then world record time. Munger gave Taylor a job and a state-of-the-art racing bicycle, trained him, and predicted Taylor would become the world's fastest man.

4

5

6

Arthur Zimmerman, a former champion, was one of Taylor's idols and another mentor; Taylor said he wanted to become the "black Zimmerman." When Taylor won the world championship in Montreal in 1899, he said that Munger's "remarkable prophecy" had come true.

Eddie "Cannon" Bald, the national sprint champion, was stunned when Taylor beat him at Madison Square Garden, in Taylor's professional debut. Bald said he never wanted to "let a nigger beat" him and became one of his fiercest, indeed nastiest, rivals.

Madison Square Garden, at 26th Street and Madison Avenue, was an architectural marvel, a showcase for the age of mass spectacles. Thousands packed the great arena to witness Taylor compete in one of the most physically punishing sporting events of the day, a six-day race.

7

Taylor's races were often promoted as "Black vs. White," as was plainly the case in the contest against Eddie McDuffee featured on this pin for a race on June 17, 1898.

Taylor trained relentlessly, forsaking alcohol and tobacco, and rigorously monitoring his diet. He used a system of pulleys, weight lifting, boxing, jump-roping, and riding to develop and maintain what he called "my always perfect physical fitness." He was one of the fittest athletes of his time. He included this picture of himself in his autobiography to demonstrate "perfect condition and perfect position." The French press marveled that he was a "bronze statue" who was "better than all description."

French promoter Victor Breyer came to Massachusetts to plead with Taylor to race in France, saying he would not "give a cent" for any other American. The belief that Taylor would draw vast crowds in France and Europe proved correct.

Taylor traveled to France in 1901 after becoming convinced that racists would prevent him from competing in the United States. He faced the only rider in the world who was considered his equal, the great Edmond Jacquelin. After losing to Jacquelin on May 16, Taylor had a rematch on May 27, and shook Jacquelin's hand before winning the contest. The victory over the Frenchman sealed Taylor's reputation as the world's fastest man.

11

12

13

Floyd McFarland, a Californian who towered over Taylor at six feet four inches, repeatedly threatened Taylor, who called him the "ringleader of the gang" plotting against him. Their clash grew so heated that Taylor made a "vicious" swing at McFarland with a two-by-four, but McFarland dodged it.

After McFarland and other white racers ganged up to keep Taylor off the racetracks, Broadway producer William Brady created his own league and made Taylor a star, putting on hugely popular matches near Coney Island.

Taylor married Daisy Victoria Morris in 1902, and the couple traveled to Australia the following two years. Their only child, Sydney, was born there and named after the Australian city. Daisy, the niece of a minister, was considered a great beauty and was a subject of fascination in magazines.

In 1903, Taylor competed against Australian champion Don Walker, right, who traveled back to the United States with Taylor and expressed shock at the racism he faced.

Taylor's comeback in 1907 was a sensation in France. A determined-looking Taylor appeared on a magazine cover and thousands flocked to see him compete, curious to know if he could still keep up with the world's best riders.

16

17

In 1909 Taylor was tormented by the absence of his wife, racing relentlessly to overcome the toll that age had taken on his body and that racism had taken on his psyche. He lost most of his European races that year before triumphing in his final race against a French champion.

18

Taylor wins a race in 1909 in Paris.

19

Taylor's last professional race was in 1910. Seven years later he competed in an old-timer's race. Taylor stands in the middle, shorter than all of his competitors; he won the race.

## Friends of Maj. Taylor, Worcester's World Champion, Rally to His Relief

Appeal Made on Behalf of
Famed Bicyclist, Now
Among the Needy

**MEETS MISFORTUNE**

None Has Reflected More
Renown on the City---
Trophies Displayed

A colored man walked down Mechanic street yesterday. His legs were none too steady and made him smile reflectively. They were the legs that won for him the famous sobriquet of "The Colored Whirlwind," legs which had blazoned his name on the sport pages of the United States and seven European countries, as well as those of Canada, Australia, and New Zealand. And now they bore his weight unsteadily.

The man was Major Taylor, and he turned into the office of Harry Worcester Smith, a friend of long standing. The legs which carried him slowly on the treacherous footing yesterday swept him not so long ago to victory over the world's best bicyclists. In America he smashed at some time every mark from the one-quarter mile to five miles. His time for the quarter mile and half-mile still remain a challenge to the world's fastest cyclists.

But now his legs are tired. Tired from a long siege of illness that has taken heavy toll of his finances also. And he is nearing the half century mark. The years have a trick of crowding a man.

Loops of evergreen hanging in the

MAJOR TAYLOR

Taylor in 1926 when he was ill, destitute, and working on his autobiography, *The Fastest Bicycle Rider in the World.* He died in Chicago in 1932, alone and largely forgotten.

20

Hamelle asked, concluding, "The face of the black demon is closed to the enemy who fights in the night."

Another *Le Vélo* writer wrote with similar condescension: "the black, naturally little disposes to the intellectual works" and makes up for it with physical strength, comparing Taylor's physique to a "living bronze." That ignored the fact that Taylor was better educated than most whites, wrote and read voraciously, and often won by outsmarting his opponents. Yet the stereotypes persisted, and the portrayal of black versus white built intense interest in the coming race. "Apart from the rivalry of the two men," a French journalist wrote, "there is for me a higher element of interest. It is the struggle of the two races, of the black race against the white race." A writer for *L'Auto Vélo* said all of France was waiting "to see the only man able to put our champion in trouble." A victory by Jacquelin would be "the final consecration of five years of unforgettable success. The negro's victory is the whole world having finally found a better man than the best." Crowds flooded into Paris from throughout the Continent. More than twenty thousand people packed into Parc des Princes, including "the best society" and many Americans who lived in Paris. Three times that number could have been seated if the capacity was available. "Never before," wrote a British publication, was a cycling event "known to create such wild excitement in Paris."

Some years later, Ernest Hemingway would attend a bicycle race while living in Paris and become enthralled with the sport. He tried time and again to write a book in which bicycle racing played a central role, laying out his idea in *A Moveable Feast*, in which he vividly described a scene similar to what Taylor experienced. Hemingway saw "the smoky light of the afternoon and the high-banked wooden tracks and the whirring sound the tires made on wood as the riders passed, the effort and the tactics as the riders climbed and plunged, each one a part of the machine." Hemingway witnessed the noisy motorized pacers, and the riders behind them "bent low over their handlebars their legs turning the huge gear sprockets." The duels between top riders "were more exciting than any racing . . . the riders elbow to elbow and wheel to wheel up and down and around at deadly speed until one man could not hold the pace and broke away and the solid wall of air that he had been sheltered against hit him." Hemingway had in this short passage captured what he accurately called "the terribly dangerous and beautiful races." Hemingway wrote that it was so exciting that there was "no need to bet," but there was, in fact, plenty of wagering as Taylor came to the starting line.

Among those watching Taylor closely was a twenty-three-year-old American, William Kissam Vanderbilt Jr., heir to one of the greatest American fortunes. He was eight months older than Taylor and hailed from a world apart. The great-grandson of the "Commodore," Cornelius Vanderbilt, "Willie" had been raised in the family's mansions, dropped out of Harvard, and had spent much of his life—like Taylor—obsessed with becoming the world's fastest man. Despite the extraordinary gulf in their upbringing, their lives had striking similarities when it came to their love of speed. At ten years old, while Taylor was riding a bicycle on the roads of Indianapolis, Vanderbilt was riding a steam-powered tricycle in the south of France. At twenty years old in 1898, while Taylor was becoming known as one of the world's fastest cyclists, Vanderbilt bought a motorized bike and whizzed along the roads of Long Island, where his family maintained a sumptuous summer estate. At twenty-two, in 1900, while Taylor continued winning bicycle races, Vanderbilt won the first automobile race held in Newport, Rhode Island. As Taylor raced in Europe, Vanderbilt made a grand auto tour of the Continent, often traveling on roads that were made for horse carts, in his newly purchased car: a German-made Mercedes, a thirty-five-horsepower red-and-white two-seater that could reach seventy-five miles per hour. Vanderbilt returned to Paris shortly before Taylor's race, checked into the Hotel Ritz, and studied the newspapers and calculated the odds. He wagered $3,000 on Taylor. Many other members of the American elite class who were staying in Paris that spring also put down their money. Harry Kendall Thaw of Pittsburgh, heir to a coal and railroad fortune—a spoiled and deranged man who five years later would become infamous for murdering the Madison Square Garden architect Stanford White in a jealous rage—bet $20,000 on Taylor. A United States senator, William Clark of Montana, who was married that year in Paris, bet what he called a "considerable" sum. Anna Gould, the daughter of Philadelphia financier Jay Gould who had become a French countess upon her marriage to Count Boni Castellane, was among those who bet on Jacquelin. Countless others bet more modest sums as race day approached.

Taylor awoke on the morning of May 16 to find that the weather was cold and raw, and he shivered despite wearing a heavy sweater as he took warm-up laps on the track. Still, he felt ready to take on "the French idol" as the pair lined up at the start for the one-kilometer race. The winner of two out of three heats would take the match.

Buckner, Taylor's trainer, brought the bicycle to the starting line and held it steady. Buckner was followed by Taylor, who took off his robe and cap, rubbed his arms, and grimaced at the cold. Nearby, Jacquelin, helped by his younger brother, Lucien, mounted his bike and placed his feet on the pedals, cherishing the cheers of the crowd.

The racers "loafed" at the start, as one writer put it, not wanting to take an early lead and tire out. With three hundred yards to go, Jacquelin made his move. Taylor followed with his jump at two hundred yards to go. Jacquelin was astonished, he wrote later, at "this Negro on my wheel, not surprised like my other opponents, fighting for it to be said that the American had beaten France! Then he came up to me, I struggled, I pushed like a demon, we were elbow-to-elbow." Then, at the very last moment, Jacquelin surged over the finish line for the victory.

In the second heat, Taylor tried a different strategy, taking an early lead, with Jacquelin on his rear wheel. The two maneuvered on the steep bank that curved above the track. Jacquelin made his move and the two were about even with a hundred fifty yards to go. Then Jacquelin used the powerful push for which he was famous, and shot to the finish line, where he won by two lengths. It was over that quickly, with no need for a third heat.

As Jacquelin took his victory lap and passed Taylor, he made two gestures that would forever outrage the American. First, he put his hand to nose. Then, as the band played the French national anthem, "*La Marseillaise*," Jacquelin turned to Taylor and delivered a military salute, mocking his rival's famous nickname. Taylor was astonished at Jacquelin's "childish" antics. "He was so carried away with his victory over me that he lost his head completely and thumbed his nose at me immediately after crossing the tape all the way around the track," Taylor wrote.

Thousands of supporters poured onto the track, and Jacquelin was hoisted upon shoulders. Taylor wrote that he had "never before suffered such humiliation as Jacquelin's insult caused me." A photographer captured a picture of a despondent-looking Taylor, wearing a cap and dressed in his long, thick robe, prompting a journalist to write of his "abject dejection" as he went "slinking away to his dressing room." It was a stark contrast to a photo of the celebrating Jacquelin. Taylor vowed to use it all as a motivation, writing that he wanted to defeat Jacquelin in a rematch so badly "that there would be no doubt, even in his mind, as to who was the better rider." Days later, after harsh condemnation for his insult to Taylor, Jacquelin wrote in *L'Auto Vélo* that "I was wrong, and I regret it." He insisted that he was thumbing his nose at those who had predicted his defeat. Taylor, he wrote, was "the most correct of all opponents."

Still, Jacquelin was shocked that Taylor wanted a rematch. "I thought I beat Taylor so obviously that there would be no need for revenge," he said. But if Taylor insisted, Jacquelin said to "tell him that I am at his disposal as many times as he likes."

For ten days, Taylor trained with Buckner, plotting strategy, pacing, timing. Journalists and fans came out to the track daily, watching Taylor and Jacquelin go through their paces. Taylor was always the first to show up. "Here is the time of the Negro!" a supporter chanted as Taylor took off his warm-up bathrobe, rounded the track, and gradually reached peak speed. "Oh, he wants his revenge!" wrote a reporter who watched Taylor train. Jacquelin trained behind a tandem bicycle powered by gasoline, his pace "always the same." The only thing Taylor felt he could not control was the weather.

The buildup for the "revenge" match was even greater than the hype prior to the first. Newspapers across Europe debated Taylor's strengths, with most concluding he would fail once again. "We exaggerated the value of the American," sniffed a writer for *L'éclair*, in a typical report, as he had "never opposed a man of the class of the French champion." Jacquelin mocked Taylor's performance, writing that he had been "amused" by the sight of Taylor "in his cloak, looking unhappy under the cold sky." This fact helped shape Jacquelin's strategy of making a slow start to keep Taylor shivering. Other publications said a hot day would make all the difference for Taylor.

On the day of the rematch, Taylor stepped outside and felt the overpowering rush of warm air. He was overjoyed. As Taylor made his way to Parc Des Princes on the morning of May 27, he found more than thirty thousand people awaiting the match, which some accounts called the largest crowd to witness a European bicycle race. Taylor took off his robe and cap, as usual, and greeted his rival, who wore "his same arrogant smile." Jacquelin held a camera. When an official barked that the race was about to start, Jacquelin asked for a moment's delay. Standing in front of Taylor, he shouted, "Do not move if you please!" Taylor obliged with a "sarcastic smile" as Jacquelin squeezed the shutter.

Jacquelin wore dark trunks and a multicolored jersey with short sleeves. Taylor wore two-toned trunks and a white, long-sleeve jersey. They readied at the starting line. Jacquelin stared down, hunched over his bike, held steady by an assistant dressed in dark clothing. Taylor glared at his rival, his bike held by an assistant dressed in white. It was Ascension Day, the fortieth day of Easter, when Christians believe Jesus Christ ascended into heaven, and some of those in the stands had come from church services to cheer Jacquelin.

The starter's pistol rang out, and the two took off—not fast, but strategically slow, agonizingly slow. Each tried to let the other take the lead, hoping to ride in his rival's slipstream and make a sprint near the end. Jacquelin was slightly ahead, and Taylor pulled one of his trickiest maneuvers, which he had practiced since he worked at the Indianapolis bicycle store, bringing himself to nearly a full stop. Then, as the crowd shouted louder and louder, Taylor pedaled half a revolution in reverse, putting him behind Jacquelin. The crowd was "in a frenzy," Taylor wrote. Jacquelin realized he had been outmaneuvered, laughed out loud, and executed his own strategic trick. Jacquelin, with the fastest sprint start of any racer, suddenly pedaled furiously and jumped ahead. Taylor was stunned, realizing "I played right into his hands." Another two hundred and fifty yards lay to the finish line. Taylor used all his power to catch Jacquelin, and suddenly, there they were, briefly side by side, and then Taylor astonished the stadium by leaping farther ahead—faster and faster down the straight stretch until he had burst across the tape a remarkable four lengths ahead of his rival. Taylor had done it, humiliating Jacquelin in the first heat. Now Taylor just had to win one of the remaining two heats.

Twenty minutes passed, and the call was made for the pair to head back to the starting line. Taylor had won the first heat on strength, and he was determined to win the second with "a bit of psychology." As the two bikes were held by assistants at the starting line, Taylor reached out his right hand and beckoned Jacquelin to shake it. Jacquelin could not refuse, but Taylor could see "from the expression on his face that he was well aware of the fact that my hand-shake was a demonstration of sarcasm pure and simple." It was similar, Taylor recalled, to two boxers shaking hands before a final round. He was that confident. As Jacquelin realized Taylor's motive, "he mumbled something, shrugged his shoulders and set his jaw," Taylor wrote. "His sneering smile disappeared and a frown encompassed his face."

The starter's gun reverberated across the track, the crowd roared, and the pair set off. Again, Jacquelin was slightly ahead as they approached the final stretch, two hundred and fifty yards from the finish line. It was here in the first heat that Jacquelin had jumped into his sprint, only to be overmatched by Taylor's response. Now, as they jockeyed for position on the banking, Taylor vaulted forward, drawing strength from what he called "the inner resentment I bore towards Jacquelin for the insult he offered me." Again, Taylor showed an astonishing jump, pulling far ahead and again winning by the same distance of four lengths. It was, as Taylor so deeply desired, a victory so devastating that there could be no question who was the better rider.

Taylor had prepared for the moment. Inside his belt, he had tucked a silk American flag. Now, with victory sealed, he dramatically pulled it out, just as a magician produces a silk seemingly from thin air, and "waved it vigorously in front of the vulgar Jacquelin while we circled the track." Decades later, Taylor remained angry at what he considered Jacquelin's "ungentlemanly conduct." As the French band played "The Star-Spangled Banner," hundreds of Americans came to Taylor's side as he rode around the track with a bouquet of roses, while French spectators applauded from their seats. As he finished his victory lap, Taylor had one more message for Jacquelin. Taylor had burned at the sight of Jacquelin giving him a "military salute" after winning their earlier match, mocking his moniker of "Major." Now Taylor turned to the crowd and gave his own salute, which he considered "ample revenge." Rarely had Taylor expressed so much anger. But the motivation, the resentment, had all combined to send him to a victory greater than any before. Jacquelin tried to make amends, bringing a bottle of champagne to his rival. "Major," he said, "I come to congratulate you. The other day I beat you, today you took your revenge." Jacquelin poured champagne into a cup for Taylor, who avoided alcohol as always and passed it back to Jacquelin, who drank it all.

Now no one could question that Taylor was the world's fastest man. He had proved that a black man could defeat every white champion he faced and completed what he called his "first invasion of Europe," winning most of his races in France, Denmark, Germany, and Switzerland. In two months of racing he won forty-two first place finishes, eleven seconds, three thirds, and one fourth, a stunning display of athletic dominance rarely seen before or since. He was hailed in newspapers across Europe. A leading Danish newspaper, *Politiken*, said in a typically effusive account that the "Holy Cyclist, as he is called," is a man "with such an unusually beautiful physique that we do not recall among all the white sports men who over the years have passed before our eyes, seeing anyone whose body bears such a fine touch of manly beauty and elegance as this young negro [who is] among the most advanced individuals of his race."

Taylor said farewell from a Paris train station, where well-wishers presented him with a bouquet, then headed to England for the steamship that would take him back to his homeland, where Daisy patiently awaited their wedding day.

# CHAPTER 15

# Voyage of the Titans

I n late June of 1901, a triumphant Taylor arrived in Southampton, England, preparing to board one of the greatest steamships of the day, the SS *Deutschland,* an even faster vessel than the one he had taken to France. The journey would be hailed as one of the most memorable in the history of the Hamburg-America line, featuring a colorful collection of some of America's wealthiest men. Newspapers were rife with talk that the titans were plotting to take control of America's financial system. Reporters tracked the departure of the ship, speculated about the parties and private conversations, and published front-page stories that featured key players. "Seldom, if ever, has one transatlantic liner brought across at one time such a number of well-known people as the *Deutschland,*" reported the *New York Times.* Taylor saw it all unfold.

Before he boarded the *Deutschland* in Southampton, Taylor had been given a rousing send-off. One observer marveled that Taylor seemed to be better known than another notable passenger, an heir to one of the world's great fortunes. "The Negro bicycle phenomenon, Major Taylor, departed from the European shore amid the huzzas of the assembled multitude," a newspaper reported. "William K. Vanderbilt, only a poor multi-millionaire, departed at the same time— unnoticed. Such, indeed, is life."

In fact, Vanderbilt would have been hard to miss. The dashing heir, who easily afforded losing the $3,000 he had wagered on Taylor's first race against Jacquelin, arrived in his newly purchased Mercedes, which he stored on the *Deutschland*. For good measure, he also brought back "two experienced chauffeurs" who were more than liveried drivers; they were experts who would help train Vanderbilt to race the car. Vanderbilt would go on to his own racing career, at least on the auto track, setting speed records at places such as Daytona Beach, and he eventually created a company that built the nation's first major paved road for cars, the forty-five-mile Long Island Motor Parkway. Having bet on Taylor in Paris and heard so much about the bicycle races during his time there, Vanderbilt could not have missed the fact that Taylor was along for the voyage on the *Deutschland*.

One after another, titans of American industry boarded with their entourages. The heads of banks and railroads and shipping lines found their cabins and made their way to the cafe, famous for its high, square ceiling of glass. The one-year-old *Deutschland* was the "queen of the seas," one of the largest ships ever built, and the fastest ever to cross the ocean. Those who loved speed were drawn to her underbelly of power. She could burn through 572 tons of coal per day, heated in 112 furnaces, fueling a horsepower of nearly 40,000, thrusting energy to a 59-foot crankshaft, hissing through cylinders, cycling through pistons, exhaling through four massive smokestacks. The ship shuddered from its strength. As she neared a top speed of 23 knots, deck chairs vibrated and passengers clung to railings as the vessel powered through the choppy seas.

The next millionaire to board was a seventy-year-old man with a steely gaze. His great nose was deformed and purplish from the disease of rosacea and related conditions. He seemed to breathe in the smoke from an ever-present Havana cigar as often as air itself. Such was the entrance of one of the world's most admired and vilified financiers, J. P. Morgan.

Morgan had joined with the Rothschild empire to bail out the US Treasury following the Panic of 1893 by providing 3.5 million ounces of gold. He controlled an array of companies; owned an assortment of houses, yachts, and estates; and spent his money on whatever pleased him. He would often be accused of colluding with a handful of other magnates in an effort to dominate world markets and enrich himself at the expense of the teeming masses who toiled for his companies—a suspicion that would only be fueled by sailing on this voyage with such a select group of men.

Morgan had come to England on a mission. He intended to buy a painting that had long fascinated him, a 1785 portrait by the English painter Thomas Gainsborough of the Duchess of Devonshire, otherwise known as Georgiana Spencer, whose descendants would include Princess Diana. The luminous oil painting had a history that seemed too bizarre even for the most imaginative novelist. The painting had been stolen in London by Adam Worth, one of the most infamous criminals in English history and the model for Sherlock Holmes's nemesis Professor James Moriarty. Worth was born in Cambridge, Massachusetts, fought in the Civil War on the side of the Union, became a pickpocket in New York City, graduated into bank robbery, stole $400,000 from a Boston bank, and moved to London under an assumed name. He created a new criminal empire that stretched to South Africa while he presented himself as an English gentleman who could afford stables and yachts and an apartment on Piccadilly. One day, the portrait of the Duchess of Devonshire came up for auction, and Worth found himself competing for it against the father of J. P. Morgan, who intended to buy it for his son's art collection. Rather than get in a bidding war with a Morgan, Worth stole the painting before the elder Morgan could complete the purchase. Worth wound up hiding the painting, and it was assumed to be lost. But J. P. Morgan never gave up on his father's dream of fulfilling the purchase; one day, news arrived that the painting had surfaced. Worth had met with the famous detective William Pinkerton, who paid off the criminal to reveal the painting's whereabouts. It had been hidden in a Brooklyn warehouse, and eventually it was transferred back to London.

Now Morgan heard that he could do what his father could not. For twenty-five years, Morgan had been transfixed by the tale of the painting and the subject it depicted. The duchess was drawn with porcelain skin, waves of golden hair tumbling beneath a fantastically large black hat, cocked at an angle like a sail in a gusty sea, clutching a pink rose in bloom, a green ribbon around her waist, the frill of the white dress shimmering from the neck—all the human perfection that the purplish Morgan was not. She was said to have been a nymphomaniac, participating in a ménage à trois at seventeen, willing to trade a kiss for a political favor. Viewers were particularly entranced by her gaze, in which she looked askance as if in the midst of a flirtation. One admirer supposedly said, "I could light my pipe by her eyes." Near the end of her life, the duchess wrote a note that would rank among the great farewells: "Before you condemn me, remember that at 17 I was a toast, a beauty and a Duchess." Morgan could not let her go again. So he traveled across the sea to place his bid and was said to have paid $150,000, a sum beyond anyone's imagination at that time for a painting. He kept the amount secret at first, explaining "If the truth came out I might be considered a candidate for the lunatic asylum."

Morgan, a man so famously hard to please, was joyous. With the portrait secured at his London home, Morgan boarded the *Deutschland*, where he accepted an offer from the captain for the use of a private suite. The financier nonetheless surprised the passengers by spending much of the voyage roaming the decks, examining the vessel, and peering over the railings into the distance. Eventually Morgan would acquire the steamship empire that would build the *Titanic*, which he would plan to board eleven years later on what would be its first and final voyage, but at the last moment would decide to stay ashore.

Finally, another of the day's great magnates, Pierre Lorillard, came aboard—or rather, was carried aboard. Lorillard's family controlled one of world's largest tobacco companies. He spent part of his fortune on a famed mansion called The Breakers in Newport, Rhode Island, then sold the estate to Cornelius Vanderbilt II and used the proceeds to build the Tuxedo Club, an exclusive country club founded in 1886 that overlooked Tuxedo Lake in the Ramapo Mountains, fifty miles northwest of New York City. He had been attending the Ascot races in England, rooting for one of his horses to win the Gold Cup, when he became seriously ill. He rashly decided that it was better to suffer an ocean voyage and get the care of his American doctor than remain in a foreign hospital.

On July 3, the day before arriving in New York Harbor, the passengers were invited to a grand dinner, to be held in the room known as the main saloon and cupola, a massive space that rose several stories, surrounded by friezes and statues and elaborate artwork. Long tables filled the interior, around which swivel chairs were placed. White tablecloths draped to the floor, crystal and silver were arrayed, and drinks were poured from the onboard stock of 12,000 quarts of wine and liquor and 15,000 quarts of beer. A crew of 550 tended to every need.

After the passengers assembled, the ship's captain ordered that the lights be turned off. Waiters scurried as the diners sat in darkness. When the lights were turned on, the guests saw that their tables were decorated in red, white, and blue. Morgan was asked to make a speech; he declined. Instead, another passenger rose and delivered a patriotic address about the progress of the United States since its founding. The speaker was Timothy L. Woodruff, the lieutenant governor of New York and prospective Republican vice presidential candidate. "A man who cannot talk at such a moment as that is not worth much as an American," Woodruff said later. "I talked." It so happened that Woodruff, in his prior position as the Brooklyn park commissioner, had been the leading advocate for the construction of bicycle paths during the 1890s, including the time when Taylor rode for the South Brooklyn Wheelmen. In gratitude for Woodruff's work, a parade of four thousand cyclists had traveled to his home, and Woodruff had vowed to support bicycling however he could.

As the passengers listened to Woodruff in the grand cupola of the *Deutschland*'s dining room, the Gilded Age seemed at its sharpest glint, even if financial troubles and turmoil were on the horizon. A new age of empire—of super ships and automobiles and expanding railroads—was inevitable. Many of the men in this dining hall would be at the center of it.

Morgan had offered an "enormous premium" for every hour that the ship shaved off its record. The *Deutschland* raced across the ocean at 22.65 knots, completing the run in five days, eighteen hours, and forty-five minutes—not quite a record, but an astonishing mark at the turn of the century. The arrival was front-page news across the country due in part to speculation about whether the industrial titans had taken the voyage to conspire on major business deals.

The *Chicago Tribune*, in a typical breathless report, said it was the largest gathering of millionaires ever to cross the ocean together, and they took over "the entire saloon deck for the purpose of discussing various plans affecting large vested interests in this country and arranging several deals among themselves." The men later denied the claim.

And then, right there on the front page of the *New York Tribune*, in a story headlined "J. P. Morgan Nearing Home" that listed the many millionaires, there was mention of another passenger. "Major Taylor, the crack bicycle rider, is also a passenger on the *Deutschland*," it reported. Another newspaper writer noted how remarkable it was that Taylor "was a passenger with the millionaires" just a few years after being seen only as a "servant" for the Brooklyn club—proof, the reporter concluded, that Taylor had been given an opportunity "to which he proved equal."

The vessel, bedecked with patriotic streamers from stem to stern in celebration of the holiday, slowly made its way toward the crowd of curious onlookers onshore. Yachts were sent to greet the *Deutschland* as it glided into New York Harbor. Detectives leaped aboard the steamship to protect Morgan and others as they prepared to step on American soil. Reporters gathered at the gangway, and hundreds of local residents were kept at a distance. Morgan was his usual circumspect self, declining to address questions about striking coal miners or the latest speculation about which company he might acquire. He confirmed that he bought "a picture or two," referring in the most casual manner to his purchase of the portrait of the Duchess of Devonshire. He added that he had decided to "do some good" by giving $1 million to Harvard. "Too much fuss is made about these things," he insisted. No deals had been discussed aboard the ship, he said. He had moved about the decks like any other passenger.

"Have you bought Windsor Castle?" a reporter mischievously inquired, to which Morgan did not smile. He turned his back and, hopping aboard a tugboat to avoid reporters, headed for his yacht, the black-hulled Corsair, in which he then sailed to his summer home up the Hudson River, in Highland Falls, New York.

Murmurs raced through the crowd as the next titan was whisked away by an entourage. It was Pierre Lorillard, the tobacco king, now even more gravely ill. He would die of a kidney disorder two days after being carried off the *Deutschland*.

Next, reporters spotted Taylor. He told the press that he was happy with how he was treated in France. A scribe from the *New York Times* eventually caught up with him, wondering if Taylor would take up another cyclist's challenge for a $500 side bet on an upcoming race. "I don't ride for my own money," Taylor responded, a comment that the *Times* reporter thought necessary to render for readers as "Ah doan' ride for mah own money." Taylor rode, he explained, "for other people's money." The *Times* reporter expressed his approval, as might have the magnates aboard the *Deutschland*. Taylor, the *Times* writer concluded, "is an excellent businessman."

There was no yacht to whisk Taylor away, no chance for him to recover from the weariness of the voyage. He hauled his bicycles and suitcases off the *Deutschland* and headed to Manhattan Beach, where he was expected to race within hours.

Taylor strode onto the familiar track, waving to the five thousand spectators who had gathered to cheer him. The event had been heavily promoted as Taylor's "First American Reappearance." The festivities included fireworks, a performance by the band of John Philip Sousa—whose compositions included the "Manhattan Beach March"—and a matinee of a play called *The Geisha*.

Taylor was slated to ride in an exhibition and then race in the evening. But the ocean voyage had left him listless, and the brutal schedule that required him to go from ship to racecourse had siphoned his little remaining energy. After completing an impressive mile behind a motorized pacing machine in one minute and thirty-six seconds, he declared himself too tired to compete and withdrew from the rest of the event. The sea voyage had left him queasy and exhausted, and he told sponsors he was ill. He headed back to Worcester.

Instead of celebrating the man who had beaten the great Jacquelin, much of the cycling world sensed a vulnerability and renewed their attacks on Taylor. The National Cycling Association fined him $100 for failing to participate in the race, even though a physician testified that he was too sick to ride. Taylor refused to pay the fine, and the association declared war. He would have to race whether he was "sick or well." Unless he showed up for his scheduled races, the cycling authorities would fine him another $100 for every missed race, and threatened to kick him out of the association. It was a bitter turn, and Taylor took out his frustration by issuing a statement from his home to the *Boston Globe,* saying he was "not well" and wouldn't be riding "anywhere" until he recovered. His doctor had told him to stay in bed for two weeks due to severe stomach problems, noting that his mother and sister had died in recent years after having similar troubles. Taylor told the newspaper that he was being persecuted due to his race, and that "if he was not a colored man, the doctor's certificate would excuse him from any meet just as it does a white man." The authorities just wanted to get rid of him. "Never again will I race," Taylor abruptly declared, although such threats—uttered repeatedly—carried less weight than the seemingly definitive words suggested.

"What rot!" wrote the *Buffalo Enquirer,* the hometown paper of his old rival, Eddie Bald. "What would Taylor do if he retired? He has made more money and received more notoriety and favorable notices than any man or any ten men of his race in the past three years. His recent trip to Europe, where he was petted and praised by men and women not of his own color, was bad enough . . . he has become unbearable."

In fact, no one attracted fans to the track like Taylor, and the sport was in danger of losing much of its revenue without him. They didn't want to admit it, but his top competitors were "just itching" for a series of championship races against him, hoping to collect huge purses. By becoming the world's fastest man, he had triumphed in his bid for racial equality. Now the real competition was one he could not win: the race against time and progress. He, like Munger, had ridden the cycling craze and made it to the top. Yet at this moment, at the beginning of the twentieth century, so much was changing. A specter loomed that threatened to upend the world that Taylor had mastered.

# CHAPTER 16

# The Caged Bird Sings

F rom the grandstands along Pennsylvania Avenue, thousands of people had shivered through a cold rainstorm to watch the second inauguration of President McKinley, a parade lasting more than four hours, with marching bands, military ensembles, and a carriage drawn by four horses carrying the reelected leader. McKinley waved his hat to the sodden masses and headed to the covered, heated reviewing area outside the Executive Mansion, as the White House was then called. After the crowd dispersed, and the bunting and flags were stored for the next great occasion, the nation's capital of 1901 reverted to being the relative backwater for which it was known. A nearby neighborhood had been called "Murder Bay" because it was so crime-infested, and only recently had many of the muddy thoroughfares been fully paved. It was the nation's fifteenth-largest city, with a population of 278,000, about half that of Baltimore and far behind New York City's 3.4 million. City leaders constantly debated ways to improve Washington, and one of the obvious needs was for a sporting arena. After the March 4 inauguration, a pair of entrepreneurs looked at the grandstands and saw an opportunity. They purchased many sections of the red-and-orange seating and moved them to a vacant plot on Capitol Hill, next to the East Capitol Street streetcar barn, a redbrick Romanesque Revival building that had been built a few years earlier. Then they constructed an oblong cycle track, one-sixth of a mile around, with seating for as many as five thousand people. The Washington Coliseum, as it was grandly called, was set to open in July.

Now all they needed was a star attraction. Taylor was the obvious choice, but in the three weeks since he returned from Europe, he had been fined for refusing to race by officials who ignored his insistence that he was too ill to compete. As Taylor recovered, the completion of the Coliseum provided an opportunity he could not resist. He paid his fines and headed south. An advertisement in the *Washington Evening Star* displayed his name in large typeface, touting "Champion of the World, Major Taylor," above the much smaller references to his competitors.

Taylor arrived on the afternoon of July 23 at the Baltimore and Potomac Railway Station, a three-story building sheathed in red, blue, and green slates, with three ornamental towers, adjacent to a series of unsightly train sheds that cut across the western side of the Mall. Exiting the train station, Taylor looked up and saw the brilliant white dome of the US Capitol, built partly by slaves and topped by the Statue of Freedom. In the opposite direction, the great obelisk of the Washington Monument reached skyward. A number of Taylor's friends met him at the depot, and escorted him to his lodgings.

The city was about one-third African American, and among the most distinguished was a man that Taylor greatly admired, the poet Paul Laurence Dunbar. It is not clear if they met on this day, but Taylor wrote effusively about how he admired Dunbar and hoped to emulate him. Dunbar was born in Dayton, Ohio, in 1872, six years before Taylor. A prodigy, he recited poetry publicly when he was nine years old, and he was the only black at Central High School, where he befriended classmate Orville Wright. Orville and his brother, Wilbur, helped facilitate the publication of Dunbar's first book of poetry, and subsequent volumes attracted international notice. In 1897, he moved to Washington, where he got a job at the Library of Congress, across the street from the US Capitol. Though he was surrounded by books, he felt deadened by his work of shelving them all day in the oppressive summer heat. The iron gratings of the book stacks suggested to Dunbar "the bars of a bird cage," his wife, Alice, later wrote. He envisioned a creature beating its wings, unable to fly. Dunbar, the son of slaves, translated the experience into one of his most famous poems, which would inspire generations of writers to come.

> I know why the caged bird sings, ah me,
> When his wing is bruised and his bosom sore,—
> When he beats his bars and he would be free;
> It is not a carol of joy or glee,
> But a prayer that he sends from his heart's deep core,
> But a plea, that upward to Heaven he flings—
> I know why the caged bird sings!

Dunbar was still living in Washington, writing poetry and novels at his home in the fashionable neighborhood of LeDroit Park, when Taylor arrived. Dunbar's acclaim was so great that he had been invited earlier in the year to join McKinley's inaugural parade, riding a horse for the first time in his life. Taylor had long admired Dunbar's realistic portrayal of the hardships faced by African Americans, and the two bore such a striking resemblance that Taylor wrote that "everybody who knew us both down in Washington said we resembled each other enough to pass for twins." Such was Dunbar's influence on Taylor that he later wrote Daisy—revealingly, if unrealistically—that he was "thinking seriously" of following Dunbar's path. "I am sure I have the makings of a great poet."

The evening after Taylor's arrival, several thousand people streamed to the Coliseum, about a dozen blocks from the West Front of the Capitol. They came by foot, horse-drawn carriage, bicycle, and street-car. There were a handful of automobiles in the city, and the idea of more such conveyances alarmed the city's leaders. The *Washington Post* reported that "horse dealers do not look upon the advent of the automobile with any degree of seriousness. It is true that society has taken up the automobile, but the dealers consider it nothing but a fad, which will not have as much permanency as the bicycle. They argue that the noise of the engine or motor will soon wear the tender nerves of the society belle or swell to a frazzle, and that the odor of the loco-mobile is not at all agreeable to the sensitive nostrils."

Indeed, one of the great controversies of the moment was a request by the city's fire department chief for five electric "motor carriages," which had top speeds of twenty miles per hour. The editorial writers at the *Post* dreaded the prospect of such a "swift and terrible approach" of "wild dashes upon the Capitol plaza" that could pose "the risk of instant death" to bystanders. Then again, the *Post* writer said, "Washington needs some excitement to stir its lethargic soul." For that, the masses headed to the bicycle races. The Washington Coliseum filled quickly, half of the spectators crowding the grassy area inside the track, and the rest taking seats in the grandstands. All eyes were on Taylor as he took warm-up laps around the bowl. Taylor lost the first race, a one-mile contest, but the main focus was on the next contest, heats of half-mile races.

Taylor's main competition in the semifinal was one of his fiercest rivals, Tom Cooper, whom he had famously beaten in the race that he had said was "run for blood." Cooper was nearing the end of his extraordinarily successful career and wanted revenge against Taylor. The former pharmacist from Detroit had earned tens of thousands of dollars from his many victories. He preferred to ride behind a motor-ized pacer but Taylor used his prerogative to insist that this race be run without them; he preferred a cat-and-mouse strategy rather than a hot pace from the start. The old rivals tried to outmaneuver each other. They jockeyed and slowly zigzagged across the track until the final lap, when they lunged full-speed for the tape. Taylor was declared the win-ner, sending him into a final heat. He won that race as well, making him national champion in the event with a time of one minute and twenty-six seconds. "Last night will doubtless go down into bicycle racing annals as 'Majah' Taylor's night," said the *Evening Star*. "He had all of the crack sprinters of the country beaten to a standstill."

No one realized it at the time, but the race would be one of Cooper's last on a bicycle. Like an increasing number of Taylor's rivals, Coo-per had seen the specter that haunted them all—the rise of the automobile—and embraced it as the future. Three months after losing to Taylor, Cooper and a partner raced a motorized bicycle in Detroit. Another man raced a different type of vehicle at the same event. His name was Henry Ford, and he drove a racing car that he had built. Cooper gave Ford advice that helped win the race.

Cooper was so impressed with the auto that he invested much of his fortune into Ford's effort to build two of the fastest race cars ever constructed: a yellow car called the 999, and a bright red Arrow, better known as the Red Devil. The result was headline news across the country, with credit going to both men. "Ford-Cooper Racing Machine," said the front-page story in *The Automobile and Motor Review*. Ford, who was assembling funds to start a new auto company, soon sold the 999 to Cooper. Months later, in October 1902, Cooper arranged for a daring twenty-four-year-old bicycle racer named Barney Oldfield— who had also once competed against Taylor—to race the 999. Oldfield, who had never driven an automobile, trained for a week and promptly set a one-mile record of one minute and four and one-third seconds. A famous picture shows Oldfield, dressed in black and wearing racing goggles, sitting in the four-cylinder 999, a stripped-down vehicle with the engine in front and a single seat in back. Next to him stands a proud-looking, thirty-nine-year-old Ford. Cooper, the cycling champion, had played a crucial role in the development of what was briefly considered the world's fastest car, and Ford, a brilliant tinkerer who once tested an engine on his kitchen table, took a major step toward building his auto business. The Ford Motor Company, formed the following year, would soon focus on a simpler vehicle that could be purchased by the masses, and Cooper joined a competitor, the Matheson Motor Car Co. The bicycle boom was mostly over in the United States, and many of those who built their career on the business saw the future in automobiles.

The morning after the race at the Washington Coliseum, Taylor returned to the train station and headed north, where he expected to continue to receive a warm welcome. Instead, he was repeatedly rejected. He stopped at a soda fountain in a Baltimore store and asked for a glass of mineral water, and the clerk refused him on account of his race. A few days later, Taylor took the train to Syracuse, New York, where he went to the four-story brick Vanderbilt Hotel, where he had previously stayed without incident. He paused in the lobby to write a letter.

A hotel clerk approached him.

"What are you doing there at that desk? Get out of here!" the clerk said.

"I guess you don't know who I am," Taylor responded. "I've stopped here several times, and if you will let me explain, perhaps you will be more friendly."

"Get out of here, or you'll be kicked out," the clerk insisted, jerking away the chair on which Taylor had been sitting.

Taylor left peaceably, but he was heartbroken. In all his travels, he told the *Worcester Telegram*, he had never been more hurt.

He tried to check into another hotel, where the clerk raised the price so high that it was evident he was trying to keep Taylor away without actually evicting him. Taylor finally found lodgings elsewhere, but lost his race that night in front of four thousand people. Taylor decided he would no longer put up with being refused lodgings. He announced he was suing the proprietor of Syracuse's Hotel Vanderbilt for $10,000. News of the lawsuit was published across the country, although the filing apparently went nowhere. As word spread, a sympathetic writer for the *New York Daily Tribune* wrote that Taylor, "who was treated so finely in Paris, has found that the color line exists in some other places besides the South."

The *New York Times*, meanwhile, saw fit to publish a letter to the editor that blamed Taylor for a string of pedestrian deaths for which he had no responsibility. The correspondent, while insisting that "I am not prejudiced," said that he "regretted that there is a colored champion" because a number of black bicycle riders in New York City were imagining themselves to be the next Major Taylor and "do reckless riding on the public thoroughfare."

• • •

Death-defying races, of course, were part of the attraction for many of the thousands who regularly turned out to see Taylor. The sport was terrifyingly dangerous, and that just added to the thrill—and the horror. Taylor believed that the odds he would be killed were even higher because competitors often forced him into dangerous maneuvers to avoid collision. In his autobiography, he named eleven fellow racers who were killed on the track. A burst tire sent a speeding rider flying on the banking; a hiccup in a motorized pacing machine could cause the trailing rider to touch wheels, creating a catastrophic collision. "I cannot help but recall the many narrow escapes I had in my races, and shudder as I think of the many brave and outstanding riders who were killed," Taylor wrote. Tom Cooper had survived the bicycle track, but several years after he joined forces with Henry Ford, he was in an impromptu race against another vehicle in New York City's Central Park. As Cooper rounded a curve near 77th Street, one of his front wheels scraped the vehicle ahead. The tire burst and Cooper lost control. Thrown from the car as it flipped on its side, he slammed into the pavement, breaking his neck. A bicycling patrolman found the lifeless Cooper twenty feet from the car.

One of Taylor's closest calls came at Charles River Park in Cambridge on August 7, 1901, as he strove to gain ground in the championship rankings. Taylor was slated to compete in two races. In the first contest, the one-third mile, Taylor was neck and neck with another rider, sometimes reaching speeds of thirty miles per hour or more, when he lost control of his bicycle, fell to the ground "in a heap," and was carried to his training room, "where he lay unconscious for some time." The serious trauma that can be caused by such head injuries was not fully grasped at the time. Cells die as the brain bounces off the skull, and the blood and oxygen flow can be curtailed, leading to a blackout. In the worst case, a concussion leads to internal bleeding, brain swelling, and sudden death. Rushing back into action after regaining consciousness can exacerbate the injury. The race promoters and Taylor himself may not have realized the danger of returning to the race. After a brief delay, Taylor was hustled back to the course for a much-promoted five-mile race against a French rider named Albert Champion, who had little sympathy for Taylor, as he himself was riding with a broken hand. (Champion would later famously launch an auto spark plug company named after himself.) After a mile, however, Taylor could not continue. Rather than question why a man who had been unconscious was so quickly returned to the track, Taylor's supporters expressed alarm that some unknown problem had occurred. "Major Taylor Losing Form," said the headline in the *Indianapolis News*, reporting that his friends "are at a loss" to understand the "sudden reversal."

The risks were great, but no rider could become a champion without regularly taking them. Few were more daring than a Taylor rival named Johnnie Nelson. Shortly after Taylor returned from Europe, Taylor faced the Chicago rider in a five-mile contest behind motorized pacers at a Worcester velodrome before five thousand people. Nelson stayed closely behind a motorized pacer, and he took an early lead in the first heat. It had been agreed that a pistol would be fired at the beginning of the fifth mile to ensure that racers knew how far they had to go. Taylor "evidently forgot" the signal, thinking the pistol's crack meant the race was over, and Nelson won easily. Then, in the second heat, Nelson set such a brutal pace, following dangerously close to the pacing machine, that he set a world's record as he once again easily outdistanced Taylor.

Shortly thereafter, Nelson raced behind a pacer at Madison Square Garden. This time, he got too close, collided with the pacer, and severely gashed his leg as he spun off his back and thudded to the track. Doctors had no choice but to amputate Nelson's injured leg. Taylor soon heard the devastating news, remembering how he had just raced against Nelson under such dangerous conditions in Worcester.

There was no time to dwell on the tragedy. Taylor was in a race at the Charles River Track in Massachusetts against a Swedish-born rival, Iver Lawson. As they circled around the packed velodrome, Lawson cut him off, and Taylor crashed to the track. The tragedy of Nelson's accident was fresh and Taylor, usually so cool with his emotions, let loose. He flung his bicycle into the center of the racing oval and "advanced toward the Swede," as the *Globe* recounted Taylor's threatening approach. A fight seemed inevitable, and Lawson put up his hands "for the colored man's onslaught." A police officer intervened and "escorted Taylor to the dressing room." Taylor got his revenge, returning to the track to win the final heat.

Two days later, Taylor learned that Nelson's amputation had been too late. The daring young rider died at Bellevue Hospital.

Taylor mourned Nelson's death, understanding it could just as easily have been him. But he still had races to run that could determine the year's championship. Awaiting him, he learned, was one of his bitterest foes, who had come up with a new plan to stop him.

CHAPTER 17

# "The Strain Is Too Great"

Floyd McFarland, a twenty-three-year-old Californian, was one of the biggest, strongest riders Taylor had ever encountered. At six foot four, he towered over the five-seven Taylor, and their contests were promoted as the giant versus the midget. McFarland grew up fifty-five miles southeast of San Francisco, in San Jose, known for its prunes and fruit and canneries and frenzied real estate sales—and its fanaticism about cycling. At the turn of the twentieth century, the city had twenty-one thousand people, twenty-eight bicycle shops, nine cycling clubs, and a velodrome. McFarland developed his strength toting thick piles of the *San Jose Mercury News* on the back of his bicycle. It was the perfect place to become a racer, with its warm climate and vast network of roads and trails. McFarland's training route included one of the most extraordinary anywhere in the United States: an endlessly curving eighteen-mile route up 4,265-foot Mount Hamilton, affording views from its mile-long ridge from the Santa Clara mountains to San Francisco Bay to Yosemite. Pedaling to the mountaintop and sweeping down into the valley, McFarland developed extraordinary legs and lungs, enabling him to specialize in multiday races—and to become one of Taylor's fiercest competitors. In time, McFarland won championships in the city, the state, and then in venues across the country.

California at the time had 1.4 million people, including around twenty thousand blacks. The African American population of San Jose was small, including a number of former slaves who had traveled west after the Civil War, but there were enough in the area that they formed their own cycling club. McFarland at some point developed deeply racist feelings, and Taylor would later say that McFarland was one of the most hateful men he ever knew on the racetrack. McFarland never hid his animosity or feeling of superiority. He carried anger, fed off it, and spewed it in hot-tempered tirades. He felt underappreciated, and was galled that Taylor was far better known. Being based in California, far from the Eastern hotbed of cycling competition, McFarland won countless races but hardly as many trophies or headlines as Taylor. The two had met a number of times, including several occasions when McFarland taunted Taylor and tried to push him off the course. A rapprochement seemed in the offing when, for financial reasons, the two had discussed teaming up in a six-day race at Madison Square Garden. The idea went nowhere when Taylor's sponsor, the Iver Johnson Company, wisely advised that he stick to his specialty of sprints. McFarland never forgave Taylor for rejecting him, and the animosity between them plunged to new depths. McFarland was part of a team that won the six-day race in 1900, and his fame finally began to match his record. President McKinley planned to visit San Jose during a national railroad tour in the spring of 1901, and McFarland arranged to lead a contingent of bicycle racers who would assemble before him in the color and form of an American flag during the Carnival of Roses parade.

McKinley's tour marked a turning point in the nation's history and its inexorable westward march. Two months after his second inauguration, McKinley left Washington on an eight-car train, planning a seven-week journey to the nation's southern, northern, and western regions, with the $75,000 cost paid by railroad companies. He was joined by his wife, Ida, an elegant beauty with wide eyes and wavy hair who suffered from epileptic seizures. Others on board were Cabinet members, three stenographers, telegraph operators, and a press corps of nine reporters and one photographer. The extensive daily coverage of the trip, sent to newspapers across the country, underscored the nation's technological turn, as readers expected complete and immediate coverage of the news. McKinley attended a parade of Confederate veterans in Memphis, went on a riverboat cruise in Louisiana, spoke to the state legislature in Texas, and visited El Paso, going to the international bridge and gazing into Mexico. McKinley used the visit to take stock of America at the dawn of the twentieth century, insisting, "there never was such unity as there is at this hour." The entourage then boarded the train and headed through mountain-ringed deserts, across the territories of New Mexico and Arizona, both of which would become states eleven years later, and arrived in Los Angeles. The president and his party then headed north, making an unscheduled stop to tend to Ida, who had become seriously ill due to an infection. McKinley nearly canceled the trip, but he was determined to speak in San Jose and celebrate the city's prosperity. Leaving his wife in San Francisco, he spoke before ten thousand cheering people in San Jose's St. James Park on May 13. As the parade including McFarland got under way, McKinley hurriedly boarded the train to San Francisco to again be by his wife's side. Most of the remaining stops on the trip were canceled, and the rerouting took the entourage across the Sierra Nevada Mountains on the return to Washington. One of the missed stops would prove fateful: McKinley had planned to stop at the Pan American Exposition in Buffalo. Instead, he made plans to go there later in the year.

McFarland, meanwhile, took a train east in his quest to win the national championship. In mid-June 1901, McFarland broke the world's record for a one-mile race at a Connecticut contest, and anticipation grew for a match against Taylor, who was soon to return from Europe. But a week later, as McFarland was riding at a "furious pace" at Madison Square Garden in a fifteen-mile contest, a motorized pacing vehicle slid from the banking and slammed into him. McFarland flew off his bicycle, hit his head hard against the track, bleeding profusely, and was rushed "semi-conscious" to the hospital. Two weeks later, McFarland had recovered, and prepared to face Taylor at Madison Square Garden. But it was at that moment that the just-returned Taylor, ill and exhausted, had declared he would never ride again, and

McFarland was deprived of the opportunity to face him. McFarland was livid. When Taylor changed his mind and reentered competition, McFarland—whose own hopes for the championship were undone by his injury—conspired with others to try to prevent Taylor from winning the title.

McFarland "was the ringleader of the gang of riders who had sworn among themselves to bring about my dethronement as champion of America at all costs," Taylor wrote. Confident that the result was fixed against Taylor, McFarland placed bets of $500 or more against him. In a race that summer at Manhattan Beach, McFarland barked instructions "to trim the nigger," urging that the race be fixed by cutting off Taylor in a manner that could cause him to be thrown to the ground. For seven laps, the riders gave Taylor no room to maneuver, but on the next turn Taylor crouched as low as possible, dropped back half a length "and at the psychological moment I kicked through like a flash." He sprinted the last three laps "for all that was in me," and won by five lengths. The crowd screamed its approval.

Afterward, McFarland roared at the cyclists in the training room.

"And you call yourself bicycle riders!" McFarland said.

One of the riders dared respond that he had once seen Taylor get around McFarland in the same manner. "Why the hell didn't you hold him in?" the rider asked. McFarland, for once, was speechless.

A few weeks later, in August 1901 at Madison Square Garden, McFarland instructed racer Owen Kimble how to beat Taylor. Once again, Taylor outmaneuvered the tactic. Back in the training room, McFarland unloaded on Kimble, screaming and cursing: "So you'd rather be trimmed by a nigger than to be defeated by a white man, would you? Well, how do you like that, how do you like that?"

Kimble, putting aside his own animosity toward Taylor, had had enough. He pleaded with Taylor to come with him to face McFarland, and Taylor reluctantly agreed. Much to Taylor's astonishment, Kimble put his hand on Taylor's shoulder and said, "Yes, Major Taylor did defeat me and he didn't have to run me off the track or foul me to do it either."

Taylor was stunned as Kimble continued to face down McFarland.

"I do not consider it a disgrace to be beaten by him because he always does it fairly and that is more than any of you can do," Kimble said. Shaking Taylor's hand, he continued, "Major Taylor, I congratulate you on winning this championship race. You're the fastest and squarest man among us."

Taylor watched the riders hang their heads, then heard several threaten to get even. In the end, that is what happened. Taylor had missed too much time due to his travels, illnesses, and injuries, and was too often beaten by McFarland's tactics against him. Frank Kramer, a racer who worked as McFarland's proxy and protégé, piled up enough points to win the championship, with Taylor in second place. Taylor had to admit that McFarland's "diabolical scheme" had been all too effective. He had stopped Taylor and enriched himself.

Later that year, McKinley made good on his promise to visit the Pan American Exhibition in Buffalo, then the nation's eighth largest city with a population of 350,000. He arrived in early September, one of 8 million visitors to view exhibits on a 350-acre site on the city's northern border that extolled the nation's progress. The symbol of the fair was the 395-foot-high Electric Tower, topped by a figurine called The Goddess of Light, which sent beams across the fairgrounds. Visitors walked along a promenade, by canals and gardens, passing brightly lit palaces, designed to be quickly built and torn down, ingeniously constructed of iron frames, wood slats, and plaster. In an echo of the W. E. B. Du Bois exhibit from Paris, the progress by blacks was displayed, but that seemed undermined by a site called Old Plantations, where African Americans played the role of cotton-picking slaves. At the Machinery and Transportation Building, an array of bicycles stood next to one of the largest exhibits of automobiles ever shown, from steam-powered carriages to gasoline-fueled cars to "electric runabouts."

On September 6, as McKinley toured the Temple of Music, a crazed anarchist, Leon Czolgosz, reached to shake the president's hand. He held a handkerchief that concealed a handgun. Czolgosz fired two shots, wounding McKinley, who died several days later. Vice President Theodore Roosevelt became president of the United States.

• • •

At Taylor's home in Worcester, it will be recalled, pictures of Roosevelt and Booker T. Washington hung on the parlor wall. As it happened, one month after Roosevelt took office, he met for dinner with Washington, the first time an African American had dined with a president at the White House. Taylor certainly would have followed the coverage, and been aware of the fallout.

The White House dinner took place on October 16, 1901, at a moment when blacks, more than seventy-five percent of whom lived in the South, faced a devastating escalation in Jim Crow tactics. The South's judicial system had been "wholly reconfigured" to coerce blacks into a permanent underclass of servitude, as historian Douglas Blackmon has written, and blacks in the region had been almost fully disenfranchised by 1901. This "neo slavery" helped keep the state coffers flush throughout the South, and propped up white-owned companies that relied on a corrupt government to furnish forced black labor. Throughout the South, few blacks served on juries or held political office, or served on police forces. "Blacks had been wholly shunted into their own inferior railroad cars, restrooms, restaurants, neighborhoods and schools," Blackmon wrote. "All of this had been accomplished in a sudden, unfettered grab by white supremacists that was met outside the South with little more than quiet assent." The promise of Reconstruction had been replaced by, as the title of Blackmon's book put it, "slavery by another name." After a number of Reconstruction-era blacks had served in Congress, whites had regained complete control; the last black to serve in Congress, George H. White, had left in March 1901, and no black would sit in that body again for twenty-eight years. African Americans increasingly looked to Roosevelt, and to leaders such as Booker T. Washington, as their best hope for progress.

Roosevelt, forty-two years old, considered Washington the most important black leader of the day, approving of his emphasis on labor, morality, and a desire to work within the existing power structure. While that fit Roosevelt's self-styled "progressive" view, it was hardly the radical approach needed to battle the white supremacism growing ever stronger in the South. Roosevelt, whose mother's family had been Georgia slaveholders, wrote to Washington that he was "confident the South was changing," and that Washington played an irreplaceable role. In fact, it would be six decades before blacks were guaranteed voting rights, among other civil rights measures.

The meeting, it would become clear, was also about Roosevelt's ambitions. Looking ahead to the 1904 election, Roosevelt believed he needed overwhelming black support to win the nomination. While disenfranchised blacks could not vote for him in a general election, black delegations from the South nonetheless played a significant role at the Republican National Convention, where they retained full rights. Roosevelt knew that inviting Washington to dinner— as opposed to seeing him in an informal setting or a business-style appointment—would send a strong signal to blacks. Roosevelt's wife and his eighteen-year-old daughter, Alice, would join the dinner, underscoring the social equality of the setting. The president had some initial hesitation, but he wrote a few weeks later that "the very fact that I felt a moment's qualm on inviting him because of his color made me ashamed of myself and made me hasten to send the invitation. I have not been able to think out any solution of the terrible problem offered by the presence of the Negro on this continent, but of one thing I am sure, and that is that inasmuch as he is here and can neither be killed nor driven away, the only wise and honorable, and Christian thing to do is treat each white man and each black man strictly on his merits as a man, giving him no more and no less than he shows himself worthy to have."

Washington wanted Roosevelt to use his power to stop Southern states from disenfranchising blacks and to stem a tide of Jim Crow laws. He also wanted Roosevelt to appoint blacks to federal positions, although on this occasion he recommended that a white Democrat, whom he believed would be sympathetic to civil rights, be picked as a judge. Roosevelt, a Republican, took Washington's advice and promised to consider blacks for other positions.

The next day, as word spread of the dinner, the Southern press attacked. It was "the most damnable outrage which has ever been perpetrated by any citizen of the United States," wrote the *Memphis Scimitar.* Southern politicians stoked the racism. "The action of President Roosevelt in entertaining that nigger will necessitate our killing a thousand niggers in the South before they will learn their place again," said Senator Benjamin "Pitchfork" Tillman, a South Carolina Democrat who had been elected after waging a years-long effort to repress blacks and support lynch mobs. Georgia governor Allen Candler said, "No southerner can respect any white man who would eat with a negro."

It was left to the African American press to hail the meeting as a breakthrough. "The First President to Entertain a Negro," said the *Washington Bee.* "No color line in the White House. An Object Lesson for the South."

Six months after his dinner with Roosevelt, in March 1902, Washington spoke at the Berkeley Lyceum in Manhattan. He hailed the generosity of white contributors to his Tuskegee Institute, the school for blacks that he expanded to twelve hundred students and fifty-six buildings. Calculating that there were more than 9 million people of African descent in the United States, he said black people "have proved their ability to look the white man in the face" and prosper when given an education. Taylor surely would have agreed. Years later, he wrote of his admiration for Washington as "the great Negro educator" who "so beautifully expressed" his thinking.

As it happened, at the same time Washington was delivering his talk at the Lyceum, Taylor was also in New York, pondering a return to Europe—and his relationship with Daisy. Given the relentless obstruction Taylor faced while racing in the United States, it was natural that he considered returning to Europe, where he had experienced his greatest victories and public adoration. Victor Breyer, the French promoter, traveled to America for the express purpose of signing Taylor to race for another season in Europe. When Taylor agreed to the contract, Breyer was ecstatic, telling New York newspapers that "I consider Major Taylor as the savior of cycling in Europe." Prior to Taylor's last tour, Breyer said, there was "every indication the great outdoor sport was dying." Taylor's arrival had given the sport "a new lease" and "drew thousands of new patrons . . . he was looked upon as an idol." As Breyer prepared to sail back to Europe with Taylor's contract in hand, he declared himself "one of the happiest men in the world."

Taylor's quest for another American championship would have to wait. He and Daisy, meanwhile, discussed whether their marriage should be delayed any longer.

Taylor was delighted to be returning to Europe but he felt exhausted. He poured out his feelings to a reporter from the *New York Sun*. He was just twenty-four years old and had accomplished more than he could have dreamed possible, yet he stunned the reporter by saying this would be his last year of racing. "The strain of continued training is telling on me," Taylor said, explaining that he had raced both in Europe and the United States during the prior years, and "it is wearing on my nerves. I had practically two seasons last year. Few appreciate what that means." He faced the same schedule this year, "and the strain is too great."

Taylor could see it coming, not just the dawning of the auto era, which he yearned to be part of, but also the decline of his own athletic ability. He wanted to "get out of the game while I am on top, and not wait till I begin to fail." He was proud that he had begun racing "without a cent. Now I have a house that I own in Worcester and a few thousands in the bank. If I can put a few thousand more away this year I shall be very well satisfied. If I can get a position and earn enough to keep me and my family and not touch the money I have saved I shall be content."

He made his decision. Taylor took a train from New York City and traveled to Ansonia, Connecticut, where Daisy was waiting for him at the home of her uncle, Reverend Louis H. Taylor, who had recently left the church he led in Worcester. The following day, March 21, the reverend married the couple, and the news was printed across the country. In one typical account, it was reported that "only a few friends" were present as Taylor got married to "one of the prettiest creoles in the state," a reference to her heritage. Taylor, the story continued "will sail for Paris with his bride." It all sounded so romantic, with Taylor showing Daisy the scene of his many triumphs, and introducing her to the wonders of Paris as they began married life together. But three days later, when Taylor boarded the *Kaiser Wilhelm der Grosse*, Daisy for the second straight year did not join him. She had gone to Grand Central Station, and then returned to the Connecticut home of Reverend Taylor. She had turned around rather than accompany Taylor to Paris, she said, because it was a "business trip," and her new husband had promised to take her throughout Europe when he was not racing.

As news spread about Taylor's return to Europe, Booker T. Washington, still in New York City, decided to show his students an exemplar of his view of what blacks could accomplish. Washington took some of his students to see Taylor before the cyclist boarded the *Kaiser Wilhelm der Grosse* "to wish him well on behalf of black Americans." Washington, born into slavery in Virginia, and Taylor, raised free in Indianapolis and mentored by a succession of liberal whites, saw each other as exemplars. Taylor always lamented that his life's circumstances and racism had prevented him from getting a formal education, and he made up for it by a lifetime of reading and learning. Washington had dedicated much of his life to enabling blacks to receive an education at Tuskegee Institute. He was forty-five years old and stood five feet nine, two inches taller and twenty-two years older than the bicycle racer. Taylor had his differences with Washington's willingness to work within the system established by whites; Taylor, after all, had spent years battling against a white-controlled system to win cycling championships. But he entirely agreed with Washington's effort to promote self-reliance through strenuous work. The two bade each other success and farewell. It would have been a proud moment for both.

From the White House, Roosevelt, too, closely monitored Taylor's journey.

Taylor's second trip to Europe aboard the *Kaiser Wilhelm der Grosse*, on which he had been seasick the year before, was only slightly less storm-tossed than the first. His fellow passengers included William Randolph Hearst, the newspaper magnate, and William M. Laffan, the editor of the *New York Sun*. Awaiting him in Paris was Breyer, who declared that Taylor was "the greatest racer and drawing card of them all." Breyer laid out a strenuous series of races in which Taylor would travel across Europe, facing the champions of every country where he appeared.

Arriving one month deeper into the racing season than he had the previous year, Taylor found the weather warmer and the crowds even larger. Storming through one European country after another, he beat the champions of Germany, England, Belgium, Denmark, and France. In Holland, Taylor faced a champion named Harri Meyers, who had announced this would be the last race of his career. A stunning showdown ensued in a best-of-three match. Taylor won the first heat, and believed he had won the second as well, but the judges said it was a dead heat. Taylor confronted Meyers about whether he thought it was a tie, and Meyers responded, "Well, they gave it to me." This enraged Taylor, who believed Meyers should have told the judges they were wrong.

"I appreciate you would like nothing better than to retire with a victory over me as a fitting climax to your brilliant career," Taylor said acidly. "Well, in the next heat I am going to try something that I never attempted before. I am going out there on the track before your home folks and intentionally see just how far I can distance you." Taylor won the race, but only by a foot, and he later complimented Meyers on staying so close, writing, "I never met a cooler rider."

Taylor's harsh dealing with Meyers underscored an intensity, a desire, that seemed unstoppable. He won every man-to-man race that season. All told, during the two-month tour, he won forty first places, fifteen second places, and two third places. It was a remarkable pace, fifty-seven races in sixty days, including some days when he competed more than once. He was paid $5,000 for making the tour, plus thousands of dollars in winnings. It was nearly all he could have hoped for, but Taylor wanted more. He returned home to Daisy and told her that he intended to compete for the American championship.

• • •

All talk of retirement vanished, and the idea of a European honeymoon was set aside. Instead, Taylor asked Daisy to accompany him to as many races as possible, to every East Coast city and burg and backwater where cycling contests were held. It was a harsh introduction to the discrimination that Taylor endured, but which Daisy rarely experienced. One day, the couple took a six a.m. train from Worcester but found no dining car on the train. Taylor and Daisy figured they would get a large lunch in Newark, New Jersey, where he would race later that day. They went to one restaurant and were refused service. Then another. Then a third. Fuming, and particularly angry that his wife had seen such humiliation even in a Northern city, Taylor returned home. On his way to the station, he ran into the race manager, who offered to take them to lunch, but Taylor turned down the offer. The manager then beseeched Taylor to race, explaining how much money was at stake. Taylor acquiesced, but he was so hungry during the race that he could not maintain his energy and lost. The manager felt so badly that he paid Taylor $400, appreciating that the race hadn't been canceled, which would have been a financial disaster.

Shortly afterward, McFarland, who had recovered from his injury, faced Taylor in Revere Beach, Massachusetts. McFarland took the lead and plotted with other racers to entrap Taylor in a pocket. Taylor expected the strategy and he bolted out of his position, passing one rider, then another, surprising his opponents by yelling as he went by, and then passed McFarland, winning the match by two lengths. As the crowd gave its "thunderous applause" to Taylor, he could hear McFarland "cursing and swearing," as he berated his two fellow riders. As Taylor took his victory lap, McFarland rode alongside him, "shaking his fists at me" and vowing "to beat me up."

Taylor took the threats seriously. Making his way to the dressing room, he picked up a two-by-four from a pile of lumber, waved it like a club, and prepared to do battle. It was, he wrote later, "the first time in my racing career that I ever lost my head to the extent of planning to fight for my rights at all costs." As McFarland approached, Taylor made a "vicious" swing at him, "but he dodged the blow." Taylor tossed the two-by-four as the other two riders arrived and fled to a corner of the dressing room where his trainer awaited. The police soon arrived and, as Taylor put it, "fortunately there was no bloodshed." But the bad blood between Taylor and McFarland only worsened.

The brawl was a turning point. Taylor became convinced that his American opponents would always work together to deny him another title. The juxtaposition between earning good money abroad and struggling at home had never been as stark. He had told the reporter from the *New York Sun* that, if he could earn enough money, this would be his last year of racing. Meanwhile, he was satisfied that he had earned the title of world's fastest man, having set a series of records. He took pride that he had "fulfilled and even exceeded the wonderful prophecy of my discoverer," Birdie Munger. His legacy seemed secure when a promoter contacted Taylor about a proposed $5,000 contract in a far-away land that had been visited by relatively few Americans. No Sunday racing was required. Taylor seized the opportunity. He told Daisy to think of it as "something in the nature of a honeymoon trip," and this time she would accompany her new husband.

# CHAPTER 18

# A Faraway Land

D aisy Victoria Taylor, raised by a single mother and then by an uncle, had worked as a housekeeper and church maid before she met Taylor. She walked along the edges of America's lines of color, proudly black, but, with her light skin and long hair, able to pass as white when needed to avoid racist encounters. She had spent most of her life in the background, serving others, but she was athletic and headstrong, and when she fell in love, she became surprised to find herself the center of attention—not only for her marriage to the famous Taylor, but also for her beauty, and for her style. Any notion that she preferred to be viewed as white was dashed when a prominent magazine called *The Colored American*, put her on its cover. The September 1902 issue showed her looking demurely downward, deep in thought, described as "Mrs. Marshall Walter Taylor—Mrs. Major Taylor." Inside, a full-page photo revealed her in a Victorian-style dress, fittingly, given her regal middle name. She wore a broad circular hat, a fringed gown that flowed to the floor, a ruffled top, and all manner of chains and jewelry. Taylor, by contrast, was only partly pictured, from the chest up, wearing a suit jacket and cravat. They were presented as the model couple in an article that ran nearly eleven pages. She was described, perhaps with some embellishment, as "the best all round girl athlete" in her youth. She was "averse to publicity," even as the magazine put her on its cover. Yet the magazine was not immune to accepting the kind of racist marketing that would later be decried;

219

it included an advertisement for "black skin remover," just like Taylor had used to such ill effect, promising to turn a black person five shades lighter to a "peach-like complexion." But the issue was filled with inspiration to "aim high . . . leave the vale of fear and doubting; sight the highlands, mount the crest!"

Taylor, by contrast to his wife, had been the subject of countless newspaper articles and photographs, yet he had an image as a solitary, driven figure, hardened by the hatred that he faced in so many corners of America. Daisy softened him, and as they prepared to take a journey across America and then the Pacific Ocean, their bond was evident. They traveled from Worcester to New York, and then switched trains and settled into a sleeping compartment for a transcontinental journey. They traversed the Plains and the Rockies, and arrived in San Francisco, where they boarded a steamship to take them to their destination on the other side of the world: Australia.

Taylor believed that this faraway land, a collection of six British self-governing colonies that had created the federation of Australia a year earlier, would welcome a black man even more readily than had been the case in Europe. But when Taylor walked up to the ticket booth in San Francisco to purchase passage on the RMS *Ventura*, the agent informed him there was a "rigid color line" in Australia. "This was the first intimation I had had that any such condition prevailed there and I was very much disturbed," Taylor wrote. The color line resulted from the Immigration Restriction Act, which later became known as the "White Australia" policy, which was aimed at preventing Chinese and Japanese laborers from taking jobs that Australian unions wanted to go to British migrants. The nation's aboriginal population of nearly one million, whose members were often referred to as black, suffered under the same kind of racism and removal policies that had forced the dislocation of Native Americans. There were few blacks of African descent in Australia. Learning about a color line, Taylor's "first thought" was to cancel the trip, fearful that he would not even be allowed to disembark. Indeed, at least one Australian newspaper expected Taylor to be turned away. But Taylor had a contract in hand, as well as a down payment, and he decided to persevere. After buying his tickets, he and Daisy headed to a hotel, only to be turned away because of their skin color. The couple was also refused service at a restaurant. With this bitter reminder of the policies of their home-land, the Taylors went without sleep or food as they waited to board the steamship on the following morning. Taylor assured Daisy that "if we could exist in America where race hatred and color prejudice are so rampant, we could undoubtedly get by in Australia." They boarded the steamship and "breathed a sigh of relief" as they sailed out of San Francisco Bay. But after a day at sea, both were terribly sick, and Taylor confessed, "for the first time in my life I was thoroughly discouraged," believing that "even nature had taken up the cudgels against us."

As the days passed, and their health improved, the Taylors fell into conversation with a ship's purser, who happened to come from Massa-chusetts and knew all about the cycling champion, and had even mem-orized his racing records. The purser introduced Taylor to a Catholic priest, who inquired about the racer's faith. "Well sir, I am a Baptist," Taylor responded. "Oh well," the priest joked, "I think you've got a chance." "Yes sir," Taylor responded, "I think I have got a chance, and a very good chance too." The purser told Taylor that while it was true that Australia had a color line, Taylor's reputation preceded him, and he needn't fear rejection.

A month after leaving San Francisco, on December 22, 1902, the RMS *Ventura* sailed through the Sydney Heads, dramatic sandstone promontories that thrust upward like a series of giant paws bursting from the seascape. It was on North Head where immigrants were quar-antined to prevent the spread of disease. As the *Ventura* sailed by the cliffs on the seven-mile journey through the harbor, Taylor and Daisy came to the deck and saw an astonishing sight. A veritable armada lay before them. Hundreds of boats bobbed in the harbor, cheered by thousands of people on the shore. For days, Taylor's arrival had been heralded in the newspapers, with stories about how he was being paid more than any sportsman in the nation's history to compete against Australia's best racers. Many Australians had never seen a black Amer-ican and came out of curiosity. The purser ran to Taylor and pointed over the railing to the many boats that flew the American flag in the racer's honor. "Do you hear those whistles and horns?" the purser asked. "Now do you think you will be allowed to land in Australia?"

"Taylor, Taylor!" the Australian sailors yelled. "Welcome, Major Taylor!"

Tears ran down Taylor's face, his wife at his side. Soon, the promoter who had brought him to Australia, a twenty-eight-year-old named Hugh D. "Huge Deal" McIntosh, climbed aboard the *Ventura*, along with a bevy of newspapermen, who listened to Taylor give an impromptu press conference. As the steamship docked, the Taylors were greeted by thousands more cheering people, and the couple was taken to the Hotel Metropole, where they were given a first-class suite, another stark contrast to Taylor's inability to find accommodation in so many American cities. Taylor was welcomed by Sydney's lord mayor, who wished Taylor success even as he hoped Australians would beat him, "although he realized that they had a very difficult task before them." Taylor delivered a speech in which he said he would try to live up to expectations, knowing that he had not trained on a bicycle for nearly two months. He promptly headed to Moore Park, where a concrete bicycle track was laid out, three laps to a mile, and banked to about thirty-five degrees. Grandstands that could hold more than twenty thousand people surrounded the oval. After several days of sightseeing, and receiving hundreds of invitations that he could not accommodate, Taylor began his rigorous preparation at the track at the Sydney cricket grounds. He took his place behind a motorized pacing bicycle, staying just behind and slightly off to the side, so close that his front wheel almost rubbed the one ahead of him. He leaned forward, back extended and flat, turning the pedals at an extraordinary pace, but also listening for danger ahead, smelling for a twitch in the engine. "He scents danger like a deer," wrote an Australian reporter after observing the training regimen. If Taylor felt something amiss, he inched to one side, ready to take an escape path if the pacer hesitated. Taylor's training speed was so consistent that it varied by only one second between rounds. He followed the pacer at one minute and thirty-three seconds, faster than observers had previously seen. Reporters were astonished that Taylor trained alongside his Australian opponents, having heard incorrectly that he preferred to prepare in secret. Australians impressed Taylor as unfailingly courteous, and he had "no worry" about racism. This, he wrote, "was a tremendous load lifted off my shoulders."

The country—its history, landscape, and people—fascinated Taylor as it had so many visitors. The continental United States and Australia were about the same size, but the former had 76 million people and the latter just 3.8 million. Most of Australia's population centered around cities near the coast, such as Sydney, Melbourne, and Adelaide, where Taylor would race; beyond that lay a stunning landscape of deserts, plateaus, mountains, basins, and plains. The next four months were some of the most pleasing and profitable of Taylor's career. The competitors were challenging and fair, the referees were unbiased, the public was adoring, and the press adulated him. The "Major Taylor Carnival," as Australians called some of the dozens of races in which he competed, was a sensation.

Daisy was delighted with Australia, thrilled with the respect given to her husband, and satisfied that she had made the right decision in traveling so far to be together. If he was treated as royalty, then so was she, right down to a carriage ride sponsored by the League of Victorian Wheelmen, rolling amid thousands of fans in the streets of Melbourne.

Taylor befriended the national champion of Australia, Don Walker, a handsome, muscular, mustachioed man who looked as if he just stepped from the Outback to the racing track. In their first competition, on January 3, 1903, Taylor, Walker, and a third racer, Bob Lewis, faced off in a quarter-mile sprint. The short race was Taylor's strongest suit, of course, and his competitors had heard about his famous "jump," in which he bolted so suddenly, jerking his handlebars, that his front wheel momentarily lifted from the ground. As the race rounded the first bend, Lewis held the lead. Then he felt something twitch; Taylor was too close behind and inadvertently bumped Lewis's rear wheel, but the two managed to stay upright. Walker, riding next to Taylor, was astonished that the American not only kept his balance but suddenly bolted ahead, victorious.

As Taylor took his victory lap, he withdrew an American flag that had been tucked into his jersey, and unfurled it as he rode around the track. This had been Taylor's standard practice in international meets, but Australians were offended. Thousands had been cheering his victory, but upon seeing the flag, they went mostly silent, seeing Taylor's behavior as unsportsmanlike crowing. Taylor was mortified at the negative reaction and stored the flag for the remainder of his time in Australia. Later that day, Taylor and Walker competed again, this time in a five-mile race that favored the Australian, who won easily. Afterward, Taylor and Walker gave interviews to a Sydney newspaper in which they heaped praise on each other. A bond was formed that would last for years, and Taylor would later say Walker was one of the finest competitors he had ever faced.

Taylor felt especially comfortable in Australia because he was widely congratulated for refusing to race on Sundays. Such contests had been banned in Australia, so Taylor didn't face the usual ridicule for skipping them. In one of his most revealing interviews, Taylor told a reporter for the *New South Wales Baptist* that he had lost the chance to win $30,000 by refusing to participate in Sunday contests. He did so, he explained, because Sunday cycling "has been responsible for a good deal of Sabbath desecration."

My people were very religious people. I was brought up Puritanical, and I've always tried to live up to it. . . . I attribute most of my success entirely to the fact that I have tried to do what was right—live fairly and squarely by every man—and any man who follows these principles is bound to succeed. The fact that I am brought among worldly people all the time—people who are inclined to look the other way—makes the fact stand out, perhaps. But I hope I have not conveyed any impression that I think myself better than anybody else. . . . I have done it because I believed it to be pleasing in the sight of God . . . when a man fears God he has no other fears, and fears nobody else. . . . God has always taken care of me, and I believe He always will.

Taylor even took the unusual step of speaking from the pulpit at churches on Sunday wherever he was in Australia, a practice that was duly reported in newspapers in Australia and back home, where the *New York Times* said in its headline that Taylor was "winning races and preaching." After a triumphant tour through Sydney, Melbourne, and Adelaide, where he won the majority of his races, Taylor left Australia with a "fortune," as the *Times* put it, estimating that an American racer in Australia could earn "far more than the best paid editors, university professors, or nine-tenths of the legal profession." Taylor wrote that he netted $10,735 in his Australia tour, and the *Washington Post* estimated he earned $25,000 by year's end. He could have made even more, but he refused to enter a $5,000 race because it would have required him to work in cahoots with other racers to produce a predetermined winner. Asked during his Australian tour about his refusal to collude, Taylor responded, "Sometimes they say to me, 'Major, how do manage to get along as you do? You never work in with any other rider on the track.'" Taylor had spent so many years having riders work in concert against him that he had no choice but to ride for himself, and in the end, that is what helped make him such a strong rider. It also meant that, when others succeeded in colluding against him, he was out of races from the start. Still, Taylor told the inquisitor that he was mistaken to say there was no friend on the track. "I always have a Friend who looks after me," Taylor said, and his meaning was as clear as his faith.

As Taylor competed overseas, a man named Branch Rickey coached the Ohio Wesleyan University baseball team. In May 1903, as the team checked into a hotel in South Bend, Indiana, to play Notre Dame, their only black player was denied a room. Rickey arranged for the player, catcher Charles Thomas, to share his room. He heard Thomas crying later that night, rubbing his hands and repeating: "Black skin, black hands. If only I could make them white."

As Rickey later told the story, he told Thomas to "snap out of it," promising, "We'll lick this one day." That day would not come until forty-two years later, when Rickey, as president of the Brooklyn Dodgers, signed Jackie Robinson, who played in the minor leagues and then debuted on the major league club in 1947. Rickey cited Thomas as his inspiration for breaking the color barrier.

Taylor, meanwhile, kept winning races, setting the stage for the legendary athletes who followed him.

Four months after his grand arrival in Sydney, Taylor and his wife departed from Melbourne, aboard the French mail steamer *Ville de la Ciotat*, and headed for Europe. They had become entranced with Australia's colorful wildlife, and they filled several cages with parrots, cockatoos, and other animals. As the steamship approached its scheduled stop in Bombay, India, where 150 cases of apples were to be delivered, it was stalled by mechanical problems. As repairs were made, Taylor visited the bustling city of 812,000 people. Across the harbor, Taylor could see the final days of construction of the city's finest hostelry, the Taj Mahal Palace Hotel, with its 240-foot-high central dome serving as a beacon to sailors. India was the pride of the British Empire, and Bombay was its vibrant, chaotic center, overflowing with masses of the poor, many of whom served the powerful elite of the military and merchant class. Carriages and ox-drawn carts rattled down the avenues, past the bazaars, picking up customers at the docks. The city was a melting pot of cultures and religions and ethnic groups, but also had its segregated quarters for Europeans, among others. Hints of anger at British rule could be found, if one listened to speeches or read the newspapers, but London saw little threat.

Taylor, unexpectedly given the chance to set foot in India, was greeted by local officials, who "lionized" him and gave him an ebony cane, which became one of his most-prized possessions. After repairs, the ship resumed its journey and headed through the Red Sea. To the west, Taylor could see the African continent, from which his ancestors had been stolen into slavery, and to the east, the Arabian Peninsula. The ship sailed through the Suez Canal, and then headed into the Mediterranean Sea, past Greece and Italy, and arrived in Marseilles.

The Taylors made their way to Paris, and a race was scheduled for the following morning. Taylor had no time to get in shape, and he fared poorly for several weeks as he traveled across Europe for a series of contests. He left Daisy behind at a hotel on Boulevard Malesherbes in the care of a Mrs. Dennis, who provided music lessons. Taylor competed from England to Austria, sending postcards with brief greetings to Daisy at every stop. "Wish you were here," Taylor wrote from the Hotel Continental in Vienna. "Will see you Wednesday," he wrote from Dresden, Germany. "Good morning," he wrote from Rotterdam, Holland. "Hope you are well," he told her from Geneva, Switzerland. "Don't sleep too much," he wrote from an Austrian village. He sent pictures of merchants in Belgium, and gardens in Denmark. Gradually he began winning, beating several of his nemeses, including Edmond Jacquelin of France and an English champion.

Returning to Paris, Taylor doted on Daisy. The couple took in the sights, walked through the Jardin des Tuileries, visited galleries, and ascended the steps to Montmartre. With his elegant wife by his side, flush with his winnings and wealthier than ever, Taylor splurged. They went shopping along the Avenue des Champs Élysée, where Daisy bought an assortment of dresses, skirts, and camisoles. Taylor was enticed into a Renault showroom and, after test-driving the roadster around the Arc d'Triomphe, became one of the first Americans to buy a French car.

In late September, returning to the United States aboard the *Kaiser Wilhelm der Grosse*, the Taylors unloaded their seventeen suitcases, shipped the car and cages of animals to Worcester, and took the train home. As Taylor stepped onto the platform at Worcester's Union Station, clasping the ebony cane that been given to him in India, he declared that he would enter "positive retirement." The headlines greeting his arrival did not exaggerate: "Returns with Honor and Cash: Major Taylor at Home From One of the Most Successful Tours of the World Ever Made by an Athlete." He was leaving on top, just as his idol, Arthur Zimmerman, had admonished him to do. Yes, he conceded, he had previously insisted he was retiring and then spent most of the year in Australia and Europe, but this was different. Bicycle racing was declining in the United States, he said, declaring that the "automobile has gained a firm hold everywhere." He wanted to settle down, have a family, and go into the automobile business himself. Newspapers across the country ran headlines that said "Major Taylor Quits Riding." He left a few weeks later on a trip for Buffalo, working for an auto company. Taylor and Daisy began renovations on their home, anticipating that they would add a baby to their family. Everything indicated Taylor would indeed call an end to his glorious career. He seemed content, riding around Worcester "in his imported automobile with his poodle dog," as one newspaper put it.

Then, as Taylor was resting at home in early November, he received a cable from "Huge Deal" McIntosh. Come back to Australia, the promoter implored, and you will earn even more than last time. The pull of Australia—the money, the acceptance, the lack of overt racism against him—all of it played with Taylor's emotions. His trip to Buffalo made him realize that he was not ready to give up cycling. He now had before him an offer that would pay him far more for a few months of racing than he likely could earn in several years of work for a manufacturer. Then there was the timing: ahead of him lay either the deep freeze of a Worcester winter, or a profitable few months of racing during the Australian summer. Daisy, having been the toast of Sydney and Paris, and perhaps unready to return so quickly to the provincial life of Worcester, must have urged on her husband. Taylor negotiated an even better arrangement than before, with fewer races and more money. McIntosh, as his nickname suggested, signed off on the huge deal. Taylor could not refuse. "It was like passing up too good a thing," he said in a story headlined "Taylor Not to Retire," which contradicted everything he had vowed just a few weeks earlier. A day after the cable arrived, Taylor and his wife were again bound for San Francisco.

As the Taylors boarded the steamship, Daisy was three months pregnant. This was hardly ideal timing, given the propensity of both husband and wife for seasickness, but the couple kept their plan. Taylor anticipated that the highlight would be a rematch against the national champion, Don Walker. He did not know that one of his bitterest rivals was awaiting him, plotting a sensational contest.

• • •

Floyd McFarland had followed the story of Taylor's financial windfall in Australia with intense interest and jealousy. He tried to land a contract to race in Australia, but could get nothing like the guaranteed fee that had been offered to Taylor. He could come, but his earnings would be based on how many races he won. He would need a huge purse to make it worthwhile. His protégé, Iver Lawson, the "Big Swede" who made his home in Salt Lake City, was planning to race in Australia, and McFarland decided to join him. For several weeks, the pair trained in Australia. They heard the news that Taylor had announced his retirement. Then they heard that McIntosh had enticed Taylor to race once again in Australia. At some point, McIntosh agreed with McFarland and Lawson that they should face Taylor. There is no evidence that Taylor was informed of this idea before he boarded the steamship in San Francisco, but McIntosh made clear Taylor had no choice other than to accept the challenge.

Taylor's second tour of Australia unfolded nothing like the first. He was not greeted by a welcoming armada, or lauded for his religious beliefs. Instead, a number of newspapers questioned why a black man was being allowed into the country that had "white Australia" anti-immigration laws. "He should be doubly challenged by the Australian Government laws—as a colored alien and immigrant under contract," wrote *The Bulletin*, whose motto was "Australia for Australians" (which was later changed to "Australia for the White Man"). Taylor was portrayed as "sanctimonious," and his religious beliefs were satirized. A cartoon mocked him with an illustration of his arms crossed and a halo-like bicycle wheel above his head. He was caricatured with the worst black stereotypes. Critics questioned why he had been guaranteed so much money and suggested that he was in effect taking cash out of the pockets of Australians. The match was promoted as a contest of white versus black. "Will the Brilliant 'Major' Succeed in Outgeneraling His Mighty Opponent?" said a poster that hung throughout Melbourne. "Or Will the Human Motor's Truly Phenomenal Stamina Wear the 'Major' Down?"

Amid all of this, as Daisy's pregnancy dominated his concerns,

Taylor learned that he would have to face McFarland. Interviewed in his dressing room shortly after his arrival in Australia, his body still glistening from a rubdown, Taylor allowed that McFarland "is better than anything you have got in Australia."

On the Saturday evening of February 13, Taylor entered a Melbourne oval cycling arena, where twenty thousand people teemed in the grandstands, shouting for local favorites. A series of stanchions, topped with powerful lights, ringed the velodrome, illuminating Taylor as he took his mark at the starting line. In the seven weeks since Taylor's arrival in Australia, this day had been marked on many calendars, a contest that was billed throughout the country as one of the greatest ever to be held. The crowd knew both competitors well by now. Taylor had kept on winning, just as he had the year before on his triumphal tour of the country, and as he had in a series of contests since arriving in late December. Just a week earlier, he had been on this track, facing an old rival, the "Big Swede," Iver Lawson—who would later in the year be crowned world champion—and beat him in two straight races.

Now, as Taylor looked askance, he saw the man that he blamed for much of his troubles in the United States, the man who encouraged other Americans to collude against him, and who regularly called Taylor "nigger" and threatened him with bodily harm. Here was the man who, a year earlier, Taylor had tried to hit with a two-by-four before seeking protection from the police.

The contest would be decided by winning two matches out of three. Taylor and McFarland took their positions, and the scene was set: deafening noise, bright lights, two of the world's best racers and most bitter rivals. The motorized pacing machines roared into action, leading out Taylor and McFarland. The spectators anticipated a flat-out sprint, as did Taylor. McFarland often tried to wear out his opponents, setting a blistering pace from the start. Taylor preferred the chess match, urging his opponent to take the lead, setting off the proverbial cat-and-mouse game. McFarland was determined to beat Taylor at his own strategy. He wouldn't sprint at the start. He inched up and down the banking, daring Taylor to go first and set the pace. No one played this better than Taylor. He employed his array of tricks learned in his youth, practically standing still on a bike by balancing on the pedals, cycling backward—anything to avoid setting an initial pace. McFarland was all brute strength and could not match Taylor in his tactics. Finally, they took off and Taylor held a slight lead for three laps. Then, as the pacers pulled away, Taylor pedaled up the banking, but McFarland refused to follow. Taylor slowly came down at an angle, another chess move. Without warning, McFarland attacked, pedaling at full speed, sensing his moment. Taylor was ready, pleased to be slightly behind, preparing for his jump. The two screamed into a straightaway. McFarland sped ahead. Taylor's jump never seemed to come. The crowd roared as McFarland crossed first over the finish line. This was not the Australia tour that Taylor had envisioned.

Taylor had to win the next heat to keep the contest alive. This time, there were no pacing machines. McFarland bolted at the start, leaving Taylor slightly behind. Then McFarland urged Taylor to take the lead, a common switch to conserve energy. Taylor refused. McFarland slowed, then climbed the banking, followed by Taylor. McFarland stalled into a track stand, but Taylor knew this trick better, and was nearly statuesque. McFarland, disgusted, reached for a light post, grabbed it, and glared at Taylor, who responded by steadying himself against a fence. Taylor "can crawl, stand still, go astern, and generally cavort as though standing on shoe leather," a journalist at the scene wrote. "Not so with McFarland. His rugged determination permits of no tricks of that sort." Suddenly McFarland pushed off from the light post, thrust down the banking, and flew toward the straightway. Taylor, lacking the leveraged push off, strained to follow. McFarland was ahead, but the referee had enough of the strange tactics. He whistled and called for the race to reset.

McFarland took the lead. Then Taylor. Back and forth it went. The final lap approached. The winner was often determined by who had the best jump, and the best legs, at this crucial point. McFarland surged forward, full speed, and Taylor struggled to keep pace. He could not find his jump; his wheel skidded twice as he tried to force his way forward. Ten yards to go, and Taylor was behind by more than a length. It seemed clear McFarland had him. Taylor suddenly found his strength, bolting forward. But McFarland raised his hand, declaring victory at the finish line.

As a reporter later put it, "Nineteen thousand, nine hundred and ninety-seven men and women said, 'McFarland,' and turned over their programmes for the next event."

Then, to the astonishment of the crowd, the judges seated at the finish line pronounced their verdict. Slowly the crowd saw two words posted on the board:

"Dead heat."

One of the judges later explained that five yards before the finish, "McFarland was leading by a wheel, but Taylor was going at twice the speed. At every revolution of his wheels he was perceptibly gaining. Both crossed the mark simultaneously . . . Taylor's last kick did it. His sprint was wonderful."

The crowd could not believe it. Yells of rage and violent threats arose against the judges. McFarland and Taylor initially were unaware no victor had been declared. McFarland "positively beamed" and felt he had won. Taylor looked crestfallen, believing he had been beaten. McFarland reached out for Taylor's hand, and Taylor returned the grasp.

Then, in another instant, McFarland realized that a dead heat had been declared. There would be no prize of thousands of dollars. Confusion reigned, and other races were held. Many in the crowd assumed Taylor and McFarland would return for a deciding match, but McFarland would not have it, convinced he had been cheated. "I've won the match, and I'm going home," he said. The crowd "swarmed over the fence and into the arena," and some ran for the judges as a ringleader shouted "thieves and rogues!" The crowd dispersed, and the judges issued an invitation for a rematch in four days. McFarland continued to insist he had won and that Taylor had congratulated him. "He rode up to me on the back stretch, took my hand and said, 'It was a good race, but you beat me,'" McFarland said. "There was a gross injustice done me last night. I beat him by full two and half feet. I want to say this about Taylor. He is a good sportsman . . . it was a big event in my life to beat Major Taylor, and it knocked out the idea that we have no chance against him alone." Taylor publicly said the judges had the best view of the finish and suggested the matter would be settled by a rematch. McFarland reluctantly agreed.

Nothing went as expected on the evening of the rematch. McFarland said he was too ill to race, which turned out to be a lie; he was perfectly healthy and eating a sumptuous dinner. The rules said that if one of the racers didn't show up, the other won by forfeit. So it seemed Taylor would win. But first, Taylor had to compete in a preliminary contest against McFarland's protégé, Iver Lawson.

Taylor beat Lawson in a close first race of a two-out-of-three contest. In the second heat, Taylor and Lawson were almost abreast when Taylor made his jump. His bike skidded and Taylor recovered, and the two again were even. Then as the two headed toward the finish, their bicycles collided. Taylor suddenly, violently, hit the track, writhing in pain. Lawson won the match while Taylor "lay helpless for several minutes." An arm and thigh were deeply lacerated, and a deep layer of skin on one of his legs had been shorn. It was one of the worst crashes of his career. McFarland now suddenly recovered from his supposed illness, and he showed up for his race, claiming that Taylor had caused the crash and forfeited the match. The judges, however, determined that McFarland had faked his illness and refused to award him a victory. Taylor filed a complaint against Lawson for illegally cutting him off, and the judges agreed, saying that Lawson's action could have caused injuries that ended Taylor's career or even killed him. Lawson was initially banned from sanctioned races for a year, an extraordinary penalty later reduced to three months. Taylor suspected that McFarland had ordered Lawson to cut off Taylor and thus cause the crash.

Taylor's body was so thick with bandages that he could barely put on his clothes. Every movement was painful. Promoters came daily, asking whether he might be able to compete in two weeks at a race in Adelaide, where he would have another chance to race against

McFarland. Taylor's doctors said no. Daisy, now six months pregnant, pleaded with him to stay off the track. McFarland, told that Taylor might try to compete against him, said, "It is almost impossible. All the skin is off his thigh, and he can't sit in the saddle."

Taylor sat in his room in Melbourne, depressed at being unable to race, and wouldn't listen. For two weeks, he lay in bed, fuming, thinking about the chance to get his revenge against McFarland. Against all wisdom, barely able to walk, he left the bustling Victorian city and boarded the Intercolonial Express. The overnight train rattled through the countryside for nearly five hundred miles and arrived in the South Australia capital of Adelaide, a city of 162,000 by St. Vincent Gulf.

After a sleepless night on the train, still limping from his injuries, Taylor went directly to the track. Word of Taylor's surprise appearance had spread overnight, and twenty thousand people filled the stands. As the crowd shouted his name, Taylor hunkered behind a grandstand with a trainer. With great pain, he took off his street clothes, revealing a mummy-like swath of bandages. He could barely move his legs. There was only one solution. He ordered the trainer to take off the bandages. Scabs had formed over bruises on his right leg, arm, and hip, limiting movement. The trainer performed a "painful operation" of removing skin and enabling Taylor to flex his arms and legs. The trainer lifted Taylor onto the bicycle, clasped shoes to the pedals, and slowly moved him back and forth, testing flexibility until a full revolution was possible. "This operation caused me great pain, and also made me bleed profusely from the injuries," Taylor wrote later. However, once the scabs were moved, "I could use my legs as freely as ever." The trainer dabbed cotton on the fresh blood. Then Taylor slowly made his way onto the racing oval, greeted by such a thunderous ovation that he momentarily forgot his injuries.

After testing his strength in preliminary bouts, Taylor sat in his dressing room when another rider approached with a secret. The rider, Bill MacDonald, had learned that McFarland had concocted a plan with other racers to ensure that Taylor could not win the one-mile championship, and he offered to help Taylor counter the strategy. Taylor thanked MacDonald for the warning but said that he preferred to win "single-handed."

Taylor and McFarland and other racers lined up for the mile championship race later that day. Taylor felt strong, hanging in second place for much of the race. As the bell rang, signaling the final lap, Taylor and McFarland prepared to jump ahead of the field. Then Taylor spied MacDonald, who had tipped him off about McFarland's plan to have other riders trap him in a pocket to ensure that McFarland would win. MacDonald sprinted at full speed, and Taylor suddenly sprang forward to cling to his wheel, but he still found himself trapped. Taylor glimpsed McFarland surging, making "a terrific bolt for the tape." Now Taylor made the move for which he was famous, shooting through a narrow inside opening, escaping from the pocket. McFarland was just ahead. Taylor pushed harder, fresh blood oozing where the skin had been torn, and caught up with McFarland, and the two tore around the homestretch. Taylor churned, found a strength deep within, and barely surged past McFarland at the finish line.

The crowd roared, standing on their seats, waving hats, as the band played "Stars and Stripes Forever," a John Philip Sousa march composed eight years earlier. Taylor "trembled with emotion" as race officials placed an enormous bouquet of roses on his handlebars, and the American flag was raised. It was the "wildest scene" Taylor said he had ever seen, "the most dramatic and thrilling incident of my racing career."

McFarland was enraged, claiming to race officials that he wanted to file a protest, charging that Taylor had colluded with others against him. Taylor was bemused that McFarland, "the arch conspirator," would make such a charge. "Imagine a man of McFarland's makeup charging anybody with collusion," Taylor wrote. The judges dismissed the claim, and McFarland stalked off the track, shouting at Taylor that he would "get" him if tried to start in another race against him that day, which Taylor had no intention of doing.

Taylor raced for another two months, while Daisy remained in Melbourne, preparing to give birth. He proposed that they leave for Sydney for the delivery and presumed it would be a boy. He suggested that the child be named Major Sydney Taylor, after the father and the city where he would be born. "Of course," Taylor wrote, "he was going to be a champion bicycle rider." The child was born on May 11, 1904, but he would not be named Major. "This child can never be the great sprinter you are," the doctor told Taylor. "Why?" Taylor asked. "Because it's a girl," the doctor replied. She was christened Rita Sydney Taylor, forever known as Sydney, and would live her own extraordinary life, to the age of 101 years old. She was, Taylor wrote, "the greatest prize of all."

Three weeks later, Taylor, Daisy, and their newborn boarded a steamship for the journey home, accompanied by Australian champion Don Walker. Taylor had regaled Walker with tales of America, and they had all planned to spend time in California. But when they arrived in San Francisco, Walker was dismayed by what he witnessed. It was a "new epidemic of Colorphobia," as Taylor put it. The Taylors were blocked from staying at one hotel after another, "insulted," and refused service at restaurants. Boarding a hotel bus at the Pacific Street wharf, Taylor was told by the driver that the effort was fruitless. "No use taking you up; there will be no room for you at the hotel," the driver said. A policeman told Taylor where he could find lodging for "colored guests," but Taylor with "a haughty glare" dismissed the suggestion that he accept racism, saying, "Not my kind of hotels."

The family searched for hours trying to find accommodations, to no avail. At one point, they encountered a man who believed that Daisy was white, and he insulted her for walking with a black man. Taylor told Daisy to take their child and go with Walker around the corner. After they were out of sight, Taylor confronted the man who had insulted his wife. A fight broke out, and Taylor "flattened him," his daughter was told years later.

Anxious to provide food for Daisy and his baby, Taylor came up with a plan. The entourage went to a restaurant where they had been denied service, and Walker went inside, reserving a large table and ordering lunch for himself and the Taylors. He paid the check when the food arrived, then fetched the Taylors, much to the "shock" of the waitresses. They gave up trying to find a place to spend the night, taking the midnight train for New York. Taylor's treatment was investigated by the *San Francisco Call*, which published a story headlined "Taylor's Money of No Account; Negro Bicycle Champion Finds That San Francisco Draws the Color Line; Cuts Short His Stay; Local Hotel and Restaurant Decline Patronage of Man Australia Lionized."

Walker was appalled.

"So this is America about which you have been boasting in Australia?" he asked Taylor. "From what I have seen of it in the past few days, I cannot understand why you were in such a hurry to get back home here. Do you prefer to live in a country where you are treated like this than to live in my country where you are so well thought of, and where you are treated like a white man, and where many inducements were made you to return to live? I cannot understand this kind of thing."

Taylor confessed that he was "unable to explain" the situation, and "the more I tried to smooth matters over, the more incensed he became."

Taylor stressed over the years that many white people had "sacrificed everything for Negros," including for him, none more so than his old friend Birdie Munger. He did not, however, hide his bitterness about how whites generally treated blacks. By now he could draw on his experiences in dozens of states, in Canada, in numerous European countries, a port of call in India, and in Australia. He had traveled hundreds of thousands of miles around the globe, by horse, car, train, and ship. He had competed against dozens of opponents in front of audiences that totaled hundreds of thousands of people. Few individuals of any race had traveled so broadly or seen so many cultures. Blacks "do not hate white people or others, but white people as a race do hate Negroes because of color," he wrote. "I am a Negro in every sense of the word and I am not sorry that I am. Personally, however, I have no great admiration for white people as a whole, because I am satisfied that they have no great admiration for me or my group as a whole." Reflecting years later on how he was so often mistreated, Taylor wrote that he kept in mind the words of Booker T. Washington: "I shall allow no man to narrow my soul and drag me down, by making me hate him."

Still, as he returned to Worcester, all the odium was about to take its toll.

## CHAPTER 19

# The Changing World

To know where one is in time is the essential tenet of racing a bicycle, either against the clock or an opponent, for to expend oneself too soon, or too late, can be the difference between victory or loss. The seconds expire relentlessly, and judgment is often difficult. So, too, for the bicyclist, in the race with time itself—are the body and mind still able and going, or has the inevitable decline begun?

As his Australian tour concluded, and 1904 lay before him, Taylor confronted such questions. His mind and body had taken enormous punishment for the past decade. There was the training, the travel, the racing, the crashes from the bike, and the psychic abrasion of confronting racism. It was draining to battle both hatred and the fiercest athletes. Taylor had already agreed to race another season in Europe, but he now had doubts about his ability. The popularity of automobile contests (and even days-long races such as the Tour de France that began in 1903) threatened to eclipse Taylor's specialty of velodrome-based cycling as a sport that mattered to the masses. He took long walks, drove his Renault around Worcester, and spent time with Daisy and Sydney. He had been racing since he was a child, he had traveled the globe twice in the past eighteen months, and his body and mind seemed to say, all at once, enough. "Not long after I reached my home in Worcester," Taylor later admitted, "I suffered a collapse and narrowly averted a nervous breakdown."

After consulting with his doctor, he reneged on his agreement to race in Europe. Robert Coquelle, the French promoter, had no choice but to sue Taylor for a $10,000 breach of contract. The American cycling association, which sanctioned races, suspended Taylor's license on the grounds that he had broken his contract. Taylor suddenly was at great financial risk, but he felt there was no way out. He was simply too exhausted and broken down. For three years he battled his demons, remained in Worcester, put on weight, and seemed forgotten.

As the bicycle boom faded and the automobile age blossomed, Birdie Munger embraced the changing world. He opened his auto business in a four-story building by the 12th Avenue docks, at 52nd Street in New York City. Munger was one of the earliest auto dealers in what had been "a thoroughly lifeless district" by the Hudson River docks, but within three years, there was "almost a solid line of motor vehicle signs" from 42nd Street to 72nd Street, known as Automobile Row, the *New York Times* reported. Just four years earlier, only eight thousand automobiles were registered in the United States. Now there were fifty-five thousand, and the American car industry pronounced itself on a par with European makers.

Munger had already spent hundreds of thousands of dollars on a new type of tire, and his fight over patents was winding its way through the courts. His new business involved assembling and selling the finest cars, which he displayed in one of the city's most lavish auto showrooms. Munger, for example, often imported a French-made chassis and finished it into an auto ready for American sales. He also specialized in retrofitting cars into more stylish vehicles for the wealthiest Americans. Among his clients was John Jacob Astor IV, who was known for building the Astoria Hotel in New York City (later joined with the Waldorf), but whose background also included his 1898 invention of a bicycle brake.

A glimpse into the life of Birdie Munger at this time can be seen from a lawsuit that was filed against his company by a wealthy buyer who felt he had been overcharged for his car. The buyer asked Munger to assemble one of the most expensive vehicles available in 1906.

Munger looked over the body, which had just been delivered from overseas for retrofitting at his factory, and said, "Well, you have got a great car there. That is the greatest piece of machinery I ever did see." After inspecting the vehicle further, Munger concluded, "I know you can go 90 miles an hour with her and I believe you can go 120." The buyer was stunned. There were few roads capable of enabling a driver to maintain that speed safely, and the newspapers were filled with stories of auto accidents. "I believe that is a little too fast," the buyer responded. Munger told the buyer not to worry: "You can go 90 miles easily." The old racer had not lost his love of speed.

A magazine called *Brooklyn Life* said Munger's firm was "among the most prominent" auto builders in New York, with "one of the most complete plants" and "very high class" mechanics. "It is worth a visit to such a plant for educational purposes alone," the magazine said. "From the machine shop in the basement to the paint shop on the top floor, everything is systematized and every piece of work has its specialists." But trouble loomed in other parts of Munger's business. His tire manufacturing company was in bankruptcy and he continued battling industry titans over the right to profit from his patents.

Taylor's financial troubles also mounted. He knew he could solve everything by agreeing to race in Europe, but for three years he had refused. Racial tensions escalated dramatically during Taylor's hiatus. In September 1906, unsubstantiated reports that black men had raped four white women in Atlanta led to race riots in which at least twenty-five African Americans and two whites died. In Mississippi, the white-nationalist governor, James K. Vardaman, said, "If it is necessary every Negro in the state will be lynched; it will be done to maintain white supremacy." In Brownsville, Texas, where the mostly black 25th United States Infantry Regiment was stationed, African American soldiers were accused without evidence of assaulting a white woman and injuring a white police officer. No arrests were made. Still, President Roosevelt, despite a plea from Booker T. Washington, supported the military's decision to dismiss all 167 black soldiers, including six Medal of Honor winners. Roosevelt's action was harshly

condemned by the black press, which viewed it as a transparent effort
to woo southern whites in the midterm elections. The warm memory
among blacks about Roosevelt's dinner with Washington at the White
House had been replaced by the reality that African Americans were
being increasingly politically isolated in a worsening racial climate.

Taylor, meanwhile, had given up on the possibility that he could be
fairly treated on an American racetrack. Then, in 1907, as the financial
pressure became unbearable, Coquelle showed up at Taylor's doorstep.
The French promoter had long been looking for ways to settle his suit
against Taylor and bring the racing star back to France. In a reprise
of many prior conversations, Coquelle told Taylor he had to race on
Sundays. "Like many other men before me I felt I was caught in a
'jam,'" Taylor recalled. He wanted the suit ended, fearing he would
lose much of his savings. "I thought of my wife and child," he wrote,
and "I weakened, as better men have done, and signed the agreement
that demanded my racing on Sunday."

Daisy had urged Taylor to take the contract, not just because of
financial need but also to end his suffering. "It was I who advised my
husband to go back," Daisy told a French newspaper in one of her rare
public comments about him. "I believe that a man at his age cannot
and should not remain inactive. He is too young to retire. And, as
nature gratified him with exceptional means, he must take advantage
of it. This job is very agreeable and is not really within the reach of
everyone in society."

Taylor stepped onto a scale and found that he weighed 198
pounds, heavy for a twenty-eight-year-old who stood five feet seven,
not to mention one seeking to be a world-class athlete. Six years earlier, arriving for the first time in Paris, he was a svelte 154 pounds.
Now his flabby stomach jutted over his belt like a pillow, and his arms
and legs had long since lost their sculpted shape. He was nothing like
the physical specimen who had astounded French doctors and made
him an iconic figure in Parisian magazines. Unless he lost 26 pounds
in a few months—still giving him a somewhat high racing weight of
172 pounds—he had no chance to compete. It was too cold to ride his
bicycle in Worcester, so, for several weeks, Taylor went on long walks

and held extended rounds of boxing matches with a sparring partner, sweating away the fat, strengthening his muscles. He lost 14 pounds. He would have to shed the rest in Paris, with Daisy and four-year-old Sydney by his side. Finally, Taylor's comeback was under way.

"The Resurrection of the Negro" announced *L'Auto,* drumming up publicity for Taylor's return. Yet as Taylor stepped onto the docks at the port of Le Havre, French journalists were shocked at his poor shape. Some wrote dismissive articles, saying he was "heavy" and "completely finished." Taylor, who thrived on being told he had no chance, made the insults part of his motivation. "I have not neglected anything to keep my muscles strong and flexible," Taylor said, insisting he had been boxing and cycling. In any case, "it's not necessary to make a lot of money." In fact, he did need to make money, but he seemed more focused on his mental state. The European tour, he said, was "just to distract me."

Arriving at the Gare Saint-Lazare, he was met by the promoter, Coquelle, and recognized by many travelers. The French greeted him warmly, but some Americans waiting for their luggage did "not hesitate to shout loudly that it's shameful to make such a reception to a Negro." A photographer snapped a picture of the elegantly dressed family, setting off a magnesium flash that frightened little Sydney. The photo was published in *L'Auto* under the headline "Major Taylor est arrivé!" Taylor checked into his hotel on the Rue des Mathurins, showing his wife and daughter to the room. Before long, however, a number of Americans staying there complained to the manager, saying they would refuse to stay in the same building with a black family. The *directeur d'hotel* promptly capitulated, ordering the Taylors to leave. Taylor was used to this treatment in America, particularly in the South, but he had stayed at the finest hotels in Europe and never been refused. Taylor was "furious," threatening to leave Paris for a city where he was welcome. His French promoters convinced him to stay and found lodgings in a "magnificent apartment" at 89 Avenue de Neuilly, near the Bois de Boulogne. The next day, many of the Paris newspapers were filled with outrage, saying it was the first time in memory that a hotel had evicted a family based on the color of their skin. Taylor, in one of the more memorable comments of his career, lectured the French that they had forsaken their history.

"In America, it would not surprise me at all, but in the country that made the Revolution and proclaimed rights of man, it overwhelms me," he said. He blamed it on the American guests and the hotel manager. It would not make him "hate the French," he said, promising to work hard and regain the racing form that had once dazzled the nation.

Taylor continued his boxing regimen, and after six weeks had lost the twenty-six pounds that he needed to shed. But too much of that weight loss came from muscle, not just fat, and it left Taylor too weak to compete effectively.

As Taylor prepared for his first race, Parisian newspapers touted a new rivalry, pitting Taylor against the current French champion Gabriel Poulain. The buildup drew tremendous interest. "For a month now, we've been talking only about a match that would bring together the famous American negro Major Taylor and the best racer on the European tracks, the Frenchman Poulain," said *Le Petit Journal*. The newspaper said Taylor looked "supple" during training, and many believed that Poulain "would succumb, despite all his efforts, to his black opponent." Taylor made a comment about the thinness of Poulain's legs, which the Frenchman interpreted as a taunt and vowed to "avenge" Taylor "by beating him," *Le Petit Journal* said. As Taylor and Poulain lined up for the match before thousands on a sunny May day at the Parc des Princes velodrome, it was clear Taylor had underestimated how much work remained to get back in racing shape. He seemed listless and unfocused. Three times, he began the race by falling in the first leg, and the match was restarted. Finally, on the fourth try, Taylor remained upright but lost badly. He would have to win the next two out of three in order to claim victory.

The second match began in Taylor's favor, and he beat Poulain. But the judges ruled that Poulain's bicycle had malfunctioned and ordered a new contest. Given a reprieve, Poulain bolted from the start, led most of the way, and easily beat Taylor. It was a humbling, humiliating start to Taylor's European tour, and it got worse as he lost his next five contests. Critics in the French press belittled his form and his fitness and suggested his career was over. Taylor was torn. He went to Daisy and told her that he had fulfilled his contractual obligation, and said they could head back to Worcester whenever she wanted. But Taylor left no doubt of his desire, telling her that he felt he was "striking my winning form" and wanted to stay.

"To leave on such a failure," Taylor wrote in a French newspaper at the time, would be "too stupid." He did not want to give satisfaction to either the Paris journalists who had doubted his abilities, or American competitors "who would have enjoyed these successive defeats." Daisy, who seemed to enjoy Paris more than any place she had lived, readily agreed. A photographer captured the family inspecting the racetrack, all three finely dressed: Taylor in a three-piece suit, tie, and hat; Daisy in a full-length dress and elegant hat; and Sydney in a lacy headdress. One photo showed Taylor lofting Sydney as the child points skyward. Daisy and Sydney attended many of Taylor's Paris matches, sitting amid crowds of more than ten thousand people, an experience that Sydney would vividly recall to the author of this book when she was ninety-six years old. "I can remember shouting, 'Daddy! Daddy!' and all the applause," she said.

Heartened by his wife's support and anxious to excel in front of his daughter, and finally regaining his strength and his form, Taylor began winning. By early August, he was ready for a rematch with Poulain. To Taylor's delight, a familiar face appeared in Paris to witness the contest. Birdie Munger was in the city, meeting with some of his French auto suppliers. In early August, Munger watched Taylor beat Émile Friol, the reigning world champion. Taylor's comeback was complete, and it seemed no coincidence that one of his crowning moments had come in front of his mentor. His reputation had been restored, and he took delight in taunting "the unjust journalists who did not trust me this year." He wrote in a Paris newspaper that he had "regularly beat the best men in Europe" and could proudly return to the United

States and not fear that critics would "make fun of the negro on his arrival." Now, he wrote, he planned to go back to his "little home" with enough money "to live quietly between my wife and my little Sydney." One day, Taylor wrote in *La Vie au Grand Air*, he would tell his daughter that "far away there in Paris there are good friends who have been so kind to her dad." Sydney, he wrote, "will like the French." The family headed to Le Havre, sailed home, and Taylor once again said he would retire.

For five years, as his name was honored throughout Europe and Australia, Taylor had refused to race in the United States, in spite of countless offers. He finally gave in as the calendar turned to 1908, signing a contract with a Boston promoter shortly after he turned twenty-nine years old. He left Worcester in January and trained for weeks, spurring intense coverage about the return of the man who was described in the *Boston Globe* as "the only colored man who can ride as a professional in this country," referring to a license he had been granted by racing officials. Crowds turned out to watch him train at the indoor Park Square Coliseum, located across from Boston Common and billed as the nation's largest exposition building, including "many automobilists" who once were connected to the bicycle industry. The *Globe* reported that Taylor had agreed to race as part of his preparation for another season of European contests, predicting "his pocket will be well lined and his limbs primed."

On February 8, Taylor lost his first race to Iver Lawson as he struggled to regain his form. Then, in a departure from his sprinting specialty, Taylor joined a team competing in a six-day race, agreeing to ride more than two hours a night, his first long race in more than seven years. Taylor "displayed great speed" when sprinting, but observers doubted his ability to go long. This version of the six-day race was akin to a relay, and at one point Taylor's partner Nat Butler faltered, and Taylor could not relieve him cleanly, costing the team a lap, and they eventually withdrew from the race.

In one of his last matches that spring, Taylor faced a local rider named James F. Moran before five thousand spectators. Few gave

Moran a chance, but he stunned the crowd by beating Taylor. "The crowd went wild with excitement when the white man won," the *Globe* reported. "Men threw their hats in the air and women screamed and waved handkerchiefs, muffs and anything else that was handy . . . the demonstration at the close of the race was the most remarkable ever witnessed in this city, for the cheering continued for almost 10 minutes and Moran was forced to make several tours around the oval before he could leave the track, and even then a mob swarmed around him and carried him in triumph." Taylor, the *Globe* said, acknowledged the victory "with bowed head."

The defeats were painful but didn't really matter. Taylor's mission was to depart for Paris in perfect condition, and he succeeded. What he could not defeat was the rise of the "automobilists," who were determined to make 1908 the year that the car was accepted by the masses.

The world around Taylor changed at an astonishing pace. On North Carolina's Outer Banks, Orville and Wilbur Wright, who got their start in the bicycle business, prepared to demonstrate that their years of effort had enabled their heavier-than-air Flyer to remain airborne and under control. They had begun their experiments on the wind-swept island five years earlier, and now, finally, they had flown their first passenger. Newspaper coverage of the flights competed with stories about Frederick A. Cook's effort to be the first to reach the North Pole, and President Roosevelt's mission to send a "Great White Fleet" of battleships around the world in a projection of American military might that presaged two world wars. Dozens of automobile companies sprung up, and Henry Ford announced the development of the first car affordable to the average American, which he called the Model T.

In Manhattan, as Munger's business on Automobile Row continued to boom, more than 250,000 people gathered on February 12 in Times Square and along Broadway to witness the start of what was billed as the greatest sporting event ever conceived: a round-the-world auto race. Until now, only a handful of bicyclists had attempted to circle the globe. At a time when relatively few roads were paved, the twenty-two-thousand-mile auto course would go across the United

States, then north through Canada to Alaska, across the Bering Strait (which promoters hoped would be frozen) to Russia, through Moscow and St. Petersburg, and on to Berlin and Paris. The contest was cosponsored by the *New York Times* and *Le Matin*. Six teams composed of a total of seventeen men drove an international roster of six cars, including one from the United States, a sixty-horsepower car called, like the Wright brothers airplane, the Flyer, built by the E. R. Thomas Motor Company of Buffalo. Munger, it so happened, was photographed in such a vehicle that same year. The Flyer was a convertible with a canvas top, retrofitted for the race with three gasoline tanks. The contest was covered feverishly for months, with the auto industry anxious to convince people that, if these cars could go around the world, then it was safe to drive one around town. In fact, the cars faced one problem after another, got stuck in mud and snow, and needed constant help from local teams of horsemen to be pulled out of quagmires. Plans to travel through Canada were abandoned. The contestants boarded a boat off the California coast and headed to Alaska, marking the first arrival of the car in that territory, and soon realized that roads—which were really sled tracks—were impassable. They skipped the crazy notion of riding across the Bering Strait, and boarded a boat for Japan. Several remaining contestants finally made it to Russia, where spring thaws made forward motion nearly impossible, and they slogged toward Paris.

Taylor, too, headed to Paris, along with Daisy and Sydney. They arrived in the spring, and unlike their prior visit, Taylor was in shape, confident that he could conquer the European racing circuit. From May to July, Taylor raced across Europe, while his wife and daughter stayed in Paris. Taylor was winning regularly by the time he got to Bordeaux, France, and raced at the local velodrome on July 13. As he rounded a curve, one of his tires burst, and he was thrown violently to the ground in one of the worst accidents of his career. His right arm was badly torn, and he could not ride for several weeks.

Returning to Paris and reuniting with his family, Taylor arrived just as the Americans in the around-the-world auto race were about to complete their quest. As the Americans left Germany in a dense fog on July 29, hoping to reach Paris that night, a coupling shaft had failed, and the team worked for sixteen hours by an apple tree trying to repair it. They finally got under way and hoped to make it to Paris on July 30.

The race was an extraordinary feat, but it had hardly extinguished the fear many had of automobiles. On the day before the American team planned to arrive in Paris, the *New York Times,* which had cosponsored the race, ran a front-page story about a horrific auto accident near Paris. The stepson of William Kissam Vanderbilt Sr. had been "roasted alive" as he sped seventy-five miles per hour to meet his family on a French road. G. W. Sands had neared Vanderbilt's estate, the Chateau St. Louis de Poissy, twenty miles from Paris, when a tire burst and the car swerved from the road into a tree, and overturned. The gasoline tank exploded, the car burst into flames, and Sands burned to death. Vanderbilt, staying at the Ritz Hotel in Paris, hurried to the scene. It was Vanderbilt's son, William "Willie" Vanderbilt Jr., who had bet on Taylor's 1901 race before joining him aboard a steamship back to America, and who in 1907 had financed the Long Island Motor Parkway, which would literally pave the way for the creation of suburbia. Now Willie's stepbrother had died in one of the year's most chronicled crashes.

The following day, even as there were more front-page stories about horrific auto accidents, the Americans completed their around-the-world race and arrived victoriously in Paris, "escorted through the boulevards by a great parade of automobilists." They had traveled twelve thousand miles on the road, journeying from New York to Paris in 170 days, hailed as one of the great feats of the age. Most of the American crew had changed several times, but one man, mechanic George Shuster, made the entire trip. Shuster had been a last-minute addition, arriving from Buffalo on an overnight train in New York City for the start, never imagining he would remain to the end. Now he was at the center of an enormous celebration, as crowds lined the streets. "*Vive le car Americain!*" shouted the Parisians, as the Thomas Flyer inched through the masses and down the avenues, propelled by the same engine that had been installed by its manufacturer in Buffalo. An American flag flew from the vehicle's rear, and the drivers strived to stop the spectators from tearing off pieces for a souvenir. Then, as the car passed the Place de l'Opera, a gendarme stopped the vehicle and told the driver: "You are under arrest. You have no lights on your car." In fact, there were two headlamps, but one had stopped working, and the officer said that amounted to a violation. Americans rushed from a nearby cafe, telling the officer that this was no ordinary car and driver; this was the winner of an around-the-world automobile race. The gendarme was unimpressed. A bicyclist then approached and offered to provide a light that he had attached to his handlebars, but he could not remove the lantern. Instead, the driver took the bicycle, placed it in the front seat, turned on the light, and insisted this would satisfy the law. The gendarme, a crowd of Americans around him, bid *adieu*, and the Thomas continued down the Boulevard des Capucines, where it was garaged while the Americans attended a supper at the Grand Hotel. Taylor, as it happened, was billeted nearby, and he could not have failed to notice the celebration, as well as what the race signified about the auto's rise.

Nearly a month later, on August 28, Taylor's wounds had healed, and he competed in a one-mile race at the Buffalo track in Paris, winning in one minute and thirty-three seconds, beating the world's record by nearly three seconds. It was an extraordinary accomplishment, erasing any doubt about whether Taylor, when trim and fit, could still be called the fastest man on a bicycle. Taylor departed for home three weeks later, telling *L'Auto* that he was forever grateful for the kindness shown him in France. He said he was "less victorious" than he liked, and his fall in Bordeaux had hurt his chances. Still, he felt lucky to leave France with his share of victories. "Thank everyone for me," Taylor said. "Let the public know that I will always keep an excellent memory of them. And see you next year."

Wilbur Wright was nearby in Le Mans, preparing to launch his latest plane, which he would fly on September 22 for ninety minutes, the world record. Newspapers in France and around the world wrote frequently about innovations in the automobile and airplane. More of Taylor's former rivals went into the auto business. Eddie Bald raced for the Columbia Motor Car Co., including a contest from Chicago to New York. He then opened the Eddie Bald Motor Co., selling vehicles made by Hudson. Bald eventually retired from the auto business, making "a couple of million dollars," according to a column by the famed journalist Damon Runyan. Interest in Taylor's world of bicycle racing faded even further, especially in America, where record speeds were regularly set at sea, on land, and in the air.

When Taylor returned home, racism was ever more rampant. Gangs roamed Taylor's birthplace of Indianapolis, targeting blacks. Although blacks theoretically were welcomed in the city's parks and on its streetcars, they risked assault if they mixed with whites. In Springfield, Illinois, where Abraham Lincoln once lived, one of the nation's worst race riots broke out after a white woman claimed she was raped by a black man. Whites rousted blacks from their homes, set fire to buildings, and engaged in a series of assaults and lynchings. A mob of five hundred weapon-wielding whites approached the house of William Donnegan, an eighty-year-old black who was "highly respected," married to a white woman, and lived in a middle-class neighborhood. The retired cobbler had known the Great Emancipator when Lincoln had lived in the Illinois capital. "Good evening, gentlemen. What can I do for you?" Donnegan asked. The rioters yelled, "Lynch the nigger!" As rioters tried to set his house on fire, someone hit him with a brick. The mob, including many boys, dragged him to a maple tree, roped him to a branch, and broke his neck. The rioters left him in this "half-standing, half-hanging" position, and he died shortly thereafter. Only later did authorities determine that the white woman who had claimed she was raped by a black man—setting off the riot—had lied in an effort to cover up an affair with a white man who had beaten her.

A landmark book was published that year called *Following the Color Line*, providing a disquieting view not just of the expected racism of the South but also of escalating prejudice in the North. The author, a white journalist named Ray Stannard Baker, said that on the surface it appeared blacks were widely accepted in Massachusetts; a black woman was principal of a school with six hundred white students; blacks served as police officers and firefighters; and blacks had no trouble getting accommodation on public transportation. Still, as he interviewed many whites about their perception of blacks, he found that even in Boston the sympathy that he had previously seen had been all but exhausted. Whites who once turned out in large numbers to support blacks were conspicuously absent. An increasing number of hotels and restaurants "will not serve Negroes, even the best of them," he wrote. "The discrimination is not made openly, but a Negro who goes to such places is informed there are no accommodations, or he is overlooked and otherwise slighted, so that he does not come again." Even in Boston's churches, there was a move afoot among integrated congregations to push blacks into their own houses of worship. A proposal was made to ban blacks from the YMCA and create a separate facility for them, just as had been the case in Taylor's youth in Indianapolis. At Harvard, which previously had a reputation as being liberal in its acceptance of blacks, and where a black student named R. C. Bruce had recently been a valedictorian, talk was heard of banning African Americans from the baseball team, and the university president spoke with "sympathy" of the Southern policy of separate education.

This was the world awaiting Taylor when he agreed later that year to once again race in the United States, hoping to stay in shape for another season in Europe. In a warm-up match, he lost a three-man race at Madison Square Garden on December 5, and then he returned to Massachusetts, having agreed to race in the increasingly hostile environment of Boston. Once again, he would compete against Floyd McFarland.

Four years had passed since Taylor faced McFarland in their bitter contests in Australia. Now, on December 20, thousands packed the Park Square Coliseum in Boston to watch them in a one-mile race. McFarland took the lead, which Taylor was happy to give, riding in the slipstream. They stayed close together for several laps, with McFarland nervously looking behind him, waiting for Taylor to make his move. Suddenly, with three laps to go, Taylor made his jump, opened a ten-yard lead, and McFarland strained to regain control. The bell sounded for the last lap, and Taylor powered ahead, winning with McFarland on his rear wheel.

The second heat began in similar fashion, but this time McFarland beat Taylor at the finish, setting the stage for the third and deciding race, a half-mile contest. Taylor took an early lead, then slowed while McFarland remained directly behind him, and the two raced in that position until the final lap. McFarland suddenly accelerated, but Taylor "turned loose a tremendous burst of speed" and won the match. Earlier in the year, the crowd had cheered at length when a white man beat Taylor. This time, the crowd chanted for Taylor.

Taylor had one more race at Park Square Coliseum, but it was hardly as satisfying. After Taylor won two of three races against an Australian champion named Jackie Clark, the referee informed him that the results were under review. Clark was managed by McFarland, who had convinced his client to protest the match. It was a sham, and Taylor said he would refuse to return to the oval to rerun the race. The referee then declared Clark the winner, fleecing Taylor of his $500 winnings, and prompting him to vow to never again race in the arena. He cleaned out his locker and took his bicycle with him. That turned out to be "a very wise move," Taylor wrote later, because the Coliseum burned to the ground the following day, and the other riders lost everything they had stored there.

Even as Taylor was increasingly confronted by indications that his prowess was in decline, news about another black athlete appeared, heartening him, and showing, perhaps, that his widely reported victories against racism were having a broader effect.

The young athlete inspired by Taylor was named Jack Johnson, of Galveston, Texas. He dreamed of being a cycling world champion, just like his hero. He won many races, and his skills began to gain notice. Then, one day, during a five-mile race, Johnson fell rounding a curve, seriously injuring his ribs and one of his legs, requiring hospitalization. He realized that he could never be a world champion like Taylor. "That accident led me to give up cycling and look for a less dangerous profession," Johnson wrote. He decided to become a boxer.

Indeed, he became one of the world's best boxers, but boxing was strictly segregated, and for years he could claim only the title of black champion. Still, inspired by Taylor, he issued a series of challenges to white champions and gained the attention of Hugh "Huge Deal" McIntosh, the Australian promoter who had brought Taylor to Australia. Hoping to emulate the way Taylor had drawn huge crowds, McIntosh arranged for a fight in Sydney between Johnson and a Canadian, Tommy Burns, for the heavyweight championship. The only way Burns would accept fighting a black man was a guaranteed payment of $30,000, win or lose. Johnson agreed to a $5,000 fee, which didn't cover his expenses, but he was willing to lose money in order to get a chance to be declared world champion.

The stage was set. At the same time Taylor raced in Boston, December 26, 1908, Johnson stepped into a boxing ring in Sydney. More than twenty thousand people watched the fourteen-round fight.

Johnson pummeled Burns, fulfilling his dream of becoming world champion, and was awarded an extra share of the gate that brought his take to $15,000. Johnson's victory set off a chain reaction of racism back in America, echoing the way many whites felt about Taylor's dominance. Popular theories of racial superiority had again been decimated, and Johnson became a target. The search began for what was called the "great white hope." As Johnson prepared to defend his title against a white fighter, the *New York Times* lamented, "If the black man wins, thousands and thousands of his ignorant brothers will misinterpret his victory as justifying claims to much more than mere physical equality with their white neighbors."

In fact, as Taylor had shown in leading the way, the black man had won, and now so had another, and the march of history—slowly, inexorably—continued.

PART THREE

# The Finish

# CHAPTER 20

# "I Need Your Prayers"

Taylor wished for one more season abroad, but his French promoters were no longer anxious to have him. He was not the great draw he once had been, or a likely winner. Still, he had made up his mind to make one more tour. He would leave behind Daisy and Sydney, much to his later regret. He barely mentioned the year in his autobiography, but it turned out to be among the most revealing of his life because it was during this journey that he wrote hundreds of pages in letters to his wife, the only correspondence between them that survives other than some postcards, revealing his innermost feelings. Her letters to him are lost to history.

Taylor arrived in New York City on April 29, 1909, a bitterly cold day that brought a brush of late-season snow, just enough to cling briefly to the flowerbeds and sidewalks, before rainstorms drenched everything. Taylor raced to the docks, where his trainer, Bert Hazard, had assembled his gear, and barely made it to the British ocean liner *Lusitania*. Taylor boarded just a few minutes before the vessel pulled out of New York Harbor, and he settled in for a rough passage. After several days at sea, Taylor wrote his location—"Deep Water"— on Hamburg-American Line stationery and began a letter to his wife and daughter. In order to avoid a scene, he had not bade farewell to his daughter, and he asked Daisy what little Sydney had said "when she woke up and Dad was gone?"

Anxiety filled Taylor as he wandered through Paris without Daisy.

He left something unstated—but understood between the two of them—in one dispatch after another. It may have been either his dashed hope that she once again become pregnant, or his sorrow over a miscarriage, as he frequently referred to a change in her appearance. He urged that Daisy not "take any foolish chances or run any risks, and I guess we will get out of this all right." This was a turnabout, as it was usually Daisy who implored him not to take foolish risks on the track. Taylor discovered a letter Daisy had hidden in his luggage, in which she wrote that she would look the same as when he left her, which Taylor said "did make me feel just a bit sad."

Something else troubled Taylor as well, and he was "very anxious" that things go well in France, and again alluded to some mysterious issue. "Think of me every minute because you know I feel that I need your prayers and sympathy just now more than ever before and of course you know why," Taylor wrote Daisy. "I feel very strange and queer about this thing and you know the reason." Taylor's greatest worry was getting killed in an accident on the track, as had happened to at least eleven of his peers during his career, and leave Daisy a widow. He asked Daisy whether she had purchased his life insurance policy, as they had discussed, signing the letter, "your affectionate husband, Marshall."

After arriving in Paris, Taylor went to the American Express office day after day in hopes of finding a letter from Daisy, only to be disappointed, leaving him thinking that she was "probably sick or very tired or that perhaps you had not fully recovered from the strangeness of it all," another elliptical reference understood only by husband and wife. Despite his worries, Taylor had to race, of course. Briefly, it appeared he was back on track. He won an early match, and his victory was trumpeted in newspapers across the United States with headlines such as " 'Major Taylor' Comes Back."

The French press, however, was unrelenting in its portrayal of Taylor as a beloved but broken man. *La Vie au Grand Air*, a sports publication that previously had lauded Taylor for his strength and physique, ran a full-page photo showing him looking weary and defeated after a Sunday race, wrapped in a blanket and wearing a cap, and criticizing him as a hypocrite who was past his prime. The newspaper speculated that Taylor was punishing himself for giving up his ban on Sunday racing that year, although Taylor wrote he had made that decision two years earlier.

In fact, Taylor arrived in Paris with an injury of some kind. In one letter to Daisy, he wrote that he had trouble standing, probably due to a problem with his joints, and said that if it continued, "I may be obliged to have you come to my aid, so you need not be surprised if you get word to come over at any time." He was "trying to make a brave fight of it," but it was "a terrible fight right from the beginning." He had proven many times that "I am no baby . . . I have a brave heart and undaunted courage, but this is a great trial, seemingly the greatest of all." In letter after letter, he pined for his wife, his home, his daughter, his bed. He put a photo of Daisy by his nightstand and placed her handiwork—a hand-stitched pillow and a blanket—on the bed. "The effect is so beautiful," he told her. "I can see you the first thing in the room when I open the door. . . . I can look at you the last thing at night and the first thing in the morning. Isn't that beautiful? And is there any wonder that I dream of you every night?"

To facilitate his training, Taylor fixed up a small cabin at the Velodrome Buffalo in Paris. He decorated it with cheesecloth and strings of electric lights. He installed a washstand and mirror, and laid wooden boards over the rough concrete. A carpet and a couple of chairs would "make it very comfortable," he wrote. Anxious to lose weight, he ate a light but protein-heavy diet, two raw eggs in Port wine for dinner, and one raw egg in Port wine for breakfast, along with a cup of cocoa with rolls. His main meal was what he called supper, a heartier repast with other riders. In his first race, which fell on a Sunday, he started well but nearly fell and bumped into his competitor. He crossed the finish first, but the referee declared he had fouled the other rider, resulting in a loss. He was still overweight, out of shape, "not strong enough just yet," he wrote Daisy. In letter after letter, he lamented her absence. "Dearie, do you remember the little kiss I used to give you, and the one you would give me, just before I would run over to the track to train?" he wrote. "Well, how I do miss it and long for it just now, and believe me dearie that is just what's the matter with me now."

He trained as hard as ever, sparring with a partner, skipping rope, and then putting on tights "and lots of shirts and a big sweater" before doing sixty laps behind a motorized pacing machine. Gradually, his conditioning improved. He wore a newfangled helmet, which he called a "mask," for the training runs, and ran on wider tires than usual in hope of avoiding a fall. Still, he told Daisy, he was obliged to take risks, and in a July race in Roubaix, he suffered one of his worst crashes. He returned to Paris, where he confirmed that, while no bones were broken, he had sprained one of his wrists. He immersed it in water "as hot as I could stand it for an hour," got a rub, and then repeated the treatment. Soon, he returned to the track.

The wrist is one of the body's most complicated joints and injuries to it invariably take time to heal. So, too, with Taylor. He could not pull with his sprained wrist, or put weight on it. Race after race, he found that younger riders had an extra bit of strength and passed him at the last moment. He performed his famous jump as well as possible but could not drive hard enough to win. Day after day, he wrote to Daisy that he was disappointed and could not comprehend what was happening to his body. "I was feeling fine, never felt better, but I was not there with the kick," he wrote after losing a June race. It was, he told Daisy, "a wicked mistake to leave you behind." Writing separately to Sydney, he asked that "you ride your bicycle every day" so that "you can go out with Daddie when I come home."

By August 1, using stationery from Hotel Bristol in Dusseldorf, Germany, Taylor confided to Daisy that he had earned only $700 with the season half over. A few days later in the elegant hotel Askanischer Hof in Berlin, he wrote Daisy that motor-paced racing had just been banned and explained the reason why: shortly before Taylor's arrival, a pacing vehicle had careened out of control with a pack of riders behind it. The six-hundred-pound vehicle jumped the track's fence, flew helter-skelter into stands filled with fans, exploded, and "mowed people down for fifteen or twenty feet." Then its gasoline tank erupted in flames, exploded again, and "burned several people to death, mostly women, underneath it." As if Daisy wouldn't be horrified enough by Taylor's vivid description, he enclosed a photograph of the conflagration. The catastrophe would not deter Taylor. He went to the track and trained shortly after the wreckage had been cleared away.

Traveling through Berlin in a "great, big roomy" taxi, Taylor marveled at how the city had become even cleaner and more beautiful since his prior visit. A week later, he arrived in Hanover, where he stayed at the Hotel Royal. He reminded Daisy they had visited there together on one of his prior tours, taking "those beautiful drives through the King's Gardens," and admiring roses that were "just the same as when you were here with me." He was treated royally, he wrote, given a large front room that looked out onto the square, and he confessed he would be sorry to leave. Amid such beauty and prosperity, it seemed unimaginable that within five years, World War I would engulf Europe.

Taylor's determination was not enough. After one race, he wrote, "I actually finished last in every heat" yet "I cannot possibly do any better. I have tried and tried, but nothing I have tried seems to be of any use. . . . I am really discouraged for once in my life." He put up with irritations that he detested, paid fines he thought were unfair. He pondered returning home but stayed in hopes of earning more money, fearing that this season would be his last due to his poor showing. As he prepared to leave Germany for Denmark, he signed his letter, "from your poor weary, homesick, lonesome, tired, and most worn out, discouraged, fat, disgusted, but game and true husband. And that does not begin to describe how I feel." He insisted he was continuing to race not for pride, but wanting to provide more for Daisy and talked of buying her a nicer house or "a beautiful little farm." Musing that he might become a "great poet," he enclosed a few verses written for Daisy. "You must not let anyone see it dearie, as I do not want it to be generally known that I am poetically inclined," he wrote. "I know you will say that I am only wasting valuable time not riding a bicycle when you read these verses, and I know it too." He suggested she sing the verses to the tune of "The Wearing of the Green," an Irish ballad about the repression of the Rebellion of 1798.

The reflective life of a poet must have seemed appealing, indeed, as Taylor faced a brutal travel schedule across Europe that left him feeling listless and defeated. Often, he woke early, took a train to a new destination, and went straight to the velodrome. He wrote Daisy that he wished he had never come back for this last season, "because if I had finished last year, you see how nice it would have been for you and little Sydney to have been with me on my last successful racing season and we could have finished by trimming them all, and on top. One thing that I am pleased for dearie, and that is you and Sydney were not here to see everybody trimming me this year."

Taylor's last European race was slated for a Sunday, October 10, yet he declared himself "happy" to compete on the Sabbath. Taylor took the train 254 miles southwest of Paris to Roanne, the hometown of Victor Dupré, the reigning sprint champion of France and the world. Dupré, a muscular, dashing rider who was featured in cycling advertisements across France, had "trounced" Taylor in August. The rematch, a best-of-three contest, was Taylor's last chance to show he could still compete with the best. Taylor and Dupré lined up for the one-thousand-meter race. The pistol cracked, and Dupré led at the start. Then suddenly Taylor reached deep, made his famous jump, and surprised Dupré, winning by a bicycle length. The second heat was a cat-and-mouse race jockeying for position, when Taylor burst through at the end for victory—or so he thought. The hometown judges awarded it to Dupré. Taylor lodged a protest, but the judges stood by their decision, setting the stage for a third, decisive heat.

It had all come down to this. One final race, the last of Taylor's career in France. He was one month shy of his thirty-first birthday, desperate to prove to himself and the world that he could still be a champion. He looked at his competitor on the starting line, at the racer who had weeks earlier claimed the title of world's fastest man. Taylor had raced like this hundreds of times, everything dependent on the final heat. He waited for the starter's gun. The familiar blast rang out, and the racers were off, hurtling around the track. Dupré took the early lead. Taylor stayed close behind, sticking to his strategy, waiting for the right moment. Taylor raised slightly off his saddle, pulled at his handlebars—the sprained wrist had finally healed—and his front wheel briefly lifted from the track. Then, suddenly, Taylor surprised Dupré and made his jump, closed the gap, and streaked to the finish line, winning by a bicycle length. It was an extraordinary moment in a life full of them, one last victory abroad, a face-saving salvation.

"Taylor Gets Revenge on Dupré in Latter's Home Town," declared the headline in an American cycling journal. Taylor was "particularly pleased" because Dupré had beaten him so badly earlier in the season. "Naturally, there was an immense crowd out to see the Frenchman trounce the American negro—a feat which did not occur, however." This victory, the reporter concluded, was "Taylor's adieu to France."

Taylor boarded *La Provence* at the port of Le Havre on October 16, and headed into the stormy waters of the Atlantic. Taylor always dreaded the seasickness that so often accompanied him on these journeys, but he had never experienced a sailing as treacherous. Three days after the departure, Taylor saw what appeared to be a tidal wave. Smashing into the wall of water, the ship's steel plates buckled and a section of handrail was torn away. As passengers panicked, the ship's orchestra kept playing, trying to maintain calm. The vessel shook uncontrollably. "When the nose of the ship pointed down after climbing over an immense wave," Taylor said, "it seemed as if it would never turn upward again." Somehow, the ship survived and completed the journey to New York Harbor.

Back in Worcester, Taylor told a reporter that he had talked with Breyer and Coquelle about returning in 1910, but his longtime promoters said they couldn't offer a decent contract after such a disappointing season, notwithstanding the spectacular finish. He would never again return to Europe. He said he could still race if he could train in the South during the winter, but the feeling was still "so strong against a negro" that he could not safely make the trip. A sense of finality set in, as the headline in the resulting story in the *Worcester*

*Telegram* seemed to make clear: "Famous Rider Too Old for Racing, Finds It Hard to Get in Condition."

The years of racing, Taylor wrote, "had exacted their toll from me."

But Taylor, like so many times before, couldn't give it up, not yet. He considered managing other cyclists but decided against it. He pondered going into the auto business but wasn't ready. Intriguingly, a newspaper said Taylor had a "secret" plan with a French racer "for the speediest and most efficient" airplane ever built, but no evidence emerged that he pursued the idea. Finally, the following year, he made one last effort to revive his racing career, in Salt Lake City. His old nemesis, Floyd McFarland, wrote a story for the *Salt Lake Telegram*, in which he acknowledged that Taylor's victories were "a bitter pill for us white boys to swallow so we immediately got together and teamed against him." McFarland vastly underplayed his brutal tactics, acknowledging only that "we did rough the Major a bit." Still, McFarland's article was mostly gracious, extolling Taylor for his tactics, his trick riding ability, and his large winnings.

The stage seemed to be set for another rematch between Taylor and McFarland. Once again leaving Daisy and Sydney behind, Taylor boarded the train, traveling to Chicago, and then headed over the Plains, across the ranchlands and Rocky Mountains of Colorado, winding through high desert and the Wasatch Range, and finally arriving in Utah, where Mormon settlers arrived by wagon in 1847 and which became a state in 1896. He headed to the grounds of the Salt Palace, an arena built eleven years earlier in Salt Lake City that included a bicycle racing track, part of an amusement park that featured a dance hall and a theater. Covered in large pieces of rock salt, the structure was a wedding cake of a building, with arches and columns and a spectacular dome, lit by hundreds of bulbs.

Taylor needed to win preliminary races in order to make it to the expected showdown with McFarland. He was heavily promoted, training hard to get in shape to face some old rivals. He was the star attraction and had demanded $500 for each race, which forced the management to raise its prices to a maximum of one dollar per seat.

"From the figures it can be seen why Taylor is called the highest priced attraction in the bike game," said the *Salt Lake Herald-Republican*. After a week of buildup in the press, Taylor raced for two laps behind a motorized pacer, but he was two seconds slower than his own record, at twenty-one and three-fifths seconds. Finally, several nights later, Taylor was set to face off against Iver Lawson, the "Big Swede." The two had a bitter history. Lawson had cut him off in races at Madison Square Garden and in Australia, the latter causing the crash that severely injured Taylor. Ticket sales set a record for what was billed as "the greatest contest of the season."

On the evening of August 16, before a crowd of six thousand, the two men lined up for a best-of-three competition in one-mile heats. Lawson knew that Taylor would try to run a tactical race, standing still to force Lawson to take the lead. Lawson took the bait, leading the race for four and a half laps, when Taylor suddenly performed "his famous jump," and shot into first place. Lawson responded with his own jump, "catching Taylor by surprise," and retook the lead, and easily won the race. Taylor's supporters insisted he was only toying with Lawson, but the Big Swede repeated his strategy and even more easily won the second heat, making him the victor in the overall match. Taylor was humbled and more than a little humiliated.

"I can only say that the best man won," he said, promising to do better in a race that was set to occur three days later. But he fared just as poorly in that contest, against Australian racer Jackie Clark, losing in two straight heats. He then agreed to race on a Sunday, again violating his old taboo, and finished second in a four-man race.

The next day, a spectacular fire destroyed the much-beloved Salt Palace, but the adjacent racing track was mostly spared, and Taylor ran yet another race, but his part in the competition was over. He had failed to make it out of the preliminary rounds, denying him a chance to face McFarland. "The famous 'black streak' has gone to the well once too often," concluded the *Salt Lake Telegram*. "Taylor showed just a wee semblance of that old jump . . . [he] has had too many years of hard campaigning and has retired too many times."

Taylor knew he had let down himself and the promoters, and as he left Salt Lake City earlier than planned, he apologized for his "miserable showing . . . I simply fell down and I was far more disappointed than the people who came to see me." He insisted his career was not over, promising to "knuckle down to the hardest kind of training," and vowing to return to Utah the following summer. "You will hear of me yet," he said. "I know I can do better."

He never raced competitively again.

For more than two thousand miles, Taylor traveled by train from Salt Lake City to Worcester, reversing the journey he had taken with such hope, back across the desert and the Rockies, the Plains and the Appalachians, and finally through the hills and valleys of Central Massachusetts, to Worcester's Union Station, where, in years past, he had so often arrived triumphantly. Now all that seemed past, and he surely ruminated during his travel across America about how far he had come and how now that glorious career had faded, even if he hadn't yet admitted it was over. Taylor wanted to provide for himself and his family while fighting for fairness for his race. Gradually, as an autumnal chill fell upon New England, painting the hillsides in yellow, orange, and red, he pondered alternatives.

Then, two months after arriving back in Worcester, Taylor learned his father had died in Chicago. This, in combination with the conclusion of his own career, marked another turning of the season in Taylor's life. His father's remains were brought by train to Indianapolis for the funeral service and burial. For decades afterward, the location of his father's gravesite would be a mystery. In fact, the old Civil War veteran was buried in Indianapolis's Crown Hill Cemetery, marked by a tablet engraved, "Corpl. Gilbert Wilhite U.S.C.T." The burial papers made clear the truth, saying the name of the deceased was "Gilbert Taylor or Wilheight," the latter being one of several spellings of the name under which Gilbert had served in the Kentucky regiment of the United States Colored Troops. Taylor had told Daisy in a letter the prior year that his father's pension would be "in the name of Gilbert Wilhite for that was the name he enlisted in the war under."

• • •

Taylor's racing career was over, but he had considerable savings, and he decided that rather than sit on most of it, he would invest it, in the American tradition of risk and reward, one that he knew well. Like Munger and many other former cycling champions, he would go into the automobile business. It was reported in a number of newspapers that he was forming "one of the largest automobile factories in France," which was no truer than the fiction that he was going into the aviation business. Somehow, these fantastical ideas took hold and were published, with no confirmation from Taylor himself. The *Chicago Defender*, a black-oriented newspaper, said Taylor was leaving the United States and was "on a fair road to become wealthy." No such business materialized, and he remained at home. Taylor was more practical. He believed he needed a business education, and he applied to Worcester Polytechnic Institute, but the school said they couldn't accept someone without a high school diploma, which Taylor never had the opportunity to earn. Taylor plunged ahead anyway with a carefully designed plan. One of the primary causes of automobile accidents was that tires frequently went flat, a danger Taylor knew all too well from bicycle racing. Munger had tried to solve the problem by improving the rim, the subject of his patent fight. Taylor studied the science and concluded that the tire itself should be reinvented, and he proposed using steel. He established a joint venture with Fred Johnson, an executive of the Iver Johnson Company in nearby Fitchburg, which had once sponsored Taylor's racing career. The two men put up $15,000 each, and other local businessmen also acquired shares in what was called the Major Taylor Manufacturing Co.

The undertaking was a huge bet for Taylor, with a considerable portion of his savings sunk in the business. The brutal perspective of history, of course, is that many such companies failed under the ruthless march of capitalism. Still, the early indication was that Taylor's gambit had a reasonable chance. In 1911, following a demonstration through the streets of Fitchburg, twenty-eight miles north of Worcester, the company said it believed every truck in the country one day would run on the tires. Three years later, Fred Johnson had taken control of the company and invested heavily in improvements.

A 1914 report said that the firm expected to raise $1 million in a stock offering. The company had made "extensive improvements in the tire invented by Major Taylor," and struck a potentially lucrative deal with the Pierce-Arrow Motor Co. of Buffalo, one of the premiere auto manufacturers of the time, to put the tire on the company's two-ton trucks. Pierce-Arrow tested the tires for twenty straight days, for a hundred miles per day, and the Taylor company expected "a big order." Johnson had also patented a lighter version of Taylor's tire for use on taxis. The article in the *Fitchburg Sentinel* said that it had been "practically decided" that a plant would be built to produce the tire. Advertisements were placed in local newspapers offering a stake in the company at five dollars per share. It seemed as if Taylor was set to participate in a key part of the booming auto industry.

But in the Gold Rush fever that follows many seemingly sure things, the company's fortunes soon floundered for reasons that were unclear. Taylor lost his entire investment. His daughter, Sydney, said years later that she was told her father "had the idea of using his money to make more money but he didn't. The things he involved himself in were things I think he didn't know enough about. He invented an automatic rubberless tire. He held a patent on it and everything. He used masses of his money to get this project off the ground, but he involved men who were supposedly his friends, and eventually they got the whole thing away from him. In the end, he lost everything and ended up going into bankruptcy." Johnson, meanwhile, was granted a patent in 1918 for a tire that sounded similar to what Taylor had envisioned, and ran a company called Pneu-Metal Tire Co., which said it manufactured a "resilient tire."

Taylor was undaunted, creating new businesses, including the Excello Oil Manufacturing Co. He gave thousands of dollars to his church and regularly helped his siblings and others in need. Inevitably his cash stockpile drained away. "In his later years I think he wanted to be nice to his family, but they only saw him as a source of money and they bled him with bills for lawyers, doctors, divorces and all that kind of stuff," Sydney said. She blamed her father's business failures on a society "where blacks weren't allowed to make money." She said

Taylor and Daisy "used to have long talks about money. His brothers and sisters sent bills, and I guess my mother had a hard time persuading him that he had to stop paying them."

Munger, meanwhile, faced his own crisis.

*Fire!*

The call came in the middle of a cold January night to the New York City Fire Department. Flames were seen inside a showroom on Automobile Row. Twenty-five fire engines streamed toward 602 West 52nd Street, aiming their hoses at the Moore & Munger automobile factory and garage. Three fireboats drew water from the Hudson River. It was the first time in city history a radio communication device was used to call out the boats.

Inside the showroom sat dozens of the most expensive cars available for sale in the United States, elaborate models with bright yellow or red wheels, black leather interior, and sleek hoods. As the firemen tried to douse the flames, someone cried out that the watchman was trapped inside. In fact, watchman A. W. Snyder, who had discovered the fire, was safe. He had driven six automobiles from the flames before the fire enveloped the structure, forcing him to flee. Now, as the blaze grew, licking outside the windows and up the walls, a fireman from Hook and Ladder Company No. 4 went inside in search of the watchman, found no one, and was showered with shattered glass, which severely cut his face and arms. One of the dozen ambulance medics on hand tended to his wounds. The fire and police commissioners rushed to the scene, where they found hoses extending for blocks. They feared that nearby gasoline tanks would explode, and ordered families in ten nearby apartment houses to be evacuated. For two hours, the blaze was watered and seemed to be under control, when it suddenly exploded upward.

Birdie Munger was asleep at his home at 79th Street and Broadway when someone alerted him. Munger raced to his factory, where he was spotted by a reporter for the *New York Times*.

"And there goes $100,000 in high-grade French cars," Munger declared. He said that the fire had gotten a second life when the flames punctured the fourth floor, where a paint shop filled with flammables was located. "And up there, we were finishing up imported cars brought over here in the rough. The practice has been for American buyers to buy the chassis of each car abroad and have the body built in this country." He had insurance, but he didn't know how much. Most of the hundred or so destroyed cars had been purchased, and the buyers had to be compensated.

A year later another tragedy befell Munger when his thirty-eight-year-old wife, Emilie, died. Munger's fortune had ebbed and flowed for years, but now everything seemed to depend on his costly court fight to protect his patents, which he still hoped would provide millions of dollars.

Like Taylor's, Floyd McFarland's career as a racer was over. He had competed for years against Taylor, making no pretense that he was anything other than a racist, but one who admired Taylor's talents. His racing days done, he had become general manager of a velodrome in Newark, New Jersey. On the afternoon of April 17, 1915, McFarland watched riders line up for a practice sprint. Nearby, a man named David Lantenberg screwed a sign into the wall near the track that advertised his refreshment business. McFarland, noticing Lantenberg, grew livid. He had banned such signs after screws had come loose and spilled onto the track, endangering riders. He confronted Lantenberg, who insisted he had the right to advertise his business. McFarland, famously bad-tempered, shouted at Lantenberg, who responded angrily and returned to screwing in his sign. McFarland grabbed Lantenberg's arm. Lantenberg whirled, and, screwdriver in hand, lunged at McFarland.

McFarland swerved his head to avoid the blow, but the tip of the screwdriver wedged into the back of his left ear, speared his skull, and entered his brain. McFarland "dropped senseless" to the ground. The riders tossed their bicycles and ran to the scene. An Australian cyclist picked up McFarland. Lantenberg insisted it had all been a tragic mistake and offered his car as an ambulance. The culprit drove his victim to City Hospital. McFarland's wife was summoned, but he never regained consciousness and died a few hours later. McFarland's career had been defined in part by his racist attacks on Taylor, but he was widely seen as one of the greatest American stars, and his death was yet another sign that an era had ended. A few days after McFarland's death, thousands lined the streets for his funeral procession.

Taylor's bitter rival was gone, and his days of racing glory were already fading from the memory of many Americans. The march of progress seemed steady, as automobiles and airplanes became more common, and electricity lit more towns and cities. But along with progress came new troubles. In 1915, the British ocean liner *Lusitania*, on which Taylor had sailed six years earlier, was sunk by a German U-boat, which would help spur the United States into World War I.

In the East Room of the White House, President Woodrow Wilson and his Cabinet screened *The Birth of a Nation*, the first time a movie had been shown in the executive mansion. Based on the novel *The Clansman*, the silent film portrayed blacks during Reconstruction taking control in the South, while it showed members of the Ku Klux Klan as heroically seeking to reinstitute white control. In the climatic scenes, thousands of white-hooded members of the KKK galloped into town on horseback, portrayed as heroes.

The three-hour epic became the first blockbuster film and helped launch a new era in Hollywood. In lieu of actor's voices, phrases were displayed on card-like transition frames called intertitles. One included a quote (slightly altered for form, not content) from Wilson, from his five-volume work *A History of the American People*: "The white men were roused by an instinct of mere self-preservation, until at last there had sprung into existence a great Ku Klux Klan, a veritable empire of the South to protect the Southern country." The film was produced by D. W. Griffith, who had grown up in Louisville, Kentucky, near where Taylor's parents had lived. Griffith's father, Jacob, joined the Confederacy and had accompanied the retreat of Jefferson Davis, the president of the Confederate states. Griffith idolized his father and the film partly was an effort—albeit one filled with inaccuracies—to justify the Confederate viewpoint. (Later in life, facing intense criticism of the film,

Griffith insisted, "The Klan at that time was needed; it served a purpose.") The film was even more harmful than many blacks had feared. The Klan was reborn and membership skyrocketed, lynchings increased, and the ballot was increasingly restricted to whites. Taylor surely heard of the outcry over the film. Booker T. Washington, in one of his last acts before he died later in the year, was among many black leaders who urged that the film be boycotted or banned. In Boston, eight hundred black women gathered at a Baptist church to protest it and riots broke out when blacks tried to enter the Tremont Theatre, where it was showing. "Army of Police Nip Theatre Riot in Bud," said the headline in the *Boston Post,* with the subhead "Two Colored Spectators Manage to Get Inside." Thousands marched to the statehouse in a final effort to stop the film, to no avail. Tens of thousands of whites in Boston, and eventually millions across the country, packed movie houses. Wilson's policies, meanwhile, led to the resegregation of the federal workforce, further emboldening local and state officials who instituted Jim Crow laws. W. E. B. Du Bois, who was among the founders of the National Association for the Advancement of Colored People and had supported Wilson's candidacy in the mistaken belief that he "will treat black men and their interests with far-sighted fairness," wrote an open letter to him six months after the inauguration, dismayed that "every enemy of the Negro race is greatly encouraged" by his policies. Du Bois cited a black government clerk who, under Wilson's segregation measure, was forced to work in a "cage" to separate him from white coworkers. Du Bois was incensed by *The Birth of a Nation* and he helped lead the NAACP's effort to ban it, which did not succeed. While much would be made of the movie's impact on filmmaking technique, it would also prove to be a landmark in the use of media for political propaganda purposes, bolstering Wilson's Democratic Party.

The harshness of the era was written into Taylor's life as well. He continued to struggle as a businessman, and his finances became increasingly bleak. Then, in the late summer of 1916, a visitor came to town. That visitor was none other than a former president of the United States, and he wanted to meet Major Taylor.

CHAPTER 21

# "My Last Race"

Theodore Roosevelt had first visited Worcester as a young man hiking through New England, as well as during his presidency, which ended in 1909, and afterward. He had lost his third-party bid in 1912 and considered running again for the White House in 1916, rejected the notion, and spent much of the year traveling the country, blasting the Wilson administration for its lack of preparedness for possible entry into the war that had engulfed Europe, calling those in Washington "96 percent feeble." On September 1, 1916, Roosevelt arrived by train in Worcester as a guest of Harry Worcester Smith, a prominent white resident who was particularly close to Taylor.

Smith had been kicked out of Worcester Polytechnic Institute for riding his horse up the steps into a third-floor chapel, and for having poor grades. He used the punishment as motivation, and eventually became so successful he donated generously to the college that had expelled him. Having made a fortune in the textile industry, Smith lived the ultimate sportsman's life, founded a country club, and became a champion horseman, winning steeplechase races and other contests. He had used his riches to build Lordvale, a two-story mansion set amid three hundred acres upon Brigham Hill, near Worcester. Smith was the sort of idiosyncratic pillar of the Gilded Age who thought it might be a good idea to let all of the inmates out of the Worcester county jail on Memorial Day so they could visit Lordvale and mingle with "the bluest blooded society folk of Massachusetts." The local sheriff nixed the idea. Now Roosevelt visited Smith at Lord-vale and posed for a photo there with several dozen of the city's leading business and government figures.

Smith drove the former president around Worcester, stopping at a newly developed area called Indian Hill, five miles from Taylor's home on Hobson Avenue. Roosevelt planted an oak tree, which still stood a century later. At one point, Roosevelt randomly walked up to a house, knocked on the door, and found a woman at home, who "was nearly knocked off her feet" when she found Roosevelt on the porch. "I just dropped in to see if you are doing everything as I think it should be done," Roosevelt told her. He assured the woman, Mrs. Emil Styffe, that everything appeared to be "bully." She compared Roosevelt's visit to the day she was married: "Very happy but so excited that I hardly knew what was happening."

It was through Smith that a meeting with Taylor appears to have been arranged. Smith had long admired the career of Taylor, his fellow Worcester sportsman, and became a friend and supporter, the latest in a long line of well-off white men who became close to him. Roosevelt had spent the day meeting "some public men of note," a category that Taylor certainly fit.

Lost to history is whether Roosevelt came to Taylor's home, where he would have seen his photo on the wall, alongside that of Booker T. Washington. Roosevelt's luster among blacks had faded, but Taylor still felt deep honor in being greeted by the former president. Taylor left no doubt that the two met in person, saying Roosevelt "grasped my hand with a hearty grip." They were two aging warriors. Roosevelt on this day wore a three-piece suit, including a high-collared vest, crossed by a chain, and a tie. His signature mustache remained intact but had grayed. In his hands he grasped a white, broad-rimmed hat. Roosevelt was fifty-seven years old and stood five foot nine, twenty years older and two inches taller than Taylor. The two men had come from different worlds, but they shared a love of adventure and travel. Roosevelt two years earlier had returned from his expedition to South America, where he had searched for the headwaters of the River of

Doubt, a dangerous mission that left him suffering from the effects of malaria and other ailments that he feared would cut short his life by a decade. Taylor, of course, had concluded his athletic career, but he still rode his bicycle and strode around town, making his appointments in his usual formal manner, wearing a suit and tie.

As Taylor later recounted it, Roosevelt spoke to him at length, saying:

> Major Taylor, I am always delighted to shake the hand of any man who has accomplished something worthwhile in life, and particularly a champion. I know you have done big things in your profession because I have followed your racing through the press for years with great pleasure. I was especially pleased and interested while you were racing abroad, defeating all the foreign champions, and carrying the Stars and Stripes to victory. Taking into consideration all the millions of human beings on the face of the earth, whenever I run across an individual who stands out as peer over all others in any profession or vocation it is indeed a wonderful distinction, and honor and pleasure enough for me.

Taylor would forever treasure the moment, writing that it was "distinction and a pleasure for me to hear such words."

Two months later, Wilson won reelection, and the United States soon entered World War I. As Worcester's factories geared up to help military production, Taylor faced a bitter reality. His savings were virtually gone, and he had no choice but to take a job as a machinist for the Persons-Arter Machine Co., which specialized in making a device that sliced steel. As American involvement in the war intensified, Taylor took a few days off to travel to Newark, New Jersey, for an old-timers race, and it was indeed like old times. The day was September 16, 1917—a Sunday, yes, but Taylor would not miss this contest. More than twelve thousand spectators filled the Newark Velodrome, where McFarland had been killed two years earlier. Eddie Bald was supposed to show up, but there is no record of him competing. Zimmerman, Taylor's hero, also was slated to compete, but he, too, didn't race.

Taylor waited anxiously for Munger, who had promised to attend. But as Munger drove to Newark, he crashed his car. He borrowed another vehicle, drove through the night, and made it just in time to send off his old friend. Taylor, wrought with emotion, said, "Well, Birdie, you started me in my first race and you're starting me in my last race." As the two men walked to the starting line, the crowd "lustily applauded," with "many a colored rooter on hand." Munger held Taylor's bike and, at the pistol's crack, set him off. Taylor easily beat the dozen competitors in the one-mile contest. He was once again "the class of the field," notwithstanding "the triple roll of fat that curved over his collar and a layer of adipose tissue around the beltline that is thicker than the armor plate on a battleship," the *Newark Evening News* reported. (In fact, a photo from that day, taken while Taylor was wearing a finely tailored dark suit and white shirt, shows him looking relatively fit for an "old timer." He stands in the middle of the picture showing nine other racers, all of them several inches taller than he was.

Taylor returned to Worcester and his job as a machinist as the war effort intensified. The military had concluded that its volunteer force was too small, and a Selective Service system was enacted that required men between twenty-one and thirty years old to register. Then, as the war continued, Congress extended the top age to forty-five, effective September 12, 1918. On that day, Taylor, at thirty-nine years old, left his home on Hobson Avenue and traveled two miles to the Boys' Club on Ionic Avenue, where an agent duly registered him. Taylor did not seek to exempt himself, as he might have tried to do, given that he was the main source of income for his family of three.

Much of the military still drew a color line, but hundreds of thousands of blacks volunteered for duty, many of them serving in regiments with white officers. The black volunteers "eagerly joined the war effort," a historian wrote, viewing it as an opportunity to prove their loyalty and that they deserved equality. Some draft boards enlisted blacks ahead of whites who wanted to avoid service. Blacks were ten percent of the population and thirteen percent of inductees. By the end of the war, about 400,000 African Americans had served, with some 50,000 engaging in combat, mainly in support roles such as laborers and logistics. About 770 were killed in the line of duty.

The war ended two months after Taylor registered for service, so he was never called up. When black soldiers returned home, many hoped the end of the conflict would be followed by a new era of equality. But the racial climate instead worsened, especially in the South, as white racists feared demands from blacks with a military background. The National Museum of the Army would later determine that race relations actually suffered in the wake of victory, with race riots growing across the country, and an increase in lynchings, including at least ten black veterans, several of whom were wearing their uniform when they were attacked.

As soldiers returned home and a postwar economy was established, the steady migration of blacks continued to the North, including those seeking work in the factories of Worcester. The city's population had surged to 180,000, largely due to the rise of industrial plants, up from about 100,000 when Taylor arrived twenty-five years earlier. The early stirrings of the Jazz Age and the Harlem Renaissance were under way, featuring a vibrant new brand of black artists. "Three Plays for a Negro Theater" had its premiere, replacing blackface stereotypes with a realistic portrayal of African American life, with the first all-black casts on Broadway.

Taylor was a prewar phenomenon, and now he faded further from public memory and slipped into a decidedly more modest life. A couple of years after the war ended, he opened Major's Tire Shop, specializing in auto tires and bicycles. An ad for the establishment said it was open evenings and offered "free air service."

Munger's fortunes seemed far better. Finally, eighteen years after filing his patent infringement case, Munger was given his chance to argue in US District Court in New York City that his idea for an easily removable automobile tire had been stolen. The case against the Perlman Rim Corporation rested in part on whether Munger could show that his wheel rim truly was unique in the way it could be separated—or "demounted"—from the tire. Munger proceeded to give a demonstration. Judge Martin T. Manton was impressed. "The removal in court was performed with ease," he wrote, and ruled in Munger's favor. It was a stunning victory after so many years of losses.

"Munger May Be a Millionaire," declared the headline in a New Jersey newspaper. Munger's lawyer said he would file a raft of similar suits against every company that had copied the idea. If the ruling was upheld, the lawyer told the *New York Times*, he could walk away with as much as $7.5 million. Munger authorized his attorney to file twenty suits, including one against Firestone Tire and Rubber Company, claiming that the firm owed him $1.5 million. A similar suit was filed against Goodrich for $1 million. Almost overnight, Munger had gone from waging a long, lonely battle against a middling company to taking on two of the most powerful firms in the auto business. They all vowed to fight Munger as long as necessary. Suddenly, he had become a target, and Firestone and Goodrich used their high-powered legal talent to win lower-court rulings.

Munger was determined to fight. The cases of Louis de Franklin Munger versus Firestone and Goodrich came to the attention of the US Supreme Court on February 20, 1920, when he filed a petition for a writ of certiorari seeking that the matter be heard. The lawyers for Goodrich and Firestone responded that Munger had failed years earlier to file the case in the proper jurisdiction, and "is alone to blame" for his "embarrassing situation . . . due to his own neglect."

All Munger could do was wait for the Supreme Court's decision. First came some good news: while he was waiting, he learned that another court had awarded him $48,000 in damages for his suit against the Perlman company. Munger was not successful, however, in his suits against Firestone and Goodrich. The Supreme Court denied his request to put the matter on the calendar. Munger's fight was over. He would not be a millionaire, but he would, to those who remembered his glory days, remain a cycling legend.

• • •

Munger had remarried and was living with his wife, Harriett, when a reporter for the local newspaper arrived at his home at 106 Chestnut Street, Springfield, Massachusetts. Though largely retired, Munger was still tinkering, promoting a patented invention he called the Radio Four-Way Switch Plug, which connected with telephones. Munger had begun his career when there was barely an automobile on the road, and now, in 1924, the Ford Motor Company alone produced 1.7 million cars, providing the masses with its black Model T. The bicycle craze was a distant memory and the auto age had transformed the nation. The reporter for the *Springfield Republican* let Munger relive the old days in a story headlined "Bicycle Champ of Other Days Living In This City," illustrated with three pictures of a young, dapper man. Munger was in a reflective mood. His wife had just received a Christmas gift of flowers that had arrived on a train from California. That prompted Munger to reminisce about how he had ridden across the continent in 111 days in 1886, on an old-fashioned English highwheeler from West to East over "nearly impassable roads." The reporter laid out Munger's extraordinary life, how he had become the world's fastest man, went into the bicycle and automobile businesses, and how he "personally trained" Taylor to succeed him as the speediest rider.

Taylor, meanwhile, watched with dismay as the rebirth of the Ku Klux Klan, spurred by the continued showing of *The Birth of a Nation*, spread across the country. He did not have to look far. The KKK saw Worcester as a breeding ground for its hate, and it began to grow there as an undeniable force, threatening blacks, Jews, and Catholics. Ethnic tension had increased in the city's factories, with large numbers of Protestants battling with the Catholic Irish. On September 27, 1923, the KKK exploited such divisions in a rally at Mechanics Hall, a Renaissance Revival building that was built before the Civil War. One of the first events held in the hall was an antislavery convention in 1857. Now, two and a half miles from Taylor's home, nineteen hundred people took their seats and filled the balconies for a rally by the KKK, awaiting the "King Kleagle," Eugene Farnsworth, to deliver his racist vitriol. Another five hundred sat in an overflow hall, and hundreds more milled around outside. Farnsworth, a Maine native who had lived in Massachusetts, had honed his performance skills by working as a stage hypnotist. He became obsessed with the idea that immigrants, especially Catholics, were taking over the country, and he saw Worcester as a prime example; seventy percent of Worcester's households had at least one foreign-born member. Farnsworth was famous for his signature line: "This is not an Italian nation, this is not an Irish nation, and this is not a Catholic nation, it always has been and always will be a Protestant nation!" Anticipation and fear built as the day of his speech approached.

An hour before the speech, Farnsworth ate a steak dinner and then lounged in his room at the Bancroft hotel. Lying in bed, he wore light brown pajamas and chewed an unlit cigar, running his hands through his graying, bushy hair. A reporter from the *Evening Gazette,* who found that his face "fairly radiated personality," followed Farnsworth to Mechanics Hall, where the crowd was being entertained by a pianist playing "Massa's in the Cold, Cold Ground." Ascending to the stage, Farnsworth dramatically took off his hat and coat, and swept his eyes over the audience. Speaking slowly, theatrically, he said, "I have been in Worcester since Noon, and near as I can find out—we're all crazy as hell!" The crowd "roared" its approval. Farnsworth then walked to the edge of the stage, where reporters had gathered. Taunting them, he told the crowd that he was going to have "a little heart to heart talk with you newspaper boys." Then began one of his many attacks.

"The press of this country is becoming discredited because it does not publish facts, does not tell the truth, does not serve the great mass of the people impartially," Farnsworth said, a canard issued by countless speakers before and since seeking to stir up a crowd. He then went after all the usual subjects and insisted the Klan members were no different from others who stick together. "If there were a thousand Negros in a community and one of them kept store, 999 of them would buy his shirts and collars in that store. That is clannishness. The Jew, too, has his invisible empire, because he believes in the Jews, and patronizes them . . . the Catholics have their invisible empire in their secret organizations. But we, native born Americans, Baptists or Methodists or whatever we are, let something happen to us fellows and we haven't a friend in the world." He insisted the Klan wasn't against all the targets of his animus, even as he insisted that the country was "teeming with alien enemies, who do not believe in our political system." Switching to sarcasm, Farnsworth insisted: "We want to give the chinks, Italians, and Jews just as must chance as we have," prompting the audience to again burst into applause. The old hypnotist knew how to stir a crowd, to prompt hatred against "the other," while insisting that it was he and his followers who were the ones under siege. Worcester was home to many Cátholics and many immigrants. It had a substantial Jewish neighborhood, centered just a few blocks from Mechanics Hall, and a long-established community of blacks. But as Farnsworth finished speaking, he was applauded loudly, and newspapers reported that the KKK expected to sign up five hundred new members. "Huge Throng Orderly As Klan Meets, King Kleagle Gives Typical Ku Klux Address, Assailing Jews, Catholics and the Press," said the front-page headline in the *Gazette*. Divisions that had long simmered burst to the surface. Farnsworth had appealed to his listeners' worst instincts, stoked their grievances, and made hatred seem more acceptable. Soon, the KKK saw Worcester as central to their efforts to grow in the region, and cross-burnings, marches, and protests were held throughout the city and surrounding area.

As the Klan gathered strength in Worcester, Taylor worked at his home on Hobson Avenue on a six-hundred-page manuscript about his life. On June 9, 1924, he sent a letter to *The Crisis*, a magazine founded by W. E. B. Du Bois that was the official organ of the NAACP, which he had helped form. Du Bois's rival, Booker T. Washington, had died in 1915. Du Bois's philosophy had become ever more influential, as evidenced by his role at *The Crisis*. Taylor, addressing the business manager of *The Crisis*, but apparently hoping to reach Du Bois, wrote, "You will no doubt remember the writer if not personally, perhaps by former reputation at least. . . . I was one of the very few athletes black or white to reach [a] World Championship." He had "retired from the sport honorably, in other words I was not prematurely forced out of the game a dissipated physical wreck," he continued. Given his extraordinary record, he saw no reason to elaborate on the difficulties of his final tour of Europe and brief effort in Utah. "I attributed my great success in bicycle racing to my always perfect physical fitness," he wrote. The book would "especially appeal to every colored man of my own race" but also to anyone who desires to excel in sports and life. He asked if *The Crisis* could consider publishing his six hundred pages in serial form. The business manager promptly passed the request on to Du Bois himself.

Nearly a quarter-century earlier, Taylor had traveled to Paris, just after Du Bois's exhibition about the accomplishment of American blacks had appeared there. *The Crisis* carried a regular column about extraordinary achievements, and Taylor had been mentioned in it numerous times; he exemplified much that Du Bois wanted to high-light. Now, however, Du Bois, as an editor, confronted an unwieldy six-hundred-page manuscript that contained many transcriptions of newspaper articles. He apparently felt he had no choice but to write the tersest letter in reply. "The CRISIS could not use any serial stories of the sort of which you speak," Du Bois wrote Taylor in July 1924. "We might use a single article if it was succinct and interesting." No such article appears to have been published. Taylor received similar rejections from other publications. It was a harsh blow, albeit one experienced by countless writers of every generation. Taylor eventually found a small Worcester company that agreed to publish a book that he was certain was needed at this very moment.

Three months later, in October 1924, the rise of the KKK in Taylor's city came to a stunning climax with a "Klonvocation" at the Worces-ter Agricultural Fairgrounds, five miles from his home, drawing fifteen thousand people, the largest such rally ever held in New England. As the Klan gathered where livestock competitions were usually held, the men, women, and children gathered at the fairgrounds heard a loud buzzing sound. They looked skyward and saw an amphibious Cur-tis biplane with a forty-seven-foot wingspan swooping above them at eighteen hundred feet. On the underside of the left wing were the letters "KKK," and under the right wing was a black cross on a white background. The pilot then performed a loop-de-loop, revealing the slogan on top of "100 percent American." Suddenly, the plane lost power, and rumor spread that a bullet had pierced the fuselage, but the problem was a mechanical difficulty of some kind, forcing a hard landing at a nearby strip. Repairs were made, and the plane took off again, its bottom lit with red electric lights in the form of a cross "glowing like a ruby in the sky." A speaker ascended the stage and declared New England an ideal place to denounce immigration laws. A Klan leader strode in front of the grandstand and made a prearranged signal. Hundreds of white-hooded Klansmen marched single file to the half-mile track, carrying candles. A torch-carrying Klansman emerged on horseback and raced around the track in a "wild gallop." The initiation ritual had begun, and more than a thousand people signed up as Klan members. An industrious reporter for the *Telegram*, banned from attendance, was curious to see if the crowd was local; he positioned himself by the entrance and counted more than two thousand cars. All but twenty had Massachusetts license plates.

By midnight, the rally was over, and Klansmen and their families piled into the cars. As word spread, some members of Worcester's large Catholic community decided they had had enough. Hundreds banded together to battle the Klan members, setting off riots that stretched for blocks. Cars were stoned, fisticuffs ensued, and bloodied Klan members wandered through the streets. "By 1 a.m., every automobile passing the center of the city that gave the least suspicion of containing klansmen was attacked in one way or another," the *Telegram* reported. When a Klansman resisted, fifty protesters "commandeered passing automobiles" and gave chase. Cars were set ablaze, and a crowd of five hundred young men in cars and trucks and on foot raced after the scattered Klan members. The city police force, largely manned by Catholics, let the violence unspool, making just a few arrests. The next day, a banner front-page headline in the *Telegram* appeared above a picture of Klansmen in their robed regalia: "Klansmen Beaten in Street, Cars Stoned, Women Injured." Taylor and his family surely were alarmed at the nearby massing of so many Klan members, and the violence of the counterprotest would have been disturbing as well, even if it provided solace that some Worcester residents had risen up against the KKK. The Klan continued to grow across the country. The sight of so many members in Worcester, a city that had so warmly welcomed Taylor three decades earlier, provided ominous evidence of the nation's continuing divisions. Less than a year later, fifty thousand Klansmen marched down Pennsylvania Avenue in Washington, D.C., watched by tens of thousands of spectators, retracing the presidential inaugural route.

Taylor, meanwhile, struggled to keep his family and his home. Daisy had clashed with him in the last few years, as Taylor continued to support relatives even as his funds dwindled, and he also spent much time and money in his effort to have his autobiography published. Still, Daisy tried to make it appear as if all was well. So, too, did Taylor. But cracks in the marriage widened. As loving and passionate as he had revealed himself to be in his letters to Daisy from Europe, he could be aloof and stubborn, especially when confronted with his failings, or those he perceived in others. Even his beloved daughter, Sydney, could feel the effect of his rigid, old-fashioned ways. She had graduated from Worcester Classical High School in 1923 "with the highest honors," an educational accomplishment that was not available to Taylor in his youth. Sydney aspired to be a physical education teacher, following her father into the athletic field. But Taylor, perhaps from chauvinism, or not wanting his daughter to experience the difficulties he had suffered, became obstinate. He pushed his daughter to go a pharmacy school, seeing it as more practical. Daisy, who had been a top athlete in her own school days, supported her daughter's choice. Taylor at one point seemed to accept his daughter's decision, writing proudly to one of his former sponsors in France that "Sydney is a fine athletic girl, and attends . . . the best school of the kind in this country. She won two firsts and a second at the last athletic meet there." But rifts continued, and Sydney would later say the last time she saw her father was in 1925, when he attended her graduation from Boston's Sargent

School of Physical Education. She recalled that Taylor did not sit next to Daisy at the event.

That same year, Taylor was no longer living at the home on Hobson Avenue. For reasons that are unclear, Taylor had put the house in the name of his sister Lena, who in 1914 sold the property to Daisy for one dollar. Then, in 1925, Daisy sold the house for the assumption of mortgages of $1,800, and unpaid taxes and water bills, according to property records. The document said that Taylor gave up all rights to the property.

Taylor apparently did not receive any proceeds from the house sale, which exacerbated his financial troubles. He sold furniture and jewelry, and moved to a modest apartment at 14 Blossom Street. Word spread through Worcester of Taylor's poverty. By 1926, his old friend Harry Worcester Smith, who had helped arrange the meeting with President Roosevelt, gave him some money and began asking others to do the same. In a humiliating but necessary gesture, Smith wrote a story for the *Worcester Telegram* titled "A Champion Laid Low: An Appeal in Behalf of Major Taylor, Veteran Sportsman, Whose Fame Was Worldwide Just a Few Years Ago." He wrote how Taylor bought a Renault in Paris and brought it home, making it one of the first automobiles in Worcester. Taylor fought racism around the world and "wrote his name in flaming letters high in the sky of sportsmanship," Smith's column said. "None ever shone brighter." He had finished his career with $35,000, and invested some of it in three triple-decker homes and a cottage. Smith told readers how Taylor went into the auto tire business, mortgaging his home to help come up with the $15,000, "and from that time on it has been a tale of sadness rather than joy." Taylor's health, meanwhile, was depleted by an insidious case of influenza that had dragged on for months, requiring a lengthy hospitalization, and his once-powerful legs were hardly able to carry him. Such cases carried serious risks; an influenza epidemic a few years earlier had killed 1,294 people in Worcester, forcing the closure of schools, theaters, and churches to prevent the disease's spread. Taylor needed help from the people of Worcester "now more than ever, and let it not be a faint echo of the deafening cheers of years ago," wrote

Smith. To publicize the cause, nine of Taylor's trophies were displayed at a store on Main Street.

A few days later, a local reporter saw Taylor walking down Mechanic Street, where he stopped into Smith's office. He was dressed as finely as ever, in a long coat, tie, jacket, and hat. He posed for a photograph, looking upward, as if lost in somber thought. The reporter was stunned at how the onetime world's fastest man now had trouble standing on his "tired legs." Taylor looked at the reporter, answered his questions, and smiled "reflectively, but not bitterly." Still, the reporter wrote, "The years have a trick of crowding a man." Daisy was still by his side, according to the reporter, living with him in the apartment, but she had been forced to take work as a seamstress during Taylor's illness, in part to pay Sydney's fees at the Sargent School of Physical Education. Daisy would soon leave, however, moving to New York City, and the marriage was over, although they apparently did not finalize a divorce.

On Christmas Day, 1926, Taylor answered a knock on his door.

He was still recovering from his illness when a visitor handed him a check for $1,138.30, including $400 from Smith and his wife. "Please thank all my friends who have worked so hard to aid me," Taylor said. "I feel all right, but I am badly in need of rest and must be quiet at all times. It is a wonderful thing to have friends come to your support in a time of need. I cannot say enough to thank them." Smith told the *Telegram* that people across the city had contacted him to donate whatever they could, including many contributions under five dollars. "Christmas has been brightened," Smith said.

Soon, Taylor's plight was told around the country and the world, and more contributions trickled in, from Toronto to San Francisco to Sydney, Australia. An acquaintance who had sold tickets to Taylor's matches at Madison Square Garden said that "the Major's courage is worth $5." Damon Runyon, the famed columnist, wrote a widely distributed feature about Taylor, which he based on a letter he had received from a Worcester resident. "It seems that the Major lost everything he owned in an auto tire he invented, but which for some reason never was put on the market . . . [even though] the tire has merit," Runyon wrote.

Taylor, meanwhile, neared completion of his autobiography. He had gathered papers he had collected during his racing career, many of which had been carefully pasted into scrapbooks. There were account ledgers, postcards, diaries and letters, ribbons and bags, currency from around the world, calling cards and photographs—strands of an extraordinary life. The sport had faded, and his championships increasingly forgotten. Yet he had a story to tell, not a self-aggrandizing story, he said, but an inspirational one, of how hard work, morality, and determination can make one a champion. He wrote to his French promoter, Robert Coquelle, seeking photographs and documents. He was particularly interested in photos showing his match against Jacquelin, displaying his sense of humor by asking, "How is the old has been?"

Now, living alone, he exhausted much of his remaining funds to print his autobiography, which would be titled *The Fastest Bicycle Rider in the World*. He added a dedication to the man who had dreamed what was possible, and who had always believed in him.

*To my true friend and advisor, Louis D. "Birdie" Munger, whose confidence in me made possible my youthful opportunities for riding. Mr. Munger prophesied that one day he would make me the "fastest bicycle rider in the world" and lived to see his prophecy come true.*

The book's reprinting of dozens of newspaper articles made for dense reading, but the writing is rich with Taylor's life lessons, his pride, and his spirit. It was sprinkled with his poetry, which Taylor composed as a way to salve his soul. "I now hang up my silent steed; That served my purpose well indeed," began one poem, a tribute to his bicycle. He hung that bike not in the cellar but in the den, so he could gaze upon it, remember, and "keep the blues away."

The lesson of his life was not bitterness at the unbearable racism he had faced, but the hope he saw in the boys and girls who looked up to him and thought: if Major Taylor can be the world's fastest man, they, too, could succeed by employing "good habits and clean living." Directing his message to the youngsters that he hoped to inspire, he wrote, "I pray they will carry on in spite of that dreadful monster prejudice, and with patience, courage, fortitude and perseverance, achieve success for themselves. I trust they will use that terrible prejudice as an inspiration to struggle on to the heights in their chosen vocations. . . . My idea in giving this word to the boys and girls of my race is that they may be better prepared than I was to overcome these sinister conditions."

The rebirth of the KKK only increased the need to hear Taylor's message. As Taylor finished his book, the 1928 presidential contest between Republican Herbert Hoover and Democrat Al Smith was under way. Hoover's victory was dismissed by some black leaders as a repudiation of the party of Lincoln. No one had done more to disenfranchise blacks and promote "race hatred" than Hoover, Du Bois said. The migration of millions of blacks from South to North continued, and growing economic problems were shadowed by the hardening of racial lines in all parts of the country. Amid this atmosphere, Taylor undertook his mission to sell his autobiography, going from store to store, town to town—an arduous task, even in Worcester, where he was so widely admired. One day, he went to Easton's, a popular eating establishment in Worcester where the city's politicians and businessmen traded gossip, and was "escorted out the door," for reasons that were never explained. The townspeople might simply have been tired of his persistent pedaling. The book received modest notice, but occasionally was highlighted for telling a triumphant tale. The *New York Age,* which mistakenly cited an earlier proposed title of the book—"The Fastest Human in the World"—concluded that "Taylor was a real champion." The premiere edition of *Abbott's Monthly,* a magazine aimed at influential blacks, published a lengthy story about the book, titled "Put in Bike Race as Joke, He Won World's Championship." The article included one of the last photos taken of Taylor. He wore a suit and tie, kerchief in his jacket pocket, and held his autobiography in his hands. His head was angled, and he appeared deep in thought as he read his words, as if reflecting on his life. Long creases under his eyes were visible. His hair had yet to gray significantly, and he had lost weight in the prior couple of years. The suit was stylish and fitted him well. He still had visions of being a poet, and the magazine published his verses. The poem "Black Versus White" included a line that was said to be its author's motto: "God has created us both, and He can best judge."

In the summer of 1929, Munger visited New York City, staying at the Dauphin Hotel, a twelve-story, 320-room landmark on Broadway and 67th Street. Sixty-six years old and suffering from heart disease, he died in his room on July 29. Munger's widow sent a telegram to Taylor, knowing her husband would want the news directly conveyed. Two days later, the *New York Times* published a two-paragraph story headlined "Pioneer Bicycle Manufacturer and Racer Dies Suddenly." Elsewhere, the great champion's passing merited bare notice.

Taylor was distraught at Munger's passing and must have felt it was all the more important to sell his book, which emphasized how closely they had worked together to make him a champion. The timing was terrible. Three months after Munger's death, on October 29, the stock market crashed, leading to the Great Depression. Few people had the means to buy a book about a black cyclist who had been a champion three decades earlier. Taylor then headed to his birthplace, Indianapolis, where he visited with family and friends, and then headed to Chicago. He had long disdained staying at places catering only to his race because he felt that was an acceptance of segregation, but now he checked into a YMCA on South Wabash Avenue that had been established for blacks, in the South Side neighborhood of Bronzeville. The sad truth was that he was without his home or family, one of the millions swallowed up by the Depression, on the fringes of society. The five-story redbrick building, in which he now had a small room, was in the center of what was called the Black Metropolis, a city within the city that symbolized the unofficial racial boundaries of the time. Every segment of society suffered in the Depression, but the once-thriving black community was particularly hard hit.

Taylor was alone, and his wife and daughter didn't know where he was.

Taylor carried little with him to Chicago except for his clothes and copies of his autobiography, which he spent many days peddling at $3.50 a copy, a high price during such desperate times. Luckily, a member of the Chicago city council, James Bowler, was a former top bicycle racer who had competed against Taylor, and he helped the old champion get settled and may have provided financial assistance. The great migration of blacks from the South had helped swell the city to 3 million people, and the economic hardships of the time were evident in long lines for food and employment. Relief stations were set up across the city, and many residents learned for the first time how to plant vegetable gardens. The city's manufacturing base had been decimated, and unemployment reached fifty percent at the height of the Depression. Thousands of people lost their homes and crowded into makeshift shelters. Organized crime was rampant, and city government was corrupt. Taylor had arrived when the need for the YMCA was never greater, and homeless and hungry patrons crowded its rooms and dining hall.

One day in March 1932, Taylor's continuing bout with illness required hospitalization. He made his way to Provident Hospital, which catered to blacks. A surgeon performed heart surgery, and Taylor was then transferred to the charity ward of Cook County Hospital. He died there on June 21, 1932, at the age of fifty-three. No one claimed the body, so he was buried in a pauper's grave in Chicago's Mount Glenwood Cemetery, which had been established twenty-six years earlier for blacks. His death certificate stated the name of his wife as unknown.

"I'm bitter because he had to die with so little money," Sydney said seven decades later in an interview. "I didn't know he died. I didn't even know where he was."

Sydney and Daisy were living in New Orleans at the time and learned of Taylor's death only when someone sent them news of his death reported in a black-oriented newspaper, the *Chicago Defender*, which had closely followed his career and learned of his passing. It was one of the few publications in the country to run his obituary. Sydney read the headline "Major Taylor, Dies Penniless; Dies Here in Charity Ward, Once Startled World on Bicycle Track." Taylor, the *Defender* reminded its readers, "is the only member of his Race, outside the field of boxing, who ever held a world title."

Sydney had not seen her father for a number of years, and it was she who informed Daisy of the death. Sydney had been bitter at what she interpreted as her father's rigidity and aloofness. Only later, she said, did she truly understand the strains he had faced—the physical one of racing for decades, and the mental one of battling racism. The combination, she believed, had slowly killed him.

Another sixteen years passed before proper respects were paid. A group that called itself Bicycle Racing Stars of the Nineteenth Century had been discussing the tragedy of Taylor's final days. They convinced Frank Schwinn, the head of his eponymously named bicycle company, to help pay the cost of giving Taylor a proper memorial. His remains were exhumed and reburied elsewhere in the cemetery. On May 23, 1948, dozens of people attended the ceremony, although not Taylor's wife and daughter. Flowers were spread, an American flag was raised, and tributes spoken. Tom Hay, the aged owner of the Indianapolis bicycle shop who had employed Taylor as a young boy, was there. Ralph Metcalfe, a world champion runner, spoke about Taylor's place in history. A bronze plaque was laid upon the grave. Underneath an image of Taylor, his biceps bulging as he hunches over a bicycle in racing form, the final honor was delivered:

*World's champion bicycle racer who came up the hard way without hatred in his heart. An honest, courageous and God fearing, clean living gentlemanly athlete. A credit to his race who always gave out his best. Gone but not forgotten.*

In truth, he had been all but forgotten at that moment. The cycling craze had passed a few decades earlier, two world wars had been fought since Taylor last competed, Jesse Owens had triumphed in the Olympics in Berlin, and Jackie Robinson had broken the color barrier in Major League Baseball a year earlier. Yet Taylor's legacy deserved to be a larger part of history, not just the narrow world of cycling records, but as a transformative figure who stood against all the racist tactics that opponents could muster, and became the world's fastest man. The nation's history of racial division would define the United States from the moment of its founding, but the nation also rose on the backs of people such as Marshall Taylor, who, inspired by the nation's ideals, powered forward, insistent that Thomas Jefferson's declaration that "all men are created equal," even if written by a slave owner who did not believe that black people were equal, meant something.

One day toward the end of his life, Taylor pondered how he would be remembered after he died, when, as he mused, "I am finally run off my feet and flattened by Father Time." He wrote that he hoped his last thought on earth would be that "throughout life's great race I always gave the best that was in me. Life is too short for a man to hold bitterness in his heart."

Writing those words, he recalled a moment from the peak of his career, in 1901, shortly after he had won the world championship and had arrived in France. It was the year in which he first lost to the French champion Edmond Jacquelin and then defeated him in a rematch. But what he remembered was an encounter with a young French racer who seemed out of his league in the competition, his body too weak, his riding too unsteady. Taylor recalled seeing something in this opponent, and he approached him after they had competed against each other. He suggested how the rider should sit in his saddle, adjust his pedals and handlebars, and told him how to train. Taylor told him to avoid alcohol and tobacco, and said that "if he trained carefully and lived a clean life," then he, too, could become a champion.

Seven years later, when Taylor had returned to France near the end of his racing career, he lined up at the starting line, and there was the young racer he had once counseled. The Frenchman had, indeed, become the champion of his country, and now he was prepared to take on Taylor. As the racers rounded the last curve of the track, Taylor could not keep up with the Frenchman, who won the match. Yet Taylor could not help but be pleased. As Taylor recounted the story, he knew that many champions felt it was better to discourage such opponents, in order to reign longer. Taylor found that idea foolish, and not just because it was bad sportsmanship. After all, he wrote, it was "through the kindness of Louis D. (Birdie) Munger" that "I became inspired and rode to American and world's championships."

It seemed fitting that his story would begin and end with thoughts of his old friend, who had shown that, despite the country's many racists, there were also fellow human beings of great decency, who believed in fairness, and who, above all else, believed that Marshall Walter Taylor could be the world's fastest man and also set an example for those he conquered—and for those who, one day, would follow him.

# Appendix 1

## *Major Taylor's Cycling Records*

Major Taylor set many world records and earned numerous championships. The following is a sampling, as many records were made and quickly broken, and different organizations and countries used various methods to calculate records. It is hard to compare records of the same distance. Not all pacing was equal; it could be a single-seat or a five-seat bicycle, and motorized pacers ran at varying speeds, all of which greatly affected Taylor's speed. Track conditions also varied greatly. Taylor's triumphs repeatedly earned him the unofficial title of world's fastest man, a feat he memorialized by titling his autobiography *The Fastest Bicycle Rider in the World*. Producing a record time was only part of Taylor's achievement. Many of Taylor's most famous races were run with a purposeful strategy of starting slowly and thus did not produce record times, including two of his most famous victories: his 1899 world championship and his 1901 defeat of Edmond Jacquelin of France.

| Sept. 2, 1896 | 1/5 mile | unpaced, flying start | 0:23 3/5 | Capital City Track, Indianapolis |
| Aug. 27, 1898 | 1 mile | paced, standing start | 1:41 2/5 | Manhattan Beach, Brooklyn |
| Sept. 6, 1898 | 1/2 mile | paced | 0:58 4/5 | Hampden Park, Springfield, Mass. |
| Nov. 4, 1898 | 1 km | | 0:57 4/5 | Willow Grove, Pa. |

| Nov. 15, 1898 | 1/4 mile | paced | 0:22 1/5 | Woodside Park, Philadelphia |
|---|---|---|---|---|
| Nov. 16, 1898 | 1 mile | paced | 1:31 4/5 | Woodside Park, Philadelphia |
| Nov. 16, 1898 | 1/3 mile | paced | 0:29 3/5 | Woodside Park, Philadelphia |
| Nov. 16, 1898 | 1/2 mile | paced | 0:45 1/5 | Woodside Park, Philadelphia |
| Nov. 16, 1898 | 2/3 mile | paced | 1:00 4/5 | Woodside Park, Philadelphia |
| Nov. 16, 1898 | 3/4 mile | paced | 1:08 2/5 | Woodside Park, Philadelphia |
| Nov. 16, 1898 | 2 miles | paced | 3:13 2/5 | Woodside Park, Philadelphia |
| Aug. 3, 1899 | 1 mile | motor-paced | 1:22 2/5 | Garfield Park Track, Chicago |
| Aug. 10, 1899 | 1 mile | | 3:02 | World Championship, Queen's Park, Montreal |
| Nov. 9, 1899 | 1/4 mile | motor-paced | 0:20 | Garfield Park Track, Chicago |
| Nov. 10, 1899 | 1/2 mile | motor-paced | 0:41 | Garfield Park Track, Chicago |
| Nov. 15, 1899 | 1 mile | motor-paced | 1:19 | Garfield Park Track, Chicago |
| Dec. 13, 1900 | 1/2 mile | unpaced | 0:55 2/5 | Madison Square Garden |
| Dec. 14, 1900 | 1/4 mile | unpaced | 0:25 4/5 | Madison Square Garden |
| August 1908 | 1/2 mile | standing start | 0:42 1/5 | Buffalo track, Paris |
| August 1908 | 1/4 mile | standing start | 0:25 2/5 | Buffalo track, Paris |
| August 28, 1908 | 1 mile | motor-paced | 1:33 2/5 | Buffalo track, Paris |

# APPENDIX 1

Taylor's consistency is evident in his overwhelming victories during his first three European tours, as recorded by Taylor and his promoters:

1901—42 first places, 11 seconds, 3 thirds, 1 fourth
1902—40 first places, 15 seconds, 2 thirds
1903—31 first places, 22 seconds, 9 thirds

SOURCE: The records in this list were compiled by Lynne Tolman of the Major Taylor Association, based on contemporaneous newspaper and magazine accounts. The compilation of records from 1901–03 comes from: Paul Hamelle and Robert Coquelle, *Major Taylor* (Paris: Montdidier, 1904 and 1907). Taylor wrote that he won forty-two first places in 1901, while Hamelle and Coquelle put the number at thirty-nine.

# Appendix 2

## *Major Taylor's Training Regimen*

One of Major Taylor's most remarkable achievements was transforming himself from a scrawny boy into a perfectly developed and muscular man who, at five feet seven inches and his ideal weight of 154 pounds, beat those who were stronger, taller, and more physically suited to the discipline of track sprints. He studied the methods of champions, learning from his mentor, Birdie Munger, and his hero, Arthur Zimmerman, who wrote a book focused on training. He adopted an exercise and nutrition regimen that was unrivaled among his peers—and still holds lessons for those who dream of following Taylor's path, or who wish simply to gain fitness. He recommended abstaining from alcohol and tobacco, eating wisely, and working simultaneously on strength and conditioning. Here is Taylor's training regimen, gleaned from advice he wrote in the *New York American*, his autobiography, various articles, and photographs.

### A typical day

- 6 a.m. Upon awakening, go through a series of stretches and light strength exercises before eating.
- 7 a.m. Breakfast, typically protein-rich with at least one egg. Rest and digest.

- 10 a.m. If Taylor was competing in middle-distance races, he would go for an extended ride on paved roads, such as a circuit from Brooklyn to Long Island. If he was preparing for his more typical half-mile and one-mile contests, he rarely went on lengthy road rides. Instead, he performed what today would be known as interval training, alternating between a rolling pace and the fastest sprint possible, increasing his aerobic capacity. Sessions typically lasted a few miles, but he would vary the routine, sometimes interspersing sprints during ten miles on a track, changing his position from high to low on the handlebars to emulate racing conditions. Then he would get a "good stiff rubdown" from an experienced trainer, who worked out the kinks and knots that would inevitably result from hunching over his bicycle for extended periods.
- Noon. A hearty midday meal, which he called supper. He took an hour or two to digest.
- 3 p.m. Repeat the morning routine, either a training ride or sprints around the track, followed by another rubdown.
- 6 p.m. Dinner. Another protein-rich meal, typically including at least two eggs.
- 9 p.m. Read, write letters, paste articles into his scrapbook, make notations in his account book, and go to sleep.

### Strength training and other exercises

- These sessions could be morning or afternoon. Taylor used a pulley machine called the Whitley Exerciser, a system of cords that could be tied to weights or a doorframe that was used to strengthen the back, chest, arms, and muscles. The system was invented by Alexander Whitley in 1894, coinciding with the beginning of Taylor's career. Holding two handles of the exerciser, Taylor could pull himself up, or pull his arms back, or perform one of many other moves to increase his strength. This was crucial because cyclists often have strong legs but weak upper bodies. Taylor knew that a strong core and back were essential to maintain his position on the bicycle and have power for a winning sprint. He supplemented the workout by lifting weights, often using a set of clubs that resembled bowling pins.

• Sparring. One of Taylor's favorite routines was boxing with a punching bag or a sparring partner, which improved his upper-body strength, sharpened his reflexes, and toned his arms. Taylor believed this practice was so important that he brought a punching bag with him to France and suspended it from a ceiling, which fascinated his competitors. He punched the bag "with a pleasure always new," he wrote in a French newspaper. "The practice . . . is an excellent exercise which strengthens the muscles." He complemented the routine by jumping rope for long stretches, which helped increase his lung capacity.

Nutrition and weight

Taylor's focus on nutrition also set him apart from his competitors, many of whom drank, smoke, and ate poorly. He was obsessive about the right amount of carbohydrates and protein, avoiding fatty foods and empty calories, a concept familiar to today's athletes but lesser known to many in the 1890s. He did not, however, skimp on food; he knew the importance of replacing the many burned calories with healthful food. "Although I use care in what I eat, I eat all I can," Taylor wrote. He weighed himself daily and fastidiously monitored his diet, believing that "a matter of ounces over or under my normal weight" would lead to defeat.

Taylor's training dedication sometimes drew as much attention as his races. In Australia, he wrote, "Thousands of people came to the track daily to watch my training preparation" and "the riders expressed astonishment at my training stunts and the great amount of work I did, all of which was new to them." In France, he was profiled in a sports magazine as one of the age's most exquisite athletes. Taylor took great pride in his training transformation. He published pictures of himself in his autobiography in which he wore only shorts, his body bulging with muscles as he emulated his riding position on a bicycle. He said that his legs were considered "the best ever developed" for bicycle racing. "Clean living and serious training," he concluded, "are necessary for the perfect condition."

# Acknowledgments

Seventeen years ago, in 2001, while working for the *Boston Globe*, I proposed writing a story for the newspaper's Sunday magazine about Major Taylor. With the enthusiastic support of the magazine's editor, Nick King, I set off in search of the story, traveling to the Indiana State Museum to read Taylor's scrapbooks, and searching the archives of the *Globe* and other newspapers. Most important, I traveled to Pittsburgh, where Taylor's ninety-six-year-old daughter, Sydney Taylor Brown, lived in a nursing home. She agreed to see me, and I was delighted to find a vibrant woman whose memory of her father was strong and filled with pride. She remembered seeing her father race in Paris, and she provided a sobering account of the difficulties he faced later in life. I also had the chance to meet Taylor's great-granddaughter, Jan Brown, who worked in Boston. The cover story in the magazine ran the weekend after the attacks of September 11, 2001. At a time when most readers corresponded by mail, I received dozens of letters, most of them appreciative of reading the story at such a difficult time for our country, and it was then I first thought about writing a book about Major Taylor. Little did I imagine that this was just the beginning of an oft-interrupted quest that would last until I completed this manuscript in the fall of 2018. I had worked on and off for years, collecting newly digitized newspapers stories that greatly expanded my knowledge, and reading histories of the Gilded Age and Jim Crow era, which provided the framework of the time in which Taylor lived.

In these intervening years, I have had the opportunity to work on four other books: coauthoring biographies of presidential candidates John F. Kerry and Mitt Romney while working at the *Globe*, and of Donald Trump at my current employer, *The Washington Post*; and authoring a book titled *Flight from Monticello: Thomas Jefferson at War*. Each of these books relied on putting the subject of the biography in the context of history. As distinct as Thomas Jefferson and Major Taylor seem to be, I viewed them as a continuum in my authorship. Jefferson famously wrote that "all men are created equal" but owned three hundred slaves in his lifetime and wrote disparagingly about blacks. Taylor believed in Jefferson's aspirational words, and disproved the thinking behind his racist beliefs. I viewed Taylor's story as the juxtaposition to history. In the same year that the US Supreme Court infamously ruled in *Plessy v. Ferguson*, legalizing separate but equal accommodation, Taylor shocked the nation by showing that given the chance for truly equal competition, he could beat the best sprinter in the world at Madison Square Garden. The story of Taylor's bicycling victories is thrilling by itself, and it provides the narrative engine of this book, but I also wanted to harness his story to understand the momentous and tortuous times in which he lived. As a white historian writing primarily about a black man, I was particularly cognizant of the need to have the broadest possible understanding of the man and his times, and I asked many people to help me understand this history.

The Taylor family has been welcoming and enthusiastic from the beginning, starting with Sydney Taylor Brown, who died in 2005 at the age of 101. She lived her own extraordinary life, helping others during decades of social work. Jan Brown, the aforementioned great-granddaughter, was a particular source of inspiration, meeting with me during the research for this book, and putting me in touch with knowledgeable sources. Karen Brown-Donovan, another great-granddaughter, was equally enthusiastic. Both Jan and Karen provided valuable thoughts after reading a draft of the manuscript. I valued conversations of other members of the Taylor family, including Barbara Brown and Joyce Bush Brown.

I am also grateful to two extraordinary journalists and friends who read the manuscript and made valuable suggestions: my *Washington Post* colleague and *Trump Revealed* coauthor, Marc Fisher, and my former *Boston Globe* colleague and author of numerous fine biographies, including a recent one of Richard Nixon, John Aloysius Farrell. My

# ACKNOWLEDGMENTS

eldest brother, Clif Kranish, who has ridden more miles on his bicycle than I ever will, also read the manuscript and provided numerous insights.

Taylor's autobiography, *The Fastest Bicycle Rider in the World*, is an essential source. In addition to reproducing many articles about Taylor, it provides insights into his thinking that cannot be gleaned elsewhere. Taylor's letters to his wife, Daisy, are extant only for 1909, but they are an unequaled source of his contemporaneous thinking, his emotions, and his humanity. (Daisy's letters to him do not survive.) I benefited from those who have gone before me in researching and writing about Taylor's life, most notably Andrew Ritchie, who in 1988 published the first biography, *Major Taylor*, and helped revive interest in the racer's career. He spent many hours with Sydney and pored over articles in the precomputer age. I learned insights from Todd Balf's *Major*, and also from Conrad and Terry Kerber's *Major Taylor* and Jim Fitzpatrick's *Major Taylor in Australia*.

I had long been an admirer of David V. Herlihy, the author of *Bicycle: The History* and *The Lost Cyclist*, and am indebted to him for reading a draft of the manuscript and making many valuable suggestions. Douglas Blackmon, the author of *Slavery by Another Name*, helped me understand the racial climate in which Taylor lived.

Lynne Tolman, an editor at the *Worcester Telegram & Gazette* who runs the Major Taylor Association as a labor of love, provided valuable insights after reading a draft of the manuscript, and she unearthed copies of newspaper stories that helped expand my knowledge. She also compiled a list of Taylor's racing records. Kisha Tandy, the associate curator of the Indiana State Museum, where Taylor's scrapbooks, letters, account books, and other papers are kept, proved to be an essential and enthusiastic source of information. She drove me around Indianapolis to help me imagine the world of Taylor's youth and provided invaluable commentary and suggestions. Gloria Hall, the owner of Taylor's home in Worcester, graciously showed me the inside of the house, provided key housing sale records, and accompanied me on a tour of the city.

Pascal Sergent, one of France's preeminent cycling journalists, met

305

with me in Lille and allowed me to comb through his unparalleled archive of articles and artifacts. He also shared his knowledge about Edmond Jacquelin, the subject of one of his many books.

I spent many hours at the New York Public Library, the New-York Historical Society, the Library of Congress, the Boston Public Library, and other institutions reading through microfilm and magazines and manuscripts, helped at each location by librarians whose work is highly valued.

Among the many books on the Gilded Age and Jim Crow era, I found a number to be particularly valuable, including *Gotham*, by Edwin G. Burrows and Mike Wallace; *Stamped from the Beginning*, by Ibram X. Kendi; *America 1908*, by Jim Rasenberger; *Drive!*, by Lawrence Goldstone; *Birth of a Movement*, by Dick Lehr; and *Up from History: The Life of Booker T. Washington*, by Robert J. Norrell. A complete list is in the bibliography.

This work was profoundly enhanced by the ongoing digitization of newspapers. Taylor kept scrapbooks that contained hundreds of stories about him, and many of them can only be read today because he painstakingly pasted them into his memory book. But he couldn't see or clip every story, and I was able to read hundreds more because so many publications around the world have been digitized. In addition to US aggregation services such as newspapers.com, newspaper archive.com, ancestry.com, and genealogybank.com, I was able to tap into archives in France, Australia, and elsewhere.

Thanks to my agent, David Black, who first heard about my interest in a Taylor book in 2003, worked with me on two other projects in the interim, and encouraged my continued interest that led to this book. Thanks also to Matt Belford, Emma Peters, and Jennifer Herrera at the David Black Literary Agency.

I am particularly grateful to be published by Scribner, where editor in chief Colin Harrison, who edited *Trump Revealed*, enthusiastically took on this project, providing countless valuable suggestions. He is one of the best in the business, and his keen eye for history, context, and character improved every page. Sarah Goldberg, a Scribner associate editor, smoothly guided the manuscript and answered my

# ACKNOWLEDGMENTS

many queries. Copyeditor Jane Herman provided superb suggestions. I am also indebted to Kathleen Rizzo, Scribner's senior production editor; Kara Watson, Ashley Gilliam, and Kelsey Manning in marketing; Abigail Novak and Brian Belfiglio in publicity; page designer Erich Hobbing; and the indefatigable leaders of the house, Publisher Nan Graham, Associate Publisher Roz Lippel, and President Susan Moldow. Martin Baron, editor of the *Washington Post*, has been an advocate of my authorship for newspapers and books from the earliest days. Thank you to all the editors over the years who have supported and improved my work.

Mike Butchko, the owner of The Bicycle Place in Silver Spring, Maryland, where I have been a patron for thirty years, patiently helped me understand how Taylor viewed the technical side of cycling. Trevor Lazarus, a native Australian, read the chapter on Australia and provided valuable insight. To my cycling friends, thanks for inspiring me and letting me tag along.

I have never raced a bicycle, but I have been riding one since I was a child. I can still turn the pedals and sometimes even keep up with my riding pals on weekend sojourns. They come from every walk of life, they wait to regroup, and they look out for one another—not a bad model for society. Ride safely, my friends.

No book is written without crucial support and understanding from an author's family. My daughters, Jessica and Laura, accompanied me when I traveled to Paris to conduct research. We spent a memorable couple of days retracing Taylor's footsteps, including a visit to the still-thriving Hotel Scribe, where a kind hotel employee let us wander and provided historical background. Jessica and Laura had heard me talk about Taylor for years, and they gave me much to think about with their curiosity and suggestions. My wife, Sylvia, patiently listened to my discoveries and provided valuable proofreading when I finally showed her a draft of the manuscript. I am forever grateful to my mother, Allye Kranish, and my late father, Arthur Kranish, who encouraged my love of history and writing. They also provided my first bike, a red Schwinn, when I was seven years old. The bicycle is freedom, which they gave me, in this and many other ways.

# Notes

Prologue

3   *one million new bikes:* Gary Allan Tobin, "The Bicycle Boom of the 1890s," *Journal of Popular Culture*, Spring 1974.

3   *the kind descriptions:* "Six Day Grind Now On," *Referee and Cycle Trade Journal*, December 5, 1896.

3   *"dark secret of Gowanus":* "Henshaw Wins a Handicap," *Brooklyn Daily Eagle*, December 6, 1896.

5   *"straining every nerve":* Ibid.


Chapter 1: Birdie Takes Flight

9   *the very future:* "Detroit Historical Society: Frontiers to Factories." Accessed at http://detroithistorical.org/buildingdetroit/curriculum_industrial.php.

9   *a foreman:* Detroit City Directory, 1844.

10  *eight thousand square miles:* Graydon M. Meints, *Michigan Railroads & Railroad Companie* (East Lansing, MI: MSU Press, 1992), 12–13.

10  *tower, turrets, and marble floors:* Accessed at http://www.historicdetroit.org/building/michigan-central-railroad-depot/.

10  *were whisked:* Northern Pacific Railroad Company, *The Wonderland Route to the Pacific Coast* (St. Paul: Northern Pacific Railroad, 1885), 9–10.

11  *"knocked out":* Lyman Hotchkiss Bagg, *Ten Thousand Miles on a Bicycle* (New York: Karl Koon, 1887), 331–32. Quotes *The Wheel*, July 17, 1885.

11  *"most remarkable race ever run":* "The Big Four Century Road Race," *Canadian Wheelman*, July 30, 1885, 2, 152–54.

13  *local riders fail to win:* "Won by a Westerner: The Twenty-Four-Hour Bicycle Record Broken," *Boston Globe*, August 2, 1885.

13  *no moonlight:* "Out Record Smashing: Bicyclists Pushing Pedals in the Moonlight," *Boston Globe*, November 21, 1885.

13  *rigged two lanterns:* "Munger Stopped by Rain," *Canadian Wheelman*, December 1885.

13  *"not at all disheartened":* "Plucky Munger," *Boston Globe*, November 11, 1885.

# NOTES

13  *"by an unlucky accident":* "Great Performance by Munger," *Canadian Wheelman*, December 1885.

13  *"delighted howl of his friends":* "Lowered Again: Munger and Huntley Break the Twenty-Four-Hour Bicycle Record," *Boston Globe*, November 22, 1885.

14  *"the life of every tour":* "The Wheel: A Champion Cyclist in Town," *New Orleans Times Picayune*, January 15, 1886.

14  *Munger was "wonderful":* "The Wheel: Munger Breaks the Fifty Miles Record," *New Orleans Times Picayune*, April 3, 1886; "Munger Beats the Twenty-Five Mile Record," *New Orleans Times Picayune*, March 3, 1886.

14  *New Orleans to Boston:* "New Orleans Historical | 1886 Cycling Tour: New Orleans to Boston." Accessed at http://www.neworleanshistorical .org/items/show/502#.UhFBfBZL6Qk. "A Long Ride on Bicycles," *New York Herald*, May 23, 1886. "Bicycle Briefs," *Cleveland Plain Dealer*, May 2, 1886. "By Bicycle to Boston: A Full Account of the Famous Trip of the New Orleans Tourists," *New Orleans Daily Picayune*, July 23, 1886.

15  *effectively been blackballed:* "The Michigan State Meet," *Cleveland Plain Dealer*, June 23, 1886.

16  *"matchless wonders":* Northern Pacific Railroad Company, *The Wonderland Route to the Pacific Coast* (St. Paul: Northern Pacific Railroad, 1885), 3.

17  *Tribes were relocated:* Estimates of the North American Indian population before the arrival of white settlers vary greatly, from 1.1 million to 18 million. The population had dropped to 600,000 by 1800, due to war and disease that came largely from interaction with whites, and there were only about 250,000 around the time Munger arrived in California in 1886.

18  *"more of a cross-country hike":* "Bicycle Champ of Other Days Living in City: Louis de Munger Winner of Many Medals and World Titles—Made First Woman's Wheel," *Springfield* (Massachusetts) *Republican*, December 23, 1924, 12. (The exact early part of the route is unclear but, given the path taken by a rider who was advised by Munger a few years later, Munger may have gone through the Mojave Desert, and the territories of Arizona and New Mexico, instead of the more northern route through the Great Salt Lake basin dominated by Mormon settlers taken by Stevens.)

19  *"I will never ride":* "'Birdie' Munger's Hardihood," *Chicago Tribune*, August 8, 1899.

20  *"the pluck of L. D. Munger":* "Women Cyclists and an Idiot," *Chicago Inter Ocean*, April 21, 1889.

## Chapter 2: The Rise of Major Taylor

21  *226,000 men, women, and children:* The Civil War Home Page. Accessed at http://www.civil-war.net/pages/1860_census.html.

22 *last name of Wilhite:* Major Taylor wrote in a 1909 letter to his wife, Daisy, that his father "had enlisted in the war under . . . the name of Gilbert Wilhite," for reasons that were not explained. See: Major Taylor to Daisy Taylor, June 1909, page 7, Major Taylor papers, Indiana State Museum. Wilhite is listed in the Kentucky adjutant general's report as having enlisted in Company A of the 122nd Colored Troops on September 30, 1864. See Report of the Kentucky adjutant general (Frankfort, KY: Kentucky Yeoman Office, 1866), 102. Information about the service of that division can be found in numerous historical documents. Wilhite's discharge in Corpus Christi, Texas, is noted in military records. See: Compiled Military Service Records of Volunteer Union Soldiers Who Served the United States Colored Troops: 56th–138th USCT Infantry, 1864–1866. Gilbert later was connected to the Soldier's Home in Marion, Indiana, according to Taylor's letter. Records at Indianapolis Crown Hill Cemetery show that a person listed as "Gilbert Wilheight" is buried there, and that his date of death corresponds with that of Gilbert Taylor, who died in Chicago on November 10, 1910, and was buried in Crown Hill shortly thereafter. Further evidence is provided in a disability document that shows Gilbert Wilheight listed his close relative as his daughter Lena of Indianapolis. That is the name of Gilbert Taylor's daughter.

22 *750,000 soldiers died:* Guy Gugliotta, "New Estimate Raises Civil War Death Toll," *New York Times*, April 2, 2012.

23 *one hundred "well men":* Roger Pickenpaugh, *Captives in Gray: The Civil War Prison of the Union* (Tuscaloosa: University of Alabama Press, 2009), 233.

23 *census worker noted:* US Census, Jefferson County, Kentucky, July 13, 1970, 162.

25 *"that big gold medal":* Marshall "Major" Taylor, *The Fastest Bicycle Rider in the World* (Worcester: Wormley Publishing Company, 1928), 3–4.

26 *"fancy and speed":* "Our City People," *Indianapolis Freeman*, August 16, 1890. In writing about the event many years later, Taylor said it happened when he was about thirteen years old, but the clipping makes clear he was eleven.

26 *older, stronger contestants:* "Wheelmen at Peoria Results of the Bicycle Contests Eastern Men Show in Hotter Form Than Their Western Competitors," *Chicago Herald*, September 14, 1890. Taylor tells of a similar event but says it was in 1892 when he was fourteen.

26 *"I finally perfected the pneumatic tire":* "Dunlop Retells Story of Pneumatic Tire," *Motor World*, June 19, 1913, 23–26.

27 *"hoots and jeers":* Taylor, *Fastest Bicycle Rider*, 5.

27 *forced to ride with solid tires:* "Bicycle Records Broken," *Chicago Inter Ocean*, September 14, 1890, 3.

28 *"couple of goats apiece":* Adam Hochschild, *King Leopold's Ghost: A Story of*

*Greed, Terror, and Heroism in Colonial Africa* (Boston: Houghton Mifflin, 1998), 158–62.

## Chapter 3: The President and the Cyclists

33 *"the history of civilization"*: Christopher Brian Booker, "The Presidency of Benjamin Harrison: Dashed Hopes for African Americans," *African-Americans & The Presidency*. Accessed at http://www.blacksandpresidency.com/benjaminharrison.php.

34 *"parade broke all records"*: "Cyclists at Their Best," *New York Times*, July 19, 1892.

34 *"their graceful riding"*: "Whirling Wheelman: They Make an Attractive Parade on Pennsylvania Avenue," *Washington Evening Star*, July 19, 1892, 6.

35 *prices would eventually drop:* Gary Allan Tobin, "The Bicycle Boom of the 1890s," *Journal of Popular Culture*, Spring 1974.

35 *"recognition of its philanthropy"*: "What Bicycles Have Done," *New York Times*, September 11, 1892.

36 *"at least one prize"*: "Close of the Meet That Has Been Very Successful," (Washington) *Evening Star*, July 20, 1892.

36 *"dangerous turns"*: "Cyclists at Their Best: A Great Meet of Wheelmen in Washington," *New York Times*, July 20, 1892.

37 *"but times had changed"*: "Whirling Wheelmen: They Make an Attractive Parade on Pennsylvania Avenue," *Washington Evening Star*, July 19, 1892.

37 *"landing with great force"*: "Tame Bicycle Races," *New York Times*, July 21, 1892.

37 *"painfully injured"*: "Close of the Meet That Has Been Very Successful," *Washington Evening Star*, July 20, 1892.

37 *his three bicycles:* "Gone Are the Wheelmen," *Washington Post*, July 24, 1892.

## Chapter 4: Birdie and Major in Indianapolis

39 *a $300 piano:* "Chicago in the Van. Peoria Bicycle Races Won by Garden City Riders," *Chicago Inter Ocean*, September 28, 1892.

39 *"may strike his fancy"*: "The Racing Men of This and Other Countries," *Wheel and Cycling Trade Review*, 10 (December 30, 1892): 36.

40 *sold for $65:* The Wright Brothers; Cycle Production and Sales, Air and Space Museum website. Accessed at https://airandspace.si.edu/exhibitions/wright-brothers/online/who/1895/production.cfm.

40 *brothers . . . Bruner:* The three cousins' mother was the former Mary Munger, Birdie's aunt.

41 *"as familiar as Shakespeare":* Consolidated Illustrating, *Indianopolis of Today* (Consolidated Illustrating Co., 1896), 158.

42 *"throughout the cycling world":* Untitled, *Washington Times,* May 14, 1899.

42 *the world's finest: Indianapolis of Today,* 158.

42 *$100 or more:* 1897 ad for Munger's Worcester Cycle, which says "It's Here! Worcester Cycle. $100. Designed by Munger. Built by skilled workmen under his supervision. It's the bicycle you have been waiting and longing for."

43 *two minutes and seven seconds:* "Anecdotes of the Racing Men," *Detroit Free Press,* September 19, 1897.

43 *"his own son":* Marshall "Major" Taylor, *The Fastest Bicycle Rider in the World* (Worcester: Wormley Publishing Co., 1928), 10–13.

44 *"that boy some day":* Ibid., 12–13, 51.

45 *"severest physical exertion"* Arthur Zimmerman and Frank Bowden, *Points for Cyclists with Training* (Leicester, England: F.W.S. Clarke), 25.

45 *Windle had grown up:* "W. W. Windle Retires," *Worcester Spy,* February 1, 1894; Ellery Crane, *Historic Homes and Institutions of Worcester County, Massachusetts,* vol. 2 (New York: Lewis Publishing Co., 1907), 116.

46 *"proudest boy in the world":* Taylor, *Fastest Bicycle Rider,* 12–13.

46 *"just and withering reflections":* "Emancipation Day at Columbus, Ind.," *Indianapolis Freeman,* August 12, 1893.

47 *diamond-encrusted gold cup:* "Zimmerman Wins an International Race," *New York Tribune,* August 25, 1893; "Capital Bike Races," *Evansville* (Indiana) *Courier,* August 25, 1893.

47 *"healthful and invigorating":* "Will Ride a Bicycle," *Washington Post,* May 19, 1897.

47 *administration of Grover Cleveland:* Alyn Brodsky, *Grover Cleveland: A Study in Character* (New York: St. Martin's Press, 2000), 452–53.

48 *banning blacks:* "Charley Murphy Reinstated," *New York Times,* February 22, 1894.

49 *unanimously opposed the ban:* J. A. Mangan and Andrew Ritchie, *Ethnicity, Sport, Identity: Struggles for Status* (London: Psychology Press, 2004), 13–16.

49 *illiteracy rate was fifty-seven percent:* National Assessment of Adult Literacy, National Center for Education Statistics. Accessed at https://nces.ed.gov /naal/lit_history.asp.

50 *"(colored cyclist)":* Major Taylor, letter to the editor, *Bearings,* February 9, 1894.

50 *"does not need":* Phoebus, *Referee & Cycling Trade Journal,* March 30, 1894, 752.

50 *"benefit of another man":* "Will Both Resort to Law: Munger and Barrett

will seek redress through the courts," *Chicago Daily Tribune*, March 24, 1893.

51   *"complete power over him":* Untitled, *Washington Times*, May 14, 1899.

52   *"great interest is centered":* "The Inter Ocean Cup," *Chicago Inter Ocean*, July 27, 1895.

52   *"very certain that no rider":* Taylor, *Fastest Bicycle Rider*, 8–9.

53   *"severing relations with the firm":* Ibid., 13.

53   *"champion rider of America":* Ibid., 13.

## Chapter 5: No Such Prejudice

55   *nearly 100,000 people:* Accessed at https://books.google.com/books?id=KKk WAQAAMAAJ&pg=PA13&lpg=PA13&dq=worcester+population+1895 &source=bl&ots=zwIwh9uZH0&sig=4j06hl635wl6W-AMLN9xwGp YYXg&hl=en&sa=X&sqi=2&ved=0ahUKEwim-92AjvrSAhVK9YMKH TMlBKsQ6AEIOjAI#v=onepage&q=worcester%20population%201895 &f=true.

56   *Worcester Cycle Manufacturing:* "Bicycle Notes," *The Iron Age*, October 10, 1895. Additional details come from Sanborn maps.

56   *on the Underground Railroad:* Janette Thomas Greenwood, *First Fruits of Freedom* (Chapel Hill: University of North Carolina Press, 2009).

57   *rounded two-story turret: American Architect and Architecture*, June 4, 1887, 566. Accessed at https://archive.org/stream/americanarchitec21newyuoft#page/n565/mode/2up.

57   *he trained for many months:* Alfred S. Roe, *The Worcester Young Men's Christian Association* (Worcester: Self-published, 1901), 81–85.

57   *"people received me":* Marshall "Major" Taylor, *The Fastest Bicycle Rider in the World* (Worcester: Wormley Publishing Co., 1928), 1, 14.

58   *"very pretty girl":* Jean Pardee-Clarke, "The Growing Popularity of Physical Training for Women," *Munsey's Magazine*, September 1896.

58   *first "physique contest":* Erwan Le Corre, "The History of Physical Fitness." Accessed at https://www.artofmanliness.com/2014/09/24/the-history-of-physical-fitness/.

58   *"cultivation of the mind":* J. M. Erwin and A. A. Zimmerman, *Zimmerman Abroad and Points on Training* (Chicago: The Blakely Printing Company, 1895), 143–68.

59   *"plane of living":* Alison Blay-Palmer, *Food Fears* (New York: Routledge, 2016), 24.

59   *rigorously planned diet:* Wilbur Atwater, H. O. Sherman, and R. C. Carpenter, "The Effect of Severe and Prolonged Muscular Work" (Washington, DC: Government Printing Office, 1901).

59   *any of his competitors:* Taylor, *Fastest Bicycle Rider*, 14.

59   *"matter of ounces"*: Ibid., 54.
60   *on his first try:* Ibid., 15.
60   *"Were it not for Munger"*: "Munger's Protégé, Major Taylor, Captures the Time Prize," *Worcester Spy*, October 20, 1895.
60   *"my old hero"*: Taylor, *Fastest Bicycle Rider*, 16
61   *"as a trick rider"*: "Munger Cycle Club," undated clipping in Taylor scrapbook.

## Chapter 6: The Bicycle Craze

63   *reached at least nine stories:* Edwin G. Burrows and Mike Wallace, *Gotham* (New York: Oxford University Press, 1999), 1050. A number of the impressions of New York City from this time period are drawn from this book.
63   *Insurance Building at 348 feet:* Ibid., 1000–1001.
64   *dumping twenty-two pounds:* Elizabeth Kolbert, "Hosed: Is There a Quick Fix for the Climate?" *The New Yorker*, November 16, 2009.
65   *dozen telephone exchanges:* Burrows and Wallace, *Gotham*, 1062.
65   *shortly after Brooklyn*: Ibid., 1111–31.
65   *Blacks had increasingly:* "Archives: New York City's 1900 'Race Riot,'" David Rosen, *Black Star News*, September 21, 2015. Accessed at http:// www.blackstarnews.com/us-politics/justice/archives-new-york-city's-1900 -race-riot.html; and https://www.census.gov/population/www/documen tation/twps0076/NYtab.pdf.
66   *cited the eugenics movement:* Dorothy Roberts, *Killing the Black Body* (New York: Vintage Books, 2016), 59–61.
66   *4 million bicycles:* "Gossip for Cyclists," *Saint Paul Globe*, December 31, 1896.
66   *arrested for dangerous driving:* Carlton Reid, "New York City Once Had the Best Bike Path in the World." Accessed at http://www.roadswerenotbuilt forcars.com/coneyislandcyclepath/.
66   *Quadricycle:* "This Day in History," June 4, 1896, History.com. Accessed at http://www.history.com/this-day-in-history/henry-ford-test-drives-his -quadricycle.
67   *"river of colored fire"*: H.T.P, "The Return of the Horse," *The Bookman* 13, no. 6 (July 1901): 425–27.
67   *"lead directly to sin"*: "Begins a Crusade Against Bicycles," *Chicago Tribune*, September 2, 1896.
67   *"had never before experienced"*: Peter Zheutlin, *Around the World on Two Wheels* (New York: Citadel Press Books, 2007), 165–68.
67   *"untrammeled womanhood"*: Ann D. Gordon, ed., *The Selected Papers of Elizabeth Cady Stanton and Susan B. Anthony: An Awful Hush*, vol. 6 (New Jersey: Rutgers University Press, 2013 ), 33–34.

68   *"swathed in tulle or lace"*: Maureen E. Montgomery, *Displaying Women: Spectacles of Leisure in Edith Wharton's New York* (London: Psychology Press, 1998), 103.

68   *"usual order of things"*: "The World Awheel," *Mumsey's Magazine* 15 (April to September 1896): 155–56.

69   *"girl friends ride there"*: William B. McCash and June McCash, *The Jekyll Island Club: Southern Haven for America's Millionaires* (Athens: University of Georgia Press, 1989), 50.

70   *advertising resorts:* Burrows and Wallace, *Gotham*, 1066.

70   Nymphs and Satyr: "Hoffman House & the Nymphs and Satyr," *Legends of America* website. Accessed at http://www.legendsofamerica.com/picture pages/PP-SaloonDecor-9.html.

70   *patents had soared:* Robert Jabaily, "Major Taylor, Colonel Pope, and the general commotion over bicycles," *The Ledger*, Federal Reserve Bank of Boston, Spring 2001, 9.

71   *"fat men, Indian chiefs"*: "Last Days of the Cycle Show," *New York Herald*, January 25, 1896.

Chapter 7: The Rivalry Begins

76   *"most attractive exhibits"*: "In Madison Square Garden," *New York Journal*, January 22, 1896.

76   *"Cannon Bald!"*: "On His Native Heath, Bald Receives the Plaudits of His Fellow Townsmen," *The Wheel*, July 17, 1896, 71.

77   *"see what was going on"*: "Vernons' Colors Go to the Front, Fifty Thousand People See Them Win the Telegram Trophy Race," *Worcester Telegram*, May 10, 1896.

77   *"a sure winner"*: "Casey the Winner," *Worcester Spy*, May 10, 1896.

79   *Catholics and Protestants:* "Louisiana's Separate Car Law," *New York Times*, May 19, 1896, 3. I was alerted to the placement of the story by a reference in: Ibram X. Kendi, *Stamped from the Beginning: The Definitive History of Racist Ideas in America* (New York: Nation Books, 2016).

79   *he was "elated"*: "Discussing the Race," *New York Times*, June 1, 1896.

79   *"some of the kindnesses"*: Marshall "Major" Taylor, *The Fastest Bicycle Rider in the World* (Worcester: Wormley Publishing Co., 1928), 16.

80   *"accident or design"*: Ibid., 17.

81   *try to ban him:* Ibid., 5–7.

81   *South Brooklyn Wheelmen:* "Cycling Clubs and Their Spheres of Action," *Outing*, August 1897, 488–94.

81   *path opened in June 1896:* "Cycle Path's Opening: Big Demonstration in Brooklyn by 10,000 Riders," *New York Times*, June 28, 1896.

82    *Patrick T. Powers:* Charlie Bevis, "Patrick Powers," *Society for American Baseball Research.* Accessed at https://sabr.org/bioproj/person/e95ef025.

82    *James C. "Big Jim" Kennedy:* Bill Lamb, "Jim Kennedy," *Society for American Baseball Research.* Accessed at https://sabr.org/bioproj/person/94ad8988.

82    *"the whole of New York":* Taylor, *Fastest Bicycle Rider,* 308–9. The citation is from an article reprinted in Taylor's autobiography, titled "Giants of the Track," by Paul Hamelle and Robert Coquelle. The writers knew Taylor and wrote a pamphlet called "Major Taylor, the King of the Cycle, his Appearance and Career."

83    *dominated Wall Street:* Edwin G. Burrows and Mike Wallace, *Gotham* (New York: Oxford University Press, 1999), 1205.

83    *his fellow multimillionaires:* Ibid., 1205.

84    *"best friend" of black Americans:* Clarence A. Bacote, "Negro Officeholders in Georgia Under President McKinley," *Journal of Negro History* 44, no. 3 (July 1959): 234.

84    *caught by Roosevelt's rider:* Theodore Roosevelt, *Autobiography* (New York: Macmillan, 1913), 187–90.

86    *"hero of the evening":* "Henshaw Wins a Handicap," *Brooklyn Daily Eagle,* December 6, 1896.

86    *"who licked Eddie Bald":* *Referee & Cycle Trade Journal* 18, no. 9 (December 31, 1896): 42.

86    *"my first money prize":* Taylor, *Fastest Bicycle Rider,* 18.

86    *highest circulation that year:* "Journals and Newspapers in the Campaign," 1896. Accessed at http://projects.vassar.edu/1896/journals.html.

87    *separate stories with headlines:* "The Major Doing Well," *New York World,* December 9 and 11, 1896.

87    *"he were a part of it":* "Taylor's Game Riding," *Brooklyn Eagle,* December 8, 1896.

88    *"better than I":* Taylor, *Fastest Bicycle Rider,* 18.

88    *collected stray horseshoes:* "Tired and Suffering from Saddle Galls, but Otherwise Feel No Ill Effects," undated clipping in Taylor scrapbooks.

89    *eleventh place:* "Hale Leads the Riders," *Brooklyn Eagle,* December 7, 1896, 12.

89    *eighteen remaining riders:* "Major Taylor Holds His Own in the Six Day Contest, *Brooklyn Eagle,* December 8, 1896, 10.

89    *"take it to the doctor":* "All suffered from the cold," undated newspaper clipping in Taylor scrapbook.

89    *"without a wink of sleep":* Taylor, *Fastest Bicycle Rider,* 19.

90    *dropped to ninth place:* "Major Taylor Continues to Be the Popular Favorite But Drops Behind," *Brooklyn Eagle,* December 9, 1896, 10.

90    *"a knife in his hand":* F. Ed Spooner, "The Crackerjacks' Corner," *Bearings,* December 24, 1896.

90   *"pass as his brother":* Jackie Clarke, "Jackie Clarke Tells of His First Experience as a Six-Day Racer," *Salt Lake Herald-Republican,* December 3, 1911. While the Salt Lake newspaper used the spelling "Clarke," Australian publications spelled it "Clark," which is widely accepted and used in the text of his book.

90   *"mobbed" the doors:* "Hale Cheered by Thousands," *New York Journal,* December 12, 1896.

90   *"developing into a fever":* "No One Can Catch Hale," *New York World,* December 10, 1896, 4.

90   *"grows every minute":* Hale Pulls Ahead," *New York World,* December 11, 1896.

90   *swerved across the track:* "Hale Cheered by Thousands," *New York Journal,* December 12, 1896.

90   *Only Teddy Hale:* "The Wonderful Legs of Teddy Hale," *New York Journal,* December 12, 1896. (While all of the newspapers at the time described Hale as Irish, and he attracted throngs of Irish American supporters, some historians later said he was born near London.)

91   *"laughing and yelling":* "Hardest Day of the Race," *New York World,* December 12, 1896.

91   *"oblivious to everything":* "Hale Looks Like a Winner," *Brooklyn Eagle,* December 12, 1896, 14.

91   *"he collapsed utterly":* "News of the Wheelmen," *Brooklyn Eagle,* December 14, 1896, 12.

91   *"greatest bicycle race in history":* "Teddy Hale Is the Victory," *Omaha World Herald,* December 13, 1896.

## Chapter 8: "Major Taylor's Life in Danger"

93   *"time and again":* "Michael Vs 'Major' Taylor," *Boston Globe,* August 27, 1897.

94   *"receiving bodily harm":* Untitled, *New York Sun,* August 15, 1897.

95   *"endangers his life":* Untitled, *New York Sun,* September 18, 1897.

95   *"they will do so":* "Taylor Says It Is So," *Worcester Telegram,* September 20, 1897.

96   *"as attractive as possible":* Treva B. Lindsey, *Colored No More* (Urbanna: University of Illinois Press, 2017). The postal service would eventually ban shipments of the skin products such as Black-No-More because it caused such damage, but the lotions would continue to be sold by other means, and a backlash against them eventually would take place. A landmark 1904 essay, titled "Not Color, but Character," urged black women to stop using the products.

96   *"before they got through with me":* "Sporting Notes," *St. Joseph Herald,* April 14, 1898.

96   *"as he was before the operation":* "Anecdotes of the Racing Men," *Detroit Free Press,* September 19, 1897.

97   *antidiscrimination laws:* Teamoh's role is highlighted in https://dataverse .harvard.edu/dataset.xhtml?persistentId=doi:10.7910/DVN/MTHDXM. A copy of the bill with Teamoh's signature is at https://iiif.lib.harvard.edu /manifests/view/drs:53243683$1i.

97   *"into a state of insensibility":* Marshall "Major" Taylor, *The Fastest Bicycle Rider in the World,* (Worcester: Wormley Publishing Co., 1928), 20.

97   *"Choked Taylor":* "Choked Taylor," *Boston Globe,* September 24, 1897.

97   *"Major Taylor Choked into Insensibility":* "Major Taylor Choked into Insensibility," *Cleveland Gazette,* October 2, 1897.

97   *"would gladly sacrifice":* "News of the Wheelmen," *New York Sun,* September 29, 1897.

98   *"a moral certainty":* "Circuit Notes," *Boston Globe,* September 17, 1897.

98   *"at the top of my form":* Taylor, *Fastest Bicycle Rider,* 20.

98   *Munger resigned:* "Strike at Middletown," *Naugatuck* (Connecticut*) Daily News,* June 15, 1897.

98   *put the company into receivership:* "Bicycle Firm's Big Debts," *New York Times,* July 13, 1897.

98   *he shifted his focus:* "Moore & Munger Co.," website history, Coachbuilt .com. Accessed at http://www.coachbuilt.com/bui/m/moore_munger /moore_munger.htm.

99   *"embraced religion":* Taylor account books, Major Taylor papers, Indiana State Museum.

99   *"his mightiest efforts":* "A Colored Orator," undated clipping in Taylor's scrapbook.

Chapter 9: The Fighting Man

102   *without means or a father:* William A. Brady, *The Fighting Man* (Indianapolis: The Boss-Merrill Co., 1916), 1–29.

102   *"Pandemonium reigned":* "Wrestlers Have a Fight," *New York Times,* May 1, 1898.

103   *"And dangerous":* William A. Brady, *Showman* (New York: E. P. Dutton & Co., 1937), 224, 231.

104   *Belleview Biltmore Hotel:* Paul Dunn and B. J. Dunn, *Great Donald Ross Golf Course* (Lanham: Taylor Trade Publishing, 2017), 44.

105   *"business was conducted properly":* Clarence A. Bacote, "Negro Officeholder in Georgia under President McKinley," *Journal of Negro History* 44, no. 3 (July 1959): 217–39; and John Dittmer, *Black Georgia in the Progressive Era, 1900–1920* (Urban: University of Illinois Press, 1980), 91.

105   *a blazing pace:* "Cowardly Writer," *Savannah Tribune,* March 12, 1898.

106  *"much to the cyclists' disgust":* "Why Major Taylor Left the South," *New York American*, March 16, 1898.

106  *"cowardly writer":* "Cowardly Writer, Writes Like a Midnight Assassin," *Savannah Tribune*, March 12, 1898.

106  *Lynchings were a real threat:* "The Complete 1898 Lynching Report," HistoricalCrimeDetective.com. Accessed at http://www.historicalcrime detective.com/the-complete-1898-lynching-report/.

106  *"only a race war will settle it":* Marshall "Major" Taylor, *The Fastest Bicycle Rider in the World*, (Worcester: Wormley Publishing Co., 1928), and "'Major' Taylor Had to Skip," undated clipping in Major Taylor scrapbook, vol. 2.

107  *"competing against him":* "News of the Wheelmen," *New York Sun*, April 10, 1898.

107  *"the color prejudice":* Taylor, *Fastest Bicycle Rider*, 20.

107  *"shucks in this business":* Untitled, *St. Joseph Herald*, April 14, 1898.

107  *"in the season of 1898":* Taylor, *Fastest Bicycle Rider*, 23.

## Chapter 10: A Rematch with Eddie Bald

109  *2,350 single bathhouses:* Lisa M. Santoro, "The Upper-Class Brooklyn Resorts of the Victorian Era," NY.Curbed.com. Accessed at https://ny.curbed .com/2013/6/27/10226192/the-upper-class-brooklyn-resorts-of-the -victorian-era.

110  *called The Homestead:* "News of the Wheelman," *Brooklyn Eagle*, May 2, 1898.

110  *"built on Manhattan Beach":* William A. Brady, *Showman* (New York: E. P. Dutton & Co., 1937), 224–25.

111  *"all the time":* Major Taylor, "Major Taylor on Bicycle Training," *New York American*, March 12, 1898.

112  *"finger's width":* "Manhattan Beach Racing," *New York Times*, May 22, 1898.

112  *two-mile race in Utica:* "Freeman Gave All the Cracks a Licking at Utica," *St. Louis Republic*, June 7, 1898.

112  *"remarkable odds":* "Major Taylor, Colored Indianapolis Boy, Attracting Attention," *Fort Wayne Daily Gazette*, June 6, 1898.

112  *Charles River Park track:* Cambridge Historical Commission letter to author. Some of the grounds would later become the campus of the Massachusetts Institute of Technology and an enormous Necco candy factory.

113  *"once invited me":* "Up to Their Old Tricks," *Worcester Spy*, July 13, 1898.

114  *"hundreds of times":* Marshall "Major" Taylor, *The Fastest Bicycle Rider in the World* (Worcester: Wormley Publishing Co., 1928), 65–66.

114  *"Taylor! Taylor!":* "Taylor Outrode All the Flyers," *Philadelphia Times*, July 17, 1898.

# NOTES

114 *"Taylor Beats"*: "Taylor Beats Champion Bald," *Philadelphia Press*, July 17, 1898.

115 *"Carries Off the Honors"*: "Major Taylor Carries Off the Honors at Philadelphia," *Los Angeles Times*, July 17, 1898.

116 *"afraid of getting licked"*: "Major Taylor Talks," *Worcester Telegram*, August 23, 1898.

116 *He chose Jimmy Michael*: "James 'Jimmy' Michael: Welsh Cycling Champion, 1877–1904," cyclehistory.wordpress.com. Accessed at https://cycle history.wordpress.com/2014/10/21/james-jimmy-michael-welsh-cycling -champion-1877-1904/.

117 *"ends the day's work"*: "Shafer's Threat," *Boston Globe*, June 9, 1898. The article mentions Michael's guarantee of $2,500 a race for six races. Andrew Ritchie, in *Major Taylor*, writes that Michael was guaranteed at least $22,500 for the season, and notes that Michael expected to earn $30,000 (page 92).

117 *in the cycling world*: "Taylor and Michael," unidentified clipping in Taylor scrapbook.

118 *"where it is most needed"*: Taylor, *Fastest Bicycle Rider*, 41.

119 *he split his earnings*: Ibid., 41–49.

119 *"overwhelming victory"*: Ibid., 50.

119 *just behind Bald*: "Circuit Cycle Races; Major Taylor Wins," *Boston Globe*, September 14, 1898.

120 *"Major's black countenance"*: Taylor, *Fastest Bicycle Rider*, 59–60.

120 *"true sportsmanship"*: Ibid., 54–58.

120 *remaining races*: "All Taylor's," *Boston Globe*, September 18, 1898.

120 *"anything else on earth"*: "War of Wheelmen on in Earnest," *Philadelphia Press*, September 26, 1898.

## Chapter 11: In Pursuit of the Championship

121 *"shut me out of tracks"*: "Taylor Will Not Join Rebellion," *Worcester Telegram*, September 27, 1898.

122 *most segregated*: Peter Irons, *Jim Crow's Children* (New York: Penguin Books, 2002), 288.

122 *postponed by darkness*: "Sunday Races in St. Louis," *Boston Globe*, October 9, 1898.

123 *this one last contest*: "Battle of Speed," *Boston Globe*, October 9, 1898.

124 *to attend rehearsals*: "Mix of the Cycle Champions," unidentified clipping in Taylor scrapbook.

124 *"leading attraction of the play"*: "Theatrical Notes," *Chicago Tribune*, September 25, 1898.

124 *agreed with him*: Marshall "Major" Taylor, *The Fastest Bicycle Rider in the World* (Worcester: Wormley Publishing Co., 1928), 28–35.

124   *"every human right":* Ibid., 32–34.

125   *"astonished the wheeling world":* "Mile a Minute," *Boston Daily Globe,* November 20, 1898.

126   *was warmly welcomed:* "Major Taylor in the Church," *Boston Daily Globe,* January 2, 1899.

126   *"any contests on that day":* *Indianapolis Sentinel,* January 16, 1899.

126   *"no experience as an actor":* "News of the Wheelman," *Brooklyn Eagle,* August 31, 1898.

127   *"a large diamond ring":* "Famous Cycler in City," *Elmira Star-Gazette,* November 10, 1898.

127   *it was "meanly small":* "How Bald Acts," *Buffalo Commercial,* November 3, 1898.

127   *"poorer constructed play":* "Criticism of Bald," *Buffalo Commercial,* November 4, 1898.

128   *"hypnotic influence":* "Tod Sloan, Jockey, Dead on the Coast," *New York Times,* December 22, 1933.

128   *collected a $400,000 check:* "Bald Is Out of It," *Buffalo Commercial,* February 4, 1899.

128   *their own train car:* "Tod Sloan Travels in a Special Car," *Evansville* (Indiana) *Courier and Press,* December 15, 1898.

128   *"president of the United States":* "Bald as a Prince," *Buffalo Commercial,* January 28, 1899.

129   *"liked the flesh pots":* "Bald Will Quit Racing," *Brooklyn Eagle,* August 9, 1899.

129   *"have a good time":* "Bald as a Prince," *Buffalo Commercial,* January 28, 1899.

130   *two minutes and eleven seconds:* M. M. Musselman, *Get a Horse! The Story of the Automobile in America* (Philadelphia: Lippincott, 1950), 92.

131   *"bad taste in their mouth":* "The McDuffee-Taylor Fizzle," undated newspaper clipping from 1899.

131   *tinkering improvements:* Eddie McDuffee, "I Beat Them All," *Yankee Magazine,* July 1955.

132   *"carried on the earth's surface":* *Brooklyn Eagle,* September 24, 1899.

132   *setting a world record:* "Taylor's Steam Machine," *Chicago Inter Ocean,* July 31, 1899.

133   *gain the world record:* "His Pace Not Fast Enough," *Chicago Tribune,* July 28, 1899.

133   *The race was on:* "Munger Talks on Taylor: Tells How the 'Major' Refused to Have His Pacing Motor Fixed on Sunday," *Boston Globe,* January 21, 1900.

133   *"hind wheel of the motorcycle":* "Breaks All Records," *Chicago Inter Ocean,* August 4, 1899.

134   *beating the mark by one second:* "Lowers Mile Record," *Boston Globe,* August 4, 1899.

# NOTES

134 *"got it in him"*: "Breaks All Records," *Chicago Daily Inter Ocean*, August 4, 1899.

134 *"when told of the fraud"*: "Munger Talks on Taylor: Tells How the 'Major' Refused to Have His Pacing Motor Fixed on Sunday," *Boston Globe*, January 21, 1900.

135 *"a tolerable citizen"*: Robert J. Norrell, *Up from History: The Life of Booker T. Washington* (Cambridge, MA: Belknap Press of Harvard University Press, 2009), 179.

135 *17,000 of African descent:* "Population and People, January 1, 1900," *Human Rights in Canada*. Accessed at http://www.chrc-ccdp.gc.ca/historical-perspective/en/getBriefed/1900/population.asp.

136 *"But I know I won"*: Taylor, *Fastest Bicycle Rider*, 87–89. (*Montreal Gazette*, August 10, 1899, quoted Taylor saying, "I believe I won.")

137 *"My national anthem"*: Taylor, *World's Fastest Bicycle Rider*, 92. While "The Star-Spangled Banner" didn't become the official US national anthem until 1931, it was not unusual for it to be called the national anthem long before then. For example, the song had been used for official purposes by the Navy ten years before Taylor heard it at the world championships, and many people considered it to be the national anthem during the time Taylor referenced.

138 *his twenty-first birthday:* Taylor, *Fastest Bicycle Rider*, 89–95.

138 *"astonished the world"*: Ibid., 111.

138 *$600,000:* "The Six Day Cycle Grind": December 6, 1899, untitled publication.

## Chapter 12: "A Race Run for Blood"

139 *"give a cent"*: "Taylor Wanted to Race in France," *Boston Globe*, December 24, 1899.

140 *"high hopes"*: Victor Breyer, *Le Vélo*, January 6, 1900.

140 *"for people of color"*: Robert Coquelle, *La Vie au Grand Air*, January 14, 1900.

140 *"lost my appetite"*: "Eddie Bald Home, Is Said to Have Spent $10,000 and He Had a Good Time," *Boston Globe*, December 24, 1899.

141 *"unrighteous in the concrete"*: "Taylor's Troubles," *Worcester Spy*, April 29, 1900.

141 *"love of fame"*: "Major Taylor Tempted," *Scranton Republican*, December 23, 1900.

141 *"Taylor Refuses $10,000"*: "Taylor Refuses $10,000," *New York World*, March 11, 1900.

141 *"not cross the ocean"*: "Will Stay at Home," clipping in Taylor scrapbook, March 10, 1900.

141 *"doing even better than they do"*: Major Taylor, letter to the editor of the *North Conway Reporter*, April 6, 1900.

142 *"I was so surprised"*: "Columbus Park Much Troubled, All Because Major Taylor Becomes Its Neighbor," *Worcester Telegram*, January 24, 1900.

143 *"sue you for damages"*: "Sporting Items of Interest," *Evansville Journal*, February 8, 1900.

143 *"Rich Neighbors"*: "Major Taylor Shocks Society," *Boston Post*, February 9, 1900; "His White Neighbors Object," *New York World*, undated clipping in Taylor scrapbook; "Major Taylor's Rich Neighbors," *Chicago Tribune*, February 4, 1900.

143 *what he paid for it*: "Columbus Park Much Troubled, All Because Major Taylor Becomes Its Neighbor," *Worcester Telegram*, January 24, 1900.

143 *"any man in town"*: "His Friends Guessing," undated clipping in Taylor scrapbook.

143 *The two-story house*: The author is indebted to the homeowner, Gloria Hall, who provided a tour and the detail about the house's construction.

144 *"driven thoughts of everything away"*: "Taylor Is at Sea on Plans," undated clipping in Taylor scrapbook.

144 *"Out for Championship"*: "Begins in Worcester," *Worcester Telegram*, June 2, 1900.

145 *The North had been served*: "By the Numbers: U.S. War Veterans." Accessed at https://www.cnn.com/2013/06/05/us/war-veterans-by-the-numbers/index.html.

145 *"Colored Troops"*: "Colored Troops," *Worcester Spy*, Major Taylor scrapbook.

146 *Arthur C. Newby*: Tiffany Benedict Browne, "Newby Oval: The Track Before the Track," *Indianapolis Monthly*, May 19, 2016. Nine years later, as cycle racing faded, Newby and Fisher and their partners constructed the Indianapolis Motor Speedway six miles away, ensuring the city remained a racing center for decades to come.

146 *"defeat me every time we met"*: Major Taylor, *The Fastest Bicycle Rider in the World* (Salem, NH: Ayer Company Publishers, 1991), 136.

146 *and won the race*: Ibid., 120–21.

147 *Taylor seemed newly energized*: "Taylor Unbeatable," undated clipping from Taylor scrapbook.

147 *won by three lengths*: "Major Taylor Adds Another to His Long List of Conquests," *Philadelphia Tribune*, October 6, 1900.

148 *"beat the little darkey badly"*: Taylor, *Fastest Bicycle Rider*, 160–62.

149 *longtime rival out of his head*: Ibid., 161–62.

149 *"If ever a race was run"*: Ibid., 164–65.

150 *An 1880 census*: US Census, Inhabitants of Hudson, New York, 8.

151 *serving on the social committee*: Calendar, Zion Church, Hartford, Connecticut, Major Taylor papers, Indiana State Museum, 71.988.190.0343. Reverend Taylor was described as Daisy's uncle in "Marriages," *Worcester Spy*, March 22, 1902. It is possible that she used the term "uncle" loosely, as some people do about a close family friend. An article in *The Colored*

*American,* September 1902, refers to Reverend Taylor and his wife as Daisy's "relatives."

151 *"very prominent":* G. Grant Williams, "Marshall Water Taylor (Major Taylor): The World-Famous Bicycle Rider," *Colored American Magazine,* September 1902.

151 *home to 1,100 blacks:* Janette Thomas Greenwood, *First Fruits of Freedom* (Chapel Hill: University of North Carolina Press, 2009), 178.

151 *"didn't approve of cycling":* Sydney Taylor Brown interview with author of this book, May 23, 2001.

152 *"mutual progress":* Douglas A. Blackmon, *Slavery by Another Name* (New York: Anchor Books, 2008), 161.

152 *"that the world has seen":* Michael P. Johnson, ed., *Reading the American Past,* vol. 2 (Boston: Bedford/St. Martin's, 2012), 116.

153 *"because of the Negro's degradation":* W. E. B. Du Bois, *The Souls of Black Folk* (New York: Oxford University Press, 2007), 38–43.

153 *"the problem of the color-line":* Ibid., 3.

153 *"take him over to France":* "La venue en France de Major Taylor," *Cyclette-Revue,* March and April, 1944.

154 *"greatest temptation of my life":* "Sunday Observance, Major Taylor's Stand, Sacrifice of 30,000 Dollars," *Adelaide Advertiser,* January 12, 1903.

154 *"cut off all negotiations":* "Taylor on Contract!," *Worcester Telegram,* January 10, 1901.

## Chapter 13: A Black Man in Paris

155 *awarded a gold medal:* "Medal for Captain of Kaiser Wilhelm Gross," *New York World,* as cited in Documents of the Assembly of the State of New York, vol. 11 (Albany: J. B. Lyon Company, 1902), 71–72.

156 *Buckner was so respected:* Jacob Pomrenke, *Scandal on the South Side: The 1919 Chicago White Sox* (Phoenix: SABR, 2015), 34. A White Sox team photo from 1915 shows Buckner in the center surrounded by white players, thirty-two years before Jackie Robinson broke the color line for baseball players. He was released from the team in 1918 after some racist players objected to his presence; one had gone after him with a baseball bat. The following year came the "Black Sox" scandal in which some players threw games, and the racist players who objected to him were gone. He was rehired the following year as the White Sox tried to emerge from the gambling scandal.

157 *the name "Worcester":* Victor Breyer, "The Negre à Paris," *Le Vélo,* March 12, 1901.

157 *"the real McCoy":* "McCoy en Europe," unidentified clipping in Taylor Scrapbook.

# NOTES

157  *"thought of protesting":* Major Taylor, "My Tour in Europe," *La Vie au Grand Air,* May 1901, 222–25.

158  *"great wandering shadows":* W. E. B. Du Bois, *The Souls of Black Folk* (Chicago: A.C. McClurg & Co., 1903), 2.

159  *"made by themselves":* David Levering Lewis and Deborah Wills, *A Small Nation of People: W. E. B. Du Bois and African American Portraits of Progress* (New York: Amistad, 2003), 18, 26.

160  *midst of the Boer Wars:* Robert Coquelle, "With Major Taylor Disappearance, a Glorious World of Track Cycling," *Le Miroir Des Sports,* July 12, 1932.

161  *"magnificent panorama of Paris":* "Courrier des Pistes," *Le Vélo,* March 17, 1901.

161  *"where art reigns supreme":* Major Taylor, "My Tour in Europe," *La Vie au Grand Air,* May 1901, 222–25.

162  *two hundred motor vehicles:* "L'Automobile club de France: un club Trés select et trés discret," passionandcar.fr. Accessed at https://www.passionand car.fr/2016/12/14/lautomobile-club-de-france-club-tres-select-tres-discret/.

162  *"are truly splendid":* Major Taylor, "My Tour in Europe," *La Vie au Grand Air,* May 1901, 222–25.

162  *Auguste Rodin:* Ruth Butler: *Rodin, The Shape of Genius* (New Haven: Yale University Press, 1993), 315.

163  *Toulouse-Lautrec:* Author visit to an exhibition of the painter's work, including the Simpson Chain painting, at The Phillips Collection, Washington, DC, 2017.

163  *"one never sees blacks in Paris":* Major Taylor, "My Tour in Europe," *La Vie au Grand Air,* May 1901, 222–25.

163  *"paraded in cabarets":* "France's first black icon makes comeback on stage and screen," France24.com. Accessed at http://www.france24.com/en/20160203 -chocolat-france-black-icon-rafael-padilla-footit-culture-circus-paris.

164  *Chocolat was the stage name:* See a 2016 French film called *Chocolat,* based on his life.

164  *"spectators' eyes turned":* "La Journee du Negre; Le Negre et Chocolate," *L'Auto Vélo,* March 13, 1901.

165  *"national character":* "France Finally Awakens," *Bicycling World,* May 30, 1901, 170.

165  *"expected as the Messiah":* "Le Programme du Negre," *Le Vélo,* January 27, 1901.

165  *"sensation on the boulevard":* Victor Breyer, "The Negre à Paris," *Le Vélo,* March 12, 1901.

165  *"to have his shoes blacked":* "Major Taylor's Trip," *Bicycling World,* April 4, 1901, 38.

165  *"the modern Babylon":* Major Taylor, "My Tour in Europe," *La Vie au Grand Air,* May 1901, 222–25.

166  *first widely published sports photographer:* Brooklyn Museum. Accessed at http://brooklynmuseum.tumblr.com/post/148151268456/the-frenchman -jules-beau-is-considered-the-first.

167  *use of halftone photography:* Jessica Stewart, "The History of Photojournalism," MyModernMet.com. Accessed at https://mymodernmet.com/photo journalism-history/.

167  *"strength, suppleness, and elegance":* Franz Reichel, "Le Negre," *Le Vélo,* May 14, 1901.

169  *"its Bohemian smoke and noise":* John M. Erwin and Arthur Zimmerman, *Zimmerman Abroad and Points on Training* (Chicago: Blakely Printing Company, 1895), 27–39.

169  *"yours may be the quicker":* "Taylor's Debut," *Boston Daily Globe,* April 7, 1901.

170  *such a welcome for a foreign racer:* "The Interview of the Two Rivals," *Le Vélo,* March 15, 1901.

170  *"not a European":* Victor Breyer, "Le Major en Piste," *Le Vélo,* March 17, 1901.

172  *"The Star-Spangled Banner":* Taylor, *Fastest Bicycle Rider,* 170–73.

173  *"had seen a negro!":* Robert Coquelle, "With Major Taylor Disappearance, a Glorious World of Track Cycling," *Le Miroir Des Sports,* July 12, 1932.

173  *10 million Congolese:* Adam Hochschild, *King Leopold's Ghost: A Story of Greed, Terror, and Heroism in Colonial Africa* (Boston: Houghton Mifflin, 1998), 233.

174  *"was the last stumbling block":* Taylor, *Fastest Bicycle Rider,* 175.


Chapter 14: "The Terribly Dangerous and Beautiful Races"

175  *"convince them forever":* "The Impressions of the Winner," *Le Vélo,* May 20, 1901.

175  *study his rival:* "Taylor's Triumphal Tour of Europe," *Cycle Age,* June 20, 1901.

176  *"Here, it will change":* "Jacquelin Attend le Negre," *Le Vélo,* January 28, 1901.

176  *"It is nothing less":* "Who Will Be King?" *L'Auto Vélo,* May 16, 1901.

176  *"The face of the black demon":* Paul Hamelle, "Noir et blanc," *Le Vélo,* March 16, 1901.

177  *"Apart from the rivalry":* Franz Reichel, "Le Negre," *Le Vélo,* May 14, 1901.

177  *"The negro's victory":* *L'Auto Vélo,* May 11, 1901.

177  *"the best society":* J. Platt-Betts and Jack Green, "Black v. White," *Cycling,* May 25, 1901.

178  *"terribly dangerous and beautiful races":* Ernest Hemingway, *A Moveable Feast* (London: Arrow Books, 2011), 51–55.

178  *He wagered $3,000:* "Americans Lost Heavily," *Boston Globe,* May 19, 1901.

179  *"the French idol":* Marshall "Major" Taylor, *The Fastest Bicycle Rider in the World* (Worcester: Wormley Publishing Co., 1928), 175–80.

179  *grimaced at the cold:* Pascal Sergent, *Edmond Jacquelin: The Life of the Most Popular Champion of All Time* (Paris: L'Harmattan, 2006), 102.

179  *"I pushed like a demon":* "The Impressions of the Winner," *L'Auto Vélo*, May 20, 1901.

180  *"Jacquelin's insult caused me":* Taylor, *Fastest Bicycle Rider*, 175–80.

180  *"slinking away to his dressing room":* J. Platt-Betts and Jack Green, "Black v. White," *Cycling*, May 25, 1901.

180  *"who was the better rider":* Taylor, *Fastest Bicycle Rider*, 175–80.

180  *had predicted his defeat:* *L'Auto Vélo*, May 20, 1901.

180  *"as many times as he likes":* Sergent, *Edmond Jacquelin*, 103.

181  *"always the same":* "Echoes of the Tracks," *Le Vélo*, May 22, 1901.

181  *"never opposed a man":* Sergent, *Edmond Jacquelin*, 104.

181  *"looking unhappy under the cold sky":* *L'Auto Vélo*, May 20, 1901.

181  *a hot day:* Sergent, *Edmond Jacquelin*, 105.

181  *"sarcastic smile":* Ibid., 110.

183  *Jacquelin poured champagne:* Ibid., 111.

183  *"first invasion of Europe":* Taylor, *Fastest Bicycle Rider*, 175–80.

183  *"Holy Cyclist":* "The Sport in Gaar," *Politiken*, June 6, 1901.

184  *a bouquet:* "Peculiar Demonstration Occurs at a Railway Station in Paris," *San Francisco Call*, June 29, 1901.

## Chapter 15: Voyage of the Titans

185  *"Seldom, if ever":* "Deutschland Greeted By Gayly Decked Fleet," *New York Times*, July 5, 1901.

185  *"Such, indeed, is life":* "Fame Is a Fickle Goddess," *Colored American*, July 20, 1901, 8.

186  *"two experienced chauffeurs":* "Mr. Vanderbilt's New Automobile," *Alexandria* (Virginia) *Gazette and Virginia Advertiser*, July 10, 1901.

186  *"queen of the seas":* The description of the *Deutschland* comes from myriad sources, including "Atlantic Liners of Today—Recent Records—The Story of the Steamship." Accessed at https://www.gjenvick.com/OceanTravel /TransatlanticShipsAndVoyages/StoryOfTheSteamship/1901/06-Atlantic LinersToday.html.

187  *hidden in a Brooklyn warehouse:* "The Disappearing Duchess," *New York Times Magazine*, July 31, 1994.

188  *Ascot races in England:* "Pierre Lorillard Dead," *New York Times*, July 8, 1901.

189  *crew of 550:* "Provisioning A Transatlantic Liner: Stocking the Steamship *Deutschland* for Voyage, 1901," gjenvick.com. Accessed at http://www .gjenvick.com/SteamshipArticles/Provisions/1901-06-29-Provisioning ATransatlanticLiner.html#axzz2aFMOxVVp.

# NOTES

189 *"enormous premium"*: "Planning to Meet Woodruff," *Brooklyn Eagle*, July 3, 1901.

189 *across the ocean at 22.65 knots*: "Prominent Men Return," *New York Tribune*, July 5, 1901.

190 *"entire saloon deck"*: "Men of Millions Reach New York," *Chicago Tribune*, July 4, 1901.

190 *"is also a passenger"*: "J.Morgan Nearing Home," *New York Tribune*, July 4, 1901.

190 *"to which he proved equal"*: "In the Wheeling World," *Omaha Bee*, July 11, 1901.

190 *"Windsor Castle"*: "Prominent Men Return," *New York Tribune*, July 5, 1901, 7.

191 *"other people's money"*: "The Man in the Street," *New York Times*, August 11, 1901.

191 The Geisha: Advertisement, *New York Sun*, July 4, 1901.

192 *"a white man"*: "Taylor's Threat: Says N.C.A. Will Force Him to Retire," *Boston Globe*, July 10, 1901.

192 *"he has become unbearable"*: " 'Majah' Taylor Retires," *Buffalo Enquirer*, July 7, 1901.

192 *"just itching"*: "Taylor's Threat: Says N.C.A. Will Force Him to Retire," *Boston Globe*, July 10, 1901.

## Chapter 16: The Caged Bird Sings

196 *Washington Coliseum*: Beth Purcell, "Capitol Hill's Coliseum," *Capitol Hill Restoration Society News*, September 2015.

196 *displayed his name*: Advertisement, "Coliseum—Grand Circuit Meet," *Washington Evening Star*, July 22, 1901.

196 *"the bars of a bird cage"*: Catherine Reef, *The Life of Paul Laurence Dunbar* (New York: Enslow Publishing, 2015), 51–52.

197 *riding a horse for the first time*: Tony Gentry, *Paul Laurence Dunbar, Poet* (New York: Chelsea House, 1989), 158.

197 *"enough to pass for twins"*: Major Taylor to Daisy Taylor, August 5, 1909, Major Taylor collection, Indiana State Museum.

197 *"horse dealers do not"*: "Horse Market Active," *Washington Post*, May 14, 1900.

198 *"risk of instant death"*: "Dutton and His Automobile," *Washington Post*, July 23, 1901.

198 *slowly zigzagged*: "Midget Is a Wonder," *Washington Post*, July 25, 1901.

198 *"beaten to a standstill"*: "Crack Cyclists Race," *Washington Star*, July 25, 1901.

199 *a simpler vehicle*: "The Birth of Ford Motor Company," Henry Ford Heritage

Association, accessed at http://hfha.org/the-ford-story/the-birth-of-ford
-motor-company/. Lawrence Goldstone, *Drive!* (New York: Ballantine
Books, 2016), 112–18. "Tom Cooper, Fastest Man in Detroit," accessed
at http://www.m-bike.org/blog/2012/11/21/tom-cooper-fastest-man-in
-detroit/. "Bike Racers Helped Create Ford Motor Company," accessed at
http://www.m-bike.org/blog/2010/04/02/bike-racers-helped-create-ford
-motor-company/. "Tom Cooper Is Defended by Ford," *Buffalo Enquirer*,
November 30, 1906. Cooper died in a 1906 auto accident in New York
City's Central Park, with a net worth estimated at $90,000.

200 *"you'll be kicked out":* "Clerk Says 'Get Out,'" *Worcester Telegram*, August 2,
1901.

200 *Hotel Vanderbilt for $10,000:* "Major Taylor to Sue; A Syracuse Hotel
Refuses Accommodations to Noted Cyclist," *Pittsburgh Press*, August 5,
1901, 8.

200 *"besides the South":* "Cycling," *New York Daily Tribune*, August 2, 1901, 5.

200 *"reckless riding on the public thoroughfare":* "Reckless Bicycle Riding," *New
York Times*, August 9, 1901.

201 *"riders who were killed":* Marshall "Major" Taylor, *The Fastest Bicycle Rider
in the World* (Worcester: Wormley Publishing Co., 1928), 420–21.

201 *breaking his neck:* "Tom Cooper Killed in Park Auto Race," *New York
Times*, November 20, 1906.

202 *"Major Taylor Losing Form":* "Major Taylor Losing Form," *Indianapolis
News*, August 8, 1901. "Champion Defeats Taylor," *Washington Evening
Star*, August 8, 1901.

202 *"evidently forgot" the signal:* "Nelson in Form, Beats Major Taylor on
Worcester Track," *Boston Globe*, July 23, 1901.

203 *"escorted Taylor to the dressing room":* "Taylor Angry," *Boston Globe*, September 8, 1901.

## Chapter 17: "The Strain Is Too Great"

205 *twenty-eight bicycle shops:* Paul Skilbeck, "California's most biker friendly
city: San Jose's storied cycling history," AXS.com, May 12, 2014. Accessed
at https://www.axs.com/california-s-most-biker-friendly-city-san-jose-s
-storied-cycling-histo-10852.

206 *Carnival of Roses parade:* "Bicyclists' Novel Plan," *Los Angeles Herald*, March
27, 1901.

206 *turning point in the nation's history:* "List of McKinley's Firsts, Part 9,"
McKinley Birthplace Museum. Accessed at https://mckinleybirthplace
museum.org/2016/08/24/list-of-mckinley-firsts-part-9-mckinley-was-the
-first-president-to-visit-california-1/.

207 *broke the world's record:* "McFarland Breaks a Record," *Los Angeles Herald,* June 19, 1901.

207 *rushed "semi-conscious":* "Nelson Wins in New York: Accident Puts McFarland Out of Race," *Los Angeles Herald,* June 25, 1901.

208 *winning the title:* "McFarland Beats Linton," *San Francisco Call,* July 9, 1901.

208 *"at all costs":* Marshall "Major" Taylor, *The Fastest Bicycle Rider in the World* (Worcester: Wormley Publishing Co., 1928), 186–87.

208 *$500 or more:* "Taylor Angry," *Boston Globe,* September 8, 1901.

208 *McFarland . . . was speechless:* Taylor, *Fastest Bicycle Rider,* 188–89.

209 *"squarest man among us":* Ibid., 196–200.

209 *iron frames, wood slats, and plaster:* "The Pan-American Exposition, Buffalo—and the Electric City and Rainbow City." Accessed at https://www2.willworkinc.com/the-pan-american-exposition-buffalo-and-the-electric-and-rainbow-city/.

209 *"electric runabouts":* "Automobiles at the Pan-American Exhibition," *The Horseless Age,* June 12, 1901.

210 *"neo slavery":* Douglas A. Blackmon, *Slavery by Another Name* (New York: Anchor Books, 2008), 7–8.

210 *"slavery by another name":* Ibid., 157.

210 *twenty-eight years:* Timeline of African American history, Library of Congress website. Accessed at https://memory.loc.gov/ammem/aap/timelin3.html.

211 *retained full rights:* Blackmon, *Slavery by Another Name,* 160–63.

211 *"the very fact that I felt":* Theodore Roosevelt to Albion W. Tourgee, November 8, 1901. Theodore Roosevelt, *Letters and Speeches* (New York: Library of America, 2004), 244.

212 *"eat with a negro":* William Albert Sinclair, *The Aftermath of Slavery* (Cambridge: University Press, 1905), 188.

212 *"Object Lesson for the South":* "The Lie Is Nailed That He Is Opposed to the Negro," *Washington Bee,* October 19, 1901. (As a racist, sectionalist backlash escalated, however, Roosevelt said, during a visit to Tuskegee Institute three years later, that the black race "must learn to wait and bide its time" and that it was up to the South to solve its problems.)

213 *"one of the happiest men":* Taylor, *Fastest Bicycle Rider,* 205.

213 *"the strain is too great":* "Taylor to Race in Europe," *Rochester Democrat and Chronicle,* March 22, 1902.

213 *"I shall be content":* "Major Taylor Going Abroad," *New York Sun,* March 21, 1902.

213 *married the couple:* "Weddings, Taylor-Morris," *Worcester Spy,* March 22, 1902. This article says that Reverend Louis H. Taylor was Daisy's uncle, and that she was his niece.

214  *"sail for Paris with his bride":* "Personal Paragraphs," *Daily Morning Journal and Courier* (New Haven, CT), March 24, 1902.

214  *"business trip":* G. Grant Williams, "Marshall Walter Taylor (Major Taylor), The World-Famous Bicycle Rider," *Colored American,* September 1902.

214  *"wish him well on behalf":* Andrew Ritchie, *Major Taylor: The Extraordinary Career of a Champion Bicycle Racer* (Baltimore: Johns Hopkins University Press, 1996), 194.

215  *William Randolph Hearst:* "Notes of Music Events," *Indianapolis Journal,* March 30, 1902.

215  *series of races:* Taylor, *Fastest Bicycle Rider,* 204.

215  *"never met a cooler rider":* Ibid., 204–9.

216  *he paid Taylor $400:* Ibid., 225–26.

217  *"fortunately there was no bloodshed":* Ibid., 227–28.

217  *"wonderful prophecy of my discoverer":* Ibid., 232.

217  *"in the nature of a honeymoon":* Ibid., 232.

Chapter 18: A Faraway Land

219  The Colored American: G. Grant Williams, "Marshall Walter Taylor (Major Taylor), The World-Famous Bicycle Rider," *Colored American,* September 1902. The magazine was purchased two years later by Booker T. Washington.

221  *"very good chance too":* "Sunday Observance, Major Taylor's Stand, Sacrifice of 30,000 Dollars," *Adelaide Advertiser,* January 12, 1903.

221  *needn't fear rejection:* Marshall "Major" Taylor, *The Fastest Bicycle Rider in the World* (Worcester: Wormley Publishing Co., 1928), 232–34.

222  *"scents danger like a deer":* "Training Notes; Major Taylor's Work," (Sydney) *Daily Telegraph,* January 1, 1903.

223  *"lifted off my shoulders":* Taylor, *Fastest Bicycle Rider,* 233–37.

224  *Walker was one of the finest:* Jim Fitzpatrick, *Major Taylor in Australia* (Karana Downs, Queensland, Australia: Star Hill Studio, 2011), 20–24.

224  *"My people were very religious":* "Sunday Observance, Major Taylor's Stand, Sacrifice of 30,000 Dollars," *Adelaide Advertiser,* January 12, 1903.

225  *Taylor was "winning races":* "Major Taylor in Australia," *New York Times,* February 16, 1903.

225  *Taylor wrote that he netted:* "General Sporting Notes," *Washington Evening Star,* March 5, 1903. Taylor, *Fastest Bicycle Rider,* 300.

225  *"who looks after me":* "Sunday Observance, Major Taylor's Stand, Sacrifice of 30,000 Dollars," *Adelaide Advertiser,* January 12, 1903.

225  *"Black skin, black hands":* Chris Lamb, "Catchers Tears Were Likely an Inspiration for Rickey," *New York Times,* April 15, 2012, Sports, 9. Thomas went on to become a dentist.

226  Ville de la Ciotat: "Major Taylor," *Mount Gambier Border Watch,* April 18,

1903. The reference to 150 cases of apples comes from: "Shipping News," *Adelaide Advertiser*, April 20, 1903.

226 *Bombay was its vibrant:* Kiran Doshi, "Here's a Snapshot of Bombay Circa 1903," *Hindustan Times*, January 14, 2016.

226 *most-prized possessions:* "Off for Europe," *Boston Globe*, September 28, 1903.

227 *sending postcards with brief greetings:* Indiana State Museum, Major Taylor Collection.

228 *"firm hold everywhere":* "Returns with Honor and Cash: Major Taylor at Home from One of the Most Successful Tours of the World Ever Made by an Athlete," *Worcester Spy*, September 23, 1903.

228 *again bound for San Francisco:* "Taylor Not to Retire," *Hartford Courant*, November 14, 1903. The day after: "Major Taylor's Farewell Words," Christchurch newspaper from Taylor scrapbook. December 23, 1903.

229 *"Australia for Australians":* The (Sydney) *Bulletin*, December 31, 1903.

230 *"is better than anything":* "A Talk with Taylor," unidentified clip in Taylor scrapbook, January 5, 1904.

232 *Taylor returned the grasp:* "Battle of Champions"; *Australian Cycle and Motor-Car World*, February 18, 1904, 5–9. "Cycling," *Melbourne Sportsman*, February 16, 1904.

233 *settled by a rematch:* "Statements by the Rivals," *Australian Star*, February 15, 1904.

233 *violently, hit the track:* "Cycling Fiasco," *The Argus*, February 18, 1904.

234 *twenty thousand people:* Fitzgerald, *Major Taylor in Australia*, 117–18.

235 *"most dramatic and thrilling":* Taylor, *Fastest Bicycle Rider*, 349–67.

236 *"greatest prize of all":* Ibid., 406–7.

236 *"flattened him":* Andrew Ritchie, *The Extraordinary Career of a Champion Bicycle Racer* (San Francisco: Bicycle Books, 1988), 202–3. The account of the fight was given by Taylor's daughter, Sydney, to Ritchie.

237 *Taylor's treatment was investigated:* "Taylor's Money of No Account," *San Francisco Call*, June 29, 1904.

237 *Blacks "do not hate white people":* Taylor, *Fastest Bicycle Rider*, 408–9.

## Chapter 19: The Changing World

239 *"narrowly averted a nervous breakdown":* Marshall "Major" Taylor, *The Fastest Bicycle Rider in the World* (Worcester: Wormley Publishing Co., 1928), 410.

240 *"almost a solid line":* "Real Estate and the Automobile Trade," *New York Times*, January 6, 1907.

240 *most lavish auto showrooms:* "Moore & Munger Company, 1904–1915, New York, New York," Coachbuilt.com. Accessed at http://www.coachbuilt.com/bui/m/moore_munger/moore_munger.htm.

240 *invention of a bicycle brake:* Accessed at https://www.google.com/patents/ US417401. (Astor would die in the sinking of the *Titanic* in 1912.)

241 *"90 miles easily":* Nicholas W. Anthony against Moore & Munger Company, *Supreme Court Appellate Division* (New York: Appeal Printing Co., 1906), 30–31.

241 *"very high class":* "Motoring-Trade Notes," *Brooklyn Life,* May 5, 1907.

241 *But trouble loomed:* "Business Troubles," *New York Times,* March 2, 1907.

241 *167 black soldiers:* Robert T. Norrell, *Up from History: The Life of Booker T. Washington* (Cambridge, MA: Belknap Press of Harvard University Press, 2009), 240–57.

242 *"I weakened":* Taylor, *Fastest Bicycle Racer,* 410. It is possible that Taylor misstated the year in which he capitulated and agreed to race on Sunday. While Taylor wrote that he made this concession in 1907, the French press wrote that it happened in 1909. Either way, there is no question that Taylor ultimately decided he had to give in to the demand in order to sign a contract.

242 *"too young to retire":* "Major Taylor est arrivé," *L'Auto,* April 20, 1907.

243 *extended rounds of boxing matches:* Ibid.

243 *"completely finished":* Major Taylor, "My Last Race Season," *La Vie au Grand Air,* August 24, 1907.

243 *"just to distract me":* "The Resurrection of the Negro," *L'Auto,* March 7, 1907.

243 *"such a reception":* "Major Taylor est arrivé," *L'Auto,* April 20, 1907.

244 *"hate the French":* "The Book of the Negro," *L'Auto,* April 21, 1907.

244 *"a match that would bring together":* "Un Match Cycliste Sensational," *Le Petit Journal,* May 10, 1907.

245 *wanted to stay:* Taylor, *Fastest Bicycle Rider,* 411–12.

245 *"successive defeats":* Major Taylor, "My Last Race Season," *La Vie au Grand Air,* August 24, 1907.

245 *" 'Daddy! Daddy!' ":* Sydney Taylor Brown interview with author, May 24, 2001. The author interviewed her at a nursing home in Pittsburgh. She was voluble and clear in her memory of her father. The interview was conducted for a magazine story for the *Boston Globe,* and helped inspire the author to collect material that eventually became this book.

246 *"will like the French":* Major Taylor, "My Last Race Season," *La Vie au Grand Air,* August 24, 1907.

246 *"as a professional in this country":* "Major Taylor to Ride," *Boston Globe,* January 13, 1908.

246 *Taylor lost his first race:* "Major Taylor Beaten," *New York Times,* February 9, 1908.

246 *his first long race:* "Ten Teams of Bikers," *Boston Globe,* February 16, 1908.

246 *"displayed great speed":* "10 Teams on Even Terms," *Boston Globe,* February 20, 1908.

NOTES

247 *"with bowed head"*: John Donovan, "Moran Beats Major Taylor," *Boston Globe*, April 5, 1908.

249 *by an apple tree:* "Thomas Car Is Delayed," *New York Times*, July 30, 1908.

249 *"roasted alive"*: "G. W. Sands Killed in Motor Accident," *New York Times*, July 30, 1908.

250 *a supper at the Grand Hotel:* "Thomas, Winner, Reaches Paris," *New York Times*, July 31, 1908.

250 *by nearly three seconds:* Untitled, *Salt Lake Tribune*, September 27, 1908, 18.

250 *"And see you next year"*: "Major Taylor Is Gone," *L'Auto*, September 20, 1908.

251 *"a couple of million dollars"*: Damon Runyan, "Runyan Says . . . 'Member Major Taylor? And the Great Bald?," (Harrisburg, PA) *Evening News*, March 31, 1927.

251 *"What can I do for you"*: Jim Rasenberger, *America, 1908* (New York: Scribner, 2007), 181.

251 *"half-standing, half-hanging"*: "The Victims: William Donnegan," *State Journal-Register*, May 31, 2008.

252 *"will not serve Negroes"*: Ray Stannard Baker, *Following the Color Line* (New York: Doubleday, Page & Company, 1908), 118–25.

253 *"tremendous burst of speed"*: "Taylor Beats McFarland," *Boston Globe*, December 20, 1908.

253 *Coliseum burned to the ground:* Taylor, *Fastest Bicycle Rider*, 416–17.

254 *"for a less dangerous profession"*: Jack Johnson, *My Life and Battles* (Westport, CT: Praeger, 2007), 17.

254 *McIntosh arranged for a fight:* Ibid., 68–73.

254 *"with their white neighbors"*: Ibram X. Kendi, *Stamped from the Beginning* (New York: Nation Books, 2016), 298.

Chapter 20: "I Need Your Prayers"

257 Lusitania: "Croker Off for Ireland": *New York Times*, April 29, 1909.

258 *"take any foolish chances"*: Major Taylor to Daisy Taylor, May 4, 1909, Major Taylor papers, Indiana State Museum.

258 *"'Major Taylor' Comes Back"*: "'Major Taylor' Comes Back," *Chicago Daily Inter Ocean*, May 17, 1909.

259 *his ban on Sunday racing:* "La Rentree de Major Taylor," *La Vie au Grand Air*, May 22, 1909.

259 *"trying to make a brave fight of it"*: Major Taylor to Daisy Taylor, May 9 and May 14, 1909, Major Taylor papers, Indiana State Museum.

259 *"not strong enough just yet"*: Major Taylor to Daisy Taylor, May 14 and 21, 1909, Major Taylor papers, Indiana State Museum.

335

# NOTES

260 *"matter with me now":* Major Taylor to Daisy Taylor, June 13, 1909, Major Taylor papers, Indiana State Museum.

260 *"as hot as I could stand it":* Major Taylor to Daisy Taylor, July 20, 1909, Major Taylor papers, Indiana State Museum. Taylor did not say which wrist he sprained.

260 *"not there with the kick":* Major Taylor to Daisy Taylor, June 14, 1909, Major Taylor papers, Indiana State Museum.

260 *"a wicked mistake":* Major Taylor to Daisy Taylor, June 13, 1909, Major Taylor papers, Indiana State Museum.

260 *"when I come home":* Major Taylor to Sydney Taylor, June 16, Major Taylor papers, Indiana State Museum.

261 *"I know you will say":* Major Taylor to Daisy Taylor, August 1, 5, 11, and 13, 1909, Major Taylor papers, Indiana State Museum.

262 *"everybody trimming me":* Major Taylor to Daisy Taylor, October 1, 1909, Major Taylor papers, Indiana State Museum.

262 *"happy" to compete:* Major Taylor to Daisy Taylor, October 1, 1909, Major Taylor papers, Indiana State Museum.

263 *"Taylor Gets Revenge":* "Walthour and Taylor Score—Taylor Gets Revenge on Dupré in Latter's Home Town," *Bicycling World and Motorcycle Review* 60 (September 25, 1909–March 19, 1910): 157–58.

263 *A sense of finality:* "Famous Rider Too Old for Racing. Finds It Hard to Get in Condition," *Worcester Telegram*, October 25, 1909.

264 *"their toll from me":* Marshall "Major" Taylor, *The Fastest Bicycle Rider in the World* (Worcester: Wormley Publishing Co., 1928), 420.

264 *"speediest and most efficient":* "Major Taylor Taking Up Aviation," *Sydney Morning Herald*, November 15, 1909.

264 *"rough the Major a bit":* Floyd McFarland, "Taylor Has Had a Great Bike Career," *Salt Lake Telegram*, August 13, 1910.

265 *"attraction in the bike game":* "Clarke Has Big Lead at Saucer," *Salt Lake Herald-Republican*, July 31, 1910.

265 *two seconds slower:* "Major Taylor Draws Out Big Crowd," *Salt Lake Herald-Republican*, August 6, 1910.

265 *"best man won":* Salt Lake Herald-Republican, August 17, 1910.

265 *"retired too many times":* Walter D. Bratz, "Sport Gossip," *Salt Lake Telegram*, August 20, 1910.

266 *"hardest kind of training":* Untitled, *Salt Lake Telegram*, September 10, 1910.

266 *"Taylor or Wilheight":* Permit for Burial, Indiana State Board of Health, No. 3811. Date of death: November 10, 1910. The whereabouts of Gilbert Taylor's remains were not known prior to the research for this book because he was buried under the name of Wilhite. The burial permit is one of several confirmations that this is the burial site of Gilbert Taylor. See also: "Obituaries," *Indianapolis Recorder*, November 19, 1910. Gilbert Taylor's death was misreported years earlier by an Indianapolis newspaper, which

said he had been killed by a train. However, newspaper stories in two publications as well as a copy of the Cook County, Illinois, death index make clear that his death occurred at this later date. Taylor wrote about his father using the name Wilhite in his letter to Daisy in June 1909. The letter is in the Major Taylor papers at the Indiana State Museum.

267 *"one of the largest automobile factories"*: Untitled, *Savannah Tribune*, September 17, 1910.

267 *"on a fair road to become wealthy"*: "Major Taylor President of Automobile Firm," *Chicago Defender*, August 6, 1910.

268 *"practically decided"*: "Road Test for New Auto Tire," *Fitchburg Sentinel*, April 9, 1914.

268 *"ended up going into bankruptcy"*: Robert Percival, "Remembering Father, The Bike Champ," *Indianapolis Star*, February 11, 1984.

268 Pneu-Metal Tire Co.: *Annual Report of the Commissioner of Patents* (Washington, DC: Government Printing Office, 1919), 275.

268 *"all that kind of stuff"*: Robert Percival, "Remembering Father, The Bike Champ," *Indianapolis Star*, February 11, 1984.

268 *"weren't allowed to make money"*: Sydney Taylor Brown interview with the author of this book, May 24, 2001.

269 *"stop paying them"*: Robert Percival, "Remembering Father, The Bike Champ," *Indianapolis Star*, February 11, 1984.

270 *"built in this country"*: "Costly Autos Burn in Factory Blaze," *New York Times*, January 25, 1914.

270 *thirty-eight-year-old wife, Emilie:* Emilie Munger, "Estates Appraised," *New York Times*, October 19, 1915.

270 *"dropped senseless"*: "Floyd McFarland Stabbed to Death; Famous Cyclist Killed," *New York Times*, April 18, 1915. Lantenberg was charged with manslaughter but was acquitted.

271 *thousands lined the streets:* "Funeral of Floyd (McFarland)," *New York Times*, April 22, 1915.

271 *"protect the Southern country"*: "The Influence of 'The Birth of a Nation.'" Accessed at https://www.facinghistory.org/reconstruction-era/influence -birth-nation. For an analysis of the Wilson quotes in the movie, see: Melvyn Stokes, *D.W. Griffith's The Birth of a Nation* (New York: Oxford University Press, 2008).

271 *Griffith's father, Jacob:* Nancy Stearns Theiss, "Film Icon D.W. Griffith Heralded Father on Grave Marker," *Louisville Courier Journal*, January 8, 2014.

272 *"The Klan at that time was needed"*: D. W. Griffith interview, as shown in PBS documentary *Birth of a Movement*.

272 *eight hundred black women:* "The Birth of a Nation Sparks Protest," *Mass Moments*. Accessed at https://www.massmoments.org/moment-details/the -birth-of-a-nation-sparks-protest.html.

272 *"Nip Theatre Riot in Bud"*: "Army of Police Nip Theatre Riot in Bud," *Boston Post*, April 18, 1915.

272 *forced to work in a "cage"*: W. E. B. Du Bois to Woodrow Wilson, September 1913. Accessed at http://teachingamericanhistory.org/library/document/another-open-letter-to-woodrow-wilson/.

272 The Birth of a Nation: For more about the impact of the movie on politics and race, see Dick Lehr, *Birth of a Movement* (New York: Public Affairs, 2014).

## Chapter 21: "My Last Race"

273 *"96 percent feeble"*: "Teddy Roosevelt Blasts Ford Pacifism, Says Wilson Unprepared," *United Press*, May 19, 1916. Wilson would go on to win reelection against Roosevelt's preferred candidate, Republican Charles Evans Hughes.

273 *a third-floor chapel*: "Harry Worcester Smith," *Worcester Polytechnic Institute News*, March 27, 2017. Accessed at https://www.wpi.edu/news/harry-worcester-smith.

274 *"the bluest blooded society"*: Jonathan M. Rourke, *An Abnormally Hard Rider* (Massachusetts: Jonathan M. Rourke, 2015), 112.

274 *appeared to be "bully"*: "T.R. Called This Woman's Home O.K.," *Boston Sunday Post*, September 10, 1916.

274 *"public men of note"*: "From the Parks Department," *American City* 16, no. 4 (April 1917): 379–80.

275 *"Major Taylor, I am always delighted"*: Marshall "Major" Taylor, *The Fastest Bicycle Rider in the World* (Worcester: Wormley Publishing Co., 1928), 421–22.

276 *pistol's crack, set him off*: New York Age, September 20, 1917.

276 *"triple roll of fat"*: Newark Evening News, September 17, 1917.

277 *thirteen percent of inductees*: Jami L. Bryan, "Fighting for Respect: African-American Soldiers in WWI," ArmyHistory.com. Accessed at https://armyhistory.org/fighting-for-respect-african-american-soldiers-in-wwi/.

277 *770 were killed*: Michael E. Ruane, "African American World War I Soldiers Served at a Time Racism Was Rampant in the U.S.," *Washington Post*, September 22, 2017.

277 *increase in lynchings*: Bryan, "Fighting for Respect."

277 *had surged to 180,000*: Accessed at http://population.us/ma/worcester/.

277 *opened Major's Tire Shop*: Worcester City Directory, 1921, 446, 1180.

278 *"was performed with ease"*: "Munger v. Perlman Rim Corp.," US District Court, New York Southern District, June 20, 1917, *Federal Reporter*, vol. 243, September–October 1917 (St. Paul: West Publishing Co., 1917), 799–805.

278 *"Munger May Be a Millionaire":* "Munger May Be a Millionaire," *Central New Jersey Home News,* June 22, 1917.

278 *$7.5 million:* "Rim Suits Against Twenty," *New York Times,* June 24, 1917.

278 *Firestone Tire and Rubber Company:* "Wants $1,500,000," *Indianapolis News,* October 6, 1917.

278 *had awarded him $48,000:* "Supreme Court Refuses Perlman Appeal," *Automobile Topics,* November 5, 1921.

279 *Radio Four-Way Switch Plug:* "Moore & Munger Co," Coachbuilt.com. Accessed at http://www.coachbuilt.com/bui/m/moore_munger/moore _munger.htm.

279 *let Munger relive the old days:* "Bicycle Champ of Other Days Living in This City," *Springfield Republican,* December 23, 1924.

279 *antislavery convention in 1857:* Mechanics Hall, National Park Service, citing *Massachusetts Spy,* April 22, 1857.

280 *Ascending to the stage:* The description of Farnsworth's speech comes from: "Huge Throng Orderly as Klan Meets" and "Kleagle Farnsworth Declares Klan Is Out to Clean Up Politics," *Worcester Gazette,* September 28, 1923; and "Klan Meeting Is Held Undisturbed, Two Halls Packed, Hundreds Outside, Leader Says 500 Seek Membership," *Worcester Telegram,* September 28, 1923.

281 *he sent a letter to* The Crisis: Letter from Major Taylor to Augustus G. Dill, June 9, 1924; letter from W. E. B. Du Bois to Major Taylor, July 29, 1924. Both letters are from the W. E. B. Du Bois papers in the Special Collections and University Archives Division of the University of Massachusetts-Amherst Libraries.

282 *the rise of the KKK in Taylor's city:* "Klansmen Beaten in Street, Cars Stoned" and "Klan Plane Is Forced Down," *Worcester Sunday Telegram,* October 19, 1924. See also: Albert B. Southwick, "KKK's History in Worcester," *Worcester Telegram & Gazette,* November 6, 2014; Raney Bench, "Maine's Gone Mad: The Rising of the Klan." Accessed at https://mdihistory.org /wp-content/uploads/Maines-Gone-Mad-The-Rising-of-the-Klan_ocr.pdf; Mark Paul Richard, "This Is Not a Catholic Nation," *New England Quarterly,* June 2009, 285–303; and "The Foreign-Born Population of Worcester, Massachusetts," Public Policy Center, UMass Dartmouth.

284 *Worcester Classical High School:* Harry Worcester Smith, "A Champion Laid Low," *Worcester Telegram,* December 14, 1926.

284 *"at the last athletic meet there":* Major Taylor to Robert Coquelle, March 3,1923, Major Taylor papers, Indiana State Museum.

284 *Sargent School of Physical Education:* Andrew Ritchie, *The Extraordinary Career of a Champion Bicycle Racer* (San Francisco: Bicycle Books, 1988), 255.

285 *Daisy sold the house:* Worcester property records examined by Gloria Hall, who owned the Taylor home in 2018.

285   *"tale of sadness rather than joy"*: Harry Worcester Smith, "A Champion Laid Low," *Worcester Telegram*, December 14, 1926.

285   *an influenza epidemic:* "Influenza Encyclopedia, Worcester," University of Michigan Center for the history of Medicine. Accessed at https://www .influenzaarchive.org/cities/city-worcester.html#.

285   *"deafening cheers of years ago"*: Harry Worcester Smith, "A Champion Laid Low," *Worcester Telegram*, December 14, 1926.

286   *"a trick of crowding a man"*: "Friends of Maj. Taylor, Worcester's World Champion, Rally to His Relief," *Worcester Telegram*, December 18, 1926.

286   *"Christmas has been brightened"*: "City's Samaritan's Lauded by Taylor," *Worcester Telegram*, December 26, 1926.

286   *"Major's courage is worth $5"*: "Do You Remember Major Taylor?," *San Francisco Chronicle*, December 30, 1926.

287   *"the tire has merit"*: Damon Runyon, "Runyon Says: Taylor a Sick Man," (Harrisburg, PA) *Evening News*, April 19, 1927.

287   *"How is the old has been"*: Major Taylor to Robert Coquelle, March 3, 1923, Major Taylor papers, Indiana State Museum.

288   *"overcome these sinister conditions"*: Taylor, *Fastest Bicycle Rider*, 426–27.

288   *"escorted out the door"*: Albert B. Southwick, "Major Taylor Was Much More Than a World Cycling Champion," *Worcester Telegram & Gazette*, May 15, 2008.

288   *"Taylor was a real champion"*: " 'Major' Taylor, Ex-Biking Champ, Tells Life Story," *New York Age*, August 31, 1929.

289   *"God had created us both"*: David W. Kellum, "Put in Bike Race as Joke He Won World's Championship," *Abbott's Monthly*, August 1930.

289   *Bronzeville:* "The Renaissance Collaborative." Accessed at https://www .trcwabash.org/history.html.

290   *performed heart surgery:* Ritchie, *Major Taylor*, 252–53.

290   *"he had to die with so little money"*: Sydney Taylor Brown interview with author, May 24, 2001.

293   *"American and world's championships"*: Taylor, *Fastest Bicycle Rider*, 428.

## Appendix 2: Major Taylor's Training Regimen

300   *"good stiff rubdown"*: "Major Taylor on Bicycle Training," *New York American*, March 12, 1898.

300   *Whitley Exerciser:* "Home Gyms in the 1800s Were a Lot Like Today's TRX Trainer." Accessed at https://www.stack.com/a/1800s-home-gym-trx.

301   *"strengthens the muscles,"* : Major Taylor, "Ma Tourneé en Europe," *La Vie au Grand Air*, May 1905.

# NOTES

301 "*all I can*": "Major Taylor On Bicycle Training," *New York American*, March 12, 1898.

301 *"matter of ounces"*: Marshall "Major" Taylor, *The Fastest Bicycle Rider in the World* (Worcester: Wormley Publishing Co., 1928), 54.

302 *"new to them"*: Ibid., 236, 411.

302 *"perfect condition"*: Ibid., 320.

# Bibliography

## SOURCES

### Manuscript Collections and Other Archival Material

Ancestry.com
California Newspaper Archive
Gallica—Bibliothèque Nationalé, French Newspaper Archive
Genealogybank.com, US Newspaper Archive
Hoosier State Chronicles, Indiana Newspaper Archive
Major Taylor Papers, Indiana State Museum
Library of Congress, newspaper and magazine archives
Newspapers.com, US Newspaper Archive
Trove—Australia Newspaper Archive

## BIBLIOGRAPHY

(Note: Many sources such as newspapers and interviews are cited in the end-notes.)

### Magazines

*Abbott's Monthly*
*The Atlantic*
*Bearings*
*The Bicycling World*
*Canadian Wheelman*
*The Colored American*
*The Crisis*
*The Cycle*
*Cycle Age*
*Harper's Weekly*
*The Horseless Age*

# BIBLIOGRAPHY

*The Journal of Negro History*
*Journal of Popular Culture*
*The Ladies World*
*Munsey's Magazine*
*Motor World*
*The New Yorker*
*Outing*
*The Referee & Cycling Trade Journal*
*The Wheel*
*The Wheel and Cycling Trade Review*
*Yankee*


## Newspapers

*The Adelaide Advertiser* (Australia)
*The Alexandria Gazette and Virginia Advertiser*
*The Argus* (Australia)
*The Australian Cycle and Motor-Car World*
*The Australian Star*
*The Boston Globe*
*The Boston Herald*
*The Boston Post*
*The Brooklyn Eagle*
*The Buffalo Commercial*
*The Bulletin* (Australia)
*The Chicago Herald*
*The Chicago Inter Ocean*
*The Chicago Tribune*
*The Cleveland Gazette*
*The Cleveland Plain Dealer*
*The Colored American*
*The Defender* (Chicago)
*The Detroit Free Press*
*The Evansville Courier*
*The Hartford Courant*
*The Indianapolis Freeman*
*The Indianapolis Journal*
*Indianapolis Monthly*
*The Indianapolis News*
*The Indianapolis Recorder*
*The Indianapolis Sentinel*
*The Indianapolis Star*
*L'Auto Vélo*

# BIBLIOGRAPHY

*La Vie Au Grand Air*
*Le Petit Journal*
*Le Vélo*
*The Los Angeles Herald*
*The Los Angeles Times*
*The New Orleans Times Picayune*
*The Newark Evening News*
*The New York Age*
*The New York American*
*The New York Herald*
*The New York Journal*
*The New York Sun*
*The New York Times*
*The New York Tribune*
*The New York World*
*The Philadelphia Press*
*The Philadelphia Tribune*
*The Pittsburgh Press*
*Politiken* (Denmark)
*The Salt Lake Herald-Republican*
*The Salt Lake Telegram*
*The San Francisco Call*
*The Savannah Tribune*
*The Springfield Republican* (Massachusetts)
*The St. Louis Republic*
*The Sydney Morning Herald*
*The Washington Bee*
*The Washington Evening Star*
*The Washington Post*
*The Washington Times*
*The Worcester Spy*
*The Worcester Gazette*
*The Worcester Telegram*
*The Worcester Telegram & Gazette*

## Books

Bagg, Lyman Hotchkiss. *Ten Thousand Miles on a Bicycle*. New York: Karl Kron, 1887.
Baker, Ray Stannard. *Following The Color Line: An Account of Negro Citizenship in the American Democracy*. London: Forgotten Books, 2015.
Balf, Todd. *Major: A Black Athlete, a White Era, and the Fight to Be the World's Fastest Human Being*. New York: Three Rivers Press, 2009.

# BIBLIOGRAPHY

Blackmon, Douglas A. *Slavery by Another Name: The Re-Enslavement of Black Americans from the Civil War to World War II*. New York: Anchor Books, 2009.

Brady, William A. *Showman*. New York: E. P. Dutton & Co., 1937.

———. *The Fighting Man*. Indianapolis: Bobbs-Merrill Co., 1916.

Brodsky, Alyn. *Grover Cleveland: A Study in Character*. New York: St. Martin's Press, 2000.

Burrows, Edwin G., and Mike Wallace. *Gotham: A History of New York City to 1898*. Oxford: Oxford University Press, 2000.

Cashman, Sean Dennis. *America in the Gilded Age*, 3rd edition. New York: NYU Press, 1993.

Consolidated Illustrating. *Indianapolis of Today*. Consolidated Illustrating Co., 1896.

Czitrom, Daniel J. *New York Exposed: The Gilded Age Police Scandal That Launched the Progressive Era*. Oxford and New York: Oxford University Press, 2016.

Du Bois, W. E. B. *The Souls of Black Folk: Essays and Sketches*. Chicago: A. C. McClurg & Co., 1903.

Finison, Lorenz J. *Boston's Cycling Craze, 1880–1900: A Story of Race, Sport, and Society*. Amherst: University of Massachusetts Press, 2014.

Fitzpatrick, Jim. *Major Taylor in Australia*. Karana Downs, Queensland, Australia: Star Hill Studio, 2011.

Gabriele, Michael C. *The Golden Age of Bicycle Racing in New Jersey*. Charleston, SC: History Press, 2011.

Gentry, Tony. *Paul Laurence Dunbar*. Los Angeles: Melrose Square Pub., 1993.

Goddard, Stephen B. *Colonel Albert Pope and His American Dream Machines: The Life and Times of a Bicycle Tycoon Turned Automotive Pioneer*. Jefferson, NC: McFarland, 2009.

Goldstone, Lawrence. *Drive!: Henry Ford, George Selden, and the Race to Invent the Auto Age*. New York: Ballantine Books, 2016.

Greenwood, Janette Thomas. *First Fruits of Freedom: The Migration of Former Slaves and Their Search for Equality in Worcester, Massachusetts, 1862–1900*. Chapel Hill: University of North Carolina Press, 2010.

Gress, Stephanie. *Eagle's Nest: The William K. Vanderbilt II Estate*. New York: Arcadia Publishing, 2015.

Guroff, Margaret. *The Mechanical Horse: How the Bicycle Reshaped American Life*. Austin: University of Texas Press, 2016.

Hayes, Kevin J. *An American Cycling Odyssey, 1887*. Lincoln: University of Nebraska Press, 2002.

Hemingway, Ernest, Patrick Hemingway, and Seán Hemingway. *A Moveable Feast: The Restored Edition*. New York: Scribner, 2011.

Herlihy, David V. *Bicycle: The History*. New Haven, CT, and London: Yale University Press, 2006.

———. *The Lost Cyclist: The Epic Tale of an American Adventurer and His Mysterious Disappearance*. Boston: Houghton Mifflin Harcourt, 2010.

Hochschild, Adam. *King Leopold's Ghost: A Story of Greed, Terror and Heroism in Colonial Africa.* Boston: Houghton Mifflin Harcourt, 1998.

Homan, Andrew M. *Life in the Slipstream: The Legend of Bobby Walthour Sr.* Washington, D.C.: Potomac Books, 2011.

Irons, Peter. *Jim Crow's Children: The Broken Promise of the Brown Decision.* New York: Penguin Books, 2014.

Johnson, Jack, and Christopher Rivers. *My Life and Battles.* Washington, DC: Potomac Books, 2009.

Kendi, Ibram X. *Stamped from the Beginning: The Definitive History of Racist Ideas in America.* New York: Nation Books, 2016.

Kerber, Conrad, and Terry Kerber. *Major Taylor: The Inspiring Story of a Black Cyclist and the Men Who Helped Him Achieve Worldwide Fame.* New York: Skyhorse, 2016.

Lehr, Dick. *Birth of a Movement: How* Birth of a Nation *Ignited the Battle for Civil Rights.* New York: Public Affairs, 2017.

Lewis, David L., Deborah Willis, and Daniel Murray Collection (Library of Congress). *A Small Nation of People: W.E.B. Du Bois and African-American Portraits of Progress.* New York: Amistad, 2003.

Mateyunas, Paul J. *Long Island's Gold Coast. Images of America.* Charleston, SC: Arcadia Pub., 2012.

McCullough, David. *The Greater Journey: Americans in Paris.* New York: Simon & Schuster Audio, 2014.

Morton, Brian N. *Americans in Paris: An Anecdotal Street Guide.* Ann Arbor, MI: Olivia & Hill Press, 1984.

Norrell, Robert J. *Up from History: The Life of Booker T. Washington.* Cambridge, MA: Belknap Press of Harvard University Press, 2009.

Northern Pacific Railroad Company. *The Wonderland Route to the Pacific Coast, 1885.* Northern Pacific Railroad, 1885.

Nye, Peter, and Eric Heiden. *Hearts of Lions: The History of American Bicycle Racing.* New York: W.W. Norton, 1989.

Pickenpaugh, Roger. *Captives in Gray: The Civil War Prisons of the Union.* Tuscaloosa: University of Alabama Press, 2009.

Pierre-André Hélène. *Hotel Scribe.* Paris, n.d.

Rasenberger, Jim. *America, 1908: The Dawn of Flight, the Race to the Pole, the Invention of the Model T, and the Making of a Modern Nation.* New York: Scribner, 2007.

Reef, Catherine. *The Life of Paul Laurence Dunbar: Portrait of a Poet.* New York: Enslow Publishing, 2015.

Reid, Carlton. *Roads Were Not Built for Cars: How Cyclists Were the First to Push for Good Roads & Became the Pioneers of Motoring.* Washington, DC: Island Press, 2015.

Ritchie, Andrew. *Major Taylor: The Extraordinary Career of a Champion Bicycle Racer.* Baltimore: Johns Hopkins University Press, 1996.

# BIBLIOGRAPHY

Roberts, Dorothy E. *Killing the Black Body: Race, Reproduction, and the Meaning of Liberty.* New York: Vintage, 2017.

Rourke, Jonathan M. *An Abnormally Hard Rider.* Massachusetts: Jonathan M. Rourke, 2015.

Sergent, Pascal. *Edmond Jacquelin: La vie du champion le plus populaire de tous les temps.* Paris: Editions L'Harmattan, 2008.

Smith, Robert A. *A Social History of the Bicycle, Its Early Life and Times in America.* New York: American Heritage Press, 1972.

Stevens, Thomas. *Around the World on a Bicycle: From San Francisco to Yokohama.* London: Century, 1988.

Taylor, Marshall W. "Major." *The Fastest Bicycle Rider in the World.* Worcester: Wormley Publishing Company, 1928.

Zheutlin, Peter. *Around the World on Two Wheels: Annie Londonderry's Extraordinary Ride.* New York and London: Citadel Press, 2007.

Zimmerman, Arthur Augustus, and Frank Bowden. *Points for Cyclists with Training.* Leicester: F.W.S. Clarke, 1894.

# Image Credits

1, 14, 15, 19: Major Taylor Collection, Indiana State Museum
2, 3: *Bearings Magazine*, 1897
4: Division of Work and Industry, National Museum of American History, Smithsonian Institution
5, 10, 11, 12, 16, 17, 18: Bibliothèque Nationale, France
6: *La Vie au Grand Air*
7: Zeno Fotografie
8: University Archives & Special Collections Department, Joseph P. Healey Library, University of Massachusetts, Boston: Bicycling realia
9: *The Fastest Bicycle Rider in the World*
13: Library of Congress
20: *Worcester Telegram*

# Index

351

# INDEX

Excello Oil Manufacturing Co., 268
exercise, 57–59
Exhibit of American Negros (Paris World's Fair, 1900), 158–59

## F

Fairchild, C. M., 15
Fairfax, Henry W., 15
Farnsworth, Eugene, 279–81
*The Fastest Bicycle Rider in the World* (MT), 281–82, 284, 287–90, 295
Fenn, W. S., 147
Fifteenth Amendment, 32–33
Firestone Tire and Rubber Company, 278
Fisher, Carl, 146
Fitchburg, 267
*Fitchburg Sentinel*, 268
flu epidemic, 285
*Following the Color Line* (Baker), 251–52
Foottit, George, 164
Ford, Henry, 40, 66, 199, 201, 247
Ford Motor Company, 199, 279
Forster, Fred, 90
Fourteenth Amendment, 77
France, 88, 135, 158
    MT decision to race in, 139, 141, 153
    MT in, 159, 160–62, 177, 179, 248–51, 258–60, 262–63
    World's Fair in, 158–59
*Freeman, see Indianapolis Freeman*
Freeman, Howard, 120
French-Canadian immigrants, 56
Friedenau Sportpark Velodrome (near Berlin), 171
Friol, Émile, 245

## G

Gainsborough, Thomas: *Portrait of Georgiana, Duchess of Devonshire*, 187–88, 190
Galton, Francis, 65–66
German immigrants, 9, 56, 65
Germany, MT in, 260, 261
Geronimo, 17
*Globe, see Boston Globe*
Goodrich, 278
*Good Roads*, 31
"Good Roads" campaign, 20
Gould, Anna, 179
Griffith, D. W., 271–72
Griffith, Jacob, 271
Grogna, Louis, 173–74

## H

Hale, Teddy, 90–91
Hamelle, Paul, 176–77, 297
Harlan, John Marshall, 4, 78–79
Harlem Renaissance, 277
Harrison, Benjamin (president), 20, 31–35, 47
Harrison, Benjamin, V (slave owner), 33
Harrison, William Henry, 33
Harvard University, 190, 252
Hay, Tom, 24–25, 291
Haynes-Apperson automobile, 130
Hazard, Bert, 257
head injuries, 201
Hearsey, Harry, 41–42
Hearst, William Randolph, 87, 215
"Hello! Ma Baby," 166
Hemingway, Ernest, 128
    *A Moveable Feast*, 177–78
Hess, Carl, 37

355

# INDEX

# INDEX

# INDEX

Native Americans, 17
nativism, 65
Nelson, Johnnie, 202–3
*Newark Evening News*, 276
Newby, Arthur C., 146
Newby Oval (Indianapolis), 146
New England Steel Company,
    55–56
New Orleans, 14–15, 77, 291
*New Orleans Daily Picayune*, 14
newspaper wars, 86–87
*New York Age*, 288
*New York American*, 111
New York and Manhattan Beach
    Railway, 109
New York City
    blacks in, 65
    Brooklyn, 65, 81
    electricity/lighting in, 64–65
    horses in, 64
    immigrants in, 65
    Manhattan, 63–66
    popularity of bicycles in, 63–64,
        66–68
    population of, 64
    tall buildings of, 63
    telephones in, 65
*New York Daily Tribune*, 200
*New York Herald*, 68, 70
*New York Journal*, 75–76, 87, 90
*New York Sun*, 94, 213, 215, 217
*New York Times*
    on auto accidents, 249
    circulation of, 86–87
    on the cyclists' parade, 34
    on the *Deutschland*, 185
    on MT, 111, 191, 200, 225
    on Birdie Munger, 13, 37, 289
    *Plessy v. Ferguson* ignored by, 78–79
    racism in, 254
    round-the-world auto race
        cosponsored by, 248–49
*New York Tribune*, 86–87, 190

*New York World*, 63, 67, 86–87,
    90–91, 141, 143
Nineteenth Amendment, 67
nutrition guidelines, 58–59
*Nymphs and Satyr*, 70


## O

Ocean Parkway (Brooklyn), 81
Oldfield, Barney, 199
Outrelon, Gaston Courbe d', 136–37
Owens, Jesse, 172, 292


## P

Pan American Exhibition (Buffalo),
    207, 209
Panic (1893), 186
Paris, 159–65, 168–69
Perlman Rim Corporation, 277–78
Persons-Arter Machine Co., 275
*Le Petit Journal*, 244
*Philadelphia Press*, 113–14, 120,
    124
*Philadelphia Times*, 114
photojournalism, 166–67
*Physical Culture*, 58
Pierce-Arrow Motor, 268
Pinkerton, William, 187
Plessy, Homer, 77–78
*Plessy v. Ferguson*, 3–4, 77–79
Pneu-Metal Tire Co., 268
*Points for Cyclists with Training*
    (Zimmerman), 44
*Politiken*, 183–84
Pope, Albert A., 76
Pope Manufacturing Co., 76
*Portrait of Georgiana, Duchess of
    Devonshire* (Gainsborough),
    187–88, 190
Poulain, Gabriel, 244–45

# About the Author

Michael Kranish is an investigative political reporter for *The Washington Post*. He is the coauthor of the *New York Times* bestseller *Trump Revealed*, *John F. Kerry*, and *The Real Romney* and the author of *Flight from Monticello: Thomas Jefferson at War*. He was the recipient of the Society of Professional Journalists Award for Washington Correspondence in 2016. Visit MichaelKranish.com.